ORAL HISTORY

ORAL
HISTORY

An Interdisciplinary Anthology

Edited by

David K. Dunaway
and
Willa K. Baum

American Association for State and Local History
in cooperation with
the Oral History Association

Second printing 1987

Publication of this book was made possible in part by funds from the sale of the Bicentennial State Histories, which were supported by the National Endowment for the Humanities.

Designed by Gary Gore

"Radio and the Public Use of Oral History" by David K. Dunaway copyright © 1984 by David K. Dunaway

"The Expanding Role of the Librarian in Oral History" by Willa K. Baum copyright © 1984 by Willa K. Baum

Library of Congress Cataloging in Publication Data
Main entry under title:

Oral history.

  Bibliography: p.
  Includes index.
  1. Oral history—Addresses, essays, lectures.
I. Dunaway, David King. II. Baum, Willa K.
III. American Association for State and Local
History. IV. Oral History Association.
D16.14.073 1984   907'.2   84-372
ISBN 0-910050-70-8

This volume is dedicated to two pathbreakers in oral history:

ALLAN NEVINS
(1890–1971)

At the time he conducted our first interview, Allan Nevins was two days shy of his fifty-eighth birthday and nearing the crest of his remarkable career. The idea "to obtain from the lips and papers of living Americans a fuller record of their participation" had haunted him for a decade and more. Every obituary pricked his conscience: "What memories that man carries to the grave with him!"

—Louis M. Starr on Allan Nevins, 1971

LOUIS M. STARR
(1917–1980)

The Oral History Collection of Columbia University is Louis Starr's enduring monument. No one was more insistent than he on giving credit to Allan Nevins as its founder, but today at Columbia we couple their names. On that foundation Louis Starr built a collection seven times larger than the one he took over. In the process he led and trained a new generation of oral historians, and he voiced ideas and ideals for his successors to explore and expand.

—Elizabeth B. Mason on Louis M. Starr, 1980

CONTENTS

III. ORAL HISTORY APPLIED:
LOCAL, ETHNIC, FAMILY, AND WOMEN'S HISTORY

IV. ORAL HISTORY AND RELATED DISCIPLINES:
FOLKLORE, ANTHROPOLOGY, AND GERONTOLOGY

V. ORAL HISTORY AND SCHOOLS

VI. ORAL HISTORY AND LIBRARIES

FOREWORD

For more years than I care to remember, those of us interested in oral history have felt the need for an anthology which brought together the significant writing and thinking on the subject. We depended on dog-eared reprints or on photocopies of loose pages, all of which vanished from our files regularly and had to be tracked down again. To those who teach oral history, what a boon to be able to refer to a single volume instead of sending students to obscure journal articles and introductions to volumes on other subjects. To all of us who write and speak on oral history, how convenient to have a compendium of the earlier writings available! Most of all, to the Oral History Association, what a useful publication to introduce newcomers to the diversity and development of a controversial field.

It is no surprise, then, that for a number of years an oral history anthology has had high priority in association discussions, but circumstances have delayed its compilation and publication until now. The Oral History Association is delighted that Willa Baum and David Dunaway have done the work at last. And what a feast they have laid before us in this volume: history, opinion, argument, and exposition are all here to be savored and considered. In oral history we often talk of filling in the gaps in our knowledge of a variety of topics; this book fills a very large gap in the field of oral history and in historiography generally.

We salute the enterprise of the editors in searching out and reprinting valuable and differing points of view. Many members of the association are represented in the pages which follow, and all will have an avid interest in the contents of the volume.

The Oral History Association is grateful to the American Association for State and Local History for its continuing interest in oral history, which has led to the publication of earlier manuals and now of this anthology. Several successive presidents of the Oral History Association have been deeply committed to this project; it becomes my privilege to express their thanks as well as my own to editors and publisher alike for the achievement of a long-sought goal.

ELIZABETH B. MASON
President, Oral History Association

July 1983

PREFACE

The ancestry of oral history in the United States extends back only fifty years, but its practice has already entered a third generation.

The first generation, led by the pioneering figures to whom this volume is dedicated, saw oral history as a tool for oral biography and autobiography and as a means to collecting critical source material for future historians.

A second generation, coming of age once the basic archives were established in the mid-sixties, built upon earlier work by expanding the number of collections and collectors. This group viewed oral history as more than a source of nontraditional materials for scholars; it employed oral history techniques to describe and empower the nonliterate and the historically disenfranchised. Throughout the seventies, many collectors of oral history used their research to promote community cohesion and ethnic diversity. In this period, oral history built a name for itself and a growing grass-roots constituency based on efforts by educators, feminists, and activists as well as local, ethnic, and regional history campaigns. While collectors in the first generation continued to direct many of the principal archives, they found the younger group of social educators virtually beating on their doors to broaden the scope of collections beyond so-called elite interviews.

Now, in the 1980s, we believe that a third generation is emerging. The new students and scholars are learning the craft of oral historiography in an era removed from both the conservative fifties and the socially radical sixties. America's principal oral history archives have set high standards for the maintenance and development of collections. New technologies such as computerized research aids and word processors have made professional oral history collections increasingly capital intensive. Many of the smaller, volunteer-oriented groups have passed the first flush of collecting and now ponder how to continue and publicize their work.

In this era, a new generation has turned its attention to the process, public use, and interdisciplinary applications of oral history. Formerly, the process of generating oral history was considered uncomplicated and the text of the interview transparent: the efforts of an interviewer to gather material of historical use from a neutral (occasionally partisan) stance. History would emerge at some later time when writers and scholars used these oral sources. Now, more theoretically oriented researchers (prompted by Ronald Grele, Peter Friedlander, and others) have speculated that the interviews *themselves* represent history: they have been compiled within a historical frame negotiated by the interviewer and narrator, within contemporary trends, within certain definable conventions of language and cultural interaction. This generation, with a wealth of previous collecting experience to draw upon, is beginning to ask tough, introspective questions of its colleagues. What is the effect of reducing a multilayered communication event (rich with gesture and intonation) to a printed page or a magnetic tape—what elements are lost or changed? What time period does such an interview represent: the time investigated or the time of the interview?

In a similar fashion, the eighties may become the decade of the public program in the oral history profession. Museums increasingly incorporate oral materials into exhibits to add a "living dimension" to presentations of research and artifacts. Libraries are reaching out beyond the stacks to establish educational programs with schools and community groups; some are midway through the transition from depositories to collecting centers generating new materials. Arts, humanities, and historical commissions are funding innovative projects involving public use of previously collected interviews: drama, multimedia exhibits, and popular publications.

Electronic mass media have come to the fore as an outlet for publicizing popular history. Documentarians in radio and television—particularly on the sparsely funded public networks—are discovering the riches available in oral history archives. Local broadcasters are airing oral history interviews to fulfill their public service obligations. Oral testimony has even been incorporated into a full-length Hollywood feature film, *Reds*. Such efforts are not new. As far back as 1934, the History Committee of the National Advisory Council on Radio in Education suggested, in terms suited to modern oral historians, that there were significant "reasons for broadcasting to the man in the street in order to develop 'historical-mindedness.' "

Interdisciplinary applications of oral history have increased steadily as disciplines such as folklore, anthropology, and gerontology explore their common ground with oral history. Each relies on oral testimony collected in a manner particular to its field; each uses that information in unique fashion—yet each shares the difficulties inherent in working with oral sources. Our selections from the various disciplines are designed to stimulate the convergence.

Oral history also has growing practical applications in administration and policy matters. The most prominent uses include those of historic preservation, land use claims, institutional and business history,

environmental-cultural impact statements, and legal actions. Policy decisions of institutions and corporations can be made more effectively by
using oral history interviews to help uncover the rationale behind earlier
actions and the precedents they set for the future.

Nearly fifty years after oral history began in the United States, these
directions and applications enliven the field and unite three generations
of professionals who use oral sources to enrich everyday historical consciousness.

Writings about oral history began in the United States in 1938, with a
paragraph in the introduction to Allan Nevins's *Gateway to History*. In the
1950s, there was a trickle of articles. Several appeared in the *American
Archivist*, with others in less widely distributed journals. By 1971, the Oral
History Association's *Bibliography on Oral History* listed 201 articles. From
then on, innumerable articles and books on oral history—or on so-called
oral history—flooded a bicentennial-conscious nation.

Yet for students of oral history and their teachers, finding the articles
(which were often buried in specialized journals of limited distribution)
posed a major task. The demand grew for a collection of readings to serve
as a base on which teachers and researchers of oral history could expand
into their own specialities. The editors of this volume, each faced with the
need to compile readings for their respective classes in oral history, first
joined forces to select and assemble their own collections, then agreed to
work with the Oral History Association (OHA) and with the American
Association for State and Local History to publish this material in book
form.

The first decision concerned the intended audience. At one time the
greatest need was for basic procedural manuals for beginning practitioners, but today a growing body of how-to-do-it books, general and specific
as to geographic area or topic, has met that need. The editors chose
instead to aim at a broad spectrum of already initiated individuals: serious
students and researchers of oral history as a methodology; practitioners of
oral history, both amateur and professional; individual researchers and
users of oral history materials; people who produce public and media
programs that could incorporate oral history; teachers who could use oral
history as an educational method; and librarians who must care for and
dispense the tapes and transcripts that are the products of oral history.

Before this thoughtful audience we intended to display oral history in
its many varieties, with some information as to how it began, who and
what shaped the directions it has taken, and how it has been used by
diverse scholars, writers, and producers of public programs. Our goal
was the upgrading of the oral history process and end product and the

establishment of reasonable expectations for the authenticity and value of oral history by users and funders.

To broaden the content and use of oral history, we have chosen articles from a variety of disciplines which collect different kinds of oral data. To stimulate critical thinking, we have included critiques of oral history. The selections represent the perspectives of both the archival collector, who collects for the use of others, and the historians and other professionals who collect for their own research. The final results of the Oral History Association's deliberations on evaluating the performance of oral history programs and a code of ethics are included in part 7.

Selecting the limited number of readings that could be included within the covers of an anthology was a difficult task. The editors solicited and received suggestions from many sources; we made the final decision ourselves. We tried to represent the major points of view in the oral history profession. In some cases, an adequate written presentation of an important school was not available or had not even been composed. We were, for example, able to find no up-to-date article on legal considerations in oral history.

To broaden the spectrum of writers represented, we decided to publish only one article per writer; in the case of some prolific scholars the choice was difficult. In a few instances, we did not receive permission to reprint an article. More often, limitations of space made it necessary to cut the longest articles substantially and to leave out many excellent pieces which had been recommended. Within a few years, there will no doubt be enough additional significant articles for a companion volume.

As far as possible, we have tried to include the entire reading in the form in which it first appeared. We felt the original format, whether a scholarly monograph or the printed version of an after-dinner speech, was essential to the integrity of the piece. Necessary cuts in lengthy articles are indicated by ellipsis points and were made with the permission of the authors. Full bibliographies and footnotes have been included as they appeared in the original (with minor editorial emendations). While some bibliographies duplicate entries, the attentive reader will find in the writers' footnotes a wealth of information and references for further reading.

We would like to express our thanks to the many members of the Oral History Association who worked on compiling and evaluating articles for inclusion. In particular, Betty McKeever Key and Martha Ross, who first proposed an OHA-sponsored anthology; Richard Sweterlitsch, Thomas Charlton, and Samuel Hand, who helped William Moss and Enid Douglass, consecutive presidents of the Oral History Association, prepare a bibliography for the Wingspread Conference on Evaluation of Oral History; the late Louis M. Starr, first editor of the anthology, whose untimely death halted the project for some years; John Neuenschwander, president of the OHA during the year of preparation, who guided us through the procedural arrangements; and most especially, Charles Morrissey, continual adviser, spur, and critic over the years of preparation. Special thanks to Betty Doak Elder, and Gillian Murrey of the AASLH, who guided us step by step through production, and to our copy editor, Marcia Brubeck. Thanks also to Emily Abbink, research assistant, and to Marta Field, typist, at the University of New Mexico. And finally, thanks to the many unnamed students who, over the years, indicated rather clearly which readings they found the most stimulating.

David K. Dunaway
Willa K. Baum

July 1983

INTRODUCTION

The book you hold in your hands attempts to assemble the most helpful oral history writings in a single volume. It seeks to acquaint newcomers to oral history with the major developments, issues, and uses in a burgeoning field as well as to spur experienced oral historians to think more deeply about why and how they record the spoken past. If this anthology is successful, it will encourage fresh thinking and a broadened literature about oral history.

The selections in this volume include much that is provocative about the untidy business of trying to persuade people to speak fully and accurately about the lives they have led and about the meanings that can be deduced by scholars and others who analyse spoken remembrances. Likewise, the book offers many statements that will inspire argument. Memory is elusive, and personal and cultural traits color the ways in which it is articulated. The interplay between spoken memories of past events and other sources illuminating the same episodes—diaries, letters, photographs, artifacts, and so forth—collectively suggests that reconstructing an authentic version of the past is extraordinarily difficult.

Moreover, oral historians argue about definitions of oral history. Some are brief, like Thomas L. Charlton's "remembered experience." Some are longer but still terse, like my personal preference: "recorded interviews which preserve historically significant memories for future use." Others, such as Imbert Orchard's interview in this anthology, use "aural" instead of "oral." But don't be dismayed: oral historians truly play it by ear. From the first national meeting of oral historians at the Lake Arrowhead Conference Center of the University of California, Los Angeles, in 1966, to the present, practitioners have argued about definitions of oral history.

Differing opinions among oral historians enliven this anthology as they do professional meetings. At national colloquia of the Oral History Association, and in the present volume, anthropologists and folklorists intermingle with a wide array of historians, and the historians have major specialties reflecting their own interests, varying from local communities, ethnic groups, women, families, medicine, and labor unionization to African tribesmen and U.S. presidents. It is instructive to compare Saul Benison's introduction to *Tom Rivers* in this book to Eliot Wigginton's introduction to *The Foxfire Book*. Benison is a perfectionist in oral history;

he contends that the interviewer must acquire knowledge of the interviewee's field of expertise (in the case of Tom Rivers, the history of virology), as well as researching all documentation pertaining to the interviewee's life, and must even persuade the interviewee to search his own files. Wigginton is a teacher in the Southern Appalachian Mountains who uses oral history as an educational tool; his students can develop language skills while learning about their mountain heritage, which is culturally jeopardized by the intrusion of the mass media. Benison and Wigginton both practice oral history but in ways that stand at far extremes from one another.

Although oral history has professionalized itself since Allan Nevins issued his call in his 1938 work, *Gateway to History,* no oral historian can completely fit the job description with all its many requirements. Such a person would need to be a psychologist in order to master the art of building rapport, conducting interpersonal conversations about the past, and interpreting nonverbal communication; this oral historian would need to be a linguist in order to understand language and its meanings (especially if tapes are "translated" into transcripts); this individual should know autobiography as a literary genre, and community and institutional studies as recommended by sociologists, and ethnographic studies conducted by anthropologists, and the skills folklorists apply to myths and intergenerational tradition. Not least, he or she would need to wrestle intellectually with philosophical questions about truth and meaning. A prospective oral historian might wisely choose a course of study to include a "how to interview" course in a school of journalism or might elect a course in evidence taught in a school of law. And explicit is the need for courses in history, political science, economics—and in library science and archival administration, too. An oral historian needs a more liberal education than is even offered by most liberal arts institutions.

Within the domain of history, the diversity of specialization is impressive. Today's oral historian is likely to be concerned with neglected aspects of the American past, for oral history allows people hitherto omitted from textbook accounts of the American experience to have their say as historical sources. In this book, turn to Theodore Rosengarten's introduction to *All God's Dangers: The Life of Nate Shaw* to understand how an illiterate black sharecropper, living in a shack by a cotton field in Alabama, was able to speak his life story in a way that begins to balance our understanding of black-white segregation in the South before the era of civil rights. Oral history allows the illiterate to contribute to historical chronicles that were previously restricted to literate people creating written documents about themselves.

Turn also to William Lynwood Montell's preface to *The Saga of Coe Ridge* for a similar example. Coe Ridge was an isolated multiracial community on the Tennessee-Kentucky border, and even though it left no heritage of written records, Montell was able, as an oral historian applying the skills of a folklorist, to capture the oral tradition of descendants of long-time residents and to document the history of Coe Ridge in a book.

Oral historians are in the vanguard of scholars trying to record and interpret what is variously called "grass-roots history," or the history of the nonelite, or demotic history, or the history of ordinary people as they lived their ordinary lives. In this anthology, Tamara Hareven is a prime example; her major book, *Amoskeag*, with photographs by Randolph Langenbach, is a social history of mill workers in the textile city of Manchester, New Hampshire. Paul Thompson's work in England has had a similar focus; he is interested, as "History and the Community" indicates, in the history of work and working people in coalmines, factories, and other industrial workpalces. Many oral historians are interested in the history of women—read Sherna Gluck's essay in this collection—because though women have been left out of orthodox history, oral history now invites them in. Indeed, one of the fascinating characteristics of the Oral History Association is the large number of women who have achieved professional success and recognition as oral historians. An explanation for their eminence is that many turned to this new field after finding traditional avenues to professional success in established historical specialties dominated by males and closed to females. Oral history is still young, vibrant, and unorthodox; it hasn't yet calcified—like many other academic pursuits—into settled ways.

As departments of history at American colleges and universities have launched "public history" programs, designed to train professional historians for nonacademic roles in museums, archives, cultural organizations, and public policy institutions, oral history has been incorporated into model curricula as a valued skill that students should master. In the public sector, oral historians are frequently employed in historic preservation programs to document the architectural heritage of American communities, and in the same fashion, oral historians are utilized to identify historical resources for environmental impact analyses. Oral historians practice their craft in "the real world"; the curricula of colleges and universities have expanded to include more oral history courses in the United States. Concurrently, the interest of teachers in using the "Foxfire Method" of Eliot Wigginton in their classrooms has prompted many teachers to attend oral history workshops. Not only is the teaching of oral history of growing interest, but regional oral history associations have formed so that practitioners of all sorts can exchange ideas. Oral history has rightfully been called "the growth industry of the historical profession" for the past decade. These developments explain why the Oral History Association asked Willa K. Baum and David K. Dunaway to compile the present anthology.

What lies ahead for oral history? In the "reel world" the prospects for oral history are enticing. Although thousands of hours have been recorded on cassettes by oral historians and millions of pages have been transcribed, many aspects of American society still merit the question-asking scrutiny of oral historians. Surprisingly, one of the most neglected areas is among the most crucial: the role of business enterprise in modern America. Businessmen have been tardy in telling the story of American business to oral historians; the story of entrepreneurism and the skills it requires has rarely been voiced on tape.

Outside the United States, the documentation of independence movements in many nations of the "Third World" invites the attention of well-trained oral historians. Many of these nations achieved independence during the decade following World War II, and after the passage of nearly three decades they may become increasingly conscious of the need to preserve the early history of their nationhood.

The term "oral history" was relatively unknown when oral historians assembled at Lake Arrowhead in 1966. Today I find myself pleasantly amazed by the large number of people who are instantly familiar with oral history. Such a broadened awareness we can attribute to several best-sellers in recent years, and two of their authors are represented in this volume. One is Alex Haley, whose *Roots*—as a book and as a television spectacular—vastly enriched the sense of family history in black and other Americans; the other is Eliot Wigginton, whose *Foxfire* books woke Americans to the heritage rapidly fading from rural enclaves bypassed by a nation rushing toward an urban-industrial society. Other "oral history books" are Studs Terkel's *Hard Times: An Oral History of the Great Depression,* which evokes in dramatic human terms the ordeal of the 1930s, and Merle Miller's striking portrait of our thirty-third president, *Plain Speaking: An Oral Biography of Harry S. Truman.*

In a halting way, many Americans today are able to combine the key elements of oral history—tape recorders and the idea of interviewing people about their historical reminiscences. Many also note their great regret that a favorite relative, neighbor, or community leader was not taped "while there was still time." I often hear sad accounts of how voices of history have been lost forever. Americans are present minded and future oriented, and our cultural consciousness has thrived, in an era of growth and technological breakthroughs, on the premise that today and tomorrow are more exciting than knowledge of yesterday's memories. But with books like this anthology, and the increasing awareness of history as a resource for understanding our varying identities as Americans, I expect that oral history will rapidly become a favorite pastime in the United States. For an institution only to commission an artist to paint a portrait of a retiring leader will be unthinkable; an oral historian will need to be retained also, to preserve the leader's record in a taped interview. A person's retirement from a lifelong career—as clerk or president, for both perspectives have value—without the communication of reminiscences to an oral historian will be considered undesirable, poor acknowledgment by the world of years of service. Oral history interviewing may become the chief genealogical tool of ancestor hunters in the upcoming decades.

Oral History: An Interdisciplinary Anthology is, in effect, both a culmination and a new departure. It offers a broad sampling of helpful articles about oral history from the bibliography that the field had developed by the early 1980s. These documents include guidelines for evaluating interview projects and suggested standards for "doing" oral history. But the essays that follow are to be read with a questioning mind, just as oral history interviewing entails a questioning mind. After reading the comments of these writers you should be prepared to interview them, thoroughly, about why they say what they say in these pieces. Read this book as an oral history interviewer with a mind full of questions.

Charles T. Morrissey
The Oral History Institute
Montpelier, Vermont

August 1983

PART ONE
The Gateway to Oral History

1

Oral History

Louis Starr

Our first selections are statements by the founders of the oral history movement in the United States, Louis Starr and Allan Nevins. Starr's essay remains the best overall introduction to the practice and history of oral history in the United States before 1977, when it was published.

Starr comments on the disappearance of traditional written sources for historical writing and notes that the term "oral history" is actually a misnomer for the process of oral data collection. His appreciation for the diverse moods and ends of oral history research, and his firsthand account of the founding of the Oral History Association (he was its first president), make this article required reading for anyone interested in the field of oral history.

Louis Starr directed the Oral History Research Office at Columbia University for twenty-four years; during that time he was a ceaseless organizer and publicist for oral sources in historical research. Starr began his career in journalism, after graduating from Yale; in the 1940s he worked on newspapers in Tennessee and Chicago. Subsequently he studied at the graduate level under Allan Nevins at the time of Columbia's pioneering efforts at oral history; his dissertation was published as Bohemian Brigades: Civil War Newsmen in Action *(1954). At the Oral History Research Office, his annual review of Columbia's program stimulated scholarly interest in oral history; under his direction the collection grew to more than half a million pages of oral memoirs. With his associate, Elizabeth Mason, he edited four editions of* The Oral History Collection of Columbia University *and taught an annual seminar which helped educate the first generation of oral history scholars.*

"Oral History" originally appeared in the Encyclopedia of Library and Information Sciences, *vol. 20 (New York: Marcel Dekker, 1977), pp. 440–63.*

ORAL HISTORY is primary source material obtained by recording the spoken words—generally by means of planned, tape-recorded interviews—of persons deemed to harbor hitherto unavailable information worth preserving.

Oral history as an organized activity dates only from 1948, when Professor Allan Nevins launched "The Oral History Project" at Columbia University. Yet the essence of the idea is as old as history itself. On the premise that it stems from the oral tradition (that body of lore by which one tribe or family knows of its past through stories repeated from one generation to the next), some scholars would argue, indeed, that it predates history. Herodotus, called by Cicero "the father of history," employed oral history in gathering information for his account of the Persian Wars in the fifth century B.C. Like most of his successors, however, Herodotus did not keep a verbatim record of what his informants told him, or if he did, it was lost. The purpose of oral history is to obtain and preserve such a record. Edmund Spenser expressed beautifully the thought that motivates the work when he wrote these lines in *The Ruines of Time* (A.D. 1591):

> For deeds do die, how ever nobile donne,
> And thoughts of men do as themselves decay,
> But wise wordes taught in numbers for to runne,
> Recorded by the Muses, live for ay.

The modern Muses, as oral historians would have it, are men and women armed with tape recorders, in quest of firsthand knowledge that would otherwise decay. This they would capture, not for their own benefit, but "for ay"—for libraries or other repositories to hold for the benefit of scholars of this and succeeding generations.

Oral History as Source Material

The verbatim record of what oral historians obtain is thus in one respect unique, in comparison with other forms of primary source materials. It is deliberately created solely for historical purposes. It can capture and preserve life stories that would otherwise be lost, by eliciting oral autobiographies that may run to a thousand or more pages. It can fill in the lacunae in one field of learning after another, by eliciting testimony from many on a single topic. It can convey personality, explain motivation, reveal inner thoughts and perceptions—serving scholars in much the same way as private letters and diaries. An oral history memoir is based on recall, and thus lacks the immediacy of these, but it can be fully as intimate, more reflective, and, if the questioner knows what to ask, quite as useful to the researcher. Obviously it is also quite as hazardous for the researcher, since memory is fallible, ego distorts, and contradictions sometimes go unresolved. Yet problems of evaluation are not markedly different from those inherent in the use of letters, diaries, and other primary sources. With *caveat emptor* ever in mind, the scholar must test the evidence in an oral history memoir for internal consistency and, whenever possible, by corroboration from other sources, often including the oral history memoirs of others on the same topic.

Inviting the comparison with private letters, diaries, and other intimate documents is doubly apropos, for it is the gradual disappearance of these in our own time that is most often advanced as the reason for the remarkable growth of oral history in the second half of this century. As early as 1950, Nevins pointed out that the telephone, the automobile, and the airliner, by enabling people to "contact" one another as readily as that expression suggests, were displacing the confidential letters of old, thereby robbing future historians of incalculable treasure.[1] Nevins was bold enough to suggest that oral history might help fill the void. If that seemed visionary at the time, the last quarter century has given it plausibility. The age of the holographic document has receded still further, jets and freeways and television have made further incursions on writing time, and oral history moves apace. The tape recorder has become omnipresent, there are oral history projects in all states of the Union and in many foreign lands, and professional associations flourish here and abroad. The oral history movement may be perceived as a conscious effort to utilize technology—not only the tape recorder, but (as we shall see) microforms, the computer, and other tools of the age—to counter the inroads of technology that Nevins deplored.

Form and Substance

Substance

In range of subject matter, particularly as it has been developing in the United States in recent years, oral history appears to know no bounds. Familiar published examples of the genre run from Theodore Rosengarten's moving evocation of a Black Alabama sharecropper's life story, *All God's Dangers*, to passages in Forrest Pogue's majestic four-volume life of General George Marshall; from Studs Terkel's interviewees talking about their jobs in *Working* to Merle Miller's version of his taped sessions with Harry Truman in *Plain Speaking*; from quotations in William Lynwood Montell's minor classic in folklore, *The Saga of Coe Ridge*, to Saul Benison's in polio research, *Tom Rivers: A Life in Science and Medicine*. If the oral history components of these books have a common bond, it is the authenticity of their firsthand testimony, delivered with spontaneity.

Each, as the vernacular would have it, "tells it like it is" (or wəs) with a candor that is the forte of good oral history, a candor emanating from the rapport which the interlocutor, each in his way, was able to establish with the respondent.

More commonly, oral history remains unpublished, awaiting researchers in libraries. Its votaries range over terrain even more varied than these titles suggest. They include New Left scholars interviewing steel workers in Gary, Indiana; law students prodding the memories of eminent jurists in New York, or of those who knew Chief Justice Earl Warren in California; social historians exploring the Jewish community of Columbus, Ohio, or of mountain people in the piney woods of Georgia; musicologists on the trail of those who remember Charles Ives or Scott Joplin or Art Tatum; and historians pursuing institutional history, be it a study of the packaging industry, of unionism in the needle trades, of the development of the computer, or of NASA. Other projects focus upon an epoch, like the occupation of Japan; an episode, like the Memorial Day Massacre during the "Little Steel" strike of 1937; or a movement, like the suffragists, or the Civil Rights Movement of the 1960s. There are oral history projects on every branch of the armed services, and on each presidential administration beginning with Herbert Hoover's. . . .

In substance, then, oral history bids fair to reflect the myriad interests of a pluralistic society—its ethnic groups, its cultural pursuits, its political leadership, its institutions and occupational groups—so far as limited resources but apparently limitless enthusiasm permits.

Form: Tapes versus Transcripts

Is the end product of oral history a tape or a transcript? For some local projects in the United States and Canada, and for most in Great Britain, the oral history process begins and ends with the tape. A written summary or some other finding aid may be prepared to guide listeners, and that is all. Some 70% of oral history centers in the United States, and many elsewhere, however, transcribe their tapes into typescript.[2] The prevailing practice is to persuade the oral author (a more precise designation than subject, respondent, narrator, memoirist, or interviewee, all of which are also employed) to verify the result, correcting the text for clarity and accuracy rather than for style. The edited transcript—completely retyped by some programs, by others left with its handwritten changes—then becomes the true end product. Indexed and cataloged, the final version takes its place in an oral history repository, subject to whatever restrictions upon access and use the oral author imposes.

Tapes versus transcripts has been a subject of lively debate among those engaged in oral history, one that is gradually moving toward resolution.

Protagonists of the tape contend that this is the true primary source. Nuances of voice, they assert, must be heard rather than left to the reader to infer from a transcript, which cannot accurately convey accent, inflection, emphasis, or manner. Those who prefer the transcript emphasize the value to the scholar of knowing that the oral author has read and corrected what he said, a process that turns what might be dismissed as hearsay into a document that has much of the standing of a legal deposition. As to nuances lost in the transcript, they hold this a small price to pay for the assurance of verification. One cannot read 20 pages of transcript, they contend, without comprehending the tone of the oral author, since this is conveyed by style, and in any case is frequently immaterial to the researcher's purpose.

The debate is subsiding in the United States largely because of the overwhelming preference of users for transcripts, calls for which exceed calls for tape in some of the larger oral history collections by ratios of a thousand to one and higher. This is not so much because those who favor the transcript have the better of the argument on theoretical grounds as because of practical convenience: to most researchers, a written document that carries page numbers, and an index to them, is vastly preferable. Whatever they wish to copy or paraphrase is before them in black and white. Tapes, no matter how carefully indexed, are awkward to use, particularly if the memoir is a massive one. Folklorists, linguists, and musicologists, nonetheless, find them indispensable.

A consensus emerges: tapes are more suitable for some purposes, transcripts for others; but so far as possible both should be preserved, allowing researchers to choose for themselves. Future generations may prove more aurally oriented.

The Oral History Movement

Antecedents

The modern roots of oral history antedate both the term itself and Allan Nevins's efforts. Several projects generated oral history (though the term was not applied) under New Deal auspices in the 1930s. One, the first of two endeavors to collect the reminiscences of former slaves, was launched by Lawrence D. Reddick under a Works Progress Administration grant in Kentucky, Indiana, and adjacent states, 1934–35. Others, done in the late 1930s for the Federal Writers Project in Georgia and other southern states, sought out Blacks and poor whites in rural areas for interviews that might enrich the state guides the agency was preparing, but this material was also perceived as having enduring archival value.[3] Like the slave narratives, these manually recorded interviews were largely forgotten in the National Archives until interest in Black studies combined with the oral history movement to resuscitate them decades later.

As for the term oral history, it appears to have been coined by a dissolute member of the Greenwich Village literati named Joe Gould, Harvard graduate, friend of the poet Maxwell Bodenheim and self-styled "Professor Sea Gull." Gould claimed to be compiling "an Oral History of Our Time," according to a *New Yorker* profile in 1942; a sequel proved this apocryphal.[4] Gould named an activity he may or may not have pursued, giving the world a misnomer now firmly embedded in the language. Suggested alternatives like oral documentation and living history have not survived the hour.

The Beginnings

The term may have slipped into Allan Nevins's vocabulary through the *New Yorker*, but his own thoughts about an ongoing interviewing effort for the benefit of future scholars germinated as far back as 1931. Engrossed in his biography of Grover Cleveland, he lamented that no one had had the wit to interview Cleveland or his associates, most of whom died without leaving historians a legacy of any kind. He discussed with friends, among them Adolf Berle and Dean Edwin F. Gay of the Harvard Business School, how the idea might be implemented, and in 1938 issued the first call for it in his preface to *The Gateway to History*:

We have agencies aplenty to seek out the papers of men long dead. But we have only the most scattered and haphazard agencies for obtaining a little of the immense mass of information about the more recent American past—the past of the last half century—which might come fresh and direct from men once prominent in politics, in business, in the professions, and in other fields; information that every obituary column shows to be perishing.

A decade passed before Nevins found the means to implement such an agency. After years of gentle persuasion on his part, his wealthy friend Frederic Bancroft, a historian who held one of Columbia's earliest Ph.Ds (1885) left the university $1½ million for the acquisition of new materials in American history.[5] A small portion of the income (initially but $3,000) helped start the work.

The beginnings were hardly auspicious. Nevins had no recording device. Limited by a skeptical faculty committee to New York City affairs, he took along a graduate student named Dean Albertson to help on the first interview, one of a series with a seasoned civic leader named George McAneny. On May 18, 1948, in the McAneny living room at 120 East 75th Street, Albertson took notes in longhand as Nevins evoked a stream of reminiscence from his subject. The young man then went home to type up a rough draft of the proceedings as best he could from his notes, and the experiment was suspended until fall.[6] Toward the end of 1948, three more memoirs had been obtained in this laborious fashion, when the pioneers of oral history got wind of an electronic device that would enable them to capture every word, the wire recorder. Judge Learned Hand was the first to speak in the presence of one of these, January 21, 1949. The process changed almost overnight. Transcribers were installed in a basement room of Butler Library, tape recorders replaced the awkward wire machines after a year or so, the horizon expanded to include national affairs, and production began in earnest.

Acquiring personal papers to complement an oral history memoir soon proved a fringe benefit, sometimes far more. Nevins's interviews with Herbert Lehman led ultimately to the gift not only of his papers, but of a model facility to house them in Columbia's School of International Affairs Library, with its own curator, catalog, and seminar rooms.

Alongside the lengthy oral autobiographies Nevins favored from the first, there soon developed a second kind of oral history—the special project. It proved fruitful. The first of these bloomed when a national organization of radio pioneers called "The Twenty-Year Club" (later "Broadcast Pioneers") helped fund an effort, 1950–1952, on the early years of broadcasting. Nevins enlisted Frank Ernest Hill for work that generated over 4,000 pages of memoirs by radio's early announcers, program directors, technicians, and executives. A second one, launched a few months later, gave oral history its first foothold elsewhere—at the Ford Archives in Dearborn, Michigan. This was by way of preliminary research for the three-volume history Nevins and Hill ultimately produced on the Ford Motor Company, and it grew into the largest of industrial oral history projects. Owen Bombard, recruited from the Columbia office, saw to the interviewing of 434 persons who descanted some 26,000 pages about Henry Ford and his empire. A third special project, conducted by Nevins and Hill in 1951, produced a wealth of material on the history of oil wildcatting in Texas, and presumably was responsible for alerting scholars at the University of Texas to the potentialities. Their project on the oil industry, begun in 1952 by William Owens at the E. C. Barker Texas History Center, appears to have been the first such by another university. The Forest History Society, under Elwood Maunder, began its oral history program the same year. The first multipurpose project after Columbia's began 2 years later, in 1954, when the Regional Oral History Office of the University of California, Berkeley, was launched. UCLA began its own in 1959.[7]

Growth remained lethargic through the 1950s, as Figure 1.1 shows. In part this was because the early emphasis on the right of an oral author to

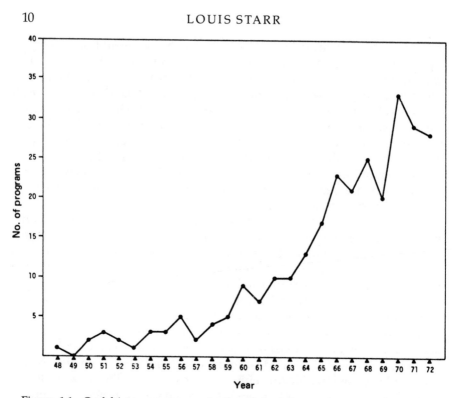

Figure 1.1. Oral history programs in the United States, by year of founding. *Source: Oral History Collections* (New York: Bowker, 1975).

close his entire memoir (rather than the sensitive parts only, as later) left oral history's pioneers with substantial holdings "in the deep freeze," as Albertson put it. Nevins, who retired in 1958, had been in no hurry to make them widely known in any case, for he conceived of the work as primarily for future generations. As for the other projects then in existence, most were wholly absorbed in creating: dissemination would come years later. (An exception was the Forest History project, which published excerpts of its oral histories in its journal, *Forest History*, from time to time.)

Growth in the 1960s

The explosive growth that ensued in the following decade cannot be wholly explained. A trickle of articles about oral history in learned journals and the popular press, which grew to a rivulet by the mid-1960s (figure 1.2) undoubtedly helped. Nor was it lost on the academic world that such scholars as James MacGregor Burns, Frank Freidel, George F.

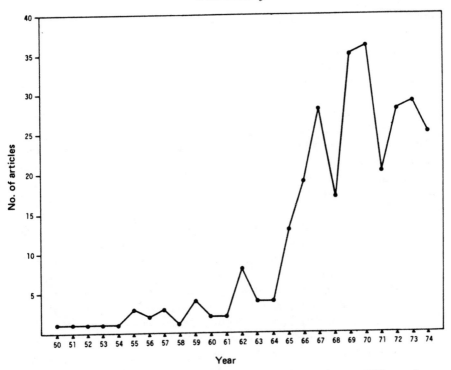

Figure 1.2. Articles on oral history, by year of publication. *Source: Bibliography on Oral History,* ed. Manfred J. Waserman (New York: Oral History Association, 1975).

Kennan, and Arthur M. Schlesinger, Jr., by the late 1950s were drawing upon oral history in their published work. Other factors include the phenomenal development of the portable tape recorder in the course of the 1960s, culminating in the cassette.

The appearance, in 1960, of the first published catalog may be noted: a slender volume titled *The Oral History Collection of Columbia University,* carrying brief descriptions of holdings then totaling 130,000 pages. Significantly, it was arranged like the catalog of a manuscript collection, a model that has been followed since. In 1961 came the first printed annual report, from the same office, both publications replacing multigraphed efforts of small circulation in the late 1950s. These reports, more widely circulated each year, served to spread the word. Scholarly traffic and inquiries from other institutions accelerated apace, and the Columbia office began a file on projects elsewhere. Its 1964 report provided brief information about oral history work in progress at the American Institute of Physics, Brandeis, Claremont Graduate School, Cornell University, Harvard (with which the JFK project was then affiliated), the Hollywood Museum, the George C. Marshall Research Library, Princeton (then beginning its project on John Foster Dulles), the University of Michigan (harboring the United Auto Workers project, begun in 1959 and shared with Wayne State), the Truman Library (first of the Presidential Libraries to enter the field, 1961), and Tulane (where the New Orleans Jazz Archive began in 1958), in addition to projects already mentioned. A survey in the wake of this resulted in *Oral History in the United States,* a state-by-state listing of 89 projects, many still in embryo, as part of Columbia's 1965 report. The "veritable movement" cited in the second edition of its catalog (1964) had indeed materialized, but it was apparent from the data that growth was not along the lines the original office had anticipated. "Oral history holds potentialities that may well give an office like ours a place in most great universities of the future," its 1961 report had ventured. Instead, museums, historical societies, corporations, labor unions, church groups, and libraries were intermingled with colleges and universities large and small, most of them engaged in a single special project as opposed to the few (notably Cornell and several California institutions) making a broad acquisitions effort on the Columbia model (table 1.1).

Was there sufficient common interest among these organizations to form a viable association? The collector of the information (and writer of this article) was doubtful. Nevins, then at the Huntington Library in San

Table 1. Oral History Centers in the United States, by Institutional Affiliation, 1973

Type of affiliation	No. of centers
Universities (public, 75; independent, 33)	108
Public libraries (city, 26; county, 15; state, 7)	48
Colleges (independent, 31; public, 16)	47
Professional, ethnic, other special interest societies	29
Historical societies, local and state	25
Federal agencies	18
Museums, hospitals, church groups	12
Private collectors	5
Corporations	4
Medical centers	3
Alumni associations	2
Bookmobile	1
Unclassified	14
Total	316

Source: From *Oral History,* annual report (New York: Columbia University, 1975), p. 4.

Marino, was convinced there was, and having failed to persuade the writer to call a meeting, he turned to James V. Mink, then in charge of oral history at UCLA. Mink had just such a meeting in mind.

The Oral History Association

With the promise of Allan Nevins as a speaker and the Columbia report as an invitation list, Mink attracted 77 persons to Lake Arrowhead, UCLA's conference facility in the San Bernardino mountains, in September 1966, for 3 days of wide-ranging discussion. It concluded with a resolve to meet again the following year and to form an association. Mink headed a steering committee which accomplished this at the Arden House meeting organized by the writer in 1967. The Oral History Association (OHA) has since published a quarterly newsletter; a *Bibliography on Oral History* (the fourth edition, edited by Manfred Waserman of the National Library of Medicine, appeared in 1975); a directory; and an annual, *The Oral History Review*. Its extraordinary growth in membership is charted in figure 1.3.

OHA has helped to alert the American Library Association, the Society of American Archivists, the Organization of American Historians, and other professional groups to the work, recruiting panel discussions on oral history for their meetings, staging exhibits at them, staffing workshops for them. Its own meetings, held in the fall in places remote from urban distraction—in 1974 at Jackson Hole, Wyoming, in 1975 near

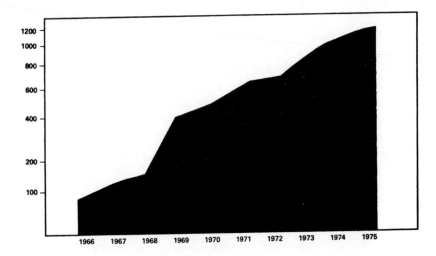

Figure 1.3. Membership of the Oral History Association, geometric scale. *Source: Oral History Newsletter, 1967–1974.*

Asheville, North Carolina, in 1976 at Le Chateau Montebello in Quebec—from the first achieved an ambiance uncommon to academic gatherings, emanating in part from a sense of creative pioneering shared by all in the field, in part from a policy of enlisting speakers outside of academe (e.g., Barbara Tuchman, Walter Lord, Alden Whitman, Daniel Schorr) as well as within it to broaden perspectives, and in part from its attraction for younger scholars. Beginning with the Fifth National Colloquium at Asilomar, California, in 1970, OHA has run workshops for initiates each year prior to its colloquium. They deal with topics ranging from the ethics of oral history interviewing, as set forth in OHA's "Goals and Guidelines," to interviewing techniques, final processing, and control of access, generally interspersed with lively debate.

Toward Wider Dissemination

The rapidity of oral history's growth led to concern among its practitioners as to how all the riches gathered were to be made widely known and put at the disposal of scholars. There has been significant progress in this direction in the 1970s. Through the OHA, the *National Union Catalogue of Manuscript Collections* (NUCMC), published by the Library of Congress, arranged to include oral history collections that met its criteria as to size, beginning with the 1970 edition. A directory of all known projects, *Oral History in the United States* (compiled by Gary Shumway of the California State University at Fullerton and edited and published by Columbia in 1971 on behalf of OHA), provided a state-by-state guide to 230 collections, with notes on their contents and a name and subject index. It is in some 3,000 libraries in this country and abroad.

This was followed in 1975 by a far more ambitious directory, *Oral History Collections*, edited by Alan Meckler and Ruth McMullin and published by R. R. Bowker. It listed in a single name and subject index the individual memoirs held in many repositories, as well as many of the topics covered in subject collections. A centers section gave data about 316 oral history centers in the U.S. Though far from complete, the guide broke a path toward comprehensive coverage in future editions.

A 1970 article on oral history observed that few projects had published descriptive lists of their holdings as yet.[8] Here, too, progress has been rapid. Study of the Bowker directory shows that by 1973 (when the data were collected) some 45 oral history centers had catalogs of their holdings (in a few instances in card rather than book form). Eight more were going to press. The third edition of Columbia's catalog, published the same year and set from computer tape to facilitate subsequent editions, carried subject and biographical indexes. Finding aids of this kind are, of course, indispensable to the researcher, for no union list can supply the detailed information they contain. The appearance of the Bowker directory is expected to stimulate such catalogs; without one, no oral history center can be properly represented in subsequent editions of this or of NUCMC.

Oral History and Microforms

A development of potentially greater significance was signaled by the establishment of The New York Times Oral History Program in 1970, whereby selected "open" transcripts are made available to libraries in both microfilm and microfiche, and to individual scholars on fiches. This came in response to complaints that oral history was both inaccessible and difficult to use because of the prohibition against copying that most centers enforce, to protect the common-law copyright of their oral authors. By obtaining assignments of copyright from the authors or their executors, centers thenceforth could look to wider distribution of substantial parts of their collections by joining the program.

By 1976, 20 oral history collections in the United States and the largest one abroad, that at Hebrew University in Jerusalem, had done so. They are included in the annual *Guide to Microforms in Print* as well as in the Library of Congress Cataloging in Publication program, making for a further increase in accessibility. Another advance was in the immediate offing: computerized name and topical indexes of some of these collections, following the general style of The New York Times Index. The first of these, covering the 200 memoirs in "Part One" of the Columbia collection on microfilm, was scheduled to appear in 1976.

Micropublication, of course, leaves "permission required" or "closed" memoirs untouched, but since all such restrictions end in due course, it appears likely that the most useful oral history transcripts in many fields will be available in microform in time for the next generation of scholars, accompanied by sophisticated finding aids.

Manuals and Guides

For all of the literature devoted to interviewing of various kinds, there was no suitable guide to the mysteries of oral history work for nearly two decades. The need was met partially, after the founding of OHA, by its printed proceedings, a series that provided hundreds of novices with their introduction to oral history. (Now out of print, the series has been micropublished by The New York Times Oral History Program. *The Oral History Review* took the place of these as the OHA's annual in 1973.)

Guides proliferated in due course. Credit for the first one belongs to William G. Tyrrell of the New York State Historical Commission, who in 1966 wrote *Tape Recording Local History*, a 12-page pamphlet issued by the

American Association for State and Local History. This was followed in 1969 by *Oral History for the Local Historical Society*, by Willa K. Baum of the University of California's Regional Oral History Office, a work that has been called the Dr. Spock of its field. Concise and clearly written, its fourth edition (1974) met the need (title notwithstanding) well enough to have become assigned reading in graduate courses on the subject.

Both more elaborate and simpler guides have come since. *An Oral History Primer*, by Gary L. Shumway and William G. Hartley, published by the Oral History Program of the California State University at Fullerton in 1973, proved useful to schools and to programs that rely on volunteer interviewers. *A Guide for Oral History Programs*, published the same year under the same auspices, set forth in detail the oral history process from funding to cataloging, as practiced by that institution. A similar volume, into which is woven an interesting history of the John F. Kennedy Oral History project, was written by William W. Moss of its staff and published by Praeger, New York, in 1974. Cullom Davis, Kathryn Back, and Kay MacLean of Sangamon State University in Springfield, Illinois, produced *From Tape to Type* as a guide for small institutions in 1975; and Joseph H. Cash (of the University of South Dakota) and associates wrote yet another, *The Practice of Oral History*, published by The New York Times Oral History Program the same year. None is likely to displace Mrs. Baum's work, with its nice sensitivity to the interests of volunteers on the one hand and to the basic needs for attainment of professional competence on the other. All served to push back the walls of ignorance about oral history.

Oral History in the Classroom

Oral history has impinged on the learning process in one way or another since its early years. William E. Leuchtenburg, Eric McKitrick, and others in the Columbia history department took to immersing their students in the Oral History Collection as a means of exposing them to the problems peculiar to it. Columbia's Oral History office, as Henry Steele Commager recalled in addressing the Second National Colloquium on Oral History, became "a kind of *Ecole des chartes* for the training of oral historians and oral archivists," but it remained for many years a very informal *école* featuring private tutoring and learning-by-doing. At the Third National Colloquium the following year, attention was given to classroom applications, but the consensus was that these remained largely unexplored. Saul Benison of the University of Cincinnati told of using oral history in lectures and assignments in a course on historiography. Charles Morrissey involved students at the University of Vermont in demonstration interviews, and Gary Shumway of California State put them to work on specific projects he was conducting. Harry Kursh, a seventh and eighth grade teacher at Lakeland Middle School, New York, told of organizing his class to obtain an oral history interview, bringing history alive to students who had no interest in it hitherto. An OHA survey in 1974 showed sharply increasing use of all applications suggested in these models, on high school, college, and graduate levels.

Like archaeology, oral history is more than a tool and less than a discipline; yet one area in which significant progress has been made recently is in the teaching of oral history itself as a disciplined activity. Ground was broken by the University of California, Los Angeles, when it obtained a federal grant for a 2-week session on oral history techniques for librarians in July 1968. Some 20 students went through the whole process, from preparing for interviews to processing and submitting them. An intensive course in every aspect of the work began at Columbia on the graduate level in 1973 and has been oversubscribed every year since. Wendell Wray, a student in the first class, transplanted it with his own embellishments to the University of Pittsburgh's Library School the same year. Jacquelyn Dowd Hall installed a similar course at the University of North Carolina, Chapel Hill, also in 1973. The *école* Commager alluded to thus spread to several campuses, suggesting that the first professionally trained interviewers and program directors presently will replace oral history's early practitioners.

A departure by William Chafe and Lawrence Goodwyn at Duke University sought to train graduate students to unearth specifics relating to Black disenfranchisement and other aspects of Black life in the South, on the premise that this buried history could be exhumed only by exhaustive digging in published sources, followed by pinpoint interviewing. While the program was a modest one, with seven students in 1974, development of this methodology for "history-from-the-bottom-up" projects attracted wide interest.[9]

Financing Oral History

"We begin with finances," Allan Nevins told the first OHA colloquium. "And sometimes we end without finances."[10] It was largely to help programs find funding that he urged they band together in the first place, yet in this area the OHA, up to 1976, had done little beyond promoting discussion. Oral history has been chronically underfinanced from the first. A survey by Adelaide Tusler of the UCLA office in 1967 showed only one-fifth of those responding had budgets of over $20,000.[11] Six years later data collected by Meckler and McMullin for *Oral History Collections* indicated a sharp increase in total expenditures for oral history, but the median for all centers providing figures fell in the $10–14,000 range. This was not enough to sustain an ongoing program without volunteer help. Volunteers, particularly as interviewers for local and regional projects, but also on occasion for some of the largest ones, have played an important role in the movement.

The cost of processing an hour of tape, from preliminary research through interviewing, transcribing, editing, indexing, and cataloging, runs from around $100 to as high as $500. This is because of wide variations in processing the material, and also in paying interviewers and transcribers. Projects employing salaried staff for the whole process, particularly if this includes elaborate editing and final-typing, obviously incur the highest costs. Those employing specialists on a per-hour basis fall in the lower ranges.

Where does the money come from? In most cases from the parent institution, the Tusler survey reported: the college, society, or other body with which the program is affiliated. Major university programs, however, have been funded largely by outside sources, public and private. Special projects, according to one study, produced 43% of all income for one major university program over a decade. These were underwritten by foundations, corporations, and individuals, as well as by various federal agencies on a "cost plus" basis, the "plus" going toward support of unsubsidized work. General support came also from foundations and from university sources, each amounting to about half the percentage from special projects. The balance came from catalog sales, royalties, and services.[12] These proportions, derived from 1957–1967 data, have remained quite stable with the exception of income from royalties, which increased substantially after the introduction of microforms.

Oral History Abroad

A 1970 report on oral history suggested that the movement would become "worldwide in the 1970s."[13] "Worldwide" may prove too inclusive, but midway in the 1970s there are signs that, taken in sum, make it arguable.

In Britain, the Oral History Society took form in 1973, meets twice yearly, and issues its own journal. Limited largely to social historians— the government's Social Science Research Council funded its first conferences—it shows signs of broadening its base. Membership reached 300 by 1976. In Canada—where leadership has been provided by Leo La Clare of the Public Archives, together with William Langlois, head of an active regional project in Vancouver—an association was formed in 1974, bringing together programs of widely diverse interests. In Australia, Joan Campbell of La Trobe University drew 85 persons to a first oral history conference in 1974, saw to the publication of its proceedings, and held another that gave birth to an association in 1975. The National Library of Australia has had a full-scale oral history operation going since 1970.

In Latin America, leadership has come from Eugenia Meyer of the Instituto Nacional de Antropologia e Historia in Mexico City. Her program has published some of its memoirs in pamphlet form, has attracted government funding, and has steadily expanded its interests. Argentina's Instituto Di Tella in Buenos Aires carried on a broad-scale economic, social, and political study of that country in an oral history effort begun in 1971, sharing its transcripts with Columbia. In Brazil, interest was sufficient to mount a highly successful course in the subject in Rio de Janeiro in 1975 to prepare scholars from Brazil and Peru for a variety of planned projects.

A survey by Elizabeth B. Mason of Columbia University for the Oral History Association in 1974 turned up 165 projects outside the United States, on every continent. In addition to those mentioned, countries where oral history activity was found included Chile, Denmark, France, West Germany, Holland, India, Ireland, Israel, Jamaica, Kenya, Lebanon, the Philippines, Rhodesia, Singapore, South Africa, Sri Lanka, and Sweden. The 1976 *Oral History Review* included reports on oral history in Australia, Brazil, Mexico, and Great Britain, and OHA's Canadian meeting symbolized its awareness of international interest.

Long-Term Significance

Oral history, if it achieves the mission its votaries have set for it, will win universal acceptance as a form of primary source material, one that is quite as pervasive, and no more and no less valid, per se, than the holographic documents it purports to replace. Its most ardent champions would not contend that this is in the immediate offing, heartening as its progress has been.

The movement has weaknesses that have prevented it from having the impact upon the scholarly world that one might expect. The experience of Eugenia Meyer in Mexico has been all too common everywhere—difficulty in "convincing historians of the value of this new source material, which was initially received quite indifferently or as 'a waste of time' because of its inherent subjective and partisan qualities." Even after academic skeptics are converted, as she has pointed out, "few are willing to involve themselves in the task of producing this type of source," save when they have books of their own in mind.[14]

In consequence, oral history has failed to receive the critical attention it needs if it is to fulfill its potentialities. Its reception is the more striking if one contrasts it with the tumultuous one that greeted another ill-named child of the technology that burst into the house of learning on its heels—

the child named quantitative history, or cliometrics. For a time, at least, its computer applications and their ramifications became a veritable obsession within the historical profession. Oral historians could argue that *All God's Dangers* was patently a more durable contribution to the history of the American South than *Time on the Cross*, the controversial attempt to apply cliometrics to the economics of slavery. They could insist that *Working*, or *By Myself, I'm a Book!*, an oral history of the immigrant Jewish experience in Pittsburgh, held values for urbanologists comparable to any that the quantifiers, or cliometricians, had given them. No matter. The critical attention accorded quantifiers, criticism that should serve to discipline their work, eluded oral history.

Should a transcript show changes made by the oral author when he reviewed it, for example, or should the final product be a smoothly edited, chaptered, completely retyped MS? Scholars worth their salt know the former is preferable. Yet they have been mute, with the result that some centers follow one procedure while others, more anxious to win the approval of their oral authors, follow another.

What of Barbara Tuchman's charge that oral history gathers trash and trivia with all the discrimination of a vacuum cleaner?[15] Defenders respond that what is trash to one researcher turns gold to another and that rapid development of finding aids will obviate her point by unearthing the nuggets. Yet they must own that standards of quality have been slow in developing, again for want of informed criticism by scholars for whom the work is intended.

What impact has the movement had upon historical literature? Manifestly, there has been an infusion of the spoken word into this tradition-bound branch of letters through the use of oral history, much of it so recent there are no studies, as yet, of the consequences. A single collection, Columbia's, has seen the number of books drawing upon it surge from 120 in its first 22 years (up to 1970) to nearly triple that total in the 6 years that followed. Notable books utilizing other collections in the same period included David Halberstam's *The Best and the Brightest* (John F. Kennedy Library oral histories); *The Devil and John Foster Dulles*, by Townsend Hoopes (Dulles oral history collection, Princeton); *Charles Ives Remembered*, by Vivian Perlis (Yale Music Library oral histories); Margaret Truman's biography of her father (Truman Library oral history collection); *Lyndon Johnson and the American Dream*, by Doris Kearns (LBJ Library oral history collection); and harbingers of more to come from these and other repositories, all of them still comparatively new.

In the same period there has been a parallel jump in the number of monographs, biograhies, and studies of current affairs that rely wholly or in part upon their authors' own interviews. It is not journalists but academics who now account for the bulk of the interviewing that is carried out with books in view, the very academics who would have been loath to risk their reputations by so much as citing oral sources a decade or so back, assuming that interviews had occurred to them at all. It is a turnabout little noted. The impact of oral history extends beyond work drawing upon established collections, insofar as these have inspired individual scholars to sally forth and do it for themselves.

Are such books the better for it? The question defies a sweeping answer, but one would have to be churlish to deny that in innumerable cases they are. Some, like George Martin's life of Frances Perkins, *Madam Secretary*, would have been impossible without oral history, as the author has said. Others, like William H. Van Vorhis's *Violence in Ulster* are "oral documentaries," distilled entirely from pools of oral history. Historical literature, then, is clearly the richer for it—richer in pungent quotation, in color, in anecdote, in personality, in insight—and beyond that there are now scores of authors to testify, as Walter Lord has, that intensive interviewing has enabled them to get to "the guts of the event, the heart of it," a point Lord has documented with examples from his own work.

Oral history's greatest growth to date has taken place in apparent defiance of the "Great Depression" engulfing the world of higher education in America (1967–). It would be a mistake to assume, however, that the movement was unaffected. Large institutions that normally could have been expected to respond to its challenge by committing themselves to the work, thereby endowing its with a stronger institutional footing, have held aloof. Oral history will continue to develop regardless. It draws vigor from a lively sense of mission, a strong professional association, and a future that excites imaginations in half a dozen disciplines. But until a better day, when more major universities and great research libraries perceive the work as central to their purpose—creating and disseminating by modern means "wise wordes taught in numbers for to runne," as Edmund Spenser put it, "for ay"—fuller assessment of its impact must wait.

Notes

1. Unpublished progress report, Oral History Research Office, Columbia University, 1950. The theme runs through oral history literature perhaps more strongly than any other.

2. *Oral History*, annual report (New York: Columbia University, 1975), p. 4.

3. Jerre Mangione, *The Dream and the Deal: The Federal Writers' Project, 1935–1943* (Boston: Little, Brown, 1972), pp. 257–58.

4. Joseph L. Mitchell, "Professor Sea Gull," *New Yorker*, December 12, 1942, pp. 28–37; "Joe Gould's Secret," *New Yorker*, September 19, 1964, pp. 61–125, and September 26, 1964, pp. 53–159.

5. Elizabeth Dixon and James V. Mink, eds., *Oral History at Arrowhead: Proceedings of the First National Colloquium on Oral History*, 2d ed. (New York: Oral History Association, 1967), pp. 36–37.

6. In April 1948, just one month before the first oral history interview, the first two American-made tape recorders, modeled on a captured German Magnetophon, emerged from Ampex facilities in California. See John T. Mullin, "Creating the Craft of Tape Recording," *High Fidelity Magazine*, April 1976, pp. 62–67. Thus tape recorders existed before oral history was launched, but the launchers were unaware of them. (They did not become generally available until several years later.)

7. Much of the information on early years has been taken from file copies of unpublished reports of the Oral History Research Office, Columbia University. Other sources are given in Louis M. Starr, "Oral History: Problems and Prospects," in *Advances in Librarianship*, vol. 2, ed. Melvin G. Voigt (New York: Seminar Press, 1971).

8. Starr, "Oral History: Problems and Prospects," p. 296.

9. "Duke U. Students Learn Interviewing Techniques of 'Oral History' to Record Lives of Ordinary People," *New York Times*, May 6, 1974, p. 41.

10. Allan Nevins, "The Uses of Oral History," in *The First National Oral History Colloquium*, ed. E. Dixon and J. Mink (New York: Oral History Association, 1967), p. 1. (See Chapter 2 of the present volume.)

11. Adelaide Tusler, "Report on Survey of Oral History Programs," multilithed (Los Angeles: University of California, Los Angeles, 1967).

12. Louis M. Starr, ed., *The Second National Oral History Colloquium* (New York: Oral History Association, 1968), pp. 113–16.

13. *Oral History*, annual report (New York: Columbia University, 1970), p. 6.

14. Eugenia Meyer, "Oral History in Mexico and Latin America," *Oral History Review* 4 (1976), pp. 56–61.

15. Barbara Tuchman, "Research in Contemporary Events for the Writing of History," in *Proceedings of the American Academy of Arts and Letters and the National Institute of Arts and Letters*, 2d ser., no. 22 (New York, 1972), p. 62.

Bibliography

Albertson, Dean. "History in the Deep-freeze: The Story of Columbia's Oral History Project." *Columbia Library Columns* 2 (1953), pp. 2–11.

Allen, Richard B. "New Orleans Jazz Archive at Tulane." *Wilson Library Bulletin* 40 (March 1966), pp. 619–23.

Bartlett, Richard A. "Some Thoughts after the Third National Colloquium on Oral History." *Journal of Library History* 4 (April 1969), pp. 169–72.

Baum, Willa K. "Oral History: A Revived Tradition of the Bancroft Library." *Pacific Northwest Quarterly* 58 (1967), pp. 57–64.

———. "Oral History, the Library, and the Genealogical Researcher." *Journal of Library History* 5 (October 1970), pp. 359–71.

———. *Oral History for the Local Historical Society*, 2d ed. rev. Nashville: American Association for State and Local History, 1974.

Benison, Saul. "Reflections on Oral History." *American Archivist* 28 (January 1965), pp. 71–77.

Bombard, Owen W. "Speaking of Yesterday." Dearborn, Mich.: Ford Motor Company Archives, 1952.

———. "A New Measure of Things Past." *American Archivist* 18 (April 1955), pp. 123–32.

Bornet, Vaughn Davis. "Oral History *Can* Be Worthwhile." *American Archivist* 18–19 (July 1955), pp. 241–53.

Campbell, Joan, ed. *Oral History 74.* Bundoora, Victoria, Australia: La Trobe University, 1974.

Catton, Bruce. "Talk Now, Play Later." Reprinted as "History-Making Idea." *Think* 31 (1965), pp. 20–23.

Challener, Richard D., and J. M. Fenton. "Recent Past Comes Alive in Dulles 'Oral History.'" *University; A Princeton Semiannual* 9 (1967), pp. 29–34.

Claremont Graduate School. "Oral History Program." Transcripts. Claremont, Calif., 1964.

Colman, Gould P. "Oral History—An Appeal for More Systematic Procedures." *American Archivist* 28 (1965), pp. 79–83.

———. "Oral History at Cornell." *Wilson Library Bulletin* 40 (1966), pp. 624–28.

Columbia University. Oral History Research Office. Annual Reports. New York: Columbia University, 1950.

———. *Oral History in the United States.* New York: Columbia University, 1965.

Conference on Science Manuscripts, May 5–6, 1960. "Case Studies of Research Experience." *Isis* 53 (1962), pp. 39–51.

Cornell University. Oral History Project. "Reports." Ithaca: Cornell University, 1962–65.

Cornell University Libraries. *Bulletin of Cornell Program in Oral History.* Ithaca: Cornell University, 1966–72.

Crowl, Philip A. "The Dulles Oral History Project: Mission Accomplished." *American Historical Association Newsletter* 5 (1967), pp. 6–10.

Curtiss, Richard D., et al. *A Guide for Oral History Programs.* Fullerton: California State University, 1973.

Dixon, Elizabeth I. "Oral History: A New Horizon." *Library Journal* 87 (April 1, 1962), pp. 1363–65.

———. "The Implications of Oral History in Library History." *Journal of Library History* 1 (January 1966), pp. 59–62.

———. "The Oral History Program at UCLA: A Bibliography." Los Angeles: University of California Library, 1966.

———. "Arrowhead in Retrospect." *Journal of Library History* 2 (April 1967), pp. 126–28.

Finnegan, Ruth. "A Note on Oral Tradition and Historical Evidence." *History and Theory* 9 (1970), pp. 195–201. (See chapter 10 of the present volume).

Fontana, Bernard. "American Indian Oral History." *History and Theory* 8 (1969), pp. 366–70.

Forest History 16:3 (25th anniversary issue, 1972). Santa Cruz, Forest History Society. (Contains editorial "Why Oral History?" and excerpts from eleven oral history interviews).

Frank, Benis M. "Oral History: Columbia and USMC." *Fortitudine* 3 (Fall 1973), pp. 19–20.

Freese, Arthur S. "They All Made History." *Journal of the National Retired Teachers Association* 25 (May–June 1974), pp. 10–12.

Fry, Amelia R. "The Nine Commandments of Oral History." *Journal of Library History* 3 (January 1968), pp. 63–73.

———. "Persistent Issues in Oral History." *Journal of Library History* 4 (July 1969), pp. 265–67.

Fry, Amelia R., and Willa K. Baum. "A Janus Look at Oral History." *American Archivist* 32 (October 1969), pp. 319–26.

Gilb, Corinne. "Tape Recorded Interviewing: Some Thoughts from California." *American Archivist* 20 (October 1957), pp. 335–44.

Glass, Mary E. "The Oral History Project of the Center for Western North American Studies: A Bibliography." Mimeographed. Reno: University of Nevada, Desert Research Institute, 1966.

Haley, Alex. "My Furthest-Back Person—The African." *New York Times Magazine,* July 16, 1972, pp. 12–16.

Harry S. Truman Library Institute. "Research Newsletter Number Ten." Independence, Mo., 1967.

Harry S. Truman Library Institute. Newsletter "Oral History: The Truman Library Approach," (Spring 1976).

Hart, Katherine. "Memories Become History." *Texas Library Journal* 45 (Spring 1969), pp. 33–34.

Hebrew University of Jerusalem. *Oral History Division, Catalogue No. 3.* Jerusalem: Institute of Contemporary Jewry, 1970.

Hewlett, R. G. "A Pilot Study in Contemporarly Scientific History. *Isis* 53 (1962), pp. 31–38.

Hoyle, Norman. "Oral History." *Library Trends* 21 (July 1972), pp. 60–82.

Kielman, Chester V. "The Texas Oil Industry Project." *Wilson Library Bulletin* 40 (March 1966), pp. 616–18.

Krasean, Thomas K. "Oral History . . . Voices of the Past." *Library Occurrent* 22 (August 1968), pp. 297, 305.

Lieber, Joel. "The Tape Recorder as Historian." *Saturday Review,* June 11, 1966, pp. 98–99.

Lord, C. L., ed. "Ideas in Conflict: A Colloquium on Certain Problems in Historical Society Work in the United States and Canada." Harrisburg, Pa.: American Association for State and Local History, 1958.

McPherson, M. W., and J. A. Popplestone. "Problems and Procedures in Oral Histories." *Archives of the History of American Psychology* 23 (1967), p. 11.

Mason, Elizabeth B., and Louis M. Starr, eds. *The Oral History Collection of Columbia University.* 3d ed. New York: New York Times Company, 1973.

Mason, John T., Jr. "An Interview with John T. Mason, Jr." *U.S. Naval Institute Proceedings* 99 (July 1973), pp. 42–47.

Maunder, Elwood R. "Tape Recorded Interviews Provide Grass Roots History." *Forest History* 2 (1959), p. 1.

Meckler, Alan M., and Ruth McMullin, eds. *Oral History Collections.* New York: Bowker, 1975.

Meyer, Eugenia, and Alicia Olivera de Bonfil. "Oral History in Mexico." *Journal of Library History* 7 (October 1972), pp. 360–65.

Miles, Wyndham D. "Usefulness of Oral History in Writing the Story of a Large Scientific Project." *Ithaca* 26 (1962), pp. 351–53.

Morrissey, Charles T. "The Case for Oral History," *Vermont History* 31 (1963), pp. 145–55.

———. "Truman and the Presidency—Records and Oral Recollections." *American Archivist* 28 (January 1965), pp. 53–61.

Moss, William W. *Oral History Program Manual.* New York: Praeger, 1974.

Nevins, Allan. *The Gateway to History.* Boston: Appleton-Century, 1938.

———. "Oral History: How and Why It Was Born." *Wilson Library Bulletin* 40 (March 1966), pp. 600–601. (See chapter 2 of the present volume).

Oral History: An Occasional News Sheet. Nos. 1–4. Colchester, Essex, England: University of Essex, 1969–74.

Oral History: The Journal of the Oral History Society. Colchester, Essex, England: University of Essex, 1973—. (Successor to *Oral History: An Occasional News Sheet*).

Oral History Association. *Newsletter*. New York: Oral History Association, 1967–.

"Oral History Collection." *North Texas State University Bulletin*, 420 (December 1970), p. 33.

Oral History Review. New York: Oral History Association, 1973–.

Perlis, Vivian. "Ives and Oral History." *Notes: Journal of the Music Library Association* 28 (June 1972), pp. 629–42.

Pogue, Forrest C. "History While It's Hot." *Kentucky Library Association Bulletin* 24 (April 1960), pp. 31–35.

———. "The George C. Marshall Oral History Project." *Wilson Library Bulletin* 40 (March 1966), pp. 607–15.

Princeton University Library. *The John Foster Dulles Oral History Project: A Preliminary Catalogue*. Princeton: Princeton University, 1966.

Regional Oral History Office. "Interviews Completed or In Process." Berkeley: University of California, 1965.

Reynoldston Research and Studies. *Oral History Developments in British Columbia*. Vancouver, B.C., Canada, 1973.

Rollins, Alfred B., Jr. *Report on the Oral History Project of the John Fitzgerald Kennedy Library*. Cambridge, Mass.: Harvard University, 1965.

Rumics, Elizabeth. "Oral History: Defining the Term." *Wilson Library Bulletin* 40 (March 1966), pp. 602–605.

Schlesinger, Arthur M., Jr. "On the Writing of Contemporary History." *Atlantic Monthly*, March 1967, pp. 69–74.

Schruben, Francis W. "An Even Stranger Death of President Harding." *Southern California Quarterly* 48 (March 1966), pp. 57–84.

Shaughnessy, Donald F. "Labor in the Oral History Collection of Columbia University." *Labor History* 1–2 (Spring 1960), pp. 177–95.

Shockley, Ann Allen. *Manual for the Black Oral History Program*. Nashville: Fisk University Library, 1971.

Shumway, Gary L. *Oral History in the United States: A Directory*. New York: Oral History Association, 1971.

Shumway, Gary L., and William G. Hartley. *An Oral History Primer*. Fullerton: California State University, 1973.

Skeels, J. W. "Oral History Project on the Development of Unionism in the Automobile Industry." *Labor History* 5 (1964), pp. 209–12.

Starr, Louis M. "Columbia's Reservoir of Source Material." *Graduate Faculties Newsletter*, November 1959, pp. 1–3.

———. "Oral History: Problems and Prospects." In *Advances in Librarianship*, vol. 2, ed. Melvin Voigt. New York: Seminar Press, 1971.

———. "Studs Terkel and Oral History." *Chicago History* 3 (Fall 1974), pp. 123–26.

Stephens, A. Roy. "Oral History and Archives." *Texas Library* 29 (Fall 1967), pp. 203–14.

Swain, Donald C. "Problems for Practitioners of Oral History." *American Archivist* 28 (January 1965), pp. 63–69.

Teiser, Ruth. "Transcriber's Fancies." *Journal of Library* 5 (April 1970), pp. 182–83.

Van Dyne, Larry. "Oral History: Sharecroppers and Presidents, Jazz and Texas Oil." *Chronicle of Higher Education* 8 (December 24, 1973), pp. 9–10.

Waserman, Manfred. *Bibliography on Oral History*. Rev. ed. New York: Oral History Association, 1975.

White, Helen M. "Thoughts on Oral History." *American Archivist* 20 (January 1957), pp. 19–30.

Wilkie, James W. "Postulates for the Oral History Center for Latin America." *Journal of Library History* 2 (January 1967), pp. 45–54.

———. *Elitelore*. Los Angeles: University of California, Latin American Center, 1973.

Wyatt, William. "Researching the South Dakota Frontier." *South Dakota Library Bulletin* 52 (October–December 1966), pp. 151–56.

Zachert, Martha Jane. "Implications of Oral history for Librarians." *College Research Libraries* 20 (March 1968), pp. 101–103. (See chapter 35 of the present volume).

———. "The Second Oral History Colloquium." *Journal of Library History* 3 (April 1968), pp. 173–78.

———. "Oral History Interviews." *Journal of Library History* 5 (January 1970), pp. 80–87.

2

Oral History:
How and Why It Was Born
The Uses of Oral History

Allan Nevins

In 1938, Allan Nevins–biographer, historian, journalist–suggested two in-novations, both of which came to pass. One was the popularization of his-tory for the multitude, an idea soon realized in the publication American Heritage *and subsequently in the many regional and topical lay history books and journals. The other was "oral history," as it came to be called. In his introduction to* The Gateway to History, *Nevins suggested establish-ing "some organization which made a systematic attempt to obtain, from the lips and papers of living Americans who have led significant lives, a fuller record of their participation in the political, economic, and cultural life of the last sixty years." Ten years later, in 1948, Nevins presided at the opening of the country's first oral history project at Columbia University, which he labored to establish.*

In the following two selections, Nevins outlines early milestones in the growth of the field of oral history. Because Nevins was an outspoken advo-cate of oral interviews as a base for "oral autobiographies," his comments on the varieties of autobiographical narratives are particularly important. Nevins's frank discussions of the difficulties of financing and providing in-terviewer comments on interviews reflect the combination of pragmatism and personal vision which made him the world-renowned "father of oral history."

Allan Nevins's career started in journalism: he wrote and edited for the New York Evening Post, *the* New York Sun, *and the* New York World. *He worked as a professor at Cornell and Columbia universities and in the course of a brilliant career wrote or edited more than sixty volumes, includ-ing an eight-volume history of the Civil War and seven biographies. His writing was twice awarded the Pulitzer Prize in biography and the Bancroft Prize in History.*

"Oral History: How and Why It Was Born" originally appeared in the Wilson Library Bulletin, *40 (March 1966), pp. 600–601. Nevins's remarks*

in "The Uses of Oral History" were made at Lake Arrowhead, California, at the First Colloquium of the Oral History Association in 1966.

Oral History:
How and Why It Was Born

"A CURIOUS THOUGHT has just occurred to me," Dr. Johnson once remarked. "In the grave we shall receive no letters." Despite such volumes as *Letters to Dead Authors*, that is indubitably true. It is equally true that from the grave no letters are sent out to the most anxious inquirers into old history or old mysteries. We can take a few precautions to prevent Time from putting too much as alms for oblivion into the monstrous wallet on his back; that is all. Oral history is one of the latest and most promising of these precautions, and already it has saved from death's dateless (and undatable) night much that the future will rejoice over and cherish.

In hardly less degree than space exploration, oral history was born of modern invention and technology. "Miss Secretary," says the President, "take a letter to the Prime Minister of———. No, stop! I'll just telephone him; quicker, easier, and above all safer. We know he has no recording device." What might have been a priceless document for the historian goes into the irrecoverable ether. The head of the great Detroit corporation, who wishes to get information on finance from several bankers, and important scientific facts from several laboratory experts, catches a plane to New York. The graphic letter that the student of social progress would prize is cut short—a telegram will do. The news-behind-the-news that a Wickham Steed once sent *The* (London) *Times* from Berlin or Bucharest does not even go on teletype; it is put on a confidential telephone wire.

All the while the hurry and complexity of modern politics, modern financial and business affairs, and even modern literary and artistic life slice away the time that men need for methodical, reflective writing. What wonderful letters Theodore Roosevelt gave the world, so full of his endless zest for life, his incredible energy, his enthusiasms and his hatreds. To go further back, what a shelf of delightful comment on a thousand subjects from the Western mastodons to the iniquities of European diplomacy, from decimal coinage to Watt's new steam engine, from slave management to Ossian's poetry, we find in the massive volumes of Jefferson's writings. No doubt great letter writers still exist. But their numbers are fewer, and the spirit of the times is hostile to them.

It was something more than a sense of these considerations that inspired the planners of oral history. It was natural that they should be rooted in the history department of the greatest university in the largest and busiest city of the continent. It was right that they should have some knowledge of what the California publisher H. H. Bancroft had done to preserve a picture of the life, lore, and legends of the youthful years of the Golden State by interviewing scores of pioneers, and getting their dictated reminiscences down on paper. The planners had a connection with journalism, and saw in the daily obituary columns proof that knowledge valuable to the historian, novelist, sociologist, and economist was daily perishing; memories perishing forever without yielding any part of their riches. They had enthusiasm, these planners. It was partly the enthusiasm of ignorance; the undertaking looked deceptively easy.

Anyway, they set to work, at first with pencil and pad, later with wire recorders, later still with early tape-recording machines. They found that the task needed a great deal of money, and money was hard to get. It needed system, planning, conscientiousness, the skill that comes with experience, and above all integrity. It was more complicated and laborious than they had dreamed. The results were sometimes poor, but hard effort sometimes made them dazzling.

And the work was adventurously entertaining. At every turn they met a new experience, a fresh view of history, a larger knowledge of human personality. They would never forget the eminent New York attorney who had once collected a million dollars in a single fee, and who interrupted the story of his career to exclaim, "This is the most delightful experience I have ever had, this reminiscing." They would always remember the labor leader who in the course of an engrossing story suddenly laid his head on the desk and burst into tears; he had come to the point where he had been sent to prison for alleged racketeering. They would always keep a picture of Norman Thomas singing a pathetic song composed by the harried tenant farmers of the Southwest, and of Charles C. Burlingham, still active at almost a hundred, recalling how as a mere urchin he had seen a Negro hanged in front of his father's parsonage in downtown Manhattan during the raging of the Draft Riots.

The original ventures had been modest, but they rapidly expanded into large national undertakings .With elation the managers watched Henry Wallace record for posterity about two thousand typed pages of reminiscences, with large diary excerpts to illustrate them; with elation they heard Mrs. Frances Perkins, who possessed an approach to total recall, record what (with additional matter she contributed) came to a memoir of five thousand typed pages. Governors, cabinet officers past and present, industrialists, and distinguished authors and editors lent themselves to the enterprise. Many of them had been badgered for years by their families to set down recollections that history would need; not infrequently they had long felt a desire to furnish their own account of an important transaction or controversial period, but had lacked time and opportunity until suddenly seated before a tape recorder with a well-equipped interviewer before them. This interviewer, upon whom half the value of the work depended, had prepared himself by reading files of newspapers, going through official reports, begging wives for old letters or diary notes, and talking with associates. Sometimes a subject possessed a fresh and copious memory, as did Secretary Stimson; sometimes his memory had merely to be jogged, as that of Governor Rockefeller; sometimes it had to be helped by extended work, as that of former Governor Herbert H. Lehman.

Now and then, too, the work originally done had to be revised and redone. This was true of the memoir prepared by that distinguished jurist and unforgettable personality, Learned Hand. His outspoken comment, his salty wit, made his original recollections remarkable. One or two sentences may be recalled. He commented on the reverence he felt for Brandeis: "I often scolded myself, when I was a young man. You eat too much, I told myself. You drink too much. Your thoughts about women are not of the most elevated character. Why can't you be like that great man Brandeis, who does nothing but read Interstate Commerce Reports?" Judge Hand's first version, however, lacked the depth and expertness supplied when a professor of law who had once been his clerk was induced to serve as a new interviewer.

Some of the anticipated obstacles never appeared. Even busy, important, and excessively modest men proved in many instances accessible; they entered into the spirit of the work. The mass of invaluable memoir material mounted. It proved possible to protect the reminiscences against intrusion; the integrity of oral history never came under suspicion, much less attack. Better and better equipment was purchased, better and better systems of interviewing, typing, and indexing were developed. About half of the memoirs were thrown open to students at once, the other half being kept under time restrictions. And the students appeared, first in scores, well accredited and watched; then in hundreds; then in more than a thousand, not a few of them writing important books.

One difficulty, however, always persisted: the difficulty of finance. It proved impossible to operate even a sternly economical but efficient office for less than $40,000 a year, and costs rose. Work had begun on funds supplied from a happy bequest to Columbia University by Frederic Bancroft of Washington, a bequest upon which the head of oral history had a special claim; and the University itself contributed quarters and money. As the project grew, certain foundations gave generous help. Other corporations made use of its skills, giving oral history not only valuable bodies of reminiscences, but a fee in addition.

Thus the material accumulated by oral history grew year by year, both in bulk and in quality. Thus the work it accomplished attracted wider and wider attention, raising up imitative agencies in various parts of the United States, and even abroad. Because New York City is an unapproachably effective seat for such work, because the office spent the utmost pains upon its methods, and because its personnel counted brilliant young men (some of whom have now made their mark elsewhere), the heads of the office on Morningside Heights believe that their accomplishment has not be̲n equaled elsewhere. They are glad, however, to see the type of activity they began in the preservation of priceless memories for the instruction of posterity copied elsewhere, and the tree they planted, like a banyan, creating sister trees in surrounding ground. May the work flourish and spread!

The Uses of Oral History

LET US begin by disposing of the myth that I had anything to do with the founding of oral history. It founded itself. It had become a patent necessity, and would have sprung into life in a dozen places, under any circumstances. I'm in the position of a guide in Switzerland. A valley in the Alps that had previously been barren was filled by an avalanche with a great body of soil and became quite tillable. A poor guide in the village had stumbled over a rock as he came down the mountain, one wintry day, and had started this avalanche that filled the valley. People pointed to him and said, "There's Jacques, he made the valley fruitful!" Well, I stumbled over a rock [laughter] and the avalanche came. It would have come anyway.

I listened this morning to the various discourses with the greatest interest. They seemed to me admirable. What I propose to do is to offer some general considerations, and to close with as spirited a defense of oral history as I can possibly present.

It struck me as curious this morning that nothing was said about what one would have ordinarily have expected a *great deal* to be said: The finances of oral history. We begin with finances and sometimes we end without finances. [Laughter] At any rate, we try to go on with finances.

This avalanche of which I spoke did begin with finances. Some of us at Columbia University were happy to know an old gentleman named Frederic Bancroft. He had been Librarian of the State Department. He had written valuable books of history. He had, more importantly, been the brother of a widower who was *Treasurer* of the International Harvester company, and this brother died while Frederic Bancroft was still very much alive, leaving his entire estate to Frederic. Frederic Bancroft grew old. He knew many of us at Columbia, for he had taken his doctoral degree there. I used often to go down to see him in Washington. He would talk about what he intended to do with the two million dollars he possessed. In the days of Franklin Roosevelt, he enjoyed pointing to the White House and saying, "My income is larger than *that man's*!" Well, as he talked about what he intended to do with those two millions, we made a few suggestions (which always centered around Columbia University). I would take him to dinner, or go to dinner at his house. He would chill my blood by saying, "I'm thinking now of giving the two million dollars to the Lowell Foundation for the Lowell Lectureships in Boston." With chilled blood, I would then call my friend Henry Commager and say, "Henry, go take Mr. Bancroft out to dinner, and make some suggestions to counter this Lowell Lectureship idea." When I presently went to Washington again, he would say, "I've been thinking more about where I shall leave my money. It occurs to me that Knox College in Illinois [laughter] would be a very good place." My blood would run cold again, until I could get Commager, or someone else, to take him to dinner once more. Well, he finally did die, and we found that the two millions had been left to Columbia University for the advancement of historical studies. I had some ideas about how to use two millions, and one was in instituting our oral history office there. . . .

We always found it necessary to earn our own way, to a great extent. Columbia possessed itself of these two million dollars, but let us have only a tiny fraction of them, and we needed an annual budget of thirty-six thousand or forty thousand dollars a year. . . . We had to scratch for money, and it's no easy task to find it; but this necessity had the virtue of instilling in us a spirit of enterprise, and I think the spirit of enterprise is very important.

It was necessary to institute specific projects which had merit in themselves. For example, we began in a small way with a project in the petroleum industry which took us into Texas and realm of the great "wildcatter," Mike Benedum, just to earn money for oral history, and then we went on to the Book-of-the-Month Club, which had a history of great importance from the literary and cultural point of view; and then we went on to the Ford Motor company, which was, of course, pivotal in the history of the whole automotive industry; and from that we went to the Weyerhaeuser Timber Company; and then we went to tracing certain government enterprises. We would not have gone into these projects if we had not been pricked by sheer necessity. If we had been given a great endowment, a few hundred thousand dollars, we might have been much more inert. . . .

It's hard to define the best interviewer. He must have a combination of traits of personality and of intellect that is hard to obtain. He must have the the Germans call *gemütlichkeit*, obvious sympathy with the person whom he interviews, friendliness and tact, as well as courage. He must work hard to prepare himself for every interview, and must have a great breadth of interests not often the possession of the candidate for the Ph.D. [laughter], such candidates as appear in our universities.

There must also be an element of integrity in recording as well as in interviewing. We used to agree, and perhaps we still agree in theory, upon the value of accompanying every interview with a set of notes made by the interviewer upon the character of the man interviewed and the circumstances of the interview. These notes would indicate whether the person interviewed has or lacks intellectual power in the judgment of the interviewer. They would include a commentary upon the candor or lack of candor evinced by the man interviewed and comments upon the intensity of feeling exhibited during the interview, whether a man showed strong convictions upon a given subject or absolute fixity of opinions upon a given personality. There should be a pretty clear indication, if possible, of any point at which the interview passes into sarcasm or irony, because a record in cold type does not disclose the sarcasm evident only in an inflection of voice. We can't preserve enough tape to show where sarcasm is employed. For example, John W. Davis gave a very useful set of interviews upon his career, before and after he was nominated for the presidency. It included some comments upon Calvin Coolidge. My impression is that a note of sarcasm crept into some of his comments upon Calvin Coolidge. [laughter] How far have we kept up our record, Louis?

LOUIS STARR (Columbia University): Well, that's a difficult problem for us, because we've always been haunted by the ghosts of the subject coming up and hoping to see and admire his memoir in the oral history collection, only to stumble upon an addendum that says that I don't think this man really leveled with us, or something to that effect—a critical comment; so that, I'm sorry to say, I've never resolved this riddle. We haven't done it as we should have, but it's something, perhaps, we can work out in the future. . . .

PHILIP BROOKS (Harry Truman Library): We have not done this in connection with our interviews. Suppose you interviewed somebody, and you had this set of notes commenting upon his candor, and then in the very near future some researcher comes along and uses that transcript. If he can't see the notes, then he's lost something that another researcher, coming along twenty years from now, may see. Well, what is your idea as to how and when these should be made available?

ALLAN NEVINS: Everything depends upon circumstances. It's an *ad hoc* question that has to be settled on an *ad hoc* basis, I should say.

WILLA BAUM (University of California, Berkeley): We write an introduction to each of our interviews, and we try to include a little bit of this, but it helps to make it a positive statement because the interviewee does get a copy and it's available to him and all his friends. So we try to word it in a positive way which the astute user can interpret. [laughter] In other words, we say sometimes that he spoke very frankly. Now if it doesn't say that he spoke very frankly, we may say that he was circumspect about his comments on his close associates, or something which, phrased in a positive way, may alert the user; but we find writing our introductions very hard.

GOULD COLMAN (Cornell University): We have, in some ways, a rather difficult situation at Cornell. We share completely your feeling about the importance of the interviewer's record of process. We want to know whether the man was sober or drunk, senile or whatever. We save all of these statements; we bind them together under the title, "Interviewer Comments." They are available to any researchers who asks for them; however, we don't advertise that we have them. This is not an entirely happy solution but it's about all we have had the courage, thus far, to undertake.

ALLAN NEVINS: That shows you have in mind the absolutely essential importance of integrity in the operation, so far as we can attain it. It must be honest. We at Columbia never felt our integrity threatened, did we, Louis? Once or twice threatened, but it was never infringed, never violated. Nobody ever went to a dinner party. . . .

LOUIS STARR: There are many problems, though, it seems to me, connected with this suggestion, and I don't know what the solution is. I think Mrs. Baum has come about as close as anyone I've heard—to write between the lines. It's sort of like reading the *AAA Guide* and trying to find out which are the places they don't think are quite so good.

ELIZABETH DIXON (University of California, Los Angeles): Maybe we could have a vocabulary which says, "Circumspect means he didn't say anything." [laughter]

PHILIP BROOKS: Professor Nevins, this is a real problem, and maybe I have the wrong impression when I said we didn't do this at the Truman Library. We do keep notes describing the circumstances of the interviews, but I'm not sure, in all cases, we've told how candid we thought that the interviewee was. I have in mind one particular interview that I did with a gentleman from another country on a subject of importance in international relations, and I don't believe what he said. I think he glossed it all over. This is very difficult to put down in writing, and, if you do, you're going to wonder who's to see it. I don't really know the answer.

ALBERT LYONS (Mt. Sinai Hospital, New York): Isn't it also true that those who hear the tapes later, for example, have to form their own conclusions, and their conclusions may be more accurate than the interviewer's because of greater retrospective knowledge, perhaps, or new information?

ALLAN NEVINS: That's certainly true. . . .

All history depends upon the great use of memoirs, autobiographies. Dependence often absolute, yet are they more trustworthy than oral history memoirs? Not a bit! Often much less trustworthy. We have been taught to enjoy Benvenuto Cellini, but do we believe all of Benvenuto Cellini's autobiography? I hope not! [laughter] Or Casanova's? I'd much rather think that a great part of Casanova's was fiction, and I suspect that it was. We've been taught to regard J. J. Rousseau's *Confessions* as one of the frankest of autobiographies. We say, "Here's something in which a man absolutely bares his own soul; tells the full truth about himself." Rousseau himself said, "This is the full truth about me. I've held nothing back." Actually we know, thanks to modern research, that Rousseau's *Confessions* comes close to pure invention. It's, in fact, one of the great works of fiction of that century. [laughter] It's full of suppressions, distortions, evasions, and outright, unblushing lies.

Here is where one advantage of oral history lies. If Cellini and Rousseau had been set down before a keen-minded, well-informed interviewer, who looked these men straight in their eye and put to them one searching question after another, cross-examining as Sam Untermeyer used to cross-examine people on the witness stand, they would have stuck closer to the path of truth.

Or take St. Augustine's *Confessions*, a much-admired book. It is one of the immortal books of religious statement, a beautiful piece of art. But does it tell us what we really want to know about St. Augustine, and does St. Augustine, though obviously a man of great rectitude, tell the truth, the whole truth, and nothing but the truth about himself? He relates, at one point, how as a young man he repulsed and abandoned his mistress, keeping for himself, and depriving her, of their child. It was St. Augustine's, it was not hers; and how the poor girl wept bitterly and swore to God that she would never let another man touch her. Well, I should think she might, after that. He gives this occurrence, which was a brief episode to him, but was a terrible disaster to the poor girl, about three lines; that is, he glosses over it. A representative of oral history would have wrung from him a little more of the facts about that occurrence, I should think [laughter]. . . .

It's true that autobiography and history have to be approached with highly critical minds, and that statements of an autobiographical charac-

ter by a group producing a history of some particular development demand even more caution and a keener critical sense. To produce a truthful
record of a man's acts, thoughts, and motives, two qualities are obviously
essential: self-knowledge and a fair amount of candor. A great many
people, however, never attain self-knowledge, but constantly deceive
themselves as to their real motives and acts; they constantly dramatize
themselves. Others are seriously deficient in candor. They don't like to
tell the truth about themselves, sometimes for good reasons
[laughter]. . . .

But in the hands of an earnest, courageous interviewer who has mas-
tered a background of facts and who has the nerve to press his scalpel
tactfully and with some knowledge of psychology into delicate tissues
and even bleeding wounds, deficiencies can be exposed; and oral history
can get at more of the truth than a man will present about himself in a
written autobiography. . . .

Another kind of candor we found in a man of much less freshness of
memory, Herbert Lehman, who was one hundred percent honest. He
wouldn't lie to himself, under any circumstances, or lie to anybody else.
He couldn't always remember what he should have remembered, but so
far as memory went, it was absolutely trustworthy; when he was
prompted by a good interviewer his memory went a long way, further
than it otherwise might have gone. I think that people who pride themselves upon the accuracy of their recollections almost invariably find, on
referring to diaries or other records of long-past occurrences, that their
memories are, in essential points, confused or erroneous. . . .

Now for the third requirement. If a man's memory is keen and vivid,
and if he does possess fairly full memoranda on his past, the array of facts
upon his career is likely to be so immense that he needs a strong faculty of
selection. In oral history, he finds useful aids to this process of selection
among the multiplicity of facts locked into his past. The autobiographer,
of course, possesses an endless array of facts about himself, if he can just
remember them, far more than the biographer can ever find out. To use
these facts well, to be his own Boswell or Lockhart, the memorist requires
an exceedingly just sense of proportion. When acumen of selection is
wanting, we get a book as prodigious and as verbose as John Bigelow's
five volumes. Volumes which nobody ever opens without a groan.

3

History and the Community

Paul Thompson

Our third selection offers the view that "history should not merely comfort; it should provide a challenge." Many recent oral history projects have reflected this populist, activist stance.

To Paul Thompson, author of a valuable text on oral history which includes historiography, theory, and practical applications, history is inseparable from its social purpose. He believes that the use of oral sources democratizes history making, and as the writing of history is broadened, so is its content. Thus oral history "gives back to the people who made and experienced history, through their own words, a central place."

While the school represented by Allan Nevins and Louis Starr searched out "significant lives" of the statesmen and the famous, Thompson and those historians he inspired have documented the unofficial, unnoticed lives of ordinary people. Out of the meeting of these two perspectives has come the contemporary practice of oral history.

Paul Thompson heads the department of sociology at the University of Essex, England. His earlier books include The Works of William Morris *(1967),* The Edwardians *(1975), and* The Remaking of British Society *(1975). He currently edits* Oral History, *the journal of the Oral History Society in England.*

"History and the Community" is the first chapter of The Voice of the Past: Oral History *(Oxford: Oxford University Press, 1978).*

ALL HISTORY depends ultimately upon its social purpose. This is why in the past it has been handed down by oral tradition and written chronicle, and why today professional historians are supported from public funds, children are taught history in schools, amateur history societies flourish all over Britain, and popular history books are among the strongest best-sellers. Sometimes the social purpose of history is obscure: for example, academics who pursue fact-finding research on remote problems without attempting to relate their discoveries to any more general interpretations, insisting on the technical virtue of scholarship and the pursuit of knowledge for its own sake, are merely concerned that they and their salaries are protected from interference, while in return they offer no challenge to the social system. At the other extreme the social purpose of history can be quite blatant: used to provide justification for war and conquest, territorial seizure, revolution and counter-revolution, the rule of one class or race over another. Between these two extremes are many other purposes, more or less obvious. Through history ordinary people seek to understand the upheavals and changes which they experience in their own lives: wars, social transformations like the changing position of youth, technological changes like the end of steam power, or personal migration to a new community. Through local history a village or town seeks meaning for its own changing character and newcomers can gain a sense of roots in personal historical knowledge. Through political and social history taught in schools children are helped to understand, and accept, how the political and social system under which they live came about, and how force and conflict have played, and continue to play, their part in that evolution.

The challenge of oral history lies partly in relation to this essential social purpose of history. This is a major reason why it has so excited some historians, and so frightened others. In fact, fear of oral history as such is groundless. We shall see later that the use of interviews as a source by professional historians is long-standing and perfectly compatible with scholarly standards. American experience shows clearly enough that the oral history method can be regularly used in a socially and politically conservative manner; or indeed pushed as far as sympathy with Fascism in John Toland's new portrait of *Adolf Hitler* (New York, 1976).

Oral history is not necessarily an instrument for change; it depends upon the spirit in which it is used. Nevertheless, oral history certainly can be a means for transforming both the content and the purpose of history. It can be used to change the focus of history itself, and open up new areas of inquiry; it can break down barriers between teachers and students, between generations, between educational institutions and the world outside; and in the writing of history—whether in books, or museums, or radio and film—it can give back to the people who made and experienced history, through their own words, a central place.

Until the present century, the focus of history was essentially political: a documentation of the struggle for power, in which the lives of ordinary people, or the workings of the economy or religion, were given little attention except in times of crisis such as the Reformation, the English Civil War, or the French Revolution. Even local history was concerned with the administration of the hundred and parish rather than the day-to-day life of the community and the street. This was partly because historians, who themselves then belonged to the administering and governing classes, thought that this was what mattered most. They had developed no interest in the point of view of the labourer, unless he was specifically troublesome; nor—being men—would they have wished to inquire into the changing life experiences of women. But even if they had wished to write a different kind of history, it would have been far from easy, for the raw material from which history was written, the documents, had been kept or destroyed by people with the same priorities. The more personal, local, and unofficial a document, the less likely it was to survive. This has remained true even after the establishment of local record offices. Registers of births and marriages, minutes of councils and Boards of Guardians, national and county newspapers, schoolteachers' log books—legal records of all kinds are kept in quantity; very often there are also accounts and other books from large private firms and landed estates, and even private correspondence from the ruling landowner class. But of the innumerable postcards, letters, diaries, and ephemera of working-class men and women, or the papers of small businesses like corner shops or hill farmers, for example, very little has been preserved anywhere.

Consequently, even as the scope of history has widened, the original political and administrative focus has remained. Where ordinary people have been brought in, it has been generally as statistical aggregates derived from some earlier administrative investigation. Thus economic history is constructed around three types of source: aggregate rates of wages, prices, and unemployment; national and international political interventions into the economy and the information which arises from these; and studies of particular trades and industries, depending on the bigger and more successful firms for records of individual enterprises. Similarly, labour history has focused on the one hand on the relationship between the working classes and the state in general, and on the other on particular but essentially institutional accounts of trade unions and working-class political organizations; and, inevitably, it is the larger and more successful organizations which normally leave records or commission their own histories. Again, social history has been concerned with legislative and administrative developments like the rise of the Welfare State; or with aggregate data such as population size, birth rates, age at marriage, household and family structure. And among more recent historical specialisms, demography has been almost exclusively concerned with aggregates; the history of the family has tended to follow the lines of conventional social history; while women's history has to a remarkable extent focused on the political struggle for civil equality, and above all for the vote.

There are, of course, important exceptions in each of these fields, which show that different approaches are possible even with the existing sources. And there is a remarkable amount of unexploited personal and ordinary information even in official records—such as court documents—which can be used in new ways. The continuing pattern of historical writing probably reflects the priorities of the majority of the profession—even if no longer of the ruling class itself—in an age of bureaucracy, state power, science, and statistics. Nevertheless, it remains true that to write any other kind of history from documentary sources remains a very difficult task, requiring special ingenuity. It is indicative of the situation that E. P. Thompson's *The Making of the English Working Class* (1963) and James Hinton's *The First Shop Stewards' Movement* (1973) each depended to a large extent on reports by paid government informers, in the early nineteenth century and First World War respectively. When socialist historians are reduced to writing history from the records of government spies, the constraints imposed are clearly extreme. We cannot, alas, interview tombstones, but at least for the First World War period and back into the late nineteenth century, the use of oral history immediately provides a rich and varied source for the creative historian.

In the most general sense, once the life experience of people of all kinds can be used as its raw material, a new dimension is given to history. Oral history provides a source quite similar in character to published autobiography, but much wider in scope. The overwhelming majority of published autobiographies are from a restricted group of political, social, and intellectual leaders, and even when the historian is lucky enough to find an autobiography from the particular place, time, and social group which he happens to need, it may well give little or no attention to the point at issue. Oral historians, by contrast, may choose precisely whom to interview and what to ask about. The interview will provide, too, a means of discovering written documents and photographs which would not have otherwise been traced. The confines of the scholar's world are no longer the well-thumbed volumes of the old catalogue. Oral historians can think now as if they themselves were publishers: imagine what evidence is needed, seek it out, and capture it.

For most existing kinds of history, probably the critical effect of this new approach is to allow evidence from a new direction. The historian of working-class politics can juxtapose the statements of the government or the trade union headquarters with the voice of the rank and file—both apathetic and militant. There can be no doubt that this should make for a more realistic reconstruction of the past. Reality is complex and many-sided; and it is a primary merit of oral history that to a much greater extent than most sources it allows the original multiplicity of standpoints to be recreated. But this advantage is important not just for the writing of history. Most historians make implicit or explicit judgements—quite properly, since the social purpose of history demands an understanding of the past which relates directly or indirectly to the present. Modern professional historians are less open with their social message than Macaulay or Marx, since scholarly standards are seen to conflict with declared bias. But the social message is usually present, however obscured. It is quite easy for a historian to give most of his attention and quotations to those social leaders whom he admires, without giving any direct opinion of his own. Since the nature of most existing records is to reflect the standpoint of authority, it is not surprising that the judgement of history has more often than not vindicated the wisdom of the powers that be. Oral history by contrast makes a much fairer trial possible: witnesses can now also be called from the under-classes, the unprivileged, and the defeated. It provides a more realistic and fair reconstruction of the past, a challenge to the established account. In so doing, oral history has radical implications for the social message of history as a whole.

At the same time oral history implies for most kinds of history some shift of focus. Thus the educational historian becomes concerned with the experiences of children and students as well as the problems of teachers and administrators. The military and naval historian can look beyond command level strategy and equipment to the conditions, recreations, and morale of other ranks and the lower deck. The social historian can turn from bureaucrats and politicians to poverty itself, and learn how the poor saw the relieving officer and how they survived his refusals. The political historian can approach the voter at home and at work; and can hope to understand even the working-class Conservative, who produced no newspapers or organizations for him to investigate. The economist can watch both employer and worker as social beings and at their ordinary work, and so come closer to understanding the typical economic process, and its successes and contradictions.

In some fields, oral history can result not merely in a shift in focus, but also in the opening up of important new areas of inquiry. Labour historians, for example, are enabled for the first time to undertake effective studies of the ill-unionized majority of male workers, of women workers, and of the normal experience of work and its impact on the family and the community. They are no longer confined to those trades which were unionized, or those which gained contemporary publicity and investigation because of strikes or extreme poverty. Urban historians similarly can turn from well-explored problem areas like the slums to look at other typical forms of urban social life: the small industrial or market town, for example, or the middle-class suburb, constructing the local patterns of social distinctions, mutual help between neighbours and kin, leisure and work. They can even approach from the inside the history of immigrant groups—a kind of history which is certain to become more important in

Britain, and is mainly documented only from outside as a social problem. These opportunities—and many others—are shared by social historians: the study of working-class leisure and culture, for example; or of crime from the point of view of the ordinary, often undetected and socially semitolerated poacher, shoplifter, or work-pilferer.

Perhaps the most striking feature of all, however, is the transforming impact of oral history upon the history of the family. Without its evidence, the historian can discover very little indeed about either the ordinary family's contacts with neighbours and kin, or its internal relationships. The roles of husband and wife, the upbringing of girls and boys, emotional and material conflicts and dependence, the struggle of youth for independence, courtship, sexual behaviour within and outside marriage, contraception and abortion—all these were effectively secret areas. The only clues were to be gleaned from aggregate statistics, and from a few—usually partial—observers. The historical paucity which results is well summed up in Michael Anderson's brilliant, speculative, but abstract study of *Family Structure in Nineteenth-Century Lancashire* (1971): a lopsided, empty frame. With the use of interviewing, it is now possible to develop a much fuller history of the family over the last ninety years, and to establish its main patterns and changes over time, and from place to place, during the life cycle and between the sexes. The history of childhood as a whole becomes practicable for the first time. And given the dominance of the family through housework, domestic service, and motherhood in the lives of most women, an almost equivalent broadening of scope is brought to the history of women.

In all these fields of history, by introducing new evidence from the underside, by shifting the focus and opening new areas of inquiry, by challenging some of the assumptions and accepted judgements of historians, by bringing recognition to substantial groups of people who had been ignored, a cumulative process of transformation is set in motion. The scope of historical writing itself is enlarged and enriched; and at the same time its social message changes. History becomes, to put it simply, more democratic. The chronicle of kings has taken into its concern the life experience of ordinary people. But there is another dimension to this change, of equal importance. The process of writing history changes along with the content. The use of oral evidence breaks through the barriers between the chroniclers and their audience; between the educational institution and the outside world.

This change springs from the essentially creative and co-operative nature of the oral history method. Of course oral evidence once recorded can be used by lone scholars in libraries just like any other type of documentary source. But to be content with this is to lose a key advantage of the method: its flexibility, the ability to pin down evidence just where it is needed. Once historians start to interview, they find themselves inevitably working with others—at the least, with their informants. And to be a successful interviewer a new set of skills is needed, including an understanding of human relationships. Some people can find these skills almost immediately, others need to learn them; but in contrast to the cumulative process of learning and amassing information which gives such advantage in documentary analysis and interpretation to the professional historian well on in life, it is possible to learn quite quickly to become an effective interviewer. Hence historians as field workers, while in important respects retaining the advantages of professional knowledge, also find themselves off their desks, sharing experience on a human level.

Because of these characteristics, oral history is peculiarly suited to project work—both for groups and for individual student enterprises: in schools, universities, colleges, adult education, or community centres. It can be carried out anywhere. In any part of the country there is an abundance of topics which can be studied locally; the history of a local industry or craft, social relationships in a particular community, culture and dialect, change in the family, the impact of wars and strikes, and so on. An oral history project will be certainly feasible. It will also demonstrate very well, especially if the project focuses on the historical roots of some contemporary concern, the relevance of historical study to the immediate environment.

In schools, projects on children's own family history have been developed which provide an effective way of linking their own environment with a wider past. Family history has two other special educational merits. It assists a child-centred approach, for its uses as the project's basis the child's own knowledge of its family and kin and access to photographs, old letters and documents, newspaper cuttings, and memories. Equally, family history encourages the involvement of parents in school activity.

A child's own family history represents perhaps the simplest type of project subject. It is more suited to suggesting than to solving a historical problem. Older groups are likely to choose some issue of more collective interest. At Corpus Christi College, Oxford, for example, Brian Harrison led a group of his students in a small research study on the history of college servants, a group of workers whose deferential respect for their employers, loyalty, meticulousness in their craft, and formality of dress and manner, are frequently perplexing to the typical modern young undergraduate. Through the project the students came to a better understanding of the college servants—and vice versa—and at the same time of the significance of history itself. As one commented: 'I found equally important and interesting . . . seeing the impact of social change in really close detail . . . how changes in the general social environment changed the style of life, values, and relationships within a traditional community.' The immediate environment also gains, through the sense of discovery in interviews, a vivid historical dimension: an awareness of the past which is not just known, but personally felt. This is especially true for a new-comer to a community or district. It is one thing to know that streets or fields around a home had a past before one's own arrival; quite different to have received from the remembered past, still alive in the minds of the older people of the place, personal intimacies of love across those particu-lar fields, neighbours and homes in that particular street, work in that particular shop.

Such fragmentary facts are not merely evocative in themselves, but can be used as the raw material for worthwhile history. It is possible for even a single student in a summer vacation project, with interviews, to make a useful extension of historical knowledge—and also to create new re-sources which others may be able to use later. With a group project the opportunities naturally enlarge. The number of interviews can be greater, the archival searches more extensive, the subject more ambitious.

The group project has some special characteristics of its own. Instead of the atmosphere of competition common in education, it requires a spirit of intellectual co-operation. Isolated reading, examinations, and lecture sessions give way to collaborative historical research. The joint inquiry will also bring teachers and students into a much closer, less hierarchical relationship, giving far more chance of informal contact between them. Their dependence will become mutual. The teacher may bring special experience in interpretation and in knowledge of existing sources, but will rely on the support of the students as organizers and field-workers. In these ways some of the students are likely to show unexpected skills. The best essay-writer is not necessarily the best interviewer—nor is the teacher. A much more equal situation is created. But, paradoxically, at the same time, by resolving—or at least suspending—the conflict between research and teaching, it enables the teacher to be a better professional. The group project is both research and teaching, inextricably mixed, and as a result each is done more effectively.

The essential value of both group and single projects is, however, simi-lar. Students can share in the excitements and satisfactions of creative historical research of intrinsic worth. At the same time they gain personal experience of the difficulties of such work. They formulate an interpreta-tion or theory and then find exceptional facts which are difficult to explain away. They find that the people whom they interview do not fit easily into the social types presented by the preliminary reading. They need facts, or people, or records which prove tantalizingly elusive. They encounter the problem of bias, contradiction, and interpretation in evidence. Above all, they are brought back from the grand patterns of written history to the awkwardly individual human lives which are its basis.

Both kinds of project also have the important consequence of taking education out of its institutional retreats into the world. Both sides gain from this. Interviewing can bring together people from different social classes and age groups who would otherwise rarely meet, let alone get to know each other closely. Much of the widespread hostility to students is based on little knowledge of what they are actually like or do, and these meetings can bring an appreciation of the serious-mindedness and idealism which is widespread among them. They can also show ordinary people that history need not be irrelevant to their own lives. Conversely, teachers and students can become more directly aware of the image which they present to the wider public. And through entering into the lives of their informants, they gain more understanding of values which they do not share, and often respect for the courage shown in lives much less privileged than their own.

Yet the nature of the interview implies a breaking of the boundary between the educational institution and the world, between the professional and the ordinary public, more fundamental than this. For the historian comes to the interview to learn: to sit at the feet of others who, because they come from a different social class, or are less educated, or older, know more about something. The reconstruction of history itself becomes a much more widely collaborative process, in which nonprofessionals must play a critical part. By giving a central place in its writing and presentation to people of all kinds, history gains immensely. And old people especially benefit too. An oral history project can not only bring them new social contacts and sometimes lead to lasting friendships; it can render them an inestimable service. Too often ignored, and economically emasculated, it can give back to them a dignity, a sense of purpose, in going back over their lives and handing on valuable information to a younger generation.

These changes made possible through oral history are not confined to the writing of books or projects. They also affect the presentation of history in museums, record offices, and libraries. These all now have a means of infusing life into their collections, and through this, of bringing themselves into a more active relationship with their community. They can set up their own special research projects, like the joint East Anglian museums' study of the sugar-beet industry, or the Imperial War Museum programmes on early aviation and on conscientious objectors. A few museums are also using tapes as a sound accompaniment to their displays, either directly explanatory or for evocative atmosphere. The display itself can at the same time be reformulated so that it comes closer to the historical original. The 'period setting' for objects becomes the reconstruction of a real room, with, for example, tools and shavings and half-made baskets left about as if the craftsman was still using it. Older local people, when they look at this room, are likely to have comments, and may even help with improvements by offering articles of their own. In one particularly lively East London museum, if an attendant hears this kind of conversation going on, he alerts one of the curators, and the old person is immediately offered a cup of tea and a chance to record some of his own impressions on the spot. And if the first impromptu session proves fruitful, others follow. Some of the recordings are later used in educational tapes lent to the local schools; and weekends have been arranged for the schoolchildren—normally Sixth Formers—to meet the old people. Thus an active dialogue develops between old people, their own local history, and a museum which has become a social centre. Here is a model of a social role for history with great potential, which needs to be taken up elsewhere.

The use of interviewing for historical presentation in broadcasting is of course long-standing. Here indeed is a fine tradition of oral history techniques which goes back many years—in fact well before the term 'oral history' was introduced. Professional historians are of course given their own chance for brief lectures in the intervals between programmes on Radio Three. But most of those I know show much more interest in those radio and television programmes which re-evoke history through the use of raw material, some of it dating from the original period, some recorded retrospectively. For the historian of the future the preservation of many of these programmes, along with others in the B.B.C. Sound Archives, will provide a rich source. It is very unfortunate that at present, by contrast, only a very small proportion of what is being broadcast on television is being preserved, and historians have shown curiously little interest in the systematic destruction of records.

In historical broadcasting it is the introduction of people, the original actors, which brings the programmes alive. Some local radio stations have deliberately used this type of programme to encourage links and exchanges with their local community. There have also been experiments with the use of the oral history approach in film making. Admittedly it presents some severe problems. A series of interwoven interviews easily becomes visually repetitive, and—despite vivid moments—lacks dramatic action. An alternative, controversial approach was tried in the filming of 'Akenfield'. Here two kinds of oral material were used. The script of the narrator was put together by Ronald Blythe from the interviews which he recorded for his original book, and was spoken by a professional actor. But all the visible actors were local people rather than professionals, and their words were unscripted. They gave their services to the film freely at weekends, and brought to each session clothes, props, and food. They would simply be warned in advance what the scene was to be about, so that they could meet in the appropriate dress and frame of mind. The result is certainly a remarkable, if somewhat puzzling film. It has moments which are deeply moving just because they are so ordinary: like the funeral sequence, with its awkward silences, the inadequacy of words when they come, the too slowly sung hymn, and afterwards the bad jokes and stories told again and again. Here is a real pathos which professional acting would not dare to achieve. On the other hand, there are clearly unsolved problems in this approach to film making. Who is it for? To the middle-class film connoisseur the ungainly 'acting' was disconcerting, and the dialect accents hard to catch. Some local audiences, by contrast, were disturbed by the many inaccuracies in historical detail—hardly surprising, since the film was made in everyday modern settings. Others simply found the film boring, ordinary, and without any obvious point. They would have been more interested had the story itself been entertaining. Most of these criticisms derive from the same fundamental difficulty. While the film may have been acted by local people, the essential direction remained in other hands. Neither its design, its plot, nor its message sprang from the collaboration which took place in its production. If there was a common purpose, it was one imposed from without.

Such a difficulty is not peculiar to film making, although it is certainly increased by the technical requirements and costs of the medium and its domination by an international professionalism. A similar problem applies especially in national broadcasting. And in practice it occurs in most other types of project, especially in education. But the co-operative nature of the oral history approach has led to a radical questioning of this one-sided process, and hence of the fundamental relationship between history and the community. Historical information need not be taken away from the community for interpretation and presentation by the professional historian. Through oral history the community can, and should, be given the confidence to write its own history. This hope has been behind some of the co-operative local oral history groups which have issued cheap cyclostyled broadsheets of transcribed extracts from recordings, adult education local history projects, or joint projects between oral historians and trade unionists.

The most radical model of this approach is provided by the People's Autobiography of Hackney. This arose from a group, originally connected with the W.E.A. (Workers' Educational Association), which met in a local book and community centre called Centreprise. Members of the group varied in age from their teens to their seventies, but all lived in or near Hackney in East London. Their occupations were very mixed. The group was an open one, brought together by notices in the local papers, libraries, and other places. Any member could record anyone else. At the group meetings they played and discussed their tapes—sometimes also recording these discussions—and planned ways of sharing what was collected with a Hackney audience. For this reason they especially emphasize publishing and have issued a series of cheap pamphlets, assisted by a local library subsidy, based on transcriptions and written accounts of people's lives, which have had a large local circulation. These pamphlets have in turn stimulated reactions from other people and led to more discussion and recordings. The group has also collected photographs, and has sufficient material, through tapes and slides, for historical presentations to audiences in the community such as hospital patients and pensioners' associations—another way of giving back to people their own history, showing them it was valued, and stimulating their own contributions. The People's Autobiography thus aims, on the one hand, to build up through a series of individual accounts a composite history of life and work in Hackney, and, on the other, to give people confidence in their own memories and interpretations of the past, their ability to contribute to the writing of history—confidence, too, in their own words: in short, in themselves.

The possibility of using history for such a constructive social and personal purpose comes from the intrinsic nature of the oral approach. It is about individual lives—and any life is of interest. And it depends upon speech, not upon the much more demanding and restricted skill of writing. Moreover, the tape recorder not only allows history to be taken down in spoken words but also to be presented through them. In a historical talk, or a museum demonstration of craft techniques, or a retrospective broadcast, the use of a human voice, fresh, personal, particular, always brings the past into the present with extraordinary immediacy. The words may be idiosyncratically phrased, but all the more expressive for that. They breathe life into history.

Something more is to be learned from them than mere content. Recordings demonstrate the rich ability of people of all walks of life to express themselves. George Ewart Evans has shown in his many books how the dialect of the East Anglian farm labourer, long scorned by the county land-owning class for his notable inarticulacy, carries a Chaucerian grammatical and expressive strength which is hard to equal in conventional English. And this kind of discovery has been shared by oral historians wherever they have worked. The tape recorder has allowed the speech of ordinary people—their narrative skill for example—to be seriously understood for the first time. Educationists a few years ago, under the influence of Basil Bernstein, were assuming that working-class speech was a fatal handicap, a constraint which imprisoned all but the simplest types of thought. Now, with the help of tape recorders, the magazine *Language and Class Workshop* can challenge Bernstein's theories with its published transcripts; and in America 'urban folklore' has become an accepted literary genre. However, it may well be a long time before such revaluations reach general acceptance. Meanwhile, one of the key social contributions which can be made by the oral historian, whether in projects or through bringing direct quotation into written history, is to help give ordinary people confidence in their own speech.

In discovering such a purpose, oral historians have travelled a long way from their original aim—and there is, undoubtedly, some danger of conflict between the two. On the level of the interview itself, for example, there have been telling criticisms of a relationship with informants in which a middle-class professional determines who is to be interviewed and what is to be discussed and then disappears with a tape of somebody's life which he never hears about again—and if he did, might be indignant at the unintended meanings imposed on his words. There are clear social advantages in the contrasting ideal of a self-selected group, or an open public meeting, which focuses on equal discussion and encourages local publication of its results; and of individual recording sessions which are conversations rather than directed interviews. But there are also drawbacks in the alternative.

The self-selected group will rarely be fully representative of a community. It is much more likely to be composed from its central groups—people from a skilled working-class or lower middle-class background. The local upper class will rarely be there, nor will the very poor, the less confident especially among women, or the immigrant from its racial minority. A truer and socially more valuable form of local oral history will be created when these other groups are drawn in. Its publications will be much more telling if they can juxtapose, for example, the mistress with the domestic servant, or a millowner with the millworkers. It will then reveal the variety of social experience in the community, the groups which had the better or the worse of it—and perhaps lead to a consideration of what might be done about it. Local history drawn from a more restricted social stratum tends to be more complacent, a re-enactment of community myth. This certainly needs to be recorded, and a self-sufficient local group which can do this is undoubtedly helping many others besides itself. But for the radical historian it is hardly sufficient. History should not merely comfort; it should provide a challenge, and understanding which helps toward change. For this the myth needs to become dynamic. It has to encompass the complexities of conflict. And for the historian who wishes to work and write as a socialist, the task must be not simply to celebrate the working class as it is, but to raise its consciousness. There is no point in replacing a conservative myth of upper-class wisdom with a lower-class one. A history is required which leads to action: not to confirm, but to change the world.

In principle there is no reason why local projects should not have such an object, while at the same time continuing to encourage self-confidence and the writing of history from within the community. Most groups will normally contain some members with more historical experience. They certainly need to use tact; to undervalue rather than emphasize their advantage. But it is everybody's loss in the long run if they disown it: their contribution should be to help the group towards a wider perspective. Similar observations apply in the recording session where the essential need is mutual respect. A superior, dominating attitude does not make for a good interview anyway. The oral historian has to be a good listener, the informant an active helper. As George Ewart Evans puts it— 'although the old survivors were walking books, I could not just leaf them over. They were persons.' And so are historians. They have come for a purpose, to get information, and if ultimately ashamed of this they should not have come at all. A historian who just engages in haphazard reminiscence will collect interesting pieces of information, but will throw away the chance of winning the critical evidence for the structure of historical argument and interpretation.

The relationship between history and the community should not be one-sided in either direction; but rather a series of exchanges, a dialectic, between information and interpretation, between educationists and their localities, between classes and generations. There will be room for many kinds of oral history and it will have many different social consequences. But at bottom they are all related.

Oral history is a history built around people. It thrusts life into history itself and it widens its scope. It allows heroes not just from the leaders, but from the unknown majority of the people. It encourages teachers and students to become fellow-workers. It brings history into, and out of, the community. It helps the less privileged, and especially the old, towards dignity and self-confidence. It makes for contact—and thence understanding—between social classes, and between generations. And to individual historians and others, with shared meanings, it can give a sense of belonging to a place or in time. In short, it makes for fuller human beings. Equally, oral history offers a challenge to the accepted myths of history, to the authoritarian judgement inherent in its tradition. It provides a means for a radical transformation of the social meaning of history.

4

Some Words on Oral Histories
Samuel Hand

Concluding our survey of the history of oral history, Samuel Hand, a specialist in the history of New England, provides an overview of practical considerations and basic controversies. Hand takes the position that the oral historian's mission is the preservation of oral documents of memory for future researchers.

This articles serves to introduce critical subjects such as the primacy of the interview's tape or transcript; the editing and annotating of transcripts; interviewee reviews of transcripts; and the publishing of oral history research in professional journals. Naturally no one article can include all the possible uses of oral history. It might also be used for community drama, for consciousness-raising, as a celebration of a life well spent, or as a program for the broadcast media.

Hand concludes by posing provocative questions for further research. Many of his points—including the need for objective evaluations of existing oral history collections—still await consideration from graduate students and practitioners in the field.

*Samuel Hand teaches history at the University of Vermont. He has writ-*ten Counsel and Advise: A Political Biography of Samuel Roseman *(1979) and has coedited* A State of History: Readings in Vermont History *(1982). He served for five years as editor of the* Oral History Review.

"Some Words on Oral History" originally appeared in Scholarly Pub-lishing *9 (January 1978), pp. 171–85.*

ACCORDING TO Lewis Hanke, a former president of the American Historical Association, the first oral history project in North America was directed by Bernardino de Sahagùn.[1] In 1558 Saha-gùn, a Franciscan missionary to Mexico, brought together about a dozen old Indians reputed to be especially well informed on Aztec lore so that he and his research assistants might interrogate them. The product of these interviews was a 'carefully organized mass of text and 1,850 illustrations on the spiritual and material aspects of the life of the ancient Mexicans as the Indians remembered them.' Distinguished above most contemporary transatlantic literature that provided 'a European view masquerading as a description of far-off peoples,' Sahagùn's 'remarkable collection of oral literature' expressed the 'soul and life of the Aztec people at the time of their greatness.' Sahagùn, of course, was not the first oral historian; the interview technique goes back at least to the ancient Greeks. Unlike Herodotus and Thucydides, however, Sahagùn became so totally immersed in research that he died in 1590 without publishing any of his monumental work. By obtaining and preserving sources of information that would otherwise not have been available to subsequent generations Sahagùn serves as a model to contemporary oral historians.

The principal rationale for oral history is to preserve and collect human memories that might otherwise be lost. Whether interviews are published directly as books or articles is secondary to the contribution they make to subsequent research. Some oral history projects even require as a condition of employment that their interviewers not publish in project-related areas. Professor Louis Starr, director of Columbia University's Oral History Office, has described oral historians as 'men and women armed with tape recorders, in quest of first hand knowledge that would otherwise decay. They would capture, not for their own benefit, but for libraries or other repositories to hold for the benefit of scholars of this and succeeding generations.'[2]

Despite Professor Starr's emphasis upon the tape recorder, Columbia's earliest interviews predated its use. The late Allan Nevins, who in the preface of the 1938 edition of his *Gateway to History* called for a 'systematic attempt to obtain from the lips and papers of living Americans . . . a fuller record of their participation in the political, economic, and cultural life,' was among the first to respond to his own challenge. In 1948, with a graduate student as his amanuensis, Nevins conducted Columbia's first interview for what is at present an archive containing oral memoirs totaling over 420,000 pages. After that first interview the student typed out an account from his longhand notes, but this cumbersome procedure was abandoned the following year when Columbia interviewers began using wire recorders from which they subsequently typed their transcripts. Shortly thereafter the tape recorder became available. By reducing the capture and storage of interviews to a portable mechanical process requiring only a small investment, it made every person a potential oral historian, or interview subject, or both. Oral history was off and running. By 1975, *Oral History Collections*, a particularly valuable reference volume edited by Alan Meckler and Ruth McMullin, described 386 projects in the United States, 30 projects in Canada, and others in Great Britain and Israel. Limited to institution-based projects and acknowledged as incomplete at the time of its publication, it nevertheless underscored the magnitude and diversity of oral history.

Although most oral history projects centre upon the careers of prominent persons or institutions, the experiences of the more obscure are also being sought. The Appalachia project, a four-college consortium based at Alice Lloyd College, in Pippa Passes, Kentucky, is an example of efforts to have people tell the story of their region in their own words. A collection of interviews conducted by the consortium over the past five years has been edited by Laurel Shackelford and Bill Weinberg and published as *Our Appalachia: An Oral History* (1977). Up to now, however, the most popular publications from the lips of ordinary folk have been by author-interviewers independent of established oral history projects. Such freelances as Studs Terkel—*Hard Times: An Oral History of the Great Depression* (1970)—and Barry Broadfoot—*Ten Lost Years 1929–1939: Memories of Canadians who Survived the Depression* (1973)—share with their more archival-minded associates the premise that great events *are* great events because they deeply influence the lives of countless persons. Not only can the memory of these influences be preserved by recording them, but for many individuals, especially the obscure and less literate, the recording is the only way that memory will be preserved. On occasion, as is illustrated by Theodore Rosengarten's *All God's Dangers: The Life of Nate Shaw* (1974), an illiterate memoirist can provide interviews remarkable enough to warrant a full-length autobiography.

The most common focus for ordinary people projects has been upon minority cultures and life styles, with Indian history the most systematically organized. In order 'to obtain history from the Indian point of view' the Doris Duke oral history project funded associated programs at seven state universities in the Unites States. The decision to establish multiple Indian oral history centres reflects an appreciation of the diversity among American Indians as to their cultural perspective and their particular historical experiences in regard to federal, state, and local agencies. *To Be an Indian* (1971), edited by Joseph Cash and Herbert Hoover, is a short collection of such interviews from the University of South Dakota and intended as a college text. Frequently the most prized of the interviews are not with 'ordinary' Indians but with those who, by virtue of their tribal or other special status, possess special knowledge of their traditional culture.

By now it is apparent that, although armed with tape recorders, most oral historians in the United States have been print-oriented, an observation that extends even to Louis Starr's scholarly pursuers, who capture knowledge not for their own benefit but for succeeding generations. Perhaps because the typescript was the only permanent record of its first interviews, Columbia has always assumed the printed record rather than the recording to be its final product. Although important theoretical objections to this practice have been voiced (as well as published), practical considerations have promoted its general adoption. Even when both tapes and typescripts are available, researchers almost invariably seek out the typescripts as easier to use. This impetus towards print has been heightened by the New York *Times* Oral History Program, which since 1970 has been micropublishing typescripts. Materials from the oral history collections of the University of California, Columbia, Stanford, Claremont Graduate School, Hebrew Union University, American Film Institute, and others are commercially available and will presumably facilitate wider distribution and more extensive use of oral history memoirs than was previously possible.

A comparable distribution system for tapes is not likely. Some reasons for this are inherent in the process by which the typescript is prepared for public access. In an ideal version of that process, each interview is transcribed and proofed against the tape by the interviewer shortly after the actual interview. Then, after all interviews have been completed, the respondent is provided with a copy of the typescripts and asked to review them for accuracy and return them along with a deed of gift releasing the interview(s) 'for such scholarly and educational purposes' as the project 'shall determine.' In the final act the interviewee makes some minor corrections on the typescript and then rushes it along with a signed contract back to the oral history office. The tape and the typescript now are made available to researchers. Keep in mind incidentally that the tape and the typescript may be different legal entities. Since the way we speak may be copyrighted separately from the words we speak, the sound recording and the typescript produced from it are not necessarily covered by the same legal agreements. Although the laws pertaining to oral history have been somewhat affected by the new U.S. Copyright Act (effective 1 January 1978), Truman Eustis' 'Get it in Writing: Oral History and the Law' which appeared in *Oral History Review 1976* contains an extremely useful discussion of these and other legal questions of particular interest to oral historians.

More to the immediate point, however, is that the scenario is never played quite in this manner. An interviewee checking her typescript for accuracy may find that although she had said 1926 was the year the Winooski River overflowed, she has since discovered from her notes that it was in 1927. Obviously her impression that Jones, who died in the winter of 1927, 'must have helped in the cleanup' is incorrect. Making these corrections on the typescript is a simple task. The interviewee can do it with a few strokes of her pen, and the page need not even be retyped. A second interviewee may specify in his contract that particular segments of his interview be closed until some future time. In this instance a typescript can usually be made available promptly with blank pages substituted for the omitted passages. Similar restrictions and emendations can be adapted to tape recordings but are more costly and technically difficult.

Apart but not distinct from these considerations are tensions arising from the interviewee's distress at discovering when reviewing the typescript that he didn't speak in written grammar; even the most forthright and articulate conversational style may appear as abominable syntax when converted from speech to print. Under such circumstances the respondent, despite all pleas to the contrary, may rewrite his interview extensively or, the ultimate disaster, even refuse to release it. To minimize these very real dangers some oral history offices 'clean up' their typescripts. Policies vary as to the extent of editorial discretion permitted, but a common practice is to delete some false starts and retain only occasional ahs, you knows, and assorted expletives for flavour. Viewed from this perspective, typescript revisions are artifices to assuage the interviewee's ego. There are those who assert, however, that judicious revision is desirable in that it makes the oral memoir more accurate and comprehensible in print than a verbatim record of an interview and that furthermore it is impossible to transcribe an interview verbatim.

Implicit in the above statement is an issue oral historians confront constantly: what is the nature of their product as source material? An oral memoir may on occasion constitute a complete record of an interview, but oral memoir and record of the interview are not synonymous terms. Some practitioners regard this as a theoretical rather than a practical distinction. Oral history, they assert, is a source that like any other source must be correlated with more conventional documentation. Researchers should bring to these sources an appreciation that oral memoirs can be as selective and self-serving as written memoirs and diaries. Human memory is fallible, and the researcher may prefer documents written while events were happning, but it is precisely the inadequacy or inaccessibility of contemporary documentation that has generated the need for oral history. Further, oral historians are prone to assert, telephones and jet travel have exacerbated the problem by obviating the need for particular forms of written documentation. Besides, even contemporary documentation should be suspect. The frequently cited *Congressional Record* systematically includes material congressmen wish they had said while deleting material they wish they hadn't.

The job of the oral history interviewer is to be sufficiently well versed in the context of his subject and knowledgeable enough in its details to formulate perceptive questions, but the final product is ultimately a record of an individual's recall. Whether the record of that recall is compiled exclusively during the course of an interview, or amended after reflection, or clarified in transcription, is information that should be provided to the researcher, but the responsibility of the interviewer ends there. It is the task of the researcher to interpret and evaluate his sources.

The most prominent dissenter from this view is Saul Bension, whose prize-winning *Tom Rivers, Reflections on a Life in Medicine and Science* (1967) is a classic among oral history memoirs. Bension, who dedicated the book to his mentor, Allan Nevins, has insisted that the interviewer prepare himself through intensive research and that he rely upon published and manuscript sources to provide the framework for the interview. His interviews with Dr. Rivers were conducted over a period of approximately fifteen months and so arranged as to facilitate continuing research. At the end of each interview Professor Benison would outline the subject matter or problems for the next interview and supply Dr. Rivers with 'copies of letters, documents, and scientific papers that might serve to refresh his memory.' On occasion Dr. Rivers would direct Bension to additional manuscript material.

Benison 'came armed' to every interview 'with relevant books and documentary material so that if the need to look at or quote from such material arose it was immediately to hand.' Despite this preparation Dr. Rivers would occasionally forget a precise date or a person's name, and the information would be inserted later at his request. Errors of fact and interpretation inevitably crept into the interview and these were retained 'even when known to be errors' since 'such mistakes were often revealing of the man and his thought.'[3] Few oral historians fault this retention policy. For anyone other than the interviewee to correct his interview is regarded as a violation of the first principle of the oral memoir: to secure the memory (aided or unaided) of some individual on a particular subject. What distinguishes Bension from most other oral historians is that he goes beyond this and uses footnotes to expand, clarify, or correct some of Dr. Rivers' statements. He also uses footnotes as devices to permit the subjects of Dr. Rivers' commentaries to defend themselves or offer a varying interpretation.

That *Tom Rivers* has been as honoured as a medical history as it has as a memoir owes at least as much to Benison's concept of his role as interviewer as to his subject's central role in medical research. Irrespective, however, of the role the interviewer assigns himself, no matter how unobtrusive he may attempt to be or how undirected his questions appear, he cannot ultimately escape becoming co-author of the oral memoir. This manifests itself in too many ways to discuss in detail here, although two can be suggested. A knowledgeable respondent is more likely to provide an informative interview to someone in whom he has confidence; if the interviewer fails to gain the respondent's confidence, subsequent researchers reviewing the memoir may well conclude that the respondent was uninformed. A similar dilemma is posed after an interviewer concludes that his subject is an uninformed source: in such instances he is prone to ask fewer questions and discourage long answers. Researchers then may well conclude from the typescript that the interviewer was inept. They may well be right.

The spectre haunting those who make conscious efforts to capture memories for succeeding generations is that it isn't readily apparent what particular questions succeeding generations will want answered and by whom. Oral historians, in effect, collect information for scholars they don't know in order to provide information for research topics they can't always anticipate. Pulitzer Prize-winning author Barbara Tuchman has suggested that the 'tape recorder, a monster with the appetite of a tapeworm,' has facilitated 'an artificial survival of trivia of appalling proportions.' 'We are,' she feared, 'drowning ourselves in unneeded information.'[4] The Columbia University Oral History Research Office, on the other hand, displays a shelf of 162 books that have drawn upon its archives. Among these are nine Pulitzer Prize winners, including Mrs. Tuchman's *Stilwell and the American Experience in China* (1971).

Oral history's contribution to any particular study will vary widely. For some authors it can provide the principal focus, for others it may verify a familiar anecdote. In either instance the existence of oral history archives is a reality with which authors must contend. Would it be appropriate, for example, to publish a work on Japanese relocation during the second world war without consulting the Earl Warren Collection at the University of California, Berkeley, or the Japanese-American Project at California State College, Fullerton? Biographers of John Diefenbaker will want to consult Peter Stursberg's two volumes on Diefenbaker's leadership and after 1980 may want to review the interviews in the Public Archives of Canada upon which the volumes were based.

Up to now published interviews have been either conducted by the author or from a project upon which the author has served. Researchers coming fresh to oral history typescripts tend to view them differently from interviewers. Much depends upon the purposes for which the researcher approaches the oral memoir, but unless he is considering a biography of the memoirist he is likely to read the interview with a specific information-gathering objective. He will primarily be seeking details and be less concerned with the interview as an artistic or intellectual unit. For his purposes reading typescripts is preferable to auditing tapes. The average rate of speech for most Americans is 125 words per minute, and most read with comprehension far in excess of that rate. Even while taking notes it is possible to read through an interview in less than half the time it would take to listen to it. Furthermore, if an interview is properly indexed it is possible to scan only the relevant portions to decide with reasonable certainty whether it deals with matters of immediate interest. To provide indexes for typescripts or published oral histories is a relatively simple task; preparing comparable aids for tapes is more difficult, and given the present level of technology the aids are more cumbersome to use.

Even a potential biographer may not bring to a memoirist a frame of reference similar to the interviewer's. The substance and style of the questions interviewers pose usually reflect their own sense of order and relevancy. Even should the replies they elicit be complete, each subsequent biographer, given his own priorities and perceptions, may prefer to have had different questions or some questions rephrased. The potential biographer will, if diligent, go beyond the typescript to the tape—the sound document—to seek information not easily transposed to print. How does one print a pause, an inflection, an ironic intonation, or distinguish a rapid flow of dialogue from a halting delivery? For that matter how does one audio-tape a sly smile, a shrug, or a vigorous nod? While the significance of non-verbal clues is open to methodological interpretation, they will by their very nature be more visible to the interviewer than to the most astute auditors of tapes and typescripts. Even when the latter has discovered an oral memoir rich in previously unpublished information, a key to reinterpretation of written documents, or indispensable in making available the perspectives of the inarticulate, he may be prudently reluctant to undertake the task of condensing, rearranging, and editing the typescripts for publication. Such tasks are better left with those who have experienced the interview.

Reference so far has been almost interchangeably to two types of publications utilizing oral history. The first and most common is books and articles that include materials from taped interviews. The interviews may be either from oral history archives or conducted by the author specifically for purposes of his research. Since oral history is more a research tool than a discipline, the range of these publications defies categorization. The second form is publication of the interviews themselves, usually, as suggested above, condensed, re-ordered, and annotated. In most instances the rationale for publishing oral memoirs is the same as for written memoirs irrespective of whether they be of the prominent or the obscure.

As evidenced from Manfred Waserman's *Bibliography on Oral History* (1975 revised edition), there is also an extensive literature about oral history. Nothing attests so vividly to its growth as a popular movement as the proliferation of oral history associations which have served to stimulate the production of oral history while simultaneously providing a sizeable audience for discussions of its objectives and practice. Articles on oral history have appeared in almost every conceivable type of publication, but most systematically in journals published by the various associations. The Oral History Association based in the United States is the largest and oldest (1965) of these. Even more recently regional societies such as the New England and Mid-Atlantic Oral History Associations have evolved, with some members also belonging to the national organization. The principal Canadian group is the Canadian Oral History Association, formerly styled Aural History Association to reflect its emphasis upon the sound document. Similar organizations have been founded in Great Britain and Australia. In nations such as Israel, France, and Mexico the movement lacks as broad a base as in the English-speaking countries and is usually dominated by a single institution engaged in some major project or projects.

The common denominator of all national associations is that they publish a journal. The United States–based group publishes the *Oral History Review* and reflects its pretentions to being *the* oral history association by regularly publishing material from oral historians outside the United States. The *Canadian Oral History Journal* and the British *Oral History* are less self-consciously international. The Australians have so far limited themselves to publishing the proceedings of their annual conferences. In addition, regional and national groups frequently put out newsletters, and occasionally individual oral history offices distribute their own periodic publications. Columbia University's annual report, usually a pamphlet of a dozen or more pages, includes material of general interest and with a distribution of over thirty thousand is more widely circulated than any other oral history publication.

Journals devoted exclusively to oral history constitute only a small minority of those that publish articles related to the field. Waserman's *Bibliography* cites almost two hundred different periodicals. Most have no special commitment to oral history, but some, such as the *Journal of Library History* and *History News*, the monthly publication of the American Association of State and Local History, feature it regularly. The total of all the words spent on oral history, however, has not added up to a distinguished critical literature. Until very recently authors tended to eschew criticism as irrelevant or counterproductive. Ronald Grele, in *Envelopes of Sound* (1975), has seen the 'dominant tendency' of historians to be 'enthusiastic in public print, and deeply suspicious in private conversation.'[5] Articles tend towards affirmations of faith and exultations of good works, of the 'How history was resuscitated in Burke Hollow through the tape recorder' variety. Variations of this include celebrations of individual projects and pleas for applying oral history to build community identity or aid in some other noble enterprise. The oral history market is saturated with these items. They are going to continue appearing because it is important to individual projects that they receive publicity and alert researchers to their particular program. Their message beyond the 'news' level has, however, become increasingly redundant to an increasingly large number of oral historians.

Ironically there is greater unanimity on the literature that oral history lacks than on what oral history is. Some definitions of oral history are so broad they include anything that involves a tape recorder and someone speaking into it. Yet despite this open admissions policy it has been moving perceptibly towards more systematic and methodologically self-conscious procedures. Only five years ago the novice might have digested Willa K. Baum's *Oral History for the Local Historical Society* (1969), the earliest and most popular how-to-do-it booklet, and rushed off to her first interview. Today's budding oral historian will still read Baum, as well as some of the many other practical manuals that have since appeared, but will seek theoretical guidance as well. Impetus for this conversion has come from many sources, but the most persistent requests for an appropriate literature have come from teaching faculties and are attributable to oral history having gained a foothold in school and college curriculums. Summer workshops are held routinely and courses are scheduled regularly. In at least one instance, 1976 at Beloit College, a baccalaureate degree was awarded to an oral history major. But although the academic community has defined its own needs most vocally, they are needs the non-academic oral historians share.

As suggested earlier, high-quality discussions of oral history are unfortunately rare, and those that were published frequently appeared in obscure or quickly out of print journals. Even the early proceedings of the Oral History Association, now available on microfiche from the *New York Times* Program, were inaccessible for some time. Under these circumstances a considerable interest in reviewing the literature with an eye towards compiling an annotated anthology has developed. The immediate value of such an effort would be to make the most pertinent articles generally available. Any such collection would be welcome and in the absence of any other single collection of readings would probably find a ready market. It would also serve to emphasize the paucity of research on many facets of oral history. Even the best articles usually lack evidence of concentrated research. They are relatively short seat-of-the-pants items prepared by veteran practitioners. Articles have seldom related to particular collections, and descriptions of particular collections, whether they appear in catalogues or as independent articles, have usually been written by an associate of the project described. Published critical evaluations of projects, and I use the term critical to mean 'exercising careful judgement or judicious evaluation,' are almost unheard of. In 1965 Alfred B. Rollins prepared such a report for the John F. Kennedy Oral History Project, but it was never publicly circulated.[6]

Systematic analyses of oral history from the viewpoints of people who have used tapes or typescripts in their research are not available. An occasional review of an 'oral history book' may raise pertinent questions, but these are usually already obvious to those engaged in oral history. Furthermore, to be truly useful analyses should involve more than one collection. To what extent, for example, do the various Doris Duke Indian projects complement or overlap each other and in what ways? Need the U.S. historian of Japanese-American relocation in the second world war research either the Berkeley or the Fullerton collections? Should he incorporate the Canadian experience from the Steveston Project? Is there a significantly distinct Canadian experience that the Steveston Project has captured? What is the relationship of these oral histories to written memoirs and documents? Do they add new facts, fill in gaps, provide anecdotes, or drown the researcher in unneeded information of dubious authenticity? Is it possible to generalize about the projects, or are they sufficiently unique to defy uniform generalizations?

Conventional wisdom dictates that the interviewer should prepare for an interview by digesting existing archival materials. What about the interviewee? Should he submit to interviews without some prior preparation or rely exclusively upon memory and the promptings of the interviewer? Tom Rivers prepared almost as much as Saul Benison, and John Diefenbaker discontinued his interviews with Peter Stursberg until he could brush up on figures and dates. How, if at all, do such interview typescripts differ from those in which the interviewee makes no special preparation? Or, a variation on this theme, does an interview with a relocation camp veteran who has steeped himself in relocation literature differ from one who brings only his own memories to the interview?

Despite the suggestion that questions such as those posed above be examined empirically from oral histories, the questions are not necessarily unique to oral history. Tradition maintains that, if oral history is a source like other sources, then the burden of evaluation rests with the researcher in his utilization of the material. Although it would be disastrous ever to absolve an author from that responsibility, he might be grateful for some additional light on the nature of oral history. Furthermore, unlike most other sources—presidential papers, business records, election returns—oral history has no function except as a guide through the past. It is generated specially for that purpose and often at great expense. (Costs from initial inception to indexing run in the neighbourhood of $200 for each hour.) To what extent oral history can best serve the needs of future scholars and whether and under what circumstances current practices might be modified to serve them better is a sticky question that by its very nature will continue to be a wager with posterity.

With well over a million pages of interviews transcribed and potential additional millions of pages stored exclusively on tape, however, it is appropriate that we take stock of the dower.

The value of such studies will transcend immediate concerns of oral historians and should attract readers with more general interests. At the most obvious levels they require explicit judgements on the quality, accessibility, and credibility of the wide range of contemporary documentary sources that would in turn stimulate expression of informed divergent views. Oral history is so broadly defined as to bring together practitioners with very little in common in terms of discipline or subject-matter within a discipline: potential users constitute at least as many diverse groups. It is perhaps inevitable that what appears as dross to the cultural anthropologist will occasionally appear as gold to the political historian. Efforts to deal explicitly with this phenomenon can contribute significantly to interdisciplinary colloquy.

There is currently an emphasis in schools and colleges upon oral history as a process through which students can experience and learn about historical research. In such instances the end product is the student's increased sensitivity to historical nuances. The typescript or the sound document is by-product. Occasionally these by-products, usually in the form of neighbourhood or family histories, gain some form of publication. Some have substantial merit, and their principal asset is frequently the special perspective of the interviewer. I strongly suspect this may also be true of projects where the typescript or sound document is intended as the final product. When an interviewer breaks into print we invariably learn a great deal about him. The interviewer for major projects is more likely to remain a name on a typescript, frequently a very obscure name. Yet if the oral memoir is truly a joint work between the memoirist and the interviewer, there are some things about the interviewer it would be useful to know. Perhaps most useful would be a short bibliography of the materials through which the interviewer prepped himself—special collections he may have consulted, and, where relevant, some indication of restricted documents to which he may have been granted access. There are also those non-verbal clues. Although it may be noted on the typescript that Ms. Weeza Matthias was present during the entire interview and spoke only once, the typescript doesn't indicate that her physical presence dominated the session so completely that at only one time did she have to resort to words to protect her husband from an inopportune disclosure. Just what, in addition to a typescript, oral history consumers may want from an interviewer is not at present apparent, and it is conceivable that project directors may not be able to deliver what is wanted most. Some observations on this would nonetheless be welcome.

Over the past few pages I have attempted to describe something of the vacuum in the literature about oral history. Most obviously lacking are critical analyses with specific and systematic reference to what has already been produced. While superficially this may appear of interest to only a highly specialized band, the issues transcend individual projects or the matter of taped interviews. Furthermore oral history itself has a large following whose professional needs—as project designers, interviewers, and teachers—would be well served by such efforts. The range of journals that would receive articles of this sort is quite broad, and oral history journals would eagerly publish them. If the studies were collected together in a book the author would probably reach a sizeable audience.

A final word is perhaps in order. I would be sorely disappointed if my remarks were interpreted as advocating an arbiter of oral history procedures or a prescribed method of operation. Sometimes, especially after some particularly serendipitous discovery, I even reject Barbara Tuchman's admonition that 'the criteria of uniqueness, importance, and significance should be applied in advance and leaf raking sternly avoided.'

Notes

1. Lewis Hanke, "American Historians and the World Today: Responsibilities and Opportunities," *American Historical Review* 80 (February 1975), pp. 6–7.

2. Louis Starr, S.V. "Oral History," in the *Encyclopedia of Library and Information Sciences*, vol. 20, (New York: Marcel Dekker, 1977). (See chapter 1 of the present volume.)

3. Saul Benison, *Tom Rivers: Reflections on a Life in Medicine and Science* (Cambridge, Mass.: M.I.T. Press, 1967), pp. xii–xiii. (See chapter 12 of the present volume.)

4. Barbara Tuchman, "Distinguishing the Significant from the Insignificant" *Radcliffe Quarterly* 56 (October 1972), pp. 9–10. (See chapter 6 of the present volume.)

5. Ronald Grele, "Movement without Aim: Methodological and Theoretical Problems in Oral History," in *Envelopes of Sound*, ed. Ronald Grele (Chicago: Precedent Publishing, 1975), p. 127.

6. Alfred B. Rollins, Jr., *Report on the Oral History Project of the John Fitzgerald Kennedy Library* (Cambridge, Mass.: Harvard University, 1965).

PART TWO
Interpreting and Designing Oral History

5

Reliability and Validity in Oral History

Alice Hoffman

In our second section, we examine the strengths and limitations of oral history from a practical perspective: the problems of interpreting and designing oral history projects. Too often, as William Moss points out later in this section, researchers overlook that fact that all documents, written or oral, require scrutiny before use as historical sources. Many written documents upon which historians have depended for centuries—memoranda of conversations, dictated letters—are generated from oral sources, a fact which makes the debate over the "worth" of oral sources more complex.

Our first essay, by labor historian Alice Hoffman, introduces a theme of later selections: reliability and validity in oral history interviewing. While Barbara Tuchman and William Cutler criticize oral history procedures in the articles which follow, Hoffman provides a framework to understand their critiques. She defines "reliability" and "validity" and suggests that the oral historian should base interviews on a thorough analysis of available historical sources. Where inconsistencies emerge between the printed and the recollected records, the interviewer should have the living sources attempt to resolve these contradictions.

Alice Hoffman, Associate Professor of Labor Studies at Pennsylvania State University, directs the oral history program there. She has coordinated projects with a number of labor unions, including the United Steelworkers, Graphic Arts International, the Philadelphia Federation of Teachers, and the national AFL-CIO. Her publications include "Oral History in the United States" (1971) and "Using Oral History in the Classroom," (1982).

"Reliability and Validity in Oral History" first appeared in Today's Speech 22 *(Winter 1974), pp. 23–27.*

ORAL HISTORY may be defined as a process of collecting, usually by means of a tape-recorded interview, reminiscences, accounts, and interpretations of events from the recent past which are of historical significance. Critics of the process have usually focused on the fallibility of human memory and questioned both the reliability and the validity of data collected in this manner.

In order to deal with this problem, it will be necessary to describe in more detail the methods used by most practitioners of the art of "oral history." Allan Nevins is usually credited with having started oral history when he established the Oral Research Office at Columbia University in 1948. The Columbia project began to conduct tape-recorded interviews with men and women who had made significant contributions in various fields and who had been in a position to observe developments in them. A tape-recorded interview was conducted, transcribed, checked for accuracy by the interviewer and his respondent, indexed, and deposited for use by researchers in the oral history collection at Columbia University, subject, however, to whatever temporary restrictions the respondent might wish to impose. By 1967 there was enough interest in this method of preserving the past that an association of oral historians was formed. From the inception of the organization, the historians in the group have been somewhat surprised to find their ranks swelled by people from a variety of academic disciplines: medical doctors, anthropologists, sociologists, psychologists, librarians, archivists, educators, physicists, ethnographers, etc.

One of the most interesting forms of oral history projects which finds representation in the Association is the variety of medical projects. These came about when doctors recognized that the most significant developments in the history of medicine have occurred within the memory of individuals still alive today. While the scientific methodology was adequately spelled out, there was a lack of information about the specific details of how the specialities were developed, the great hospitals created, and the new techniques introduced into the practice of medicine. Therefore, a number of the specialties are conducting tape-recorded interviews with the pioneers in these fields; some of these interviews have been videotaped.

Another type of project which we have represented in the Association is what might be called "Famous People and Their Friends and Associates." There is, for example, a most significant project centered on the life and activities of General George C. Marshall. Since Franklin Roosevelt, each president, as he left office, has set up a library for the preservation and deposit of the materials associated with his presidency; and each of these libraries, beginning with the Truman Library, has an oral history office.

Then there are a large number of projects which deal with regional and cultural history. The project at the University of California in Berkeley is called the Regional Oral History Project and is devoted to collecting and preserving information on a wide variety of topics from forestry to the development of the wine industry in California with all their attendant social, political, and economic ramifications. In this connection, a number of state archives have initiated governmental and social oral histories related to the development of their state.

Ethnic history finds significant representation in the Oral History Association, and there are oral history projects on the history of the Jewish people in the United States, and the history of various Indian tribes; and one very important recent development is a number of projects focused on black history. The development of oral history projects in these areas leads to one general observation about all of them. That is, oral history projects tend to come about where significant developments occur and where there is a paucity of archival or written records about them; black history serves as a case in point. We have developing in the United States a new sense of racial pride among blacks, and they are desperate to recover their own past; but there is very little information. Black archives are virtually non-existent so that the only means of getting at the past is to interview people who were slaves or who were the children of slaves; with few exceptions, the only means of finding out what it was like to move into the northern ghettos in the twenties is to interview these people.

Finally, oral history offices are involved in organizational history. Organizations of a wide diversity, ranging from International Business Machines to the United Steelworkers of America, have become involved in oral history as a means to recovering and preserving their origins and development. One potential advantage of the organizational history approach—and one not to be dismissed as mundane inasmuch as it may involve the very survival of an oral history project—is that an organization or institution is often willing to provide funding for such a series of interviews. . . .

One of the persistent challenges presented by scholars to oral history regards the reliability and the validity of the interviews. In this connection reliability can be defined as the consistency with which an individual will tell the same story about the same events on a number of different occasions. Validity refers to the degree of conformity between the reports of the event and the event itself as recorded by other primary resource material such as documents, photographs, diaries, and letters. Now, while it is conceivable that an oral report might be a true description of an event, its validity cannot really be tested unless it can be measured against some body of evidence. Without such evidence, an isolated description of an event becomes a bit of esoterica whose worth cannot be properly evaluated.

When viewed in this fashion, an oral history informant is reliable if his or her reports of a given event are consistent with each other. For example, in 1966 the Pennsylvania State University Oral History Project conducted an interview with an employee of the Carnegie-Illinois Steel Company. An employers' organization had attempted to recruit him to provide undercover information on the union activities of his fellow employees. In the interview he described the means used to recruit him and the methods by which he was paid for his services. In 1935 Robert R. Brooks conducted research on the early organization of trade unions in the steel industry and published in his book, *As Steel Goes*[1], an anonymous interview with the same individual. Both the published account in Brook's study and the transcribed interview done thirty years later read almost word for word the same.[2] Thus we are assured of the interview's reliability. Its validity, however, must be measured against other testimony and documents; for example, the accounts of industrial espionage uncovered by the LaFollette Senate Committee to investigate the Violation of Civil Liberties[3] and the accounts of other respondents in the Penn State Oral History Project. When compared with these accounts this particular interview also appears to be essentially valid, but there are discrepancies between his testimony and the preponderance of other available sources. An informant can therefore be reliable (the same story emerges each time it is called for), but the story may or may not be a valid representation of the original events as judged by comparison with other sources. If, however, an informant is unreliable, the validity of the reports must be suspected. In short, in historical assessment, as in the area of psychological assessment, a data-gathering instrument can be valid only to the extent that it is also reliable.

David Musto at the Fourth National Colloquium of the Oral History Association presented a summary of research findings on the reliability over time of the information which parents gave with respect to the medical and training histories of their children. There was a common thread running through these studies: although many facets of the reports were found to be quite reliable, especially the "hard data" (for example, reports of the baby's birth weight), certain aspects of the reports, such as those dealing with the parents' attitudes and emotions, were less reliable.[4]

Moreover, in one study cited, a test of the validity of these oral reports was also made. At New York University there is a large and long-term study of child rearing, so that it is possible to compare parents' reports with clinical records over time. Again certain factual information was quite accurate; but where there was distortion, it tended to be in the direction of recommendations by child care experts.[5]

This tendency toward conformity with acceptable norms is probably characteristic of all human reports, and it both requires and receives special attention by the practitioners of oral history. When David Musto presented his data at the Fourth National Colloquium, the first question he was asked was as follows:

Question: I would like to ask if, in any of these studies, the interviewee was faced with the apparent inconsistency in the record.

Musto: To my knowledge this was not done.[6]

Unlike the interviews that Musto reported where parents were not confronted with the inconsistencies in their reports, a well-trained oral historian will invariably familiarize himself with the available records on the matter under discussion and will raise the issue when inconsistencies arise. This practice was described by one of the Colloquium participants:

Question: My experience indicates that, if you confront a person with a contradiction or inconsistency, he very often is able to resolve it. It will turn out that it had to do with a change over time in the understanding of the definition of a word, or it has to do with the context in which one event took place as opposed to another event. I think that in setting up an oral interview one of the basic motivations for agreeing to do this with you is to set the record straight. If you have a letter or a document which indicates that he was very angry at someone and he's now saying that he really thought he was a very nice fellow, if you challenge him or present him with these inconsistencies, he will often be very glad to have the opportunity to show you how his thinking changed. And that's very important material to record. If you have convinced him of your basic sensitivity and willingness to cooperate with him in the whole business of setting the record straight, I don't think he will be put off by making challenges to him.[7]

This, of course, reflects the difference in purpose of the studies Musto cites and the work of an oral historian. Those studies sought to assess the limits of reliability in the clinical reports made by parents uncontaminated by the corrections that would be induced if parents were faced with their inconsistencies. An oral historian, on the other hand, seeks a valid representation and hence uses the interview to enhance the opportunity to obtain a valid report.

It is unlikely, however, that in any given interview the oral historian will be entirely successful in this venture. Recognizing this, many oral historians assert that they are not historians at all but rather oral archivists and that the oral record is what the philosophers call a "memory claim"; that is, it is one person's claim as to what happened and, as such, is simply another primary resource to be stored by archivists along with the more traditional items in the archives to be evaluated and compared with documents, letters, etc., by future historians to assess its significance.

In this sense the oral record has certain advantages over the written document. One advantage is that there can be no doubt as to its authorship. In government circles in Washington it is standard operating procedure that an important letter may be the work of many individuals except the one who signs it. In that connection the journal *Science* recently reported that the letter written by Franklin Roosevelt suggesting the creation of the National Science Foundation was not actually authored by Roosevelt but by two young Washington lawyers: Oscar Ruebhausen and Oscar S. Cox.[8]

Another advantage of the oral interview is that it is not a written document and often contains the freshness and candor which is more typical of direct conversation.

Its most important advantage in my view, however, is that it makes possible the preservation of the life experience of persons who do not have the literary talent or leisure to write their memoirs. In this way it facilitates a new kind of history—a history not of the captains, kings, and presidents but of farmers, workers, immigrants, and the like. Interviews with people who have been foot soldiers in various important movements of social change but have heretofore been unrecorded may now be preserved and hence their impact assessed. In that connection, it has been interesting to observe the frequency with which we have collected evidence that many policies developed by the United Steelworkers of America have been the result of the experience, knowledge, and suggestion of a much lower level of leadership than is commonly reported in historical studies of the Union or in contemporary journalistic accounts.

In sum, then, one might say that oral history is simply one among several primary resources. It is no worse than written documents. Archives are replete with self-serving documents, with edited and doctored diaries and memoranda written "for the record." In fact, when undertaken in the most professional way, oral histories may be superior to many written records in that there is always a knowledgeable interviewer present actively seeking to promote the best record obtainable. Norman Hoyle in an article on oral history has defined the interview as "a kind of social transaction in which each party has a direct, though perhaps indeterminate, effect upon the other. The whole array of stimuli emitted by the interviewer—his age, his appearance, his manner of speech, his actions, his preparations, his credentials—will determine how he is perceived by the person being interviewed. And the way he is perceived will in certain measure determine the content, style, and quality of the response he elicits."[9] While the presence of the trained interviewer provides certain advantages, it also obviously colors the results in somewhat unpredictable ways. In this connection oral historians stand to benefit greatly from contact with professionals in the area of speech communication. Our colleagues in this area understand the parameters of the kind of communication represented by an oral interview, and they could provide insights which would greatly enhance the reliability and validity of oral histories.

Notes

1. Robert R. Brooks, *As Steel Goes . . . Unionism in a Basic Industry* (New Haven: Yale University Press, 1940), p. 9.

2. John Mullen, oral interview conducted by Alice M. Hoffman, February 1966, PSU-USWA Archives, pp. 8–10.

3. U.S. Senate, Committee on Education and Labor, *Violations of Free Speech and Rights of Labor, Hearings*, 75th Cong., 1st sess., pt. 14 (Washington, D.C.: U.S. Government Printing Office, 1937).

4. David F. Musto and Saul Benison, "Studies on the Accuracy of Oral Interviews," in Gould P. Colman, ed., *The Fourth National Colloquium on Oral History* (Warrenton, Va.: Oral History Association, 1970), pp. 167–72.

5. *The Fourth National Colloquium*, p. 173.

6. *The Fourth National Colloquium*, p. 176.

7. *The Fourth National Colloquium*, p. 180.

8. "Historical Footnote," *Science* 182 (October 12, 1973), p. 116.

9. Quoted in James E. Sargent, "Oral History, Franklin D. Roosevelt, and the New Deal," *Oral History Review* 1 (1973), p. 93.

6

Distinguishing the Significant from the Insignificant

Barbara Tuchman

A major problem in using oral sources for history is the public misconception that recording reminiscences is the same as sifting and melding them into a work of history. Barbara Tuchman, Pulitzer Prize–winning historical writer, underlines the point by sharply criticizing those who collect oral data indiscriminately, thus confusing history gathering with history making.

Tuchman writes as a historian who conducts interviews for her own research; whereas many oral historians collect information not for their own work, but for future scholars working after the narrator is gone. For this reason, the archival oral historian must cast a broader net than the thesis-minded historian.

The author fears that tape recording will mean "a downgrading both of source material and what is made from it" and considers that in early oral history work, thanks to the apparent ease of tape recording, "a few veins of gold and a vast mass of trash are being preserved." On the other hand, Tuchman acknowledges that some of her best sources have been "verbal interviews" conducted by historians. Thus she validates the field while at the same time criticizing it for a lack of selectivity and self-discipline. Ultimately, she makes the same point that William Moss and Gary Okihiro do in later selections: oral history must be based firmly on research.

Barbara Tuchman is one of the most vivid and successful writers of history in the United States. Educated at Radcliffe College, she has achieved prominence through a series of historically astute, popularly written books, including The Guns of August *(1962),* Stilwell and the American Experience in China *(1971); both received the Pulitzer Prize. A collection of her essays on the craft of history is* Practicing History *(New York: Alfred Knopf, 1981).*

"Distinguishing the Significant from the Insignificant" first appeared in Radcliffe Quarterly 56 *(October 1972), pp. 9–10.*

HOW DOES RESEARCH in contemporary history differ from research into past history? My own opinion is, that apart from the obvious physical difference of interviewing live people instead of reading their published memoirs or unpublished papers, the difference in *research* is not very great. The real difference is in the stance and the intent of the historian. Where does he stand in relation to the events? Is he writing from inside or out, as participant or as observer? Is his intent basically apologia, or an attempt to collect the whole story and stand back from it so that he can see it in the round? The answer determines the research, or rather what is done with it, for what finally counts is not the research *per se* but what you do with it after you've got it.

I am not concerned here with diaries and memoirs which are the *stuff* of history, that is, primary source material, but with the ex post facto account, that is, the work of the conscious historian. As told by a participant, these accounts belong in a great tradition from Flavius Josephus to the Earl of Clarendon to Winston Churchill, but they are all apologia; some more, some less but all special pleading, as history by a participant is bound to be. Research in such cases, especially if the author played a central role in the events, is usually designed to fit a desired result as for example in the account of 1914 by General Joffre, or the latest entry in the field of contemporary history by the Texas historian, Mr. Lyndon Johnson, two works, incidentally, that closely resemble each other. Both are based on the work of teams of researchers and both come up with an equally fanciful result: a never-never hero, idealized beyond recognition.

The participant's advantage in research is his special access to sources. The normal historian, of course, does not have the whole staff of the General Staff or a federally subsidized twelve-story library at his personal disposal, which is perhaps just as well—Thucydides, too, like the rest of us, did his own work. I have had no experience in the research of special advantage, that is, the insider's research, because I have never written as a participant—except perhaps once, as an emotional participant, so to speak. My first book *Bible and Sword*, which, to give you an idea of the subject, was subtitled, *Britain and Palestine from the Bronze Age to Balfour*, came to an end at 1918. Since it was written after the achievement of statehood by Israel in 1948, the publisher was insistent on an epilogue bringing it up to date. I spent six months on research in the period of the Mandate, the White Papers, Ernest Bevin, and the barring of the refugees and all that, but when I came to write it, the result was a disaster. Even I could see that. I was too angry to write history, so I tore it up, and the book came out without an epilogue. Since then, whenever someone, about once a year, proposes that I *must* write the history of modern Israel or the Six-Day War, I am not tempted because I know that an emotional participant is no historian.

I have never come nearer to contemporary history than a perspective of 25 years. The book on Stilwell concerned events of my own time and research involving people still alive, but except for the technique of interviewing, I did not find the problems of research very different for this book than for the others. The memories of the living, one soon discovers, are no more reliable or free of wishful recollection and the adjustments of hindsight than the memoirs of the dead.

The chief difficulty in contemporary history is over-documentation or what has been called, less charitably, the multiplication of rubbish. Ever since the advent of mechanical means of duplication there has been an explosion of material that cannot be dealt with by less than teams of researchers. The 20th century is likely to be the doom of the individual historian. (Actually I do not really believe that. Though the doom seems logical, I believe somehow the historian will illogically survive.)

With the appearance of the tape recorder, a monster with the appetite of a tapeworm, we now have, through its creature Oral History, an artificial survival of trivia of appalling proportions. To sit down and write a book, even of memoirs, requires at least *some* effort, discipline, and perseverance which until now imposed a certain natural selection on what survived in print. But with all sorts of people being invited merely to open their mouths, and ramble effortlessly and endlessly into a tape recorder, prodded daily by an acolyte of Oral History, a few veins of gold and a vast mass of trash are being preserved which would otherwise have gone to dust. We are drowning ourselves in unneeded information. I should hastily add here that among the most useful and scintillating sources I found were two verbal interviews with General Marshall tape recorded by Army historians in 1949. Marshall, however, was a summit figure worth recording, which is more than can be said for all those shelves and stacks of oral transcripts piling up in recent years.

In my interviews I failed to take advantage of technology and did not use a tape recorder, chiefly I suppose, because a machine makes me quail. This may have something to do with being female. A woman is accustomed to entering upon a conversation as a personal thing, even with a stranger—perhaps more so with a stranger—and I can't imagine myself plunking a machine down in front of someone and saying, "Now, talk." Besides I am quite certain I would not know how to make it work. So I took along a notebook instead, one that fitted into my purse and so was always handy for planned or unplanned need. The loose-leaf pages, being the same size as my index cards, could be filed conveniently along with the other research material.

Taking notes of an interview, like taking notes on reading, is a crystallizing process which is part of the writer's business. You are practicing the essential function of the historian—distinguishing the significant from the insignificant—as you go along. It is true you miss a lot by not having the taped transcript. In skilled hands and in needful circumstance, the tape recorder is unquestionably useful, but its effect in the long run, as it proliferates, will I think be a downgrading both of source material and what is made from it.

Technology has made two additions to historical method: oral history via the tape recorder and quantitative history via the computer. Quantification in history is the business of feeding vast multiples of data into a computer which sorts it, packages it, and returns it gift-wrapped, as it were, in a suitable historical generalization, usually one that the unassisted human would have no difficulty in arriving at by ordinary deduction or intuition. An interesting moment in my career was a visit some years ago by two quantitative historians from California and, I think, Wisconsin who had been working for several years in a group spread over two universities on a project dealing with the origins of World War I. They had collected *all*—and I mean all—the diplomatic messages of the crisis period of June-July 1914 between sovereigns, ambassadors, foreign offices, etc.; had classified them according to various decimal-point degrees of friendship, suspicion, concealed or overt antagonism; and had fed these into the computer, and tabulated the result in three or four mimeographed bound volumes. The conclusion reached by the study was this: that the likelihood of war increases in direct proportion to the increase in expressed hostility.

Actually I do not wish to discount the contributions that may be made by the quantitative method in some more useful study than the 1914 endeavor. In a field susceptible of quantification—wage and price levels, migrations, demography—anything that can be counted, they may discover principles not known before or cause a revision of accepted theories—like the professor at a recent conference I attended who, by quantitatively comparing the price movement of cotton and of slaves, discovered something very significant about the cause of the Civil War, though I forget what.

An incomparable and, I think, indispensable source for contemporary historians is film, both for the physical realities of places and people that one cannot get any other way, and for flashes of insight and understanding through visual means. I think I learned more about Chinese propaganda from a film of the military parade staged for Wendell Willkie in Chungking, and more about Stilwell from a film showing him lying in the dust next to a Chinese soldier at the Ramgarh training ground and demonstrating how to handle a rifle, than I could have in any other way.

In the research for the Stilwell book, among the most valuable insights I gained were one from a verbal interview, one from unpublished letters, and one from published but obscure material found almost by accident.

Of course the most vivid and difficult to deal with were the diaries—
difficult because they bring events down to too small a scale. It was as if I
had been a cartographer trying to draw a map on a scale 100 miles to the
inch and working from surveys detailed down to one mile to the inch. I
might almost advise a putative biographer to find a subject who did *not*
keep a diary.

7

Accuracy in Oral History Interviewing

William Cutler III

Critiques of oral documentation come from both writers, such as Tuchman, and professional academic historians, such as the author of this next essay, William Cutler. This article, published in 1970, was one of the earliest critiques of oral history interviewing. Cutler suggests that factors inherent in the interview process—forgetfulness, self-delusion, and reticence of narrators; the biases of interviewers; the inaccuracy of human memory—all make the creation of history from oral sources a questionable proposition.

In later selections professional oral historians answer Cutler's arguments through a self-evaluation of the oral interviewing process. Yet Cutler's critique raises questions worthy of consideration; many individuals in the historical profession publicly (or privately) profess a suspicion of oral sources and share Cutler's reservations.

While some practitioners felt Cutler's article depended on marginally relevant studies, others found his arguments provocative. This essay inspired a healthy debate about the importance of historical standards (and better public relations) within the oral history profession.

William Cutler III is associate dean of the Graduate School and associate professor of history and education at Temple University. His writings include The Divided Metropolis: Social and Spatial Dimensions of Philadelphia: 1800–1975 *(1980) and "Oral History in the Study of Education in the 1980s," in* Historical Inquiry in Education: A Research Agenda, *ed.*

"Accuracy in Oral History Interviewing" originally appeared in Historical Methods Newsletter *3 (June 1970), pp. 1–7.*

SINCE 1948, when the technique of oral history originated at Columbia through the work of Allan Nevins, its practitioners have searched for ways to make the memoirs which they produce as accurate as possible. The chief obstacles, of course, have been the human failings of the people interviewed. Forgetfulness, dishonesty, or reticence have frequently introduced errors of fact or emphasis into oral history tapes.[1] Interviewers, too, have not been faultless, and misunderstandings have undoubtedly resulted in many distortions by confused respondents. But unlike those librarians and scholars who collect and use documents from the past with no guarantee of their accuracy, the oral historian can exert at least some control over his primary resource, the respondent, and strive to minimize the number of errors in the memoir which is produced.

Recent work in such fields as medicine, psychology, and sociology suggests that accuracy in interviewing is not easy to achieve. In one disquieting study of conservationists done a decade ago, researchers interested in the reliability of the human memory found that when asked the same seven questions one year apart, fifty-nine respondents showed an overall consistency in their responses of only 63.6 percent. Three of the questions were factual, and logically enough, they were answered more consistently than the other four, which tested attitudes.[2]

Likewise, other investigators at New York University and the University of Pennsylvania discovered that after several years parents recalled the facts concerning their children's infancies more reliably than their own attitudes as new parents.[3] But the evidence is not conclusive that attitudes are remembered better than facts; nor were Wenar and Coulter at Pennsylvania convinced by their data that time always dulls the memory. Because most of the mothers they questioned knew the details of their children's illnesses but had forgotten the facts of their own health during pregnancy, it was hypothesized that, regardless of its affective content, a brief and completed activity, like a child's one-time bout with the mumps or measles, might be "more reliably recalled than one which is continuously present over long periods of time."[4]

That time is not the oral historian's only enemy is further borne out by psychological findings of an important connection between the culture and values of an era and human perception and memory. In the study done at NYU by Lillian C. Robbins, mothers tended to remember having practiced demand feeding as advocated by Dr. Spock when, in fact, many had not fed on demand, for scheduled feeding was still in vogue at the time of their children's infancies.[5] Researchers interested in the past might still conclude from this study that respondents ought to be interviewed as soon as possible after an event in question, but even that view must be qualified by some findings reported in 1961 on the powerful and enduring cultural stereotype of the ideal American family. Among a matching group of parents, half the couples and their children were observed for nearly six years, while half were merely questioned once about the chief characteristics of their family life. While their observations told them otherwise, the researchers, Joan and William McCord, learned from those they asked that in their family everyone loved each other, and father was a "decent" man who provided faithful leadership.[6] Similarly, other psychologists have found a close relationship between the social desirability of a given trait as seen by a group of respondents and the probability of its later being highly rated by them as one of their own characteristics.[7]

The cultural milieu is not the only bad influence on the accuracy of perception and recall. The spurious features of a research situation can damage the validity of any study, as Roethlisberger and Dickson demonstrated in analyzing the now famous Hawthorne experiments. Published in 1939, their book, *Management and the Worker,* stressed the importance of social relations to worker performance and hypothesized that the synthetic nature of the experimental work group was primarily responsible for the increases in output of the laborers studied.[8] Because the interviewing milieu is fundamentally unnatural, comparable distortions are entirely possible in oral history, resulting in unintentional exaggerations or timidity. The potential for such errors in oral history can hardly be eliminated, since interviewers and respondents must interact at least somewhat, but measures can be taken to neutralize or diminish their effect. Interviewers can diversify their inquiries into a given subject to expose unconscious distortions or ask indirect questions to bypass sources of accidental error. Knowing the difficulties of extensive self-awareness, the oral historian might, for example, inquire about a person's feelings on an issue and hope to infer his beliefs from these. And yet making the interviewing situation as natural as possible may be the simplest and surest way of suppressing this elusive kind of error. Oral historians are great believers in personal rapport with respondents and often try to interview them in their homes or offices where the setting is familiar and the tape recorder may be less menacing. But caution is advised, for too much good fellowship can distract attention from the serious work at hand and even encourage respondents, who might otherwise be honest, to disrespect the occasion and twist their answers deliberately in their own favor. Enough will try this anyway when interviewed for posterity, and the oral historian must be watchful and prepared to minimize it.[9]

The research milieu can also cause intentional distortions in the opposite direction. A respondent may deflate his role in an event or even refuse to discuss it to avoid embarrassment should his recollections ever become known to friends or associates. The same man might also bend the truth in an interview for fear of reprisal, as industrial sociologists have learned from questioning workers who will not always be honest or complete without assurances of privacy from management.[10] The best defense against all dishonesty by respondents is the well-informed interviewer.

Poll takers know the value of removing threatening questions or surroundings, while balanced questions which allow respondents to praise
as well as criticize can sometimes loosen fearful tongues.[11] In oral history
interviewing legal options guaranteeing confidentiality have often per-
suaded the apprehensive. To be able to restrict the use of a memoir for a
stated number of years is to be able to discuss openly and truthfully what
otherwise might be too controversial or revealing at the time of recording.
In 1968 approximately 20 percent of Columbia's oral history transcripts
were partially or totally closed; and while most of these probably contained little or nothing earthshaking, such limitations undoubtedly have
saved much important information for the historian.[12]

Because it is commonly assumed that a warm and friendly atmosphere
is conducive to frank conversation, rapport is often cited as another key to
accuracy in touchy interviewing. By increasing a respondent's confidence, it can discourage dishonesty or reticence, even when an interviewer must eventually ask a threatening question. Public opinion takers
believe that good rapport can also neutralize the biasing effects of wide
social distance between the participants in an interview. However, if the
social distance is too great, an interviewer is hard-pressed to hide obvious
distinctions and to prevent distortion. Oral historians do not normally
face this problem since they and their respondents are usually well-
educated, but they ought to know about it and remember as well that too
much rapport can easily become interviewer bias and have damaging
effects, especially where social distance is a factor.[13]

Interviewers should always try to know their biases and conceal them
as far as possible. Prejudiced remarks, emphatic intonations, or even a
simple affirmation, if consistently applied, can distort a respondent's
account of the past. Interviewers themselves are vulnerable to error because of their own biases since a strong point of view, if unrecognized,
can induce a narrow plan of questioning accidentally tailored to suit private principles and assumptions.[14] Those same prejudices can also cause
an interviewer to make hasty judgments about respondents, branding
them with a stereotype which can then wrongly guide the rest of an
interview. Poll takers know that canvassers sometimes mark their ballots
on the basis of what a respondent is supposed to say and not in accord
with what is actually said. In oral history the use of tape recorders eliminates this kind of clerical error, but interviewer expectations can still
mean overlooked opportunities and an incomplete, invalid memoir.
When social or ideological differences are readily apparent, it is all too
easy to neglect to probe unusual responses or fail to ask questions for
which the stereotype provides an answer. Such expectations may even
rub off on respondents and influence them to falsely match the interviewer's stereotype.[15]

There are then many internal sources of error in oral history interviewing, but ultimately accuracy begins before the tape recorder is turned on, with foresight in the selection of topics and respondents. Ideally, a project should be pursued only when there are knowledgeable people to interview as well as existing manuscripts or corroborating witnesses to provide checks on what respondents say. Nor should hearings be sought with those whose obvious biases would surely overpower their ability to "tell it like it was." But ideal conditions seldom prevail, and the oral historian should be capable of hard work and ingenuity. Before an interview he ought to have a clear idea of his purposes and learn as much as he can about his prospective respondent. If there is to be a run of interviews with the same person, he should first discuss them with the respondent, without a tape recorder. Respondents should be encouraged to use their files to refresh their memories, although such conscious preparation can tempt dishonesty. Therefore, in extended projects it is important to include further research and reevaluation between taping sessions.[16]

With such groundwork the oral historian can more effectively bring out the fullest amount of accurate recall and reporting. In actual interviewing, broad-based questions are initially preferable to ensure a common understanding of fundamental concepts and prevent the bypassing of unanticipated essentials. But later on the well-prepared interviewer is better able to avoid enticing his respondent with questions which he cannot answer. He has the background to probe sensitive areas with precision and knows which questions to repeat for the amplification or verification of previous responses. If done with tact or a reasoned explanation of its importance, such repetition can catch and clarify deliberate errors or accidental inconsistencies and even rescue information first given off the record. It can connect related topics, separately discussed, and above all promote greater respondent enthusiasm and participation by attesting to the interviewer's interest and involvement.[17]

If backed by research and re-evaluation, the leading question is yet another technique to improve the accuracy of any interview, including those done by oral historians. Traditionally interviewers have shied away from such questions for fear of prejudicing responses. But in a recent study by three public opinion experts, the same people in a test group gave a comparably small number of distorted answers to both leading and straightforward inquiries. Furthermore, correct premises or assumptions in questions can increase honesty and candor by convincing respondents that only a frank answer will satisfy the interviewer.[18] The particular reluctance of the aged to discuss matters of peripheral importance to their lives can be overcome by insightful leading questions, but should they miss their mark, the reverse can occur, especially if the respondent is old, impatient, or too eager to please. Oral historians, who often interview the aged, must be conscientious and bear the burden to be well-informed.[19]

What other qualifications good interviewers share are moot among the experts, who seem able to agree only on the value of some experience. People from a variety of backgrounds have produced good results as oral history interviewers, and this without the benefit of standardized interviewing techniques. The resulting problems of comparison of oral history interviews have not troubled most oral historians, perhaps because historians as a group have let the special nature of their evidence preclude concern for the statistical accuracy of their generalizations. Recently, though, some oral historians have become concerned with their inability to compare responses in different interviews. To overcome this difficulty, one Cornell oral history project is subjecting the same respondents to both open-ended interviews for depth and penetration and standardized questionnaire-type interviews for comparability.[20] But there is room for much improvement. Oral historians must become more familiar with proper sampling techniques to ensure that in any project dealing with broad ranges of opinion the respondents selected represent the population under study as closely as possible.

With so many special ways for oral historians to increase accuracy, it seems a shame that both careless typing and overzealous editing can diminish the credibility of oral history manuscripts. Most oral history programs in the United States today transcribe their interviews to ease the process of editing by respondents and handling by scholars. The average typist needs careful supervision, and editing should be minimal and done in ink on the original transcript to show researchers what was said on the tape and what was not. Elaborate or concealed revisions give a distorted picture of an interview and may even lead the researcher to unwarranted conclusions.[21]

Despite the merit of these criteria, few oral historians ever meet them all, and probably many often meet very few, indeed. Inaccuracies are common in oral history interviews, but if the researcher can identify them, especially those resulting from dishonesty or reticence, he can profit handsomely, for sometimes they provide an important avenue of insight into a respondent's state of mind. In fact, some claim that oral history is valuable chiefly because of the light it can shed on a respondent's past state of mind and thereby on the milieu of an era in history, and not because of any facts which might be derived.[22] But as has been noted, recent work in sociology and psychology suggests that attitudes may be forgotten even faster than facts, and thus the researcher must constantly beware. He must always remember that oral history transcripts are raw material to be treated with the same care as any other primary source. Extra wariness may even be in order because of the potentially biasing effects of the research situation. Yet oral historians will not cease to refine their craft, and meanwhile, despite its imperfections, oral history must continue to be done if our increasingly electronic society is to supply the future with both a full and human account of itself.

Notes

1. See, for example, Francis W. Schruben, "An Even Stranger Death of President Harding," *Southern California Quarterly* 48 (March 1966), pp. 57–84; "Is Oral History Really Worthwhile?" *Ideas in Conflict: A Colloquium on Certain Problems in Historical Society Work in the United States and Canada*, ed. Clifford L. Lord (Harrisburg, Pa.: American Association for State and Local History, 1958), pp. 17–57; R. G. Hewlett, "A Pilot Study in Contemporary Scientific History," *Isis* 53 (March 1962), pp. 35–36.

2. In this study the authors defined "consistency" as "an identical response to identically or highly similarly worded questions asking for the same information, of the same respondent, on different occasions" (Ralph Dakin and Donald Tennant, "Consistency of Response by Event-Recall Intervals and Characteristics of Respondents," *Sociological Quarterly* 9 [Winter 1968], pp. 73–84). See also R. J. Van Zooneveld, "An Orientation Study of the Memory of Old People," *Geriatrics* 13 (1958), pp. 532–34; Gladys Palmer, "Factors in the Variability of Response in Enumeration Studies," *Journal of the American Statistical Association*, 38 (June 1943), pp. 143–52.

3. In the study done at NYU the time elapsed was three years, while at the University of Pennsylvania the differential was three to six years (Lillian C. Robbins, "The Accuracy of Parental Recall of Aspects of Child Development and of Child Rearing Practices," *Journal of Abnormal and Social Psychology* 66 [March 1963], pp. 261, 264–67; Charles Wenar and Jane B. Coulter, "A Reliability Study of Developmental Histories," *Child Development* 33 [1962], pp. 453–62). See also Ernest Haggard, Arne Brekstad, & A. G. Skard, "On the Reliability of the Anamnestic Interview," *Journal of Abnormal and Social Psychology* 61 (November 1960), pp. 311–18.

4. Wenar and Coulter, "A Reliability Study of Developmental Histories," *Child Development*, pp. 460–61.

5. Robbins, "The Accuracy of Parental Recall," *Journal of Abnormal and Social Psychology*, p. 261.

6. Joan McCord and William McCord, "Cultural Stereotypes and the Validity of Interviews for Research in Child Development," *Child Development* 32 (1961), pp. 171–86.

7. See, for example, Allen L. Edwards, "The Relationship Between the Judged Desirability of a Trait and the Probability That the Trait Will Be Endorsed," *Journal of Applied Psychology* 37 (1953), pp. 90–93. See also Bernard S. Phillips, *Social Research: Strategy and Tactics* (New York, 1966), pp. 108, 112; Stephen A. Richardson, Barbara S. Dohrenwend, and David Klein, *Interviewing: Its Forms and Functions* (New York, 1965), p. 132.

8. Marie Jahoda, Morton Deutsch, and Stuart W. Cook, *Research Methods in Social Relations* (New York, 1958), p. 60; Fritz J. Roethlisberger and William J. Dickson, *Management and the Worker* (Cambridge, Mass., 1939), pp. 183–84, 575. Recently, critics have argued with the conclusions of Roethlisberger and Dickson, one claiming that economic factors and not the dynamics of the social situation caused the changes in production discovered in the Hawthorne experiments. See Alex Carey, "The Hawthorne Studies: A Radical Criticism," *American Sociological Review* 32 (June 1967), pp. 403–16. Whether Carey is right or not, however, oral historians would be unwise to ignore the artificialities of the research milieu and their possible effects on accuracy in interviewing.

9. Jahoda, Deutsch, and Cook, *Research Methods*, pp. 154–55, 160–64.

10. *The Third National Colloquium on Oral History* (New York, 1969), pp. 25–26. See also Herbert H. Hyman, *Interviewing in Social Research* (Chicago, 1954), pp. 311–13.

11. Phillips, *Social Research*, p. 119.

12. Oral History Research Office: Columbia University, *The Oral History Collection* (New York, 1964); OHRO: Columbia University, *The Oral History Collection: Recent Acquisitions and a Report for 1966* (New York, 1966); OHRO: Columbia University, *Oral History: The First Twenty Years* (New York, 1968); Louis M. Starr, "History Warm," *Columbia University Forum* 5 (Fall 1962), pp. 27–30.

13. Hyman, *Interviewing in Social Research*, pp. 22, 285, 308–10; J. Allen Williams, Jr., "Interviewer Role Performance: A Further Note on Bias in the Information Interview," *The Public Opinion Quarterly* 32 (Summer 1968), pp. 287–88; Barbara S. Dohrenwend, John Colombotos, and Bruce P. Dohrenwend, "Social Distance and Interviewer Effects," *The Public Opinion Quarterly* 32 (Fall 1968), pp. 419–22.

14. Richardson, Dohrenwend, and Klein, *Interviewing: Its Forms and Functions*, pp. 132, 201–03, 227, 232, 242.

15. Harry L. Smith and Herbert H. Hyman, "The Biasing Effect of Interviewer Expectations on Survey Results," *The Public Opinion Quarterly* 14 (Fall 1950), pp. 491–506; J.J. Feldman, Herbert H. Hyman, and C.W. Hart, "A Field Study of Interviewer Effects on the Quality of Survey Data," *The Public Opinion Quarterly* 15 (Winter 1951–52), p. 761.

16. See, for example, Owen W. Bombard, "A New Measure of Things Past," *American Archivist* 18 (April 1955), p. 128. Elwood R. Maunder, "Tape-Recorded Interviews Provide Grass Roots History," *Forest History* 2 (Winter 1959), pp. 1, 15. For further references, see Donald J. Schippers and Adelaide G. Tusler, *A Bibliography on Oral History* (Los Angeles: Oral History Association, 1978).

17. Richardson, Dohrenwend, and Klein, *Interviewing: Its Forms and Functions*, pp. 157–58. Sociologists call interviews which begin on a general level and gradually close in on a specific topic "funneled," or "focused," interviews, as first described by Robert K. Merton and Patricia Kendall in "The Focused Interview," *American Journal of Sociology* 51 (May 1946), pp. 541–57. See also Phillips, *Social Research*, p. 118.

18. Richardson, Dohrenwend, and Klein, *Interviewing: Its Forms and Functions*, pp. 185–92, 196, 214, 240–42.

19. See Kenneth J. Gergen and Kurt W. Back, "Communication in the Interview and the Disengaged Respondent," *Public Opinion Quarterly* 30 (Fall 1966), pp. 385–98.

20. Hyman, *Interviewing in Social Research*, pp. 291, 300–301; Feldman, Hyman, and Hart, "A Field Study of Interviewer Effects," pp. 749–51, 758–59; *Bulletin of the Cornell Program in Oral History* 2 (December 1969), pp. 3–4.

21. Some oral history programs, most notably Berkeley's, entirely retype all of their transcripts but alert researchers to the extent of the editing in a preface to every interview. Since the Berkeley program also reorganizes many of its interviews to coordinate their content, such warnings are, in my view, minimal at best.

22. Saul Benison, "Oral History and Manuscript Collecting," *Isis* 53 (March 1962), pp. 113–17; Corinne L. Gilb, "Tape-Recorded Interviewing: Some Thoughts from California," *American Archivist* 20 (October 1957), pp. 335–44; Doyce B. Nunis, Jr., ed., "Recollections of the Early History of Naval Aviation: A Session in Oral History," *Technology and Culture* 4 (Spring 1963), pp. 149–76; Donald C. Swain, "Problems for Practitioners of Oral History," *American Archivist* 28 (January 1965), pp. 63–69.

8

Oral History: An Appreciation

William Moss

In response to charges of inaccuracy in oral history interviewing, this next article on oral historiography spells out the need for evidentiary standards for oral history and for a more precise documentation on the conduct of the interviews.

William Moss, chief archivist for the most distinguished oral history project among presidential libraries, suggests four principal types of historical records: transactional (contracts, licenses, written instructions); selective records (notes, memoranda, audio and visual recordings); recollections (the stuff of oral history, short- and long-term); and reflections (self-evaluations of the past, which oral historians should avoid because of their subjectivity). He goes on to propose a method whereby historians can evaluate the content and conduct of an interview.

Moss's article, published in 1977, summarizes many of the concerns of archivists since the First Colloquium of the Oral History Association in 1966 and a survey made not long after by the Society of American Archivists. The present article helped prompt the OHA to convene a meeting of experienced professionals to develop the evaluation guidelines included in the appendix to this volume.

William Moss was for many years chief archivist of the John F. Kennedy Library in Boston; he is now affiliated with the Smithsonian Institution. His Oral History Program Manual *(1974) remains one of the best guides to organizing a large-scale project. His extensive lectures on oral history, delivered in the United States and abroad, have resulted in surveys such as "Archives in the People's Republic of China" (1974) in the* American Archivist.

"Oral History: An Appreciation" first appeared in American Archivist *40 (October 1977), pp. 429–39.*

IN THE GENERATION since Allan Nevins demonstrated the great potential of personal narratives as sources for writing history, much time and effort have been spent, and much money, in the activity that has come to be called "oral history." But the product of all this effort and expense remains largely untested in terms of its promise. Broad and undiscriminating charges of wasteful triviality or of biased and self-serving narrations do little to improve or clarify the situation. Nor do naive and enthusiastic praises of its potential serve to prove its worth. Even the occasional use of oral history information by biographers does not establish its validity as an important source. The promise remains impressive in the abstract, but the product is still untested. Yet, if oral history is to be a reliable research tool, if it is to be respected historical evidence, and if it is to justify a national association in its name, then those who produce oral history, the scholars that use its product, and the institutions that finance its projects must have some means of under-standing its proper role and of evaluating what is being done in the field. We need to know more about the place of oral history in the system of historical analysis, and we need to understand better the contribution that oral history can make to the writing of history. Clues are scattered in the literature on oral history. This essay attempts to bring them together and to place oral history in its proper context, to give it a proper value as historical evidence, and to offer some ideas for critical testing in order that the product may justify the promise.

The Evidentiary Value of Oral History

To understand its proper place in the system of historical analysis, we must examine oral history in relation to other kinds of historical evidence. For purposes of this thesis, it is suggested that there are five types, or levels, of source material that go into the writing of history: transactional records, selective records, recollections, reflections, and the analyses that are written by one's predecessors.

From the usual meanings of these five terms we can recognize an as-cending scale of sophistication and abstraction. There is also a counter-scale of evidentiary value. As abstraction increases and we get farther away from the immediate reality, the evidentiary value of the information decreases. The simple thesis that evidence and abstraction are in an in-verse relation to one another often is forgotten because it is so elementary; but it is crucial to an understanding of the value of oral history.

The historian is engaged in the task of mastering the past. The disci-pline of history is a means by which we may keep from kidding ourselves about what has happened. It is axiomatic that such discipline is essential to coping with the present and planning for the future. If the discipline of history in general and the tool of oral history in particular are to be employed successfully, then we must have some systematic means of relating evidentiary and abstract values and of distinguishing them from each other. An examination of the five levels of sources is necessary to achieve this understanding.

Transactional Records

Transactional records are not so much abstractions of human actions and interactions as they are the actions themselves. They may be abstract in the sense that they are symbolic representations of agreements or communications, but the documents produced are the transactions as well as their records or reports. Any document that embodies in its text the sum and substance of the action it represents is a transactional record and is the authoritative basis for any action arising from or dependent upon the transaction recorded. Constitutions, laws, contracts, deeds, wills, treaties, diplomas, certificates, licenses, patents, proclamations, orders, instructions, advertisements, and similar documents are transactional records. They are primary evidence. An order never obeyed and an advertisement never responded to are nevertheless actions that occurred. Unless they are forged, we may accept the documents at face value, as primary evidence. There is no interpretive or selective process between the document and the reality it represents, beyond that inherent to the transaction itself. No interpretive element intrudes between the document and the observer other than the observer's own bias and perception.

Selective Records

Selective records are attempts to preserve and to communicate to others descriptions of what is happening at a given time. Concurrency is important in order to distinguish this level of evidence from recollections, discussed below. Audio, video, or cinematic recordings of actions as they unfold, stenographic notes of conversations as they are taking place, still photographs, and even recorded running descriptions (such as that of a sports broadcaster) may be included in the category of selective records. They are selective in that there is a selective or interpretive process between the reality and the record. We are so accustomed to accepting electronic or film recordings as substitutes for reality that we tend to confuse them with reality. In fact, the technical limitations of the camera and tape recorder are not unlike those of human perception. The human observer records in his memory not exactly what is happening, but rather what his predisposition toward people and events make him capable of recording. The mechanical or photographic or electronic device records only so much as its technical range and capacity will allow. There is not a truly one-to-one relationship between the reality and the record. Some interpretation through selection, decision, or translation is unavoidable.

Selective records, because of their contemporary nature, are highly valued as historical evidence, but their evidentiary value must always be somewhat less than that of transactional records. The very interpretive nature of the selective class of records, however, produces commensurate value for the historian. Selective records are, after all, primary evidence of what someone decided to record or was capable of recording. If we further suppose that such recordings are generally more deliberate or purposeful than whimsical or random, then we may infer some contemporary value to what is recorded. What is recorded is what someone contemporary to the events believed to be important or worth recording. The first step away from primary evidence and into abstraction has been taken. Selective records are abstracts of reality. In the next category we take a much larger step away from reality and into abstraction.

Recollections

If the human memory is a selective record, then recollections are still further selective and selection is compounded to a second degree. It might be fairer to subdivide recollections into those emerging soon after the events recalled, and those emerging later. The distinction is one of degree rather than kind, and it begs the question of where to draw the line between sooner and later. Nor is it important to this thesis. Into the category of recollections we may place any accounts that are first-hand and yet are not concurrent to the subject or event described. Recollections include diaries, information solicited from eye witnesses by investigators, tales told by grandfathers to little children, and information supplied by oral history narrators.

Recollections are clearly another step removed from reality into abstraction. As evidence they must be considered less reliable than either transactional or selective records. They may perhaps be all a historian has, and therefore a *sine qua non* to his research; but this value must not be confused with the relative evidentiary value. For too often a recollection is used as the basis for a historical thesis simply because it is the only evidence available. Because it is the only evidence available does not mean that we may rely on it as we would a transactional record or a selective record. The distinction is an important one in terms of mastering the past, and the values are far too often confused.

Several factors contribute to the decreased evidentiary value of recollections vis-à-vis transactional or selective records. Recollections may, and often do, include secondhand accounts and hearsay, or will at least be colored by the impact of such information on the witness/narrator re-counting a description from memory. Furthermore, intervening events in the experience of the witness/narrator, or his prior receptivity to certain ideas and not to others, may induce him to diminish the importance of some evidence and perhaps to enhance beyond proper proportion the importance of other evidence. We also have in the process of recollection an intrusion of purposes that may affect the evidence: to inform a group; to secure one's own dignified position in history; to prosecute or defend a case; to sell a newspaper or book; to instruct a grandchild; or even to enhance the collection of a library. All are purposes that may overtly or subtly affect the character and nature of the evidence presented.

Historians clearly must be careful about using recollections as evidence. They must understand that a recollection is itself a complex piece of evidence. Three levels are included. There is the initial event or reality, there is the memory which is a selective record at least one step removed from reality, and there is the further selective and interpretive account recalled from memory by the witness/narrator. Furthermore, when an interviewer deliberately questions a person to solicit information as evidence, a fourth level of selection and potential for intrusion enters the process. The questions that an interviewer asks and the apparent purpose of his interviewing have a direct bearing on what is being called up from memory, and why.

Crucial to a sound understanding of oral history is that the record produced by an interview should never be confused with the original events, nor even with the memory of that event. The record is a selective one that itself selects information from the selective record of the witness/narrator's memory of past events and subjects. Whatever other values oral history may have for journalists, novelists, dramatists, educators, and propagandists (and these values may be many), the historian must understand and respect the evidentiary limitations of recollections if he is to use them honestly in his attempts to master the past. He must understand that the evidence has been refracted several times before he confronts it in an oral history recording.

Yet, even as we move further from reality, recollections provide the historian with a corresponding abstractive value of fascinating richness. We may infer from what is recalled what it is that people believe to be significant enough to remember and to recount about the past. One of the historian's tasks in analysis is to assess the importance of past events in terms of subsequent developments. The selective recollections of others may contribute insight and understanding to the task. Even when erroneous or misguided, recollections may in their very errors provoke understanding and insight. Furthermore, the aggregate recollections of many people can provide a rough means for approximating historical truth where no transactional records or selective records exist. But it requires many accounts from a good cross-section sample of witnesses to endow this kind of evidence with a reliability even approaching that of transactional or selective records.

Reflections

It is necessary to distinguish reflections from both recollections and analysis. Reflections go beyond simple recollections of facts in that they are what an individual person thinks spontaneously about the past, the values and affective impressions with which he characterizes the past and makes it relevant to his own present situation. Although deliberate, reflections are subjective and emotional and are not usually characterized by the thorough and systematic weighing of evidence required by historical analysis.

Reflections are usually recorded along with recollections in an oral history interview or diary; but, like recollections, they must not be confused with the past on which they focus. A reflection is a contemporary event of contemplating and evaluating the past, but it is not the past which is the subject of the evaluation. The historian must use reflections with the same caution that he uses recollections, as clues to the significance and meaning that past events have for people in the present. Reflections are hardly to be classed as evidence about the past at all, and thus they must be separated from recollections as a level of historical evidence. They may certainly provoke insight and understanding, and usually do so more directly than recollections. The significance attributed to past events in reflections does not mean that the events had that particular importance when they occurred, nor does it mean that they necessarily ought to have such meaning for us now or in the future. They are useful to analysis as a record of what people have thought about the past, and they may be the basis for inferences about the meanings of events. As with recollections, isolated reflections make poor foundations for analysis, and an aggregate of many concurring values is necessary before a historian may rely on the interpretation with any confidence.

Analysis

Analysis is the process by which form and order are brought to the chaos of evidence about the past, to bring meaning and understanding not only to the individual historian but to many people with differing subjective views of reality. Analysis requires a rigorous accounting of all the evidence, of all levels and kinds, available to the historian. It requires the making of hypotheses about how and why things happened as they did and why they occurred in the sequence that they did. Analysis may be good or bad, sound or weak, honest or biased, depending on how good the evidence is, whether or not all the available evidence has been accounted for, whether or not all possible hypotheses have been tested against the evidence, and whether or not the analyst's own private interests intrude unfairly to distort the evidence and analysis.

Analysis goes far beyond the simple collection, preservation, and retrieval of information. It goes beyond the mere description of events, people, places, and things. Nor is analysis merely the repetition or aggregate of notions that have occurred to others about what might be personally or universally significant about the past. Analysis requires the comparing and testing of different records against each other, weighing the relative values of insight and evidence that they contribute in fair proportion, forming theoretical structures from the information (both evidence and insights), and then testing these new hypotheses against the evidence again and again to see if it can survive critical examination.

Analysis is performed not only by historians but by journalists, writers of government reports, and others. Analysis inevitably has a limited perspective based on the purposes for which the analysis was performed and the subjective interests of those performing the analysis. But analysis can be fair and honest if all the evidence has been accounted for, the hypotheses rigorously tested, and the author's bias well defined and accounted for in the process. It is true that not only journalists and government report writers but also historians can and have misused analysis to serve subjective prejudices and ideologies. But,when they do, they are no longer masters of the past but rather creators of new mythologies in the present. Such efforts may have value in documenting present prejudices and interpretations, but they cannot properly be called good history that masters the past. Enhancing or suppressing particular bits of evidence not on the basis of relative evidentiary or insight value but rather in the service of a subjective purpose is inimical to mastering the past with the integrity that must be demanded by the discipline of history. Moreover, because of the authoritative pretensions of historical analysis to mastering the past, its conclusions, when erroneous, may compound the illusion every time they are quoted or relied upon uncritically by subsequent scholars. The stronger the analysis and the more it rests on comprehensive accounting of all the evidence and on proper evaluation of evidence and insight, the more likely it is to produce a more reliable and more enduring mastery of the past.

The Lesson for Oral History

Oral history has a proper place in the system of evidence, experience, and analysis that produces good history, and properly used it can make an important contribution. Improperly used it can be mischievous and destructive. Oral history, to be most effective, must itself be well-grounded in sound analysis and in a thorough knowledge and understanding of all the other available and pertinent sources, if it is to produce the best and most reliable oral documentation. Figure 8.1 illustrates the

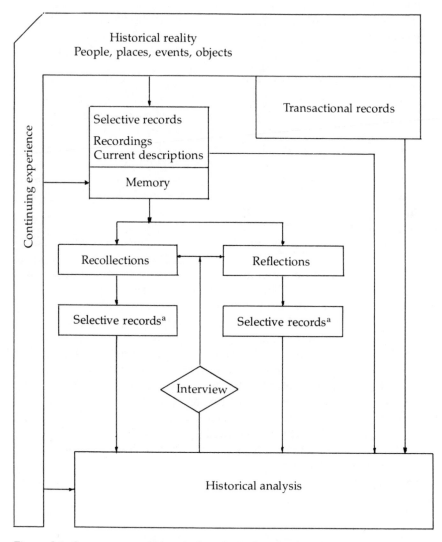

Figure 8.1. Components of historical analysis: Levels of evidence and the place of oral history interviewing in the process. [a]Includes diaries and retrospective writings as well as tape recordings of oral history interviews.

place of the oral history interview in the system and its relationship to the other component elements. Each arrow in the diagram indicates not only the direction of influence and effect, but also the intrusion of a selective or interpretive factor between reality and analysis.

Systematic Evaluation of Oral History

In order to evaluate oral history properly we must first distinguish it from other forms of oral documentation. Essentially, there are three classes of oral documentation. The first is the recording of performances in which the participants are following a prepared script (which provides additional documentation about the event). Performances include political speeches as well as dramatic presentations. The second class of oral documentation is the recording, sometimes surreptitiously, of unrehearsed events in which the speaking of the participants is spontaneous and dynamic and entirely concerned with immediate purposes or plans. Finally, there is the oral documentation that has come to be called oral history: the recording of a special kind of event, the interview, in which historical information, insight, and opinion are sought deliberately and are deliberately preserved as a historical source. The third category must be evaluated somewhat differently from the other two.

There are two steps in the evaluation of any record: determining its genuineness, authenticity, and integrity as a record; and determining the value of its content information against known and previously established facts.

Evaluation of the record itself is the same for all three categories of oral documentation. The historian needs to know a number of things to establish that the recording is just what it purports to be, is complete, and has not been altered or changed. He must know when the recording was made, and under what circumstances. He should know why it was made. He should know, if possible, what kind of equipment was used to make the recording. If the tape or film of an event is a second, third, or fourth generation copy of the original recording, then the historian should know something of the equipment, procedures, and conditions involved in making the copies. The historian needs to know if the voices on the tape are indeed those of the people they are represented to be. (We may find a growing role for the electronic voice-analysis devices for authenticating oral documents.) In order for the historian to have full confidence in the recording being offered as evidence, he must have a full and authenticated record of its creation, preservation, processing, and custody. He needs assurances that the recording was not tampered with, falsified, or edited—or if it was, then by whom, under what circumstances, to what extent, and why? In this the tape recording is no different from traditional written documents, for which the historian needs similar kinds of information and assurances about its provenance. In many cases a full record of provenance is not available, and the historian must perforce rely on the reputation of the producing or custodial institution for integrity.

Once the integrity and authenticity of the recording have been established, the historian's evaluation turns to the contents. Once a performance has been identified as a performance, the historian's task is a relatively simple one. The value is clearly that of a contemporary selective record and ranks very high on the scale of evidence. With the unrehearsed event, the historian does have a very important first question to ask. Even if the record is fully authenticated, is this truly an unrehearsed event and not a performance? In our current age of dramatized history and electronic simulations on television, the historian must truly ask himself if the creation of the recording was not somehow deliberately manipulated to leave a biased record. He must find reassurances that the participants were indeed acting spontaneously and not with half a mind on the tape recorder. He must find reassurances that the whole thing was not prepared in advance and stage managed for the sake of producing a distorted historical record. But, the same can be said for written minutes of meetings, on which historians have traditionally relied, so there is really nothing new here.

The oral document produced by an oral history interview, however, presents the historian with a far more complex problem of evaluation. Its effective and proper use in historical analysis requires special understanding and a lot of hard work. It cannot be accepted quite as readily as the first two categories of oral documentation. Interviews depend on memories, and we know memories to be tricky with respect to reality. The historian, faced with the information content of a recorded interview, really has no way of knowing, from the record itself, whether the record is faulty or true, distorted or accurate, deliberately falsified or spontaneously candid. The historian is at the mercy of the witness who is testifying, and the historian does not have the opportunity to stop the testimony to cross-examine. He must rely on the interviewer to do that for him.

Faced with such risky evidence, the historian must approach oral history documentation warily and with great skepticism. He must find means to determine if the witnesses are reliable. A particular problem with the modern process of recording oral testimony for historical use is that so many of the narrators are unknown, are of unproven reliability, and there exists little with which to test their evidence. So much of the evidence is personal and unique that there is not a body of data against which to cross-check the information. In some published works relying on personal interviews the contributing witnesses are anonymous. Nor, in his assessment, should the historian neglect the need to evaluate the interviewer. Although the interviewer may seek to be objective and unobtrusive, he must inevitably play a dynamic role in the creation of the interview record, and the way he plays his role often determines not only the tone and character of the record produced but also the substance of the record content. Narrators frequently respond with what they think the interviewer wants to hear. The apparent aims and objectives of the interview may have much to do with the way the interviewee perceives his role and therefore with the way he responds to the interview as a whole and to individual questions in particular.

Further, the historian must compare the content information, both questions and answers, with other sources on the same subjects to see if both participants know what they are talking about. He must not impute authority to a statement or an assertion in an interviewer's question (even if the respondent does) simply on the assumption that the interviewer must know what he is talking about. Interviewers often test hearsay, and its repetition in a question should not be construed as corroboration unless it is supported by adequate responses from the interviewee. Interviewers, too, like interviewees, may on occasion be whimsical or frivolous. The historian must discover discrepancies in the accounts presented and must try to account for them or (perhaps reluctantly) discard those accounts. He must identify unique information and attempt to obtain corroboration from additional sources. Ultimately, in the case of truly unique information, he may have to make a leap of faith; but it should be an informed leap, based on an accumulated sense of the reliability of the witnesses as proven by their testimony on other and related subjects.

In order for the historian to develop such confidence about any given interview or any collection as may permit him to make these leaps of faith in the absence of corroborating evidence, we require a regular and continuing process of systematic and critical evaluation and review of the oral history documentation that is being produced; not only of published books directly or loosely based on interviews, but of interviews. Since it is the deliberate interview that makes oral history unique as a historical source, it is proper that critical examination should focus primarily on the content and conduct of the interview. There are a series of questions that can be asked and must be answered in any thorough evaluation of the content or conduct of an oral history interview.

Evaluating Content

Evaluating content focuses on three groups of questions familiar to most historians. These questions may be applied either to a single interview or to a group of interviews dealing with a common theme.

1. How sound is the evidence presented? Are several sources in corroboration? Is the evidence presented at variance with previous evidence, and if so, why? Does the testimony ring true not only in the subjective judgment of the reviewer but also with the whole pattern of evidence? Does the testimony seem contrary and out of place, and if so, why? To what extent are the facts presented credible in the light of the known consequences of the actions and events recounted? In the light of subsequent events, does the story make sense?

2. Is the interview a thorough one? Does it cover all possible relevant themes? Are all topics probed in depth for detail, amplification, and appreciation? Do both interviewer and interviewee seem to be aware of gaps in recorded history and conventional wisdom? Do they deal with the topics and the omissions candidly? What has been omitted from the interview that ought to have been included, and why was it left out? Does the interview work on both the rational or logical level of facts and conclusions and also on the affective, emotional level of opinions, with clear indications of the value of each?

3. Is the information provided really needed, or is it superfluous and redundant? In what ways does the interview provide a unique contribution to history? Is there unique information? Is there a unique perspective on the past? Does the interview provide the historian with a unique arrangement or concentration of information that is enlightening or at least helpful? Does the interview provide corroboration or challenges to previously held notions, and how should these be valued? Does the interview contribute richness of detail and description, or perhaps a richness of affective response and commentary that aids insight?

Evaluating Conduct

The interview is not a passive document that merely accepts evidence. It is a dynamic process in which the observer-collector (interviewer) has a marked effect on what the witness-narrator (interviewee) produces in the way of information and opinion. The historian must ask a number of questions about the way in which any given interview or any given group of interviews was conducted, and the first of these questions shakes the practice of oral history to its very roots.

1. Is an interview, after all, the best means of acquiring the evidence produced? Is it, perhaps, the only means? If not, what other means exist and have they been used? If not, why not?

2. Does the interview get the most possible out of the interviewee; or does much appear to have been held back, omitted, suppressed, or distorted? How effectively did the interviewer exercise the opportunity for critical challenge within the interview?

3. Do both interviewer and interviewee appear to understand, to be committed to, and to be able to pursue the inquiry for the sake of historical integrity and truth, or are other purposes being served? Why? To what effect? How does history suffer or benefit from either?

4. Do both interviewer and interviewee appear to be knowledgeable about the subject under discussion? Are they in command of the information? If they are guessing, then to what effect?

5. Do both interviewer and interviewee use a variety of approaches to the subjects and bring to bear a variety of perspectives, or do they seem to be limited to rigid, one-dimensional discussions? Do they both seize upon and appreciate the clues provided by associating ideas? Do they pursue trains of thought thoroughly, or is the inquiry essentially a lazy one?

6. Does the narrator seem to have been an appropriate one for the subjects discussed? What were his strengths and weaknesses? What about the interviewer with respect to the same questions?

7. Do the interviewer and interviewee seem to be well-matched so that they excite each other to produce the best and most complete possible record? Do they bring to bear the most productive combination of empathy and critical judgment?

8. Is either participant really a disinterested party? If not, what personal interests or biases are apparent and why? What effect do they produce and how must the historian handle it?

Evaluating Projects

Of less immediate concern to the historian's research topic but nonetheless important is the evaluation of and the confidence the historian may have in the project that produced the interviews. A rather different approach must be taken to evaluating projects. Even when the individual interviews and the aggregate collection can pass critical inspection, there are still additional questions about the project that the historian must find satisfactory answers to before he can have full faith and confidence in the material.

1. Does the project have a well-defined set of purposes and objectives? What are they? Are they compatible with and do they contribute to honest historical inquiry or are they distorted by bias? What are the real objectives of collecting the information and how do they affect the information collected? What other influences may tend to tilt the information produced toward a particular attitude or character over the whole aggregate collection?

2. Are the interviews and interviewers that have been chosen to produce the records appropriate to the purposes of the collecting agency?

Are they the best available, or were compromises made and, if so, why? Where could the choices have been improved? Which significant narrator-witnesses were omitted, and why?

3. Are the policies and procedures of the program consistent with providing accurate information on the provenance of the material produced? Are the procedures designed to produce the most accurate and undistorted record of the interviews for use by the historian? If not, to what effect, for the purposes of historical analysis were the procedures designed?

4. What is the availability of the interviews collected, and what restrictions on access (if any) are there? How do these affect the aggregate picture presented by the material that *is* available? Who may use the material? Is the researcher population limited? By what criteria? What effect does the limitation have on the critical reception of the material to date? How have the interviews been used by researchers, and what contributions have they made thus far to historical writing?

5. What kinds of finding aids are provided to the researcher? Are these adequate to the purposes of most researchers or only to a few? How could they be improved and why?

6. What other kinds of information resources does the collecting agency or institution provide that the researcher can use to test and corroborate or refute the information found in the oral history interviews?

7. Does the project provide information about both the interviewees and the interviewers in sufficient detail to help the researcher make judgments about reliability?

Summary and Conclusion

Oral history interviewing and the documentation that it produces are a logical part of the system and process by which we transform the evidence of reality into the composition of history that masters the past. As evidence, oral history is less than transactional or selective records; but it makes a significant contribution to insight and understanding, and in the absence of primary evidence an aggregate of testimony may serve to approximate historical certainty. To be effective, oral history interviewing must proceed from a base of primary evidence and sound analysis. Producers and users of oral history must be critical when they deal with this source. Only when they can provide or obtain the answers to a large number of questions about the character of the material can the kind of confidence in it needed for good history be developed.

A continual and regular process of critical review, not only by institutions that sponsor oral history projects but also by the historians who use the material, is essential to the continued improvement of oral history sources. Oral history can be done well, and it can make an important contribution to history; but in order to do so it must be properly understood and rigorously tested, and those who produce it must measure their efforts against, and strive to meet, the highest standards of evidentiary value.

9

Oral Tradition
and Historical Methodology

Jan Vansina

While few practitioners of oral history work with oral tradition (unwritten knowledge passed verbally through successive generations), the next two sections discuss the historical worth and reliability of oral sources from nonliterate societies. The traditional nature of much orally elicited data tends to be overlooked by students of oral history, for narrators are themselves often unable to distinguish between accounts of witnesses to historic events and accounts based upon generalized knowledge or anecdotes and folklore told within a community.

Oral history is in a number of ways similar to oral tradition: error or falsification can be introduced in the same ways as in oral narratives; differing oral documents need to be evaluated for veracity by comparison with each other or with written documents, where available; and many interviews show the performance associated with oral tradition, as a result of the narrator's wish to create an explainable experience.

This excerpt from Jan Vansina's classic Oral Tradition: A Study in Historical Methodology *provides criteria useful to historians distinguishing between community story-telling and historical fact. Based on field research in Africa, where oral tradition remains a living force, Vansina's insights into the types and functions of oral narrative can be applied to the survivals and new creations of tradition in an electrified, post-literate society. His comments on interpreting history on the basis of oral sources may apply equally to interviewers working on Wall Street or along the Amazon.*

Jan Vansina's writings about oral tradition have been translated from French into English, Spanish, Italian, and Arabic. He is the author of a dozen books on African history, and his The Children of Woot *(1978) tested oral tradition against other historical sources in Africa. A member of the Royal Academy of Overseas Sciences and a consultant to UNESCO, Vansina is Vilas Research Professor of History at the University of Wisconsin.*

"Oral Tradition and Historical Methodology" is excerpted from Oral

Tradition: A Study in Historical Methodology [De la tradition orale
(1961)], *trans. H. M. Wright (Chicago: Aldine, 1965).*

ORAL TRADITIONS are historical sources of a special nature. Their
special nature derives from the fact that they are 'unwritten'
sources couched in a form suitable for oral transmission, and
that their preservation depends on the powers of memory of successive
generations of human beings. These special features pose a problem for
the historian. Do they *a priori* deprive oral tradition of all validity as a
historical source? If not, are there means for testing its reliability? These
are precisely the questions to which the present study seeks to find an
answer, and I hope to show that oral tradition is not necessarily un-
trustworthy as a historical source, but, on the contrary, merits a certain
amount of credence within certain limits.

In those parts of the world inhabited by peoples without writing, oral
tradition forms the main available source for a reconstruction of the past,
and even among peoples who have writing, many historical sources,
including the most ancient ones, are based on oral traditions. Thus a
claim for the practical utility of research on the specific characteristics of
oral tradition, and on the methods for examining its trustworthiness, is
doubly substantiated. . . .

I should like to make it clear that my examination of the topic is primarily based on traditions still alive among peoples without writing, since
sources of this kind preserve the essential nature of oral tradition better
than traditions found in literate societies. Among peoples without writing, oral tradition continues to exist at the very heart of the environment
that gave rise to it. It has not yet been supplanted, nor had its main
functions taken over, by written documents, as is the case in a society
where writing has taken pride of place. Nor has it yet been torn from its
natural context, as happens once traditions have been committed to writing. For these reasons, and also because of the opportunities open to me, I
have based this study mainly on the oral traditions of the Kuba, the
Rundi, and the Rwanda, among whom I carried out field researches from
1955 to 1956, and from 1957 to 1960. . . .

The first thing to note about the historical information that can be
obtained from oral traditions is that it varies according to the type of
tradition. A survey of the typology of traditions and an outline of the
characteristics of each type show that the types vary widely, and that all
have a given historical bias which imposes certain limitations, but which
gives each type its own particular usefulness in providing information
about certain particular aspects of the past. Next, oral tradition as a whole

can be shown to have its limitations, as well as certain tendencies towards bias due to the influence of the political system—which accounts for the very existence of many traditions—and also due, to a lesser extent, to cultural factors. The limitations of the information that can be derived from oral traditions are real, and must be accepted by the historian; but he can attempt to make up for them by using data supplied by other historical sources, such as written documents, and the disciplines of archaeology, cultural history, linguistics, and physical anthropology. Each of these disciplines furnish data which in themselves are limited; but by putting together all the available information, the area of the past about which we can acquire some knowledge is greatly extended. Nevertheless, even if all these techniques are used, we can never arrive at a complete knowledge of all the events of the past. We can never do more than touch upon a small part of past history—namely, that part which has been preserved in the various surviving historical documents. But this statement must not be taken as an excuse for abandoning the study of history on the grounds that perfection can never be attained.

The Interpretation of History

. . . oral traditions are historical sources which can provide reliable information about the past if they are used with all the circumspection demanded by the application of historical methodology to any kind of source whatsoever. This means that study of the oral traditions of a culture cannot be carried out unless a thorough knowledge of the culture and of the language has previously been acquired. This is something which is taken for granted by all historians who work on written sources, but it is too often apt to be forgotten by those who undertake research into the past of pre-literate peoples.

In these final remarks I shall make several observations about the interpretation of the facts obtained. The layman is too often inclined to entertain a completely false idea as to the powers of the historian, and is apt to regard any historical reconstructions offered as absolutely valid. He fondly imagines that written sources reveal events of the past which can be accepted as fact, but considers that oral sources tell of things about which there is no certainty—things which may or may not have happened. He forgets that any historical synthesis comprises an interpretation of the facts, and is thus founded upon probabilities.

I must apologize in advance to those historians who are only too familiar with the reflections which are here offered for their perusal. I make them in order to refute a prejudice which is commonly found among all those who have raised objections to the use of oral traditions as a historical source.

There is no great difficulty in accepting the proposition that history is always an interpretation. An example will prove the point better than abstract argument. If a Rwandese source tells us that a certain king conquered a certain country, what does this statement mean? It may mean that a cattle raid was carried out in enemy territory and was highly successful; or that the chief or king of the enemy country was deposed or killed, and his territory annexed, in theory, by Rwanda, while local government was left as it was; or it may mean that the conquered chief remained in power, but recognized the suzerainty of the king of Rwanda. Or yet again, it may mean that the king of Rwanda occupied the country, incorporated it as part of the states over which he ruled, and replaced the administration from top to bottom. Any one of these possibilities could be inferred from the statement, and this is still leaving out of account the subsidiary question as to whether the measures taken were temporary or final. That stating the problem in this way is not merely the sign of a Byzantine finicalness is shown by the following factual example from Rwanda. A certain King Ndabarasa conquered Gisaka, a country bordering on Rwanda. This meant in effect that he carried out several raids there with the intention not only of bringing back cattle, but also of weakening the military power of the enemy and disorganizing the government—a project in which he succeeded. His great grandson, Mutara Rwogera, also 'conquered' the same country, and succeeded in killing or exiling all the various chiefs who ruled there, thus ending the country's existence as an autonomous state. But it was his successor Rwabugiri who first founded administrative centres there of the kind found in Rwanda, and who appointed Rwandese to high government posts. In 1901, Rwabugiri's son was faced with a rebellion there, and it was not until this ended in 1903 that all the native chiefs and subchiefs were deprived of their rights, and the entire administration was taken over.

Thus every historian is obliged to interpret the sources he is dealing with. He does not and cannot have an unlimited knowledge of history, and there is usually more than one interpretation possible of the facts at his disposal. In addition, the historian adds something of his own to these facts, namely, his own particular flair, which is something more akin to art than to science. The only concession to history as a scientific discipline he can make here is to ensure that he discloses what his sources are, so that his readers will be informed as to the reasons for the choice he has made in his interpretations of the texts.

Interpretation is a choice between several possible hypotheses, and the good historian is the one who chooses the hypothesis that is most likely to be true. In practice it can never have more than a likelihood of truth, because the past has gone for good and all, and the possibility of first-hand observation of past events is forever excluded. History is no more than a calculation of probabilities. This is true not only as far as the interpretation of documents is concerned, but for all the operations of historical methodology, and above all for the most important ones. How shall one decide whether a statement is an error, or a lie, or is 'veracious'? Each of the three hypotheses has a varying degree of probability, and the historian will choose the most probable one. Or if, in comparing two texts, resemblances between them are found, the historian must judge whether the resemblances imply that the texts have a common origin or not. Here again what he does is to assess possibilities and weigh probabilities. Historical science is a science of probabilities. Nor is it the only science of this kind. A large number of present-day scientific disciplines make use of the concept of chance and of probability.

From what has been said, it follows that there is no such thing as 'absolute historical truth', and no one can formulate an 'unchanging law of history' on the basis of our knowledge of the past. The truth always remains beyond our grasp, and we can only arrive at some approximation to it. We can refine our interpretations, accumulate so many probabilities that they almost amount to certainty, and yet still not arrive at 'the truth'. We can never hope to understand everything, and indeed do not even understand all that we experience personally. We cannot arrive at a full understanding of the past because the past is something outside our experience, something that is other. It has been said that it is possible to describe historical events because history is a science which deals with mankind, to which we ourselves belong, whereas a scientific description of bees does not make sense, since we cannot imagine what it is like to be a bee. This is true. But is also true that we cannot understand the past because the men who lived then were different from us, and however great an effort we make, we cannot ever completely enter into the mentality of someone else. We can never understand his motivations, and thus we can never pass judgment on them.

What the historian can do is to arrive at some approximation to the ultimate historical truth. He does this by using calculations of probability, by interpreting the facts and by evaluating them in an attempt to recreate for himself the circumstances which existed at certain given moments of the past. And here the historian using oral traditions finds himself on exactly the same level as historians using any other kind of historical source material. No doubt he will arrive at a lower degree of probability than would otherwise be attained, but that does not rule out the fact that what he is doing is valid, and that it is history.

10

A Note on Oral Tradition
and Historical Evidence

Ruth Finnegan

This selection continues our exploration of oral tradition as historical evidence. Ruth Finnegan, one of the foremost experts on oral literature, suggests that a given oral tradition should be analyzed for its function as either literature or history before historical generalizations are drawn. She also notes the impact of what the folklorist calls the performance context of oral tradition: how the audience's (and the peformer's) desires influence the ways in which a tradition is told—which, in turn, influence an oral historian's or ethnohistorian's interpretation of a given text in reconstructing history when few print sources exist.

Historians reading transcripts face a similar task in determining how an interview's sociolinguistic elements (pauses, verbal emphases, gestures not included in the transcript) affected the "performance" of the narrator. While there is clearly a distinction between oral literature and the authorized, formalized accounts produced by oral historians in developed nations, Finnegan's study opens up useful avenues for comparing the two forms.

Ruth Finnegan was trained at Oxford University and has taught in Rhodesia, Nigeria, Fiji, and England at the Open University (since 1969). She has written seven books on ethnography, anthropology, and oral tradition, including Oral Literature in Africa *(1967),* Oral Poetry: its Nature, Significance, and Social Context *(1977), and* Conceptions of Inquiry *(1981).*

"A Note on Oral Tradition and Historical Evidence" was first published in History and Theory *9(October 1970), pp. 195–201.*

THERE ARE A number of assumptions about the nature of oral tradition in Africa which are sometimes made by historians and others. Two of these will be discussed in this Note—the assumption that "oral tradition" is something unitary and self-evident and that it is somehow impervious to many of the factors which historians usually take account of in critical assessment of sources. These (and other) assumptions about the nature of oral tradition are generally unconscious, but—perhaps because of that—they have often seriously affected its use as a source in African history. Of course not all historians make the assumptions discussed here, but they are common enough to warrant some general comment.

The common assumption that "oral tradition" is something uniform, something that can be treated as an undifferentiated and self-evident entity, leads to the tendency of some historians[1] and others to speak of "oral tradition" generally as a source, without apparently feeling the need—which would be obvious in the case of documentary sources—to describe and analyze the detailed source material. In practice a number of very disparate sources have often been lumped together under the name "oral tradition." Broadly one can list three main classes of oral tradition: recognized literary forms, generalized historical knowledge, and personal recollections.

First there is what has been called "oral literature." Though hard to define precisely, this class is composed of various types of both prose and poetry which correspond to literature in literate societies. Oral literature is relatively formalized, in the sense not of verbal accuracy but of genres clearly recognized in the society, and is sometimes—poetry especially—regarded as the product of specialist activity. A brief survey of the forms of oral literature follows.[2]

Praise poetry is one of the best known forms, occurring in most of the traditional centralized states of Africa. Since its main theme is eulogy (most often of the ruler) it is political propaganda, and we cannot expect any very direct historical information, in the sense of exact description or narration. Nevertheless, praise poetry can lead to insight into the values and ideals of the society, or of one group, at least. Religious poetry, particularly if by highly trained specialists, can be conservative and thus potentially a good source; for the history of earlier times the problem, of course, is to sort out not only which are the older poems but which parts of these preserve earlier references and which not—which is difficult to do without knowing a lot about the earlier history already. Lyrics—songs for weddings, dance, work, love, and so forth—can throw light on values and personal preoccupations in a society at a particular time, but of course tend to be ephemeral. Topical and political poems can be an excellent source *if* they are recorded at the time they spring up; essentially short-lived, they are seldom or never feasible sources for arguing back to an earlier period.[3]

All in all, poetry in non-literate as in literate societies can be illuminating for the historian—of direct relevance for the intellectual history of the time and indirectly useful for other aspects of society, provided the historian avoids literalistic interpretations and proceeds circumspectly, bearing in mind all the elements of propaganda, idealization, personal whim, exaggeration, artistry, and desire to please that variously characterize different kinds of poetry. In non-literate societies there is the additional and often overwhelming difficulty that unless a poem is recorded at the actual time being studied—which few have been—there is usually no way of knowing from a later poem whether it is the same as or even slightly similar to versions in the earlier period. Normally the safest assumption can only be that it is not.

It will have been noticed that I have said nothing about "historical poetry" or about "epic." Surely these provide the best and most relevant source fo the historian? The truth is that this type of poetry seems surprisingly uncommon in Africa. Certainly there are some exceptions, and there are of course a number of well-known instances of *written* historical poems under Arabic influence. But in general terms specifically "historical poetry" seems rare as an oral form, and even apparent instances turn out to be basically more like panegyric, the element of narration being subordinate to that of eulogy. True "epic," in spite of widespread assumptions about its being the natural form in many nonliterate societies, is hard to find.[4]

Prose literature can be discussed more briefly. It tends to less specialization than poetry in African oral literature. Unlike poets, the performer/composer of prose is seldom an expert, and often genres are not recognized. The outside analyst could list several main categories. First there are obviously fictional narratives concerned with people, imaginary beings, or animals. These clearly give little clue to the historian, though scholars still steeped in the idea that they date from the immemorial past purport to find traces of earlier ages and ideas in them. "Myths," or narrations about creations, deities, and so on, do not occur in the wide-ranging sense in which they appear among, say, the Polynesians or American Indians, but have nevertheless been spoken of by a number of writers. These narratives are admitted to be of little direct historical relevance: they tend to reflect present realities and preoccupations rather than those of earlier periods.[5] If recorded at the time, however, they can be useful for a later historian by throwing light on local attitudes rather than as literal statements.

The narrations often termed "legends" or historical narratives again are unfortunately rather less promising as sources than they might seem at first mention. The common picture of formalized historical accounts being passed down from generation to generation by specialists whose duty is to recite and transmit them accurately turns out to be not so widely applicable as one might expect; in fact it appears that the concept of historical narrative as a definite literary form distinct from other genres is relatively rare, except in societies much influenced by Arabic culture. This exception is of course not an unimportant one, as it affects many of the societies in the huge Sudan area across Africa and on the East African coast. Here historical accounts not infrequently took a written form and there was mutual interchange between oral and written versions.[6] There are also perhaps some other exceptions in states where, like Dahomey, Kuba, or Rwanda, the king kept close control over a centralized and authoritative version of the history.

Even these exceptions, however, involve their own difficulties. Were they really handed down "word for word"? There is almost no way of checking this (for even if one earlier version coincides closely, this cannot prove that still earlier ones did too) the fact that unfortunately local people believe that accounts are given accurately is not necessarily evidence. Again, the fact that such accounts are often the versions authorized by those currently holding political and/or religious power and, furthermore, are often mingled with praise of the ruling house and its ancestors, means that one must treat them with caution as an historical source.[7] In addition one has to be chary of taking such accounts literalistically. A narrative about first arrival in an area—a common topic—need not necessarily be interpreted as the migration of a whole people. Even if the account of actual arrival is accurate it may really only refer to one influential family coming to an already populated area. One good example of this is in Gabon oral tradition. If the traditions of specific "migrations" were taken literally "the history of Gabon would begin with an empty forest only 300 years ago, into which various peoples penetrated abruptly"; in fact it is clear from documentary and archaeological evidence that the area was inhabited long before this.[8] Travels, conquests, and arrivals are in any case common themes in stories, even among long settled peoples, and one must always be cautious about accepting them literally as the record of either wholesale migrations or specific military engagements.[9] Nevertheless, these professed historical narratives can be useful for the relatively recent periods when the description is usually less steeped in supernatural elements than the early portions of such accounts.

However—to return to the main point—there seem in fact to be relatively few specifically historical formal narratives in Africa. Some of the apparent exceptions rest on a misunderstanding. Many of the texts presented as "local historical accounts" are in fact elicited rather than spontaneous narratives. In other words, an answer is being given to a particular researcher which would not be naturally given in other circumstances and therefore does not form part of the formal transmission of traditions in that society. An elicited narrative of this kind is of course particularly subject to current preoccupations and conflicts, the status of an attitude to the inquirer, the present political situation and so on. This is not to say that such narrations are useless. But they are clearly a different kind of account from one formally handed down and authorized by the society or a dominant group in it. Too often we are not told by the researcher which type of "historical narrative" he is relying on; we may thus be given the impression that what was in fact an elicited version is really an authoritative and formalized account.

So far we have been concentrating on the first broad category of oral tradition—recognized literary forms. The second category is rather different. This is the general historical knowledge in a particular society which is not normally crystallized into actual recitations.[10] This knowledge may consist of beliefs about recent events or may include references to the more remote past. In each case such beliefs or references are less subject to formal requirements than the "oral literature" type, and are perhaps particularly subject to modification or embroidery in the light of current fashions, interests, events, or the availability of written accounts.

Informal historical knowledge includes not only general notions of what happened in the past, but also a few elements which, though not eligible for the term "oral literautre," can take a somewhat formalized shape. These include items like place names, praise names, or genealogies. Again, such sources have both uses and limitations.

Genealogies are a good case in point. There are a few instances in which genealogies are formally recited in, say, prayers or praises, but most often they merely form part of the general knowledge of a society or group. As such, they might seem an excellent source as far as they go. Some of their drawbacks, however, are well known.[11] There is the tendency to telescope, i.e., for links to fall out and be forgotten; there may be grafting on of extraneous links—as in Koranko genealogies going back to Noah and Adam, Fung pedigrees claiming descent from the Prophet,[12] or others from locally well-known but equally unrelated personages; or early ancestors may be rationalized in terms of current ideas or claims so that, say, early chieflets or village heads are presented as equally Paramount Chiefs or kings with their descendants. All these points arise from the inherent changeability of oral forms.

Perhaps less well known are the dangers of the way apparently objective genealogies are in fact closely tied to current—and ephemeral— political or social realities. An example can illustrate this.[13] The Tiv of Nigeria are a people who have traditionally had an uncentralized political system largely based on lineages and for whom, therefore, genealogies are of the utmost importance. They believe that they are all descended from one man (Tiv) through fourteen to seventeen generations of known ancestors. Yet these genealogies are constantly in dispute, and one even finds the same person citing different and contradictory genealogies on different occasions. These changes are dependent not on lapses of memory or on what Vansina would call "distortions," but arise merely because their actual use is always tied to some practical issue; there is never recitation or learning of genealogies as a whole for their own sake. Genealogies are thus used to fit particular facts and are constantly being modified in the light of the current situation. One incident illustrates this very clearly. A certain law case involved a question of genealogies. The details do not concern us, but roughly, the question of whether a certain man (X) received compensation or not turned on the exact position of one of his ancestors, Amena, possibly his great grandfather. But it was not agreed by the elders whether Amena was in fact one man, two men, or even perhaps a woman. It was first decided on a priori grounds that he was not a woman, but the issue still remained: if he was one man, then X was not due compensation; if two, then he was due it. In the event, he was not compensated, because none of the relevant property happened to be currently available. Two days later, however—and this is the point—the elders all agreed that Amena was only one person *on the grounds that* the compensation had not been paid. The genealogy was thus directly dependent on the result of the law case. This is a particularly striking example of the variability of genealogies, but many similar cases could be mentioned. [14]

   Leaving the discussion of this flexible type of general historical knowledge, we come to the third broad category of oral tradition—personal recollections. In many ways these are the best sources of all. Of course, there are still obvious safeguards to be observed—exactly the same kind as for similar recollections in literate societies. There is the need to cross-check and to allow for personal prejudices, romantic memories, special interests, lack of direct involvement, exaggeration, and so on. But clearly this kind of source is much nearer the primary facts than similar accounts which have been handed down through several generations.
   In using oral tradition as an historical source, it is important to make clear in each instance under which of these three broad categories a particular item falls: formalized oral literature, informal historical knowledge, or personal recollections. The reason for this is an obvious one. Each type has its own particular dangers or limitations, and critical use of sources involves making these explicit—something which it is impossible to do without differentiating between the categories. The idea that "oral tradition" is something unitary and can be treated as such runs counter to all the normally accepted historical procedures of assessing each type of source on its own merits.

The notion that when using "oral tradition" one can suspend many of the normal critical canons of historical research is, despite the caution of more experienced historians, surprisingly prevalent.[15] Perhaps this is because the various assumptions about oral tradition coming down word for word, about its unitary nature, or about its supposed freedom from individual originality or artistry seem to add up to the conclusion that oral tradition is somehow impervious to the kinds of factors of which historians are so aware with other sources—the effects of, say, prejudice or propaganda, personal interests or fantasies, aesthetic forms, or just the variations between different types of sources.

I would suggest that the opposite of this assumption is in fact true. Oral sources are in many ways even more open to such factors than written ones. A written document is certainly liable to many influences as it is written down, but once written it can be taken as permanent. Oral forms, on the other hand, are open to all these influences, not only on the occasion of the first formulation and delivery, but on every single occasion of delivery afterward. Because they *are* oral, and thus can exist only as and when they are rendered by word of mouth, obviously they are closely affected by a number of additional factors that do not apply to documentary sources.

First there is the whole aspect of performance. The oral speaker is by definition a performer, and all the arts of drama, rhetoric, display, and verbal facility may be relevant in his performance. Furthermore, since speakers vary in these arts, so too will the style, structure, even content of what he says. Unlike the author of a written document, the author of an oral historical account does not always remain the same; in the case of traditions handed down over long periods he is necessarily different; and different individuals have different ways of presenting the facts, different prejudices, different interpretations. Over any length of time at all this is likely to lead to many changes and in a very complicated way.

Oral forms, are, secondly, deeply affected by the kinds of audiences to which they are addressed on any particular occasion. The audience is there, fact to face, inescapable; it may be members of the family, friends, the king, children, a government official, a foreign researcher—and in each case the version may be different. Those whom local people rightly or wrongly associate with the government are particularly likely to have special versions given to them. In parts of Nigeria local people gather the evening before to prepare a version for delivery to the researcher the next day, and government officials frequently find that different accounts of history are being given by contending families or areas to bolster their own claims to some desired benefit. This is a consideration which makes one doubtful about the value of hasty recording of oral traditions. One example that springs to mind is Meyerowitz's research in Ghana; she visited over 130 towns and villages within nine months to record their traditions of origin—and this at a period when European visitors were associated with the government and regarded with suspicion.[16]

Oral tradition is also more constantly subject to outside influences because of its close connection with the current social situation. Each performance is on a specific occasion, and each occasion is in turn subject to the whole changing social background. This means that there is constant interpretation and reinterpretation in terms of the current situation. One example of this is provided by the Tiv genealogies already mentioned. Another is the story of the founding of the kingdom of Gonja in northern Ghana. One version of this was recorded around 1900, a period at which Gonja was divided into seven administrative divisions. The story tells how the state was first founded by a certain Jakpa who came to the area in search of gold, conquered the local inhabitants and became king by right of conquest; his seven sons and their descendants became the seven divisional chiefs. About 1960 the "same" story was recorded again. By that date two of the old divisions had disappeared, leaving only five; and the tale speaks of only five sons, with no mention at all of the other two.[17] A narrative like this is obviously influenced as much by present realities and power relationships as by historical considerations.[18]

The idea therefore that oral tradition is somehow impervious to all the kinds of influences of which historians must take cognizance in other sources is far from the truth. Oral tradition, being inherently variable and unfixed, is in certain ways peculiarly susceptible to such factors, and this is something of which an historian using these sources must take special account.

Notes

1. Not some of the more rigorous analysts, however, like J. Vansina, *Oral Tradition: A Study in Historical Methodology*, trans. H. Wright (London: Routledge and Kegan Paul, 1965; see chapter 9 of the present volume); P. D. Curtin, "Field Techniques for Collecting and Processing Oral Data," *Journal of African History* 9 (1968), pp. 367–85; E. J. Alagoa, "Oral Tradition among the Ijo of the Niger Delta," *Journal of African History* 7 (1966), pp. 405–19; G. S. Were, *A History of the Abaluyia of Western Kenya* (Nairobi: Uniafric House, 1967).

2. The list makes no attempt to be comprehensive. Further types are discussed in Vansina, *Oral Tradition*, and R. Finnegan, *Oral Literature in Africa* (London: Oxford University Press, 1970).

3. The Mau Mau political songs, for instance, were thus recorded and should prove extremely useful to the historian of this period.

4. For a further discussion of this problem, see Finnegan, *Oral Literature*, note to chap. 4, pp. 108–10.

5. For an instance of this, see below on the "myth" about the founding of Gonja.

6. With the corollary that some of these written chronicles must be subject to the same cautious treatment as oral accounts.

7. A point well discussed in Vansina, *Oral Tradition*, p. 155, but often neglected (see, for instance, M. Southwold's acceptance at their face value of claims in official Ganda king lists that those who succeeded to the kingship by rebellion were all in any case highly qualified to succeed [*History and Social Anthropology*, ed. I. M. Lewis (London: Travis-Tock Publications, 1968), p. 130]).

8. H. Deschamps, "Traditions orales au Gabon," in *The Historian in Tropical Africa*, ed. J. Vansina (London: International African Institute, 1964), p. 175.

9. For a critique of the concept of migration as an explanatory device, see H. S. Lewis, "Ethnology and Culture History," in *Reconstructing African Culture History*, ed. C. Gabel and N. R. Bennett (Boston: Boston University Press, 1967), pp. 32–33, and references given there.

10. The "elicited narrations" just mentioned properly fit into this category.

11. See the account in Vansina, *Oral Tradition*, pp. 153–54.

12. E. F. Sayers, "The Funeral of a Koranko Chief," *Sierra Leone Studies*, o.s., 7 (1925), p. 24; B. A. Ogot, "The Impact of the Nilotes," in *The Middle Ages of African History*, ed. R. Oliver (London: Oxford University Press, 1967), p. 51.

13. This account is based on L. Bohannan, "A Genealogical Charter," *Africa* 22 (1952), pp. 301–15.

14. For some further examples of changes in genealogies, see E. E. Evans-Pritchard, *The Nuer* (Oxford: Clarendon Press, 1940), pp. 199–200; *Tribes without Rulers*, ed. J. Middleton and D. Tait (London: Routledge and Kegan Paul, 1958), pp. 10, 42ff., 198ff., 218; J. Middleton, *Lugbara Religion* (London: International African Institute, 1960), pp. 8, 235–36, 265; J. van Velsen, *The Politics of Kinship* (Manchester, England: University Press of Manchester, 1964), pp. 268–69; and the references given in J. A. Barnes, "Genealogies," in *The Craft of Social Anthropology*, ed. A. L. Epstein (London: Pergamon Press, 1967), pp. 118–21.

15. See the warnings in, for example, Vansina, *Oral Tradition*, and Curtin, "Field Techniques."

16. E. Meyerowitz, *Akan Traditions of Origin* (London: Faber Press, 1952), pp. 15, 17.

17. J. Goody and I. Watt, "The Consequences of Literacy," *Comparative Studies in Society and History* 5 (1963), p. 310.

18. An aspect brought out by the common point in social anthropological writings that such accounts are "mythical charters" for the existing social and political situation.

11

Oral History Project Design
David Lance

The design and evaluation of the research goals of an oral history project are subjects often slighted in how-to manuals. As a result, many beginning interviewers overlook the need for a balanced collection of sources and ignore relevant earlier work in their area, leaping with their microphones before looking at previous collections. The next five articles provide guidance on practical and theoretical considerations in designating (and attaining) realistic project goals.

Archivist David Lance dissects one English oral history project to demonstrate the research which necessarily precedes and informs the interviews. He indicates the necessity for a thoughtful analysis of potential research problems before beginning interviews and provides a matrix design to assure a balanced sample of narrators. Novices to oral history, as Charles Morrissey has written, frequently confuse the tape recorder and the vacuum cleaner. David Lance's article, however, explores an area which even experienced interviewers occasionally neglect. Lance offers compelling suggestions on research procedures and topic selection.

David Lance has been the secretary and the president of the International Association of Sound Archives (IASA). For the last fifteen years he has worked as the keeper of sound records at the Imperial War Museum in London; there he not only established a department of sound records but helped produce documentaries for the British and Canadian Broadcasting Corporations using oral sources. Some of his writings are "Oral History: Legal Considerations" (1976) and "Oral History: Perceptions and Practice" (1980), published in the British journal Oral History.

"Oral History Project Design" is an excerpt from An Archive Approach to Oral History *(London: Imperial War Museum and the International Association of Sound Archives, 1978).*

THE ORGANISATIONAL methods on which this section is based have been applied across a wide subject and chronological range. They can be adapted for much oral history research which is concerned with the history of particular social and occupational groups. In order to allow readers to relate the various phases of project management to specific examples it is convenient, however, to concentrate on a single project. The project used for illustrative purposes was concerned with the experiences and conditions of service of sailors who served on the lower deck of the Royal Navy between the years 1910 and 1922.

(1) Preparation

The organisation of any project should be set within realistic research goals. Since oral history recording is dependent for worthwhile results on human memory, this fallible faculty must be accommodated by careful preparation. The planning of the project should, therefore, be based on as thorough understanding of the subject field (and of the availability of informants) as the existing records permit.

It is prudent, first, to fix a research period which is historically identifiable as being self-contained. In the lower deck project, for example, the so-called Fisher Reforms of 1906 altered several important aspects of naval life; the First World War stimulated further changes during the early 1920s; and the Invergordon Mutiny in 1931 was another watershed for Royal Naval seamen. The combination of these three distinct periods in a recording project, would have made it extremely difficult for sailors who served throughout them to avoid confusion on many details of routine life which, for research purposes, might be of critical importance. Three distinct periods of social change within a single career of professional experience are clearly difficult for informants to separate with few points of reference beyond their own memories. By setting the general limits of the lower deck project at 1910 to 1922, a reasonably distinct period of naval life was isolated as appropriate for oral history research.

The research problems which are created by rapid social change can seldom be eliminated entirely from oral history recording. It is for this reason that historically unsophisticated interviewing can result in information of uncertain reliability. Therefore, the project organiser's responsibility is to minimise the dangers implicit in such situations by his own common sense and historical sensitivity, and he should always apply the question 'Is this reasonable?' to the goals which he sets. Some practical examples of the application of this principle in oral history research are given overleaf.

The chronological scope of an oral history project should be fixed before any recording begins, bearing in mind the age of the likely informants as well as the historical character of the subject field. By the time the lower deck project began in 1975, men who saw service in the Navy as early as 1910 were in their eighties, and thus the opportunities for preceding this date were limited. This basic consideration affects all oral history recording. The informants who are actually available to be interviewed, also predetermine many of the topics which may be sensibly raised. Thus, owing to the slowness of promotion in the Royal Navy there was little point in introducing questions about, for example, conditions in petty officers' messes in 1910. Only informants into their nineties would have had the necessary experiences to be able to answer them. The chances of locating a sufficient number of interviewees of this great age, were sufficiently slight to preclude this—and many similar topics—from being a practical aim within a systematic research project.

Similarly, the project organiser must take into account the structure of the particular group of people he is concerned with. For example, a battleship of the Dreadnought era—with a complement of some 700 men— might carry one writer (*ie* account's clerk) and one sailmaker. The odds against tracing such rare individuals more than fifty years after the events eliminated some aspects of financial administration and some trade skills aboard ship from the range of what it was likely to be able to achieve.

The selection of and possible bias among informants, are related factors which have to be appreciated. Between 1914 and 1918 the total size of the Navy increased threefold owing to the needs of war. A substantial proportion of those who served for hostilities only may not have accepted the traditional *mores* of regular lower deck life. At the end of a carefully organised and conducted project, the organiser had no clear idea of whether wartime personnel generally adopted the attitudes of those who had been in the service since they were boys, because the original selection of informants simply did not permit systematic investigation of their particular prejudices. An appropriate selection of sailors to be interviewed would have produced a representative sample of these kinds of informants and thereby provided suitable evidence from which conclusions about this particular question could be drawn. This obviously does not devalue the information for the purposes for which it was recorded, but it does eliminate the range of hypotheses to which this body of data is open. Thus, the project organiser must take into account the relationship between the subject matter of the project and his selection of informants and—at one stage yet farther removed from recording—this involves being clear about the kind of research evidence he is actually seeking to collect.

(2) Specification

The list of topics which guided the interviewers' work in the lower deck project is given below, as one example of subject delineation in oral history research. The field of study was first broken down into the following main areas:

a Background and enlistment	j Traditions and customs
b Training	k Foreign service
c Dress	l Home ports
d Ships	m Pay and benefits
e Work	n Naval operations
f Mess room life	o Effects of the war
g Rations and victualling	p Family life
h Discipline	q Post service experience
i Religion	

Each of these topics was examined in some detail, the extent and nature of which may be demonstrated by one example. Thus, in dealing with the subject of 'Discipline', the following questions influenced the interviewers' approach:

a. What was the standard and nature of discipline on the lower deck? Who influenced it? Did it vary much?

b. What were the most common offences? What were the most extreme? How were they punished?

c. Was the discipline fair? Was it possible to appeal effectively against any unfair treatment, if it occurred?

d. What was the lower deck's attitude to naval police? How much and what sort of power did they have? Did they ever abuse their authority?

e. What were relations like between the lower deck and commissioned officers, 'ranker' officers, NCOs and the Marines?

f. Was there any code of informal discipline or constraint on the lower deck? What kind of behaviour was considered unacceptable and how would it be dealt with?

g. Who were the most influential members of the lower deck? Was their influence based on any factors other than rank?

(3) Application

While there can be no question that the purposes of oral history research need to be very carefully defined, the way in which project papers should be used is open to variation. Some important work has been done[1] in which listed questions are much more numerous and refined than in the above example and the resultant paper used in the form of a social research questionnaire. While such methods may serve the purposes of some historians, for the wider aims of collecting centres . . . formal questionnaires have not been found suitable. Partly this is because no questionnaire is sufficiently flexible to accommodate, in itself, the unexpected and valuable twists and turns of an informant's memory; and partly it is due to the fact that a questionnaire can become an obstacle to achieving the natural and spontaneous dialogue that is the aim of most oral historians.

But, short of a questionnaire, lists of topics can provide useful guidelines for interviewers to work to. The more interviewers there are engaged on a particular project, the greater becomes the need to ensure consistency of approach. As a device for obtaining such consistency, topic lists have a practical value throughout a recording project. Even with a project which is in the custody of one historian, the construction of a formal research paper is still valuable for reference purposes, because consistency is no less important and only somewhat more certain with one interviewer than with many, in the course of a recording project of any significant scale.

(4) Monitoring

It is possible, simply by drawing the interviewers together and taking their reactions, to get an impression of the progress that has been achieved at various stages of the recording programme. However, for the effective monitoring of the project more systematic aids should be introduced. These are needed because the creation of oral history recordings usually far outstrips that of processing the recorded interviews. Cataloguing, indexing and transcribing generally lag so far behind recording that the customary aids which give access to the material are not available when they would be most useful for project control.

As an intermediate means of registering the project information as it is being recorded, simple visual aids can be designed which are appropriate to the work which is being carried out. In the case of the lower deck project the chart reproduced opposite was useful as such a tool. When projects are geared to preparatory research papers and control charts of the kind reproduced in figure 11.1 oral history recording can be effectively monitored and sensibly controlled. At the beginning of the project, the research paper represents the academic definition of the project goals. By careful application in the field academic prescription and practical possibility can begin to be reconciled. Thus, in the light of early interviewing

Informant	Clarke	Ashley	Holt	Boin	Maloney	Burke	Boughton	Clarkson	Basford	Ford	Pullen	Heron	Lazenby	Hutchings	Cox	Leary	Halter	Masters	Adshead	Roberts
Port division	A	B	C	A	A	B	C	B	C	B	A	A	B	B	A	A	C	C	B	C
Branch	B	E	A	C	E	D	C	C	E	F	B	A	B	E	D	A	D	C	F	B
Service: from 19	09	13	17	17	16	08	17	15	08	11	11	18	17	13	18	13	11	12	03	13
to 19	25	19	30	20	19	10	32	37	32	23	24	40	31	22	33	19	24	36	26	25
Interview period	B-C	A-C	B-C	A-B	A-C	C	B-C	B-C	C	B-C	A-C	A-C	B-C	A-C	A-A	B-C	A-C	A-C	C	A-B
Motivation	✓	✓		✓	✓	✓	✓	✓			✓	✓	✓	✓	✓	✓		✓	✓	✓
Boy training	✓	✓	✓	✓	✓	✓		✓	✓	✓		✓	✓	✓	✓	✓		✓	✓	
Man training	✓	✓	✓		✓	✓		✓	✓	✓	✓		✓			✓	✓	✓		✓
Dress	✓	✓	✓	✓	✓	✓	✓	✓	✓	✓			✓					✓		✓
Work		✓		✓		✓	✓			✓			✓		✓	✓	✓		✓	✓
Mess room life		✓			✓	✓	✓		✓	✓	✓	✓			✓		✓		✓	✓
Food			✓					✓				✓								
Discipline	✓	✓	✓	✓	✓	✓		✓	✓		✓	✓	✓	✓					✓	
Religion	✓							✓		✓									✓	✓
Traditions and customs					✓			✓		✓					✓	✓				✓
Foreign stations	AD	AC	CE	AD	A	AC	C	CE	AC	B	C	AD	CE	DE	A	C	AC	D	A	AD
Home ports	✓	✓	✓	✓	✓			✓	✓		✓	✓	✓	✓	✓	✓				
Operations	✓		✓	✓			✓	✓		✓						✓		✓	✓	✓
Effects of war	✓						✓								✓	✓		✓	✓	✓
Pay		✓	✓	✓	✓	✓	✓			✓							✓			
Family life			✓							✓	✓	✓	✓			✓		✓	✓	✓
Post service experience	✓	✓	✓			✓	✓	✓	✓		✓		✓		✓	✓		✓		✓

1. Port division		2. Branch		3. Interview period		4. Foreign stations	
Portsmouth	A	Signals	A	Pre-war	A	China	A
Devonport	B	Torpedo	B	Wartime	B	Cape	B
Chatham	C	Engine room	C	Post-war	C	Mediterranean	C
		Gunnery	D			N. America	D
		Artisan	E			S.E. America	E
		Other	F				

Figure 11.1. Sample control chart

experience, the list can be altered after some initial application. Certain questions may be modified, some removed or new questions may be introduced into the initial scheme, until a more refined and useful document emerges. Sensible alterations to the scope of a project cannot be made without a systematic approach of the kind that is implied in the formulation of a project paper.

As recording progresses, a chart of the information being collected permits the monitoring of the project's interim results. The value of the original topics—and their various divisions—should not be treated as inviolate until the work has run its full course. A common experience is that the collection of information in some subject areas reaches a point of saturation before many of the others. Such lines of questioning may be discontinued when there is reasonable certainty that their continuation would be unlikely to add significantly to the information that has already been recorded. The converse is also facilitated by a framework which permits the interim analysis of results. That is to say, areas in which the collection of information has proceeded less satisfactorily can more easily be singled out for greater attention.

Devices of the kind described above are usually essential in the effective management of oral history research. Unless the resources of the collecting centre are untypically lavish, there is usually no other means by which it can be established that the interviewing and recording is achieving the results which were originally sought. It is obviously necessary, through such methods, to be able to control the course of the project and to judge when it may be terminated

(5) Documentation

For the proper assessment and use of oral evidence, the collecting centre should systematically record the project methodology. Without this background information the scholar may not be able to use appropriately the information which has been recorded. What were the aims of the project organiser? By what means were informants selected for interview? What was their individual background? How were the interviews conducted? How was the work as a whole controlled? The more information there is available to answer such questions as these, the more valuable oral history materials will be to the researcher and the more securely he can make use of them in his work.

A formal paper, of the kind recommended earlier, can tell the user a great deal about how the project was structured. A working file will be even more useful, if it reveals the way in which the work evolved (recording what changes were introduced at what stage in the development of the project). Such files should be maintained and regarded as an integral part of the research materials which may be needed by historians.

Individual informant files should also be accessible for research. They should contain biographical details of the informant and also be organised in such a way that the user can correlate tapes or transcripts with places and dates which are covered by the interview. In this respect, interviewers are in a uniquely valuable position to secure a documentary basis of the information they record. Often the informant's memory, photographic and documentary materials in his possession, reference sources and the interviewer's own subject expertise, can be combined to formulate quite a detailed chronology. This will support and give background to the recorded interview.

Similarly, the interview itself should be used as a means of establishing the kind of background information that will give additional significance to the information the informant provides. Thus, in addition to the specific project information the interviewer is seeking, he can with advantage also record details of the informant's place of birth and upbringing, his family background, economic circumstances, educational attainments, occupational experiences and so on.

Much that an informant says during the course of an interview he may wish to correct, amend or amplify subsequently. No documentation system would be complete without providing him with the means so to do. The opportunity to listen to or read the completed interview often provides the informant with a considerable stimulus to add to the information which has already been recorded. Once committed to an oral history interview, most informants feel the need for historical exactitude. Collecting centres can maintain their transcripts in pristine condition, whilst also giving informants full opportunity to supplement with written notes the information they have already given, and filing such notes along with the final tapes and transcript.

Note

1. The outstanding British example of this kind of approach is Dr. Paul Thompson's (University of Essex) study of family life and social history in Edwardian Britain.

12

Introduction to *Tom Rivers*
Saul Benison

An oral history project would ideally engage as a researcher and interviewer someone trained both as a professional oral historian and as an expert in the subject being examined. Our next selection shows what can be realized under these conditions, given substantial financial support.

As Samuel Hand noted in part 1, Saul Benison's biography of Tom Rivers demonstrates the results possible when a specialist designs a closely researched agenda of questions. Benison's approach requires an exactingly prepared interviewer who not only shapes the reminiscence with background facts but also annotates it by including footnoted material which contradicts or explains his narrator's comments. The reader should observe the ways in which the author's notes stand in an unusual counterpoint to Dr. Rivers's recollections.

This introduction affords an example of a carefully executed interview history, describing the circumstances of the interview and the character and mood of the interviewee as they relate to the interview context and indicating the approach taken to editing.

Saul Benison is professor of the history of science and environmental health at the University of Cincinnati. He is currently finishing an oral history memoir of Dr. Albert Sabin and the first volume of a biography of Dr. Walter Bradford.

This selection appeared as the introduction to Tom Rivers: Reflections on a Life in Medicine and Science *(Cambridge, Mass.: M.I.T. Press, 1967).*

Whoever elects to study history, as far as I am concerned, may bring to bear the most pathetic and childish belief in the classifying power of our spirit and methods, but apart from this and in spite of it he should have respect for the incomprehensible truth, reality, and singularity of events. To deal with history my friend is no jest and no irresponsible game.

—Hermann Hesse, *Magister Ludi*

Historyans is like doctors. They are always looking f'r symptoms.
Those iv them that writes about their own times examines th'tongue
an' feels th' pulse an' makes a wrong dygnosis. Th' other kind iv
histhry is a post mortem examination. It tells ye what a counthry died
iv. But I'd like to know what it lived iv.
        —Peter Finley Dunne, *Observations by Mr. Dooley*

O N FEBRUARY 5, 1962, one hundred distinguished micro-
biologists, virologists, and biochemists, including four Nobel
laureates, met in a New York hotel to pay tribute to Dr. Thomas
Rivers, a member emeritus of the Rockefeller Institute for Medical Research. A fifth Nobel laureate, Dr. John Enders, ill in Boston and unable to
attend the festivities, telegraphed the following message to Dr. Rivers:
"We the members of the church salute the apostolic father."

The recognition that Dr. Enders and others accorded Dr. Rivers that
day was singularly appropriate. For a period of almost forty years, Dr.
Rivers had been a dominant figure both as an investigator and as an
administrator in virus research in the United States. Three months later,
at the age of 73, he was dead. Dr. Rivers' death did not mark the end of
one era in virology or the beginning of another. His career in essence
spanned the development of virology from its status at the beginning of
the twentieth century as an adjunct to bacteriological study to its current
position as an independent discipline, as much concerned with the fundamental problems posed by molecular biology as with the diseases
caused by viral agents.

This oral history memoir is an attempt to chart the evolution of Dr.
Rivers' career. Oral history is a relatively new phenomenon in American
historiography, and a note as to its development, purpose and procedures may serve to put Dr. Rivers' memoir in perspective. In 1938 Professor Allan Nevins, in his handbook of historiography, *The Gateway to
History,* urged his fellow historians to establish an organization which
would make a systematic attempt to obtain from the lips and papers of
living Americans an expansive personal record of their participation in
the political, economic, and cultural life of the nation. It was his hope that
in this way a unique archive of autobiographical material might be prepared for the use of future historians. There was precedence for Professor
Nevins' proposal. Autobiography was an old and vital tradition in western historiography. Further, during the nineteen twenties several notable
projects had been organized for the collection of autobiographies to
elucidate the history of psychology and medicine. Equally important,
other social scientists, in particular anthropologists and folklorists, had

long demonstrated the usefulness of oral traditions for historical research.

Professor Nevins' proposals, however, elicited little enthusiasm from his contemporaries. Some voiced reservations about the wisdom of having historians gather memoirs from the living. They felt that such a procedures would of necessity compromise the historians' objectivity and in the end lead to the production of self-serving, partisan accounts of recent events. Others argued that historians had neither the skills nor funds necessary to capture autobiographical interviews verbatim. In spite of these and other objections, Professor Nevins continued to proselytize for his idea. In 1948, soon after the tape recorder was perfected for commercial use, he secured funds from several foundations and established an oral history research office at Columbia University to carry out the plans he had projected a decade before. Professor Nevins' persistence not only showed a belief in his own original vision and purpose, it also reflected the growing need of those who worked in contemporary history to find a way of coping with some of the complexities created for historical research by modern technology.

Historians are agreed that modern society rests in part on foundations created by printing and paper making. These are important not only because they rank among the oldest of modern industrial processes but because they also serve as catalysts of human thought. Newspapers, magazines, books, and a vast mechanically produced correspondence all testify to the pervasiveness of print and paper communication in all facets of our daily public and private life. Indeed the one constant result of both business and government seems to be the production of new records. It is a condition that has provoked some archivists to make the irreverent suggestion that the best possible thing that could happen to modern historical records was a good fire.

Paradoxically, the industrial process which has created this superabundance of records has also produced a technology which threatens to deprive the historian in future of a great deal of the substance, detail, and variety usually found in the process of human events. This technology, of which the automobile, airliner, radio, television, and the telephone are but a part, has created a revolution in communication that has made the world smaller, changed the tempo of living, and transformed the nature and uses of time. Its hallmark is talk. As a result of new sound and visual communication, much of the detail of human experience, which was previously put to paper because of the exclusive nature of print and writing communication, has today been sapped from the record and become fleeting and ephemeral. Such experience, if preserved at all, is only to be found in the memory of living men. It is this paradox of simultaneous plenty and scarcity in contemporary records that in large measures defines the tasks of those who work in oral history.

In an important sense oral history is misnamed. While it is true that the oral historian helps gather an oral memoir, it is equally true that such an account is based on a written record. It is precisely this record which ultimately determines the course and substance of his work. That work may be divided into four parts. Once a subject has been chosen to be interviewed, the oral historian, like any other historian, must prepare himself in extant primary and secondary source material so as to see and define relevant historical relationships and problems. Second, armed with a tape recorder, he must so handle himself and his preparation as to spur the chosen subject's memory of past events. Third, he must gather from his subjects, and other people, supporting documents of contemporary demonstration, both as a check on the tenuousness of memory and to supplement the account gathered. Fourth, he must edit or aid the subject in editing the final preparation of the memoir so that it says what the subject wants it to say.

The memoir that emerges as a result of this process is a new kind of historical document. Although it has been created by a participant in past events, it is also the creation of the historian-interviewer who has in fact determined the historical problems and relationships to be examined. This mutual creation contributes to both the strength and weakness inherent in oral history memoirs. And it is for this reason that the circumstances surrounding the production of any given memoir must be clearly set forth. The events leading to the creation of Dr. Rivers' memoir were these.

In the spring of 1961, soon after beginning research on a projected history of poliomyelitis and The National Foundation, I asked Dr. Rivers, then Vice President for Medical Affairs of The National Foundation, to allow me to record his memoirs. This was not the first such request I had made of Dr. Rivers. Five years before, while gathering medical and other scientific memoirs for the Oral History Research Office at Columbia University, I had presented a similar petition and was refused. This time he consented. I was helped in obtaining that decision by an untoward circumstance. A short time before I had approached Dr. Rivers, he was operated on for a malignancy in one of his lungs. It so happened that on the day I met with him he was more than usually bored by the inactivity that convalescence had forced on him, and he seized on my request as a way of escaping the confinement of recovery. Dr. Rivers' consent was not without restrictions. Although he agreed to talk with me about his career in science, he stipulated that under no circumstances would he speak to me of his family or his private life. When I remonstrated that posterity would never believe that he had appeared, fully grown and armed, from Zeus's forehead, he agreed to tell me a little about his father and mother, but nothing more. Both the circumstance of Dr. Rivers' illness and the restrictions he placed on our talks are important because they serve to explain some of the content of his memoirs.

By nature Dr. Rivers was a curmudgeon.[1] He had a keen critical mind, possessed a waspish tongue, and loved a good fight. His illness accented some of these characteristics. Further, from the beginning of his illness he knew he was suffering from a malignancy. While he initially hoped that the operation he had undergone might stem its development, by the end of the summer of 1961 he knew he did not have long to live. These circumstances not only contributed to his candor about himself and his work, they also encouraged him to make uninhibited comments and judgments about people he knew in science—comments that in ordinary circumstances might have been more discreet. His illness affected the conduct of the interviews as well. Although on several occasions I saw Dr. Rivers socially in his home, at no time would he permit interviews to be held there. All interviews were held in his office at The National Foundation or his offices and sickroom at the Rockefeller Hospital. I felt that he insisted on this for two reasons. First, it allowed him to keep the interviews on a formal plane, and second, by arranging interviews in his office he created an added incentive for himself to carry on his daily activities as he had before his operation. In the last seven months of his life he came into his office at The National Foundation five days a week until his illness required hospitalization two weeks before his death.

I particularly regretted Dr. Rivers' decision not to speak about his family and private life, because it meant that I was unable to examine with him his home environment and the larger social environment of the New South in which he came of age. More important, it prevented me from discussing with him his social beliefs or to examine the impact of his scientific career on those beliefs.

As a result of both Dr. Rivers' restrictions and my ultimate purpose in writing a history of poliomyelitis and The National Foundation, I concentrated my interviews on four basic subjects or problems: the development of Dr. Rivers' medical and scientific education, the evolution of his virus research, an examination of those scientific institutions and organizations in which he had played a singular or important role, and finally an examination of problems in the administration of scientific research, as exemplified by the development of polio research during the nineteen forties and fifties.

My preparation for the interviews began several months before the first interview actually took place and was continued throughout the course of the interviews, a period of approximately 15 months. Interviews were so arranged as to facilitate research and were usually held at the beginning and end of each week. In general, the interviews ran for no longer than an hour, though an occasional one ran for an hour and a half or an hour and three quarters.

At the end of each interview I would not only outline for Dr. Rivers the subject matter or problems that the next interview would cover, I would also supply him with copies of letters, documents, and scientific papers that might serve to refresh his memory. For his part, Dr. Rivers would frequently direct my attention to material that he thought might be useful to me in my preparation. In this sense the interviews were "prepared." At every interview I came armed with relevant books and documentary material so that if the need to look at or quote from such material arose it was immediately to hand. On several occasions Dr. Rivers quoted passages from such documents or books or asked that such material be inserted later in the memoir. Once an interview was completed, it was immediately transcribed.

While the end product of oral history often looks neat and logical, the process itself isn't, because man's memory and the course of conversation are frequently untidy. Although I tried to examine all subjects and problems with Dr. Rivers chronologically, so as to establish a rudimentary outline of development, I was not always successful. Often during the pursuit of a subject, both Dr. Rivers and I were led by the nature of conversation and subject matter into making digressions. At times Dr. Rivers would repeat himself. On other occasions he would forget a precise date or name of a person. At such times he would ask me to find the date or name and insert it in the memoir. Such forgetfulness is common at any age and was in no sense characteristic of Dr. Rivers' memory. His recall of substantive matters was prodigious—so much so that it was often a conversation piece among his long-time colleagues at the Rockefeller Institute and his associates at The National Foundation.

When interviews on a given subject were completed, I edited that portion of the transcript and submitted it to Dr. Rivers for his approval. My editing chores in the main consisted in arranging the material in chronological and chapter order, eliminating repetitious material, and inserting blank dates and names. No attempt was made to alter Dr. Rivers' language, to make him grammatical, nor were the expletives and other expressions he was fond of eliminated. Errors of fact and interpretation, even when known to be errors, were kept because such mistakes were often revealing of the man and his thought. These I have footnoted passim.

In the end my method of proceeding chronologically and editing the transcript while the interviews were still in progress worked against me, because Dr. Rivers died before I could carry my investigations and interviews much beyond 1958. I was unable therefore to examine with Dr. Rivers at least two important subjects, the development of the Sabin vaccine after 1958 and the scientific background of the decision of The National Foundation to enter the field of birth defects and arthritis.

After Dr. Rivers' death, I sent portions of his memoir to several of his former colleagues and friends mentioned in the text for critical comment. Among those who commented on the manuscript were Dr. Peter Olitsky, Dr. Peyton Rous, Dr. John Enders, Dr. Joseph Stokes, Jr., Dr. Albert Sabin, Dr. David Bodian, Dr. Hilary Koprowski, Dr. Thomas Turner, Dr. Jonas Salk, Dr. Joseph Smadel, Dr. Harry Weaver, and Dr. Walter Schlesinger. They sent valuable critical material which is appended in various footnotes throughout the text.

It is an impertinence to tell a reader how to read a book. The nature of a book, however, must be understood. Dr. Rivers' oral history memoir is an account of some aspects of the recent history of American virology from a particular moment in time filtered by individual experience. In no sense is it presented as an exclusive historical source. It is rather a corroborative source and guide. As such it is a beginning of interpretation, not an end.

Note

1. Dr. Richard Shope, a long-time associate of Dr. Rivers at the Rockefeller Institute, characterized him as follows in a biographical notice he wrote soon after Dr. Rivers' death. "Although Dr. Rivers was by nature a friendly person, he had the capacity of being irascible and pugnacious. He was a difficult and formidable person to oppose and could be stubbornly inflexible in maintaining a position. His discussion at scientific meetings of findings with which he disagreed could on occasion be so stinging that the audience, even though realizing the correctness of Rivers' position, often had their personal sympathies entirely with Rivers' opponent. Many of those who have known Dr. Rivers best have felt the sting that he could so picturesquely deliver in an argument. Few of us have had the nerve openly to side with his opposition in one of these 'knock down' and 'drag out' discussions" (R. E. Shope, "Tom Rivers," *Journal of Bacteriology* 84 [1962], pp. 385–88).

13

Theory, Method, and Oral History
Peter Friedlander

Our third approach to oral history project design is a theoretical essay from The Emergence of a UAW Local *by historian Peter Friedlander. The author challenges the prevailing view of the oral history interviewer as the miner of facts from an interviewee's memory. Instead, Friedlander suggests, we should rethink the process: the interviewer (by his or her questions) and the interviewee (by his or her answers) participate jointly in the manufacture of a historical fact—"The problem of the interpretation of facts is bound up with the manner of their production: they arise out of a matrix of meaning."*

In this complex work of oral historiography, Friedlander borrows insights from linguistic and anthropological theory to pose some tough questions for oral historians: What is the significance of the collaboration between interviewer and interviewee in generating history? Does the structure of human memory affect history made of reminiscence? The following text represents only a small portion of the introduction to this important book, which has attracted attention among the more theoretically inclined researchers studying oral history.

Peter Friedlander's research crosses the boundaries of anthropology and history. He is currently at work on an article, "The Origins of the Welfare State, 1910–1937." He teaches at the Weekend College of Wayne State University in Detroit, Michigan.

"Theory, Method, and Oral History" is excerpted from the introduction to The Emergence of a UAW Local, 1936—1939: A Study in Class and Culture *(Pittsburgh: University of Pittsburgh Press, 1975).*

THIS ACCOUNT of the emergence of Local 229 of the United Automobile Workers is based on a lengthy and detailed collaboration with Edmund Kord, the president of the local during most of its first eighteen years. Because there is little documentary evidence bearing directly on the history of this local,[1] I have had to rely almost entirely on

Kord's memory. For this reason I think I owe the reader an explanation of the nature and extent of these discussions and communications with Kord, so that the limitations of this study will be clear.

In December 1972 Kord and I spent eight days together on the east side of Detroit. At that time I took notes of our discussions, and Kord showed me the plant and the surrounding neighborhood in Hamtramck, pointed out the important bars, and described such details as the configuration of workers in front of the gate during strikes. I wrote a draft based on this material and on Tonat's dissertation. I sent this to Kord, along with a set of questions, for comments and criticism. On the basis of his response to these I constructed a further set of questions and sent them to him. Later, in late June of 1973, we spent a week together. This time I recorded our conversations on about eight hours of tapes. These were then transcribed and reordered in a rough narrative sequence and in this form became the basis for the major series of communications: an extensive correspondence occupying seventy-five pages. A draft of the first three chapters was then drawn up and submitted to Kord for comments and corrections. Following this we met for a week in January 1974 and two days in March 1974. Again the conversations were recorded. Finally, to fill some gaps that became apparent in the course of drawing up the final draft, Kord and I had six recorded telephone conversations totaling about four hours. What follows, therefore, is the outcome of a lengthy collaboration extending from December 1972 to March 1974.

The extent of Kord's knowledge of events in the plant varied in relation to the location of those events. Kord, who was a grinder in the torch-welding department, had an intimate knowledge of his own department and a substantial, but less intimate knowledge of the adjacent press departments, based on direct contact and close observation. His knowledge of the front of the shop—front-welding and departments 16 and 18—was gained mainly through discussions at the time with activists and leaders in that part of the shop, although he possesses a good deal of direct knowledge even there. However, Kord's knowledge of both the toolroom and the inspection department in the early period of the union's history, with which the first chapters of this book are concerned, is limited not only by their physical distance from his own department, but also by the resistance to unionization exhibited by these two departments.

Nevertheless, because of the nature of the questions that I sought to answer in this study, the limitations imposed by the character of the evidence have little significance: not only is the necessary information unavailable except in the form of the memories of participants; it emerges only through a critical dialogue.[2] Therefore I did not simply ask questions of Kord or solicit his reminiscences. On the contrary, I sought to bring to bear on Kord's experience a number of theoretical and historical conceptions that I thought critical to an understanding of the CIO—conceptions that I found myself forced to alter as my increasingly concrete information obstinately refused to fall into some of my prefabricated categories.

Even if, for example, a certain amount of "hard" evidence were available, say in the form of census data for the plant, it would be of almost no use. The census would only distinguish between foreign-born and native-born of foreign or mixed parentage. Yet among the latter, it turns out, there were at least three distinct groups of young, unskilled second-generation Polish workers: (1) those who were helpers in front-welding and who expected to be promoted to welders (the most highly skilled production work in the plant), (2) those unskilled press operators who were in their middle twenties, who had left their parental homes, and who were married or planning to get married, and (3) those who were just out of high school (or who had dropped out) and who were members of neighborhood gangs and barroom cliques. Obviously, this kind of information cannot be gleaned from available documentary evidence.

The same problems emerge in regard to other major questions. What was the subjective, psychological content of relationships to authority, and how did this change in the course of the organizing effort? Who were the leaders: what was the inner structure of leadership, conceived of as a social formation, and how did it emerge from the matrix of social relations in the plant? What was the role of leadership, and to what extent did the leaders act or seem to act independently of their followers? How did the various groups of workers conceive of their struggle for power, and what impact did that struggle have on their personal lives and social outlooks? Until recently, the major current in labor historiography has been frankly institutional in orientation, yet the emergence of institutions is only an aspect of a more complex social process. What are the sources of institutionalization, and what is its relationship to the broader social process out of which institutions emerge? . . .

The foregoing briefly summarizes the theoretical intent of this study. Because of the nature of this investigation, however, the problem of methodology is intimately connected with the pursuit of these theoretical purposes. Since this work is almost entirely dependent on oral sources and on memory, questions emerge about the structure and reliability of memory and about the nature of the interview process itself—a problem that occupies the middle (and perhaps hybrid) ground between epistemology and linguistic philosophy, on the one hand, and more orthodox historiography on the other. For the problem that we face arises not so much out of the interpretation of data as in its creation. And because the interview process is above all linguistic, language itself becomes a methodological problem.

Superficially, of course, Kord and I shared the same language: everyday English. Moreover, Kord's cultural and social background is fairly close to that of my own family, so that, even if the results of this study might be called ethnographic, the environment I chose to study was familiar. Thus, in the collaboration that we undertook, I brought my own curiosity, informed and disciplined by a specific body of knowledge, a theoretical framework, and a rudimentary method of investigation. To these Kord added his own background in history and theory, the consequences of his father's Socialist culture, his mother's broad intellectual and cultural interests, his own schooling, his intellectual experience in the Socialist party, and, above all, his experience not merely as a participant but as the architect of Local 229. Because of Kord's cosmopolitan, rationalist background, we were able to establish a theoretical framework within which to discuss and interpret such cultural phenomena as the differences between Polish immigrants and their children. Such a theoretical framework is a vital necessity if a discussion is to get beyond the primitive stage of collecting anecdotes.

Yet in spite of this common ground, we initially had considerable difficulty with language and meaning: for history as a discipline has its own language, its canon of interpretation, its collection of problems occupying the forefront of contemporary inquiry. And my approach, a Hegelian Marxism greatly influenced by phenomenology, linguistic philosophy, and structuralism, at first only intensified this problem. Yet if the work of generating a theoretically meaningful account of the development of Kord's local union was to progress, a common language had to emerge out of our collaboration, one whose logic and terms of description would be clear and unambiguous to each of us, and within the framework of which our discussion could proceed with precision. While explicit discussion of theory would help to clarify the problems that I was concerned with, the actual emergence of our common language, and its verification, came only after months of "practice."[3] If at first our discussions seemed unclear and unfocused—if we had difficulty understanding each other—by the mid-point of our collaboration we had arrived at a sufficiently clear language and had eliminated a number of extraneous or irrelevant avenues of investigation, so that both question and answer seemed increasingly to be complementary moments in a more integrated historical discourse involving the two of us. The clarify of theoretical focus that developed, in fact, was an important part of the development of our common language.

It was within the framework of linguistic interaction that "data" was produced: since few facts existed, we had to create them. This is less arbitrary than it seems. A census enumerator, for example, does not merely collect data. Rather, standing behind him are not only the census

bureau and its staff of statisticians, but also a cultural matt
administrative purpose which give a specific shape to certain pe
of family structure, nationality, education, etc. Likewise, a ni
account is hardly "factual"; it is a reporter's impression, which is
outcome of his predisposition to view people and situations in a certain
way. Even the "obvious" fact that there were a certain number of paid-up
members in the union at a particular time is a fact only because someone
looked at the situation in a certain way and made an observation. (Even
such hard observations can dissolve into a welter of complex, uncertain
shadings and contradictory meanings when one begins to focus more
closely on the phenomenology of social processes.) If, for example, the
designer of the census was oblivious to the fact that Lutheran Slovaks
lived in a different cultural, political, and social world than Catholic
Slovaks, and that Bohemian Freethinkers were quite unlike both, the
resulting category, Czechoslovak, is not only limited in its historical usefulness, but is misleading and mythological.

Thus, the historian who deals with artifacts is restricted to bringing his
own intellectual apparatus to bear, not on the object itself (an epistemo-
logical fantasy at any rate), but on another object: the result of a previous
process of abstraction. The limitations of depending on traditional sources
are therefore obvious. . . .

How reliable is Kord's memory? This is a problem that encompasses
any oral history project, and it must be dealt with forthrightly. Kruchko
has observed that, in his interviews with veterans of the struggle to organize UAW Local 674 in Norwood, Ohio, "the memories of the men . . .
even down to small details, were surprisingly accurate."[4] I found the
same to be true of Kord. The depth and intensity of his involvement was
such that even now, thirty-six years later, his remembrances are both
vivid and detailed.

Nevertheless, memory does not provide us with the kind of pinpoint
accuracy found in documentary evicence. Kord's margin of error in the
precontract period, he estimates, is of the order of several days to two
weeks. Thus, I refer to a meeting which was held during the last part of
February, for example. How important such a margin of error is depends
upon how well Kord could recall the dramatic sequence of events not only
in terms of order, but also in terms of the tempo and dynamic of development. In this regard Kord's memory was generally clear and unambiguous, and he was quite certain of all but a handful of minor points.
Nevertheless, in addition to the external verification, which was found in
the few sources that relate to Local 229 and which appears in the footnotes, a system of internal checking was also used. As the broad picture
began to emerge in the course of our discussions and correspondence, I in
effect "cross-examined" Kord. In general, the contradictions that I found

were relatively minor, more often than not based on misunderstandings. In addition, these contradictions were ironed out early in the course of our work: Kord, having become deeply involved in this endeavor, began to do his own checking. Wherever any uncertainty has remained, it is indicated.

Yet if the contents of memory are simply "facts" as discussed above, we would find ourselves in the same situation that obtains when dealing with more orthodox sources. But while the structure of memory is related to the structure of perception and the latter is itself rooted in culture, education, and experience (native American informants, for example, are extraordinarily unperceptive about Slavs), memory itself is a vast welter of impressions and feelings, as well as a more structured, rational schemata. Many impressions either were not important to Kord in 1937 or did not appear to make any sense; yet, as we brought them to the foreground their possible interconnectedness and meaning emerged. Furthermore, the elaboration of this matrix of meaning and the gradual construction of the history of the local reacted back upon the original source, Kord's memory. As a consequence, Kord's recollections became richer and more precise, and the elaboration of a number of hypotheses gave a critical focus to his effort to recall. And precisely because memory is richer than the rational narrative superstructure to which it is often reduced, the whole enterprise remained open-ended: there were numerous ways of structuring the material. What it would become depended on how we approached our work, what leads we followed, and what problems concerned us. For example, I continued to press for cultural and psychological data on as many workers as Kord could remember, especially the primary and secondary leadership. Certain Freudian and Weberian concerns led me to ask particular kinds of questions (e.g., about personal habits such as drinking). These questions themselves emerged in my own thought only over a period of many months, and the responses to them were by no means immediately intelligible. I was looking for patterns and relationships. At first, however, the material was necessarily fragmentary; then, after more such questions and answers had accumulated, the material became less fragmentary, but it was still difficult to penetrate. Only gradually did patterns emerge relating some characteristics of personality with certain aspects of the history of the local.

Two further examples help clarify the relationship between memory and theory. In the course of our first series of discussions in December 1972, Kord made a remark about "new hires" in department 19 (in the spring of 1937). The remark registered, but I let it go by. Later, as we continued to discuss the situation in the plant, "new hires" came up again. What gave the department where these employees worked its peculiar character was the fact that they were members of neighborhood gangs. Yet what I had at this point was not a concept of a social group, but rather the understanding that very likely these gang kids were in fact a group, that they had to be studied further, and that out of all this a concept might emerge. In the next series of discussions and in the seventy-five pages of letters that I sent to Kord, whenever relevant I brought up questions relating to these young workers. What did they say to the foreman under certain circumstances? What forms of recreation did they engage in? Where did they live, and under what circumstances? What were their attitudes toward the union effort at specific times? How did they react to the five-cent raise? The results of such inquiry are contained in the body of the book.

Another determination I sought out more purposefully. I was convinced that there were significant ethical or moral differences between the Appalachian migrants, the first-generation Slavs, and the wildcatters among the second generation. Twice in the course of our second series of discussions (July 1973) I raised this question. Twice Kord replied negatively. The third time, however, something clicked. Kord briefly but cogently described actual confrontations, quoted typical statements made by representative members of the three groups, and described the interrelationship of these groups within the union and their different relationships to the leadership in confrontation situations. Further, he discussed their varying attitudes toward authority, both that of the management and that of the union leaders, and their conceptions of society, of the individual, and of standards of behavior.

This example illustrates both the obstacles to and the immense potential of this kind of investigation. The process of searching, guessing, hypothesizing, and probing that the historian must undertake depends for its success on the degree to which his collaborator is willing to get involved in these questions. Often the relevance of what I asked was not obvious, and some of the more exciting questions were obscure and even ambiguous. To make sense out of some of my questions required that Kord search his memory for any evidence that might have had a bearing on the question, sort it out, and verbalize it. If these cultural differences were not clear at the time, then Kord's cognitive processes did not organize his perceptions along such lines. Such an organization of perceptions, drawn from the complex welter of memory, was precisely what I asked of Kord. And it was here that a real dialectic unfolded, in the course of which we collectively shaped both concept and perception, batting ideas and observations around exploring their significance, and conceiving of new questions as material developed.

From the foregoing, it is obvious that, if certain problems are to be explored at all, they must be investigated through the use of oral history techniques: the usual sources that historians traditionally rely upon simply fail to throw any light on some of the most fundamental historical processes. Yet even in those areas of data collection where the census is thought to excel, oral history techniques are far more accurate than any but the most accurate hypothetical census. For example, we have already seen one of the problems with the census—its tendency to amalgamate under a single category (such as Czechoslovak) several distinct and often contradictory social groups. Beyond this, however, even if the ethnic composition of a factory were known to a high degree of precision, its relevance would remain dubious. Of what value would be the knowledge that 30 percent of the workers in a particular plant were Polish, if we knew from previous investigations that this geographical unit was far too large to be meaningful? On the other hand, the response of an informant that a single department, say metal-finishing, possessed a work force that was 90 percent Polish might be off by a few points, or even by as much as 10 or 15 percent, but it would be far closer to the truth than the census estimate, which would be unable to go any farther than specifying that 30 percent of the workers *in the plant* were Polish. When one realizes that each department possessed a very specialized ethnic structure, it becomes obvious that if one is to write the social history of the organization of a factory, one must have this information; and from the standpoint of the historian, such data, regardless of the greater margin of error of this technique, is far more useful and indeed, from a historiographical standpoint, far more accurate than the results of a hypothetical census based on plant-wide surveys.[5]

To meaningfully describe patterns of behavior or to analyze the structure of an event are objectives that often lie beyond the reach of orthodox uses of data, particularly when one's interest shifts from the various intellectual, social, and political elites to the industrial working class. In the present study, for example, a critical union action inside the plant is met with strikingly different positive responses on the part of the first- and the second-generation Poles. Such occurrences provide invaluable materials out of which to develop a sense of the interaction of the various political cultures within the plant—or they even permit one to define such cultures in the first place.

Nevertheless, in the conduct of a series of interviews it is important to maintain a critical attitude. Failure to cross-examine can lead to astonishing reversals of fact. For example, in an interview by Jack Skeels of Frank Fagan, a unionist active in the Murray Body plant during the formative years of the UAW, an entirely different story emerges from that found in my own interviews with Fagan.[6] In the Skeels version, an incident in 1933 in which Fagan organized a petition campaign among thirty welders asking for company-supplied leather armlets to protect their clothing and arms from red-hot sparks resulted in the firing of Fagan and another worker. This event, according to Fagan, "broke the back of the men." In this section of the interview, Skeels himself intervened very infrequently, resulting in long periods of unbroken reminiscences which were left to stand as they were, with no effort made at cross-examination or elicitation of detail. Unprepared for what was to follow, I reopened the question of the leather armlet incident with Fagan, mainly in order to investigate the ethnic background of the workers involved and the structure of the event. This eighteen-minute section of the interview began with a discussion of the year. Fagan thought that it was 1935. I told him that in his previous interview he had said 1933. He was unable to remember that interview, but began to fix the leather armlet incident in relation to other events, finally settling on 1935 as the most likely year. The story then unfolded in great detail; I constantly asked for more bits of information—the names of people, descriptions of the welding process and the problem it posed in terms of burning holes in the welders' shirts, etc. Then I asked Fagan to remember as many individuals as he could who were working on the same line and who got involved in the petition incident. At this point the interview makes for poor reading: long periods of silence, punctuated first by one name—about whom I asked such details as ethnic background and union experience—then by another name, the whole liberally sprinkled with remarks by Fagan that this was a long time back and was hard to remember, yet at the same time that he could visualize all of the welders involved in the incident. Nevertheless, he succeeded in remembering eight others besides himself. He described the incident itself: the misgivings of many of the workers about signing the petition, its delivery, and the response of the personnel manager to Fagan and his coworker Udata as he politely threw them out onto the street. From this point on, however, the story directly contradicts the earlier version told to Skeels. Following the firing of Fagan and Udata, some of the welders began a job action, letting the arcs of flame get too big and burning holes in the automobile bodies, as a result of which production of the entire plant was piling up in the repair shop. The foreman told all the welders to go home and to behave themselves when they returned the next day. Alex Faulkner replied (as was reported to Fagan a few days later) that Fagan and Udata both better be at work too. Within a couple of days the company had gotten in touch with Fagan and rehired him. When Fagan returned to work, however, the other workers wanted to know where Udata was, and Fagan, after a visit to Udata's home, ascertained that Udata had gotten another job, not wanting to return to Murray Body. Only then did the tension subside.

The point of retelling this story is to illustrate some of the pitfalls of writing oral history. Memory is a treacherous thing, as more than one of my informants has remarked. The necessity for cross-examination, digging for details, and even confronting an interviewee with contradictory evidence, is critical. It is important *before* the interview to get deeply into the documentary materials relevant to an interviewee's experience, to anticipate several strategies of questioning, and to be prepared with a battery of questions that are derived from the historian's special understanding of social phenomena. It is equally necessary to be alert to the possibility that an offhand remark may contain an important clue, the consequences of which may be totally unexpected and even contrary to some basic assumptions. In general, the historian must counterpose his *intensive* approach to the *extensive* narrative that tends to be the spontaneous response of most informants. Thus, in the Skeels interviews, there are numerous junctures in which an informant reveals something of critical significance. Instead of interceding and sharpening the focus of the discussion, Skeels let these things go by. In fairness of Skeels, of course, we should remember that many of these theoretical concerns are of recent origin. Nevertheless, as the leather armlet incident indicates, there may be some question about the accuracy of interviews conducted in an expansive narrative style, rather than through intensive cross-examination.

Notes

1. This evidence includes Constance S. Tonat, "A Case Study of a Local Union: Participation, Loyalty and Attitudes of Local Union Members" (M.A. thesis, Wayne State University, Detroit, 1956), which is based on a study of Local 229; a few brief notices which appeared in the *United Automobile Worker* between 1938 and 1940; and a collection of correspondence found in the George F. Addes Papers on deposit at the Archives of Labor History and Urban Affairs at Wayne State University (henceforth cited as Archives).

2. The material contained in the Archives pertaining to Local 229 is sparse. Even in regard to two of the most thoroughly documented locals—Local 51 (Plymouth) and Local 3 (Dodge)—the materials available are of such character as to render impossible any attempt at answering the questions posed in the present study.

3. The problem of language as practice in this sense is one of the central points of Ludwig Wittgenstein, *Philosophical Investigations* (Oxford: Basil Blackwell, 1963).

4. John G. Kruchko, *The Birth of a Union Local: The History of UAW Local 674, Norwood, Ohio, 1933–1940* (Ithaca, N. Y.: New York State School of Industrial and Labor Relations, Cornell University, 1972),p.iii.

5. The following is an example of the generation of data. The excerpts are from my interview with Frank Fagan of August 9, 1974. Fagan was active in Murray Body during the formative years of the UAW.

FAGAN: In Murray there was a predominance of Polish people. And I always had the feeling that they—although I don't know this to be a fact—they're all pretty close. Nearly all lived in Hamtramck, which was near by. . . . There seemed to be a predominance of Polish—I realized that when I first got active in the union when we actually got recognized and I had to keep book as a steward.

FRIEDLANDER: Steward in the welding department?

FAGAN: Well, the body in white. I covered quite a large building. I'm talking now about after we organized the union . . . later 1937, late '36. I know I had a predominance of Polish there, because I had trouble with the names. . . .

FRIEDLANDER: When you shouldered union responsibilities and you were going around and checking up on people, how widely did you travel in body in white?

FAGAN: The whole thing.

FRIEDLANDER: I assume you know that best then?

FAGAN: Yeah. . . .

FRIEDLANDER: I find that there's a lot of Hungarians floating around metal-finishing. Now is that true here?

FAGAN: I, I don't . . . I'm sitting here thinking about the metal-finishing gang, all the guys on the different floors that I knew. I don't recall a metal finisher that wasn't a great big strong Polish fella in Murray Body.

FRIEDLANDER: So they're all Polish in Murray Body?

FAGAN: Yeah. Come to think of it. . . . I'm just thinking about all the lists of names of the metal finishers, because I used to list them for wage negotiations, always trying to get them up higher.

FRIEDLANDER: I just want to double-check something. There's no chance of your confusing a Polish name with some other Slavic nationality?

FAGAN: There's that possibility, but not very great possibility. I knew everyone.

FRIEDLANDER: Between Yugoslav on the one hand, and Rumanian and Hungarian on the other hand. . . .

FAGAN: No, I don't think I could have made that mistake. There might have been some, but I doubt it very much. It just seems to me they were nearly all Polish. Even the foremen. . . . I don't think—I can't recall any one that I don't know—because we had a lot of affairs going where we needed their names and that sort of thing.

6. Interview with Frank Fagan, February 19, 1963, Archives, pp. 10–11.

14

Oral History and the California Wine Industry

Charles Morrissey

The design of an effective oral history project requires not only a knowl-edge of the key questions in your area but also a way to make sure these questions have been answered: evaluation. Yet the evaluation of oral his-tory on a project-by-project basis is relatively untried. When this essay ap-peared in 1977, it was the only published review of an entire oral history project.

Morrissey had conducted the sort of outside evaluation called for by Wil-liam Moss and other authors in this collection. Perhaps one reason for the scarcity of his procedure is the difficulty of finding the right evaluator, one who is trained in both the content area studied and in the profession of oral history.

By analyzing in depth one series of transcripts from a leading oral his-tory office, Morrissey raises questions—about editing, interview histories, and factual errors in transcripts—which apply to most oral history projects. Should editing involve rearranging the interview narrative? Should it in-clude questions and answers from subsequent correspondence? What are the most effective ways of correcting the interviewee's obvious errors of fact without putting words in his mouth?

A careful reading of this article will provide one set of answers to these questions. Reading this essay alongside the evaluation guidelines in part 7 will assist the practicioner in beginning a critique of previous work in his community and in raising the overall standards of oral history research.

Charles Morrissey has worked as an oral historian at the Truman and Kennedy libraries and directed interview projects for the Ford Foundation, Harvard University, and Dartmouth College. Currently he edits Vermont Life *magazine and teaches oral history at the University of Vermont.*

"Oral History and the California Wine Industry" appeared originally in Agricultural History *51 (July 1977), pp. 590–96.*

HISTORIANS WHO labor in the vineyards of scholarship have often been dubious about the growth of oral history. That uncertain crop, they say, usually brings a meager harvest. Time and weather can twist memory and spoil its true flavor. Oral history, in the judgment of some detractors, is hardly a rich source of nourishment; they dismiss it as producing only the junk food and cheap wine in Clio's cupboard.

But an oral historian has been laboring in the vineyards of California, and the grapes she has harvested are now available as mellow wine. She is Ruth Teiser, an interviewer for the Regional Oral History Office (ROHO) of the University of California at Berkeley, and a San Francisco journalist who has written about wines since the 1940s. As director of the California Wine Industry Oral History Project her task has been "to preserve the history of the California wine industry in the twentieth century through tape-recorded interviews with men who have had a formative influence upon the state's wine industry." She recorded twenty-four separate interviews in this series (a final memoir is still in process) and had them bound in twenty volumes (nineteen of which are now open for research).[1] The taste varies, understandably, from volume to volume, but none of these can be dismissed as cheap wine.

Fourteen of these memoirists have been major figures in the California wine industry since the Prohibition Era (1920–1933) and even before that "noble experiment" was launched. If one accepts Vincent P. Carosso's assertion in *The California Wine Industry: A Study of the Formative Years, 1830–1895* (University of California Press, 1951; rpt. 1976) that "between 1890 and the passage of the Eighteenth Amendment there were few major structural or commercial changes in the industry" (p. vii), the careers of these men link early California viticulture with its modern growth. The soaring popularity of California wines is one of the most dramatic trends in the recent history of American business, and per capita consumption may continue to rise until wines exceed spiritous liquors, perhaps as soon as 1980. All who savor California wines will recognize many of the names of these successful vintners—Martini (father and son), Petri, Wente, Gallo, Perelli-Minetti, Rossi, and Brother Timothy of Christian Brothers. Five of the other ten memoirists are viticulturists and enologists at the University of California (four at the Davis Campus, one at Berkeley) who have done much of the crucial research underlying the development of the California wine industry since 1933. Of the remaining five, two are bankers with the Bank of America in San Francisco, one is an attorney specializing in state and federal legislation affecting winemaking and sales, another is a wine merchant, and the last is a publicist who organized both the Wine Institute and the Wine Advisory Board and whose writing has done much to persuade Americans to drink California wines.

Funding of $37,600 for recording these interviews was provided by the Wine Advisory Board, which administers the marketing of wine in California under the authority of the California Department of Food and Agriculture. Credit for launching this series lies primarily with Ernest Gallo, although this is ironic because he was the only interviewee to close his transcript (until 1995), and Julio Gallo, his brother, was the only participant in the project to withdraw his copy. Actually, the degree of cooperation by long-time vintners was extraordinary: thirteen of the fourteen men identified as the most important of all prospective respondents did consent to interviews. The only person to demur was Walter E. Taylor, an organizer of California Fruit Industries in the 1930s, and his refusal is noted in several places so readers of this series will not fault the project director for overlooking a significant informant. Moreover, an alternative for Taylor, Philo Biane, was able to speak about matters which also figured in Taylor's career. Teiser wisely kept her interviewing focused on the key figures identified beforehand and avoided a deficiency of other oral history projects which recorded interviews with anybody who walked within distance of a microphone regardless of the role played in the events being documented. (Some oral historians are so captivated by electrical gadgetry that they have yet to distinguish between tape recorders and vacuum cleaners.)

This series of interviews is also noteworthy because it demonstrates how an industry or trade association can fund a project without inhibiting the oral historian who probes its history. It is a model for others to emulate. Several food and beverage producers in America should be urged to follow this ROHO example and commission oral history projects with major innovators and leaders in their industries. Time doesn't wait while this prospect is contemplated abstractly; among California winemakers the "actuarial imperative" (a euphemism used by oral historians at ROHO) has inexorably been in motion. Louis M. Martini, who was interviewed between 1969 and 1972, died in 1974; Edward A. Rossi, interviewed in 1971, died later that year; Victor Repetto, interviewed in 1970, suffered declining health shortly afterwards and left his transcript unedited when he died in 1973; Burke H. Critchfield of the Bank of America died six months after his interview in 1970; Professor William V. Cruess of Berkeley died one week after the transcripts of his seven interview sessions were delivered to him.

Oral historians who have recorded interviews on other aspects of American business might regret one oversight in the research design which encompasses these interviews. "These recollections are of particular value," Teiser writes, "because the Prohibition period saw the disruption of not only the industry itself but also the orderly recording and preservation of records of its activities." But apparently the early planners of this project did not intend to survey and describe what records do exist in order to ascertain how interviewees might be queried about confusion in them, or how gaps might be filled by first-person testimony. From time to time interviewees refer to such printed sources and thereby guide historians to valuable holdings. Brother Timothy, for one, cites the *St. Helena Star* as a source for Napa Valley history over the past one hundred years: "I believe that their files are absolutely complete from the first day they started to print." Professor Harold P. Olmo of Davis remarks that he has kept notes and diaries of all his trips abroad. Records pertaining to passage of the Wine Control Act of 1935 (which Lucius Powers describes in his memoir) and other federal enactments affecting the industry should be examined and described. A survey of archival sources is a plodding and undramatic task but essential for those who view oral history as basically an effort to supplement and enrich existing documentation. Fortunately Teiser did thorough preparation for these interviews in published materials.

As products of one of the most professional and experienced oral history offices in the United States these transcripts are neatly and expertly presented. Yet one wonders if the practices developed at ROHO warrant broader systematization to assure that a large number of transcripts reflect more consistency in format. Editing, for instance, usually retains the spoken character of the actual interviews as recorded on tape, but the eight sessions with Louis M. Martini are transcribed into a single narrative with portions rearranged from the original sequence in which they were recorded. Also, some of the questions and answers are extracted from written exchanges, not from the dialogue on tape. The result is a final document which varies from the materials assembled to create it.

In other transcripts, however, portions are footnoted to alert readers to more reminiscences on the same topics which can be found elsewhere in the same volumes. The editing of these memoirs did not entail a reordering of passages to put them in a sequence based on progression from one subject to another. In some instances the portions lie many pages apart because the conversations moved to other matters before returning to the subjects which merited more elaboration. These cross references are helpful, but annotation of passages which are murky and cry for elucidation, or which would benefit by editorial comment citing sources elsewhere in the literature bearing on what the interviewees discuss, might also be worthwhile.

This suggestion isn't as simple as it appears because editorial comments which imply that a respondent's memory is faulty won't please the memoirist—and he is free to withdraw totally from the oral history process if he is discomfited by the way the experience damages his own idea of his ability to remember accurately and speak coherently. In many oral history projects the interviewer, as editor, tries deftly to resolve these uncertainties in the text by proposing alternative ways to phrase passages in the transcripts. This in turn raises problems for the readers of transcripts—the ultimate consumers of the oral history harvest—because the respondents have had their memories improved for them by a diligent interviewer-editor who has embodied his own scholarly knowledge in transcripts without signifying to readers how this has upgraded the original versions on tape.

In this series of interviews on the California wine industry the problem arises most notably in the interview with Maynard Amerine, an enologist at Davis. He remarks that a congressman from either North Carolina or South Carolina—he can't remember his name or specific state—was a prohibitionist who vehemently opposed wine research by the U.S. Department of Agriculture and was able to prevent federal funding of enology from being authorized in the USDA budget appropriation. Should the oral historian have done thorough research on this congressman and informed the respondent of the findings so a specific identification could be inserted into the first draft of the transcript? Or instead of clarifying the respondent's memory should the oral historian have conveyed the findings in a footnote and leave the actual passage unrevised? Or should the footnote point out that Leon Adams says on page 30 of his book, *The Wines of America* (Boston, Houghton Mifflin, 1973), that the congressman who played this role was Clarence Cannon of Missouri?

The practice of identifying factual errors in Introductions to each volume—in this series usually prepared by Professor Amerine—can create problems as well as provide guidance. Amerine notes that Horace O. Lanza in his memoir confused Paso Robles with the Paicines Area ninety miles to the north, but surprisingly, in a series about harvesting grapes for wine, nobody detected Lanza's other error, on page 59 of his transcript, where he attributes the origin of the famous Concord grape to Concord, New Hampshire, instead of Concord, Massachusetts.

The custom of writing an "Interview History" for each respondent has limited value, moreover, because tactful interviewers express themselves cautiously, or obliquely, in order not to offend memoirists by commenting frankly about their inability to remember clearly, speak articulately, and edit sensibly. An "Interview History" which is critical might, in the interest of fairness, be balanced by a rejoinder written by the interviewee. But this might jeopardize the rapport so carefully nurtured from the time the prospect of an oral history interview was first broached. An interviewer who represents an interviewee as disingenuous might be rebutted by the interviewee accusing the interviewer of becoming giddy during the interview because the wine served as a refreshment was too heady to absorb. Interviews, like wine glasses, are easily up-ended and sent spilling. In this series the "Interview History" prepared for Burke Critcu. field's transcript seems more candid than the others; if this impression is valid can it be explained because Critchfield was no longer alive to read it?

The vignettes which emerge from these interviews should be treasured by scholars who write about the California wine industry. Sometimes a phrase illuminates a personality—Leon Adams recalls the mercurial Louis M. Martini exclaiming "And if you agree with me, I'll change my mind!" Many scenes are depicted more vividly than formal records could possibly suggest. Harry Baccigaluppi describes how he brought Anglo and Chicano laborers together for Christmas parties in Delano despite the warnings of his foremen that boisterous behavior might get beyond control and ruin this venture to lessen intergroup tension. Jefferson Peyser recounts how as a young attorney attending a meeting of vintners in San Francisco in the 1930s he proposed that they call themselves "wine growers" instead of "wine manufacturers." "Well," he remembers, "you could have heard the laughter all the way to Los Angeles." But they indulged their young legal adviser and told him to revise the terminology if he could persuade legislators to change the language in the statutes. He did so, and a few years later, during World War II, the Office of Price Administration greatly aided the industry when it recognized the wine men as "growers" instead of "manufacturers," and their products as agricultural commodities instead of manufactured items.

Most revealing in these memoirs is the picture of the wine industry when Prohibition was repealed in 1933: "we were just about at the same point in 1934 as they were in 1880 when the viticultural work started," recalls Professor A. J. Winkler of Davis. "They thought anything wrapped up in a grape skin would make wine." Maynard Joslyn echoes this: "We were amazed at the large numbers of inept winemakers in the field, and these had to be trained." Ernest Wente describes this situation from the viewpoint of the producers: "They got their wines infected and when they were shipped to the East, why California received one of the worst reputations. Bum stuff." Brother Timothy remembers that he was chosen in 1935 to be the wine chemist for the Christian Brothers in Napa because he was teaching high-school chemistry (along with English and Religion) at the time and that served as his major qualification for the assignment.

The quest for respectability was arduous. Leon Adams quotes one of the Giannini brothers at the Bank of America—he can't remember which one—as saying, "Oh, these wine men. They're just a bunch of ex-bootleggers!" Jefferson Peyser felt Washington bureaucrats were equally unkind: "The federal people absolutely in my opinion at least, for ten years after Repeal, still treated the industry as though they were a bunch of bootleggers." But the story has a happy outcome. Philo Biane, a southern-California vintner, expressed it with a measure of eloquence:

"The wine business of the United States—not only California, but *all* the wine business of all our states that are making wine—has now moved into its rightful position of being a very honorable profession, and not only that, one that is looked upon with envy because it is a profession that lends itself to the dignity of man. We are using things that are made available to us—the grapes, the sunshine, the water—everything that is involved in wine making. You create something from this that is enjoyed by the masses. It's gratifying. I am thankful that I have endured long enough to see this take place, because for many years I didn't know if we were going to make it or not."

While Sidney Block provides an informative memoir about selling wines, one wishes there was more in this series about how wine has been advertised and marketed as a suitable item for the American palate. The records of advertising agencies and the memories of advertising executives contain valuable information about the foods and fluids which Americans consume, but unfortunately this material is not being preserved adequately by archivists and oral historians. Otto E. Meyer of the Paul Masson vineyards mentions in his interview how physicians have been urged to speak well of wine as a health-inducing tonic, but this campaign to win medical endorsements is not recounted in detail by any of these memoirists.

The transcripts will be appreciated by scholars interested in the history of Italian immigration to the United States and in many other topics not related to the wine industry. Antonio Perelli-Minetti, for example, planted vines in Mexico and conferred over breakfast with Pancho Villa just before his raid on Columbus, New Mexico: "Villa hated the Americans, and I could get anything because to him I was still an Italian." Horace Lanza has a revealing segment about how his Italian-born mother believed in traditional roles for males and females when she was raising her family in Fredonia, New York. If her sons showed any interest in household chores she would berate them. "And she'd say, 'Get out of here! Get out of here!' She'd say, 'By jingo, even if I am dead and gone and I hear that you're going to wear dresses and let some poor woman's daughter do the man's work, I'll get up from my grave and raise hell with you." And she meant it. [Laughter]"

These nineteen bound volumes vary in price from eighteen dollars to thirty-three dollars and may be ordered from ROHO. The total number of pages is 2,063. To date copies of the hard-bound volumes are already available at six other libraries in California and at the University of Wyoming and the National Agricultural Library in Beltsville, Maryland. Since ROHO is planning to make all of its unrestricted oral history transcripts accessible on microfilm and microfiche through the *New York Times* Oral History Program it will soon be possible for libraries everywhere to obtain the California wine series at a lesser price. For any scholar who wants to update the history of the California wine industry by writing a sequel to Carosso's book the wider availability of these transcripts will be a helpful service.

Hubert Howe Bancroft would be pleased to know that ROHO, as a division of The Bancroft Library, has preserved the memories of these major figures in the California wine industry. In his quest a century ago to preserve the recollections of early Californians, such as Governor Juan Alvarado, Bancroft covered expenses by offering gifts of wine fermented from California grapes. ROHO continues to document California's history in similar fashion, and a hearty and sparkling glass raised to toast this achievement is surely appropriate. ROHO tills a fertile vineyard, and the labor is productive.

Note

1. Regional Oral History Office, Bancroft Library, The California Wine Industry Oral History Project, interviews conducted by Ruth Teiser, 23 interviews in 19 vol., 1971–1976 (bound indexed volumes are available to scholars for research and to manuscript libraries for deposit, $500 the set; for further information, contact ROHO, Room 486, Bancroft Library, University of California, Berkeley, Calif. 94720).

15

Reflections on Ethics
Amelia Fry

*The final essay on designing oral history discusses ethics, a part of proj-
ect design often overlooked in the initial stages of planning. The national
scandal concerning Richard Nixon's presidency provides the backdrop for
this statement by Amelia Fry, veteran interviewer of twenty-four years' experience.*

*Taking in turn the rights and responsibilities of interviewees, interview-
ers, and institutions, Fry discusses the dilemmas that arise daily during efforts to work within the principled guidelines of the profession, the Goals
and Guidelines of the Oral History Association included in part 7 of this
volume. The author sets up a dialogue with the reader, posing real-life difficulties which bedevil professional oral historians. Like Friedlander, Fry
recognizes the collaborative nature of the oral history process, which requires interviewers—as the more experienced partners—to educate narrators
as to the implications of their accounts. Just as doctors try to obtain an
"informed consent" before operations, so oral historians should be sensitive
to the danger of victimizing or harming interviewees in the quest for historical fact.*

*Amelia Fry has conducted interviews and directed projects for the Re-
gional Oral History Office at the University of California, Berkeley, since
1959. She has taught oral history institutes and workshops for the Oral History Association and the University of Vermont and has contributed articles
on oral history to a wide variety of professional journals. She is presently
writing a biography of Alice Paul, a spin-off from her oral history project
on the Suffragists.*

"Reflections on Ethics" first appeared in the Oral History Review 3
(1975), pp. 17–28.

*Reflection: an action of the mind whereby we obtain a clearer view of
our relation to the things of yesterday and are able to avoid the perils
that we shall not again encounter.*
—Ambrose Bierce, The Devil's Dictionary

WATERGATE HAS made us question anew the ethics governing American life. Oral history, too, has received its share of scrutiny. Although stemming partially from Watergate, it has also sprung from an accumulation of questions oral historians have evolved from years of collective experience.

Uncertainty about fair practices was a recurring theme of the 1974 Oral History Workshop and Colloquium at Jackson Lake Lodge. Discussions ranged from lively rump sessions in the lobby to hushed debates in hallways outside the meetings, to the formal sessions themselves. One of the first acts of the new president, Samuel Proctor, was to appoint a committee to revise, and, if necessary, augment the OHA's present one-page statement of ethics called *Goals and Guidelines.*

A concrete ethical question related to the Nixon tapes has confronted some individual oral historians. They have been called upon to provide affidavits verifying that inaccuracies are inherent in interpretation when the transcriptions cannot be checked against their tapes—the one precept that probably would receive unanimous agreement by all OHA members who have ever checked a transcript with its tape. The underlying issue here is whether the question of public access to the Nixon tapes is relevant to oral history. Consider the facts that the tapes are conversations recorded with knowledge of the President (the person in charge of taping) but kept secret from others being taped; that the conversations were released only by the person who taped, in disregard of any wishes of those unknowingly recorded. Should an oral historian allow himself to be called upon, *as an oral historian,* for an opinion that will facilitate the public release of tape recordings produced in a manner that violates the code passed unanimously by the OHA? Does OHA's *Goals and Guidelines* give him, in fact, any relevant goals and guides for this question? Should it?

Part of the confusion is voiced in the guidelines' initial statement (a sort of preamble) as a fact of life: oral historians have a dual nature as both producers and users of the tapes. To quote in full:

The Oral History Association recognizes Oral History for what it is—a method of gathering a body of historical information in oral form usually on tape. Because the scholarly community is involved in both the production and use of oral history, the Association recognizes an opportunity and an obligation on the part of all concerned to make this type of historical source as authentic and as useful as possible.

It is this inherent schizophrenia that gives us two views of the Nixon tapes. As users, we want them made available to the public. As producers, we can never approve of the methods used by the White House.

The main body of the ethics document is organized around a sort of Trinity: the researcher, the interviewee, and the sponsoring institution. The fact that there is a set of guidelines for each of the three implies reciprocal do's and don'ts. A basic question is, Are they a delineation of principles precise enough to apply to concrete situations, and broad enough to cover all varieties of oral history and changing techniques?

Saith Guideline Number One, on behalf of the interviewee:

The person who is interviewed should be selected carefully and his wishes must govern the conduct of the interview.

This guideline was written in the belief that it takes two to produce an interview and that they should have equal rights. In addition to the philosophical underpinnings, this one has a practical base, too: you are not likely to have a good session if your interview is not conducted in agreement with the basic arrangements. In addition, it stands also as a reminder to those of us who come to feel that it is *my* interview, *my* skillful technique that elicits the answers—a point of view that results from our abiding concern with interviewing techniques. However, the information we are after is the interviewee's. It is in her memory cells and frequently in her private files. If she wants something sealed for five years, that is her prerogative and your responsibility. And, as William Manchester will sadly attest, her prerogatives and desires should be agreed upon beforehand, lest tremors of disagreements and even litigation fall upon your head afterward. Number Two says as much:

Before undertaking a taped interview for the purpose stated above, the interviewee (or narrator) should be clear in his mind regarding mutual rights with respect to tapes and transcripts made from them. This includes such things as: seal privileges, royalties, literary rights, prior use, fiduciary relationships, the right to edit the tape transcriptions, and the right to determine whether the tape is to be disposed of or preserved.

One might note that if our former president had followed that procedure, the taped evidence in the Watergate cover-up would have been quite different, or—more likely—not created in the first place.

Many oral history offices now send to the prospective interviewee an informal agreement letter, which is signed by each party and which spells out these rights and conditions for each reference by each party during the course of the interview; others simply tape record the agreement at the first session.

If the interviewee wants a passage sealed, this means you have to remove the sealed passage from your transcription to locked storage with the opening date noted, then, if you wish to keep one available for public access, erase that portion from a tape which you have copied. The original tape you lock up with the sealed pages of the transcript. True, precious staff time is required for searching out the place and going through this process. In addition, the sealed passage presumably resides in your memory cells and must be held there with no leaks.

However clear-cut this guideline appears, a "yes, but" (hereafter called a yesbut) arises when the material on the tape is likely to backfire on the interviewee, or to damage your project or your institution—and she does not want it sealed. An example (partly fictitious):

When you interview Professor Curt, recently deposed from the deanship, she criticizes another professor with an eloquence that is born only of a person wronged. The controversy is still warm; you can see that these transcripts would create history right on the spot if the interview is released, and you envision a sudden escalation of the strife, with a spin-off of secondary charges that the oral history office is doing at least one portion of the faculty no good. Or, even if the oral history office survives the controversy, a certain sector on campus will view the transcript as a collection of unsubstantiated accusations and will demand to tape its side—and that disrupts the office budget for the year. In addition, future narrators in other subjects would be more inhibited, less candid, after witnessing this spectacle.

So, are you being irresponsible if you leave the material open for anyone to use: the opposition, the campus newspaper, or the local daily bugle?

You point out to Professor Curt that she could be dismissed, that jobs are hard to find, that she should seal it for a couple of years. She says absolutely not, that this is the way she was railroaded and she wants the world to know—now.

Is it ethical to press for sealing, as your part of the mutual right? You could seal it unilaterally, of course, but that would be an open disregard of her privilege as a coauthor with equal rights. Although in many projects, like the Berkeley office, either party has the *legal* right to seal, the question here concerns ethics, not legalities.

If it comes to a choice, would you risk sacrificing your project on the altar of that first guideline—*her* wishes "governing the conduct of the interview"? Should this guideline be softened, perhaps, to read wishes "*mutually arrived at* governing the use of the interview"?

A stickier yesbut is, What do you do when she gives you information that is confidential and that she refuses to put on tape? It is presumably for your ears only and important as background. You probably make a note of it, mark it confidential, and stick it in your own private files. *Should* you write it down? Can you keep it in your private papers that are then sealed for your lifetime—or a time specified far enough in the future that the reasons for the confidentiality will no longer exist? In the meantime, should you use it as a source on which to base a line of questions when interviewing someone else? Off-tape information is not specifically dealt with in the guidelines. Perhaps it should be.

Probably most of the infractions of guideline number 2 issue from the oral historian's chronic disease of insufficient time: we are in a hurry and neglect to schedule a period with the narrator in which we make clear to her what her options are and negotiate the agreement before interviewing. Sometimes the legal agreements are themselves cause for quandaries. For example:

Shortly after completing the taping, your interviewee has a stroke and is too debilitated to sign the final agreement. The transcript and the agreement fall into the hands of a conservator who is either incompetent, over-protective, or suspicious. You realize he is never going to sign. You are caught between two commitments: one to the interviewee to finish processing her interview and deposit it as she expected you to do (a responsibility that may also extend to a granting foundation that underwrote the project); on the other hand you are legally committed not to release it until she or her conservator sign.

And there is the now-classic oral history nightmare in projects that transcribe: What happens when the interviewee dies and the agreement is there on her desk awaiting her signature? You have, again, a responsibility to her to finish it and make it available, but you are legally restrained from doing so.

The third guideline for the memoirist can be evoked to help her distinguish between an oral history interview for an archive or serious research as opposed to a television-type interview for entertainment:

It is important that the interviewee fully understand the project, and that in view of costs and effort involved he assumes a willingness to give useful information on the subject being pursued.

Underlying this is the recognition that your own preparation alone can never achieve the rich tapestry of overtones, the warp and woof of interrelationships, the unexpected leads that you can get only if you have a serious and well-prepared narrator.

The second section of the trinity—the guidelines for the interviewer— is also riddled with yesbuts. It begins by providing a procedural goal rather than an ethical guideline:

It should be the objective of the interviewer to gather information that will be of scholarly usefulness in the present and the future.

Then follows an attempt to reconcile the dual and sometimes conflicting nature of the oral historian as both creator and consumer of his product:

The interviewer who is collecting oral history materials for his own individual research should always bear in mind this broader objective.

All of us are depressingly familiar with the limitations of time and funding that most researchers have to accept. Visualize an interviewer who is teaching half-time, doing faculty committee work half-time, and supposedly using another half to write a book on the migratory farm workers in the Imperial Valley of California. She tape records Caesar Chavez. She may not have the time to expand the interview to include the childhood of Chavez or the broader story of Chavez's efforts nationwide. Again, the interviewer's commitments conflict: the Guidelines Number One is pitted against her obligations to her institution and publisher to use her time efficiently and keep her research to the point. Yet the archives will be the poorer in that collection of transcripts or tapes that she will eventually donate.[1] Dealing as it does with a basically irreconcilable dichotomy produced by one researcher wearing two hats, this guideline is probably as precise as is realistically possible. To "always *bear in mind* this broader objective" is as much as anyone can demand from the harassed interviewer-writer.

Number Two stems from the perennial question, "How much research is enough?" and also from the recognition that broad variations in interview preparation exist among the diversity of projects, each embodying different goals. The statement reads:

In order to obtain a tape of maximum worth as a historical document, it is incumbent upon the interviewer to be thoroughly grounded in the background and experiences of the person being interviewed, to select the interviewee carefully, and, where appropriate and if at all feasible, to review the papers of the interviewee before conducting the interview. In conducting the interview, an effort should be made to provide enough information to the interviewee to assist his recall.

If you are funded with a sufficient grant over several years and a staff of graduate students, you may research every scrap of relevant paper and produce an unsurpassable oral history memoir, as has been done in *Tom Rivers, Reflections on a Life in Medicine and Science.*[2] It is a magnificent use of oral history. Forrest Pogue from his intensive research and years of interviewing is producing a multivolume biography of General George Marshall that is the ultimate in scholarship.[3]

Most of us, however, dig down in our pockets and realize that we have to settle for less grant money, fewer staff, shorter time, and pressures for greater quantitative output. This Number Two guideline was meant to discourage those unfortunate interviews which result from someone buying a $60 tape recorder and then calling on his favorite community character. Or what about the interviewer who goes to his senator armed only with blank tapes and background research similarly blank except for the *Who's Who* vaguely in his memory? Those who developed the guidelines believed it is not fair either to the interviewee or to future scholars to tape with only slight preparation. This makes a victim of the memoirist, it clutters libraries with superficial and usually redundant material, and it creates difficulties when a serious interviewer tries to get an appointment with the victimized memoirist.

Nor is it *fair* to put the burden of the interview on the narrator. She is giving her time and brain power to this; you, the interviewer, are doing the research, which you then share with her to help her recall those far-off dates and names. Such a joint effort will more likely produce a document of which both of you will be proud. And, on the purely practical side, you will more likely avoid difficulties getting a release signed.

Yesbuts lurk here, too. For instance, what do you do when you want to interview a public official who has just gone out of office, and her papers have been sealed until her death? She feels that she cannot give one person special access to those papers; you feel you must use them or you cannot be adequately prepared. Is your alternative not to interview her at all? That would be a loss to history. So what do you do? You might compromise; you can dig around in collections of her contemporaries, where you may find letters and references to her. You can talk to her old friends, and enemies, and of course to her, to help you prepare topical outlines. Sometimes you can confer with a scholar who has researched areas relating to her career and who will contribute questions for the interview.

Yesbut two: What if her papers *are* open, but they fill 350 unorganized filing cabinets in a warehouse? Are you going to go through these? They are not even catalogued yet. Here it is pertinent to bring up a point in reference to Interviewer's Guideline Number Two: there is a difference in preparation when your objective is to draw up *questions*, as distinguished from a scholar's research for dependable answers for his book. In oral history, you are not aiming at making final judgments; the historian who later uses your interview is the one who has to assess the evidence and draw conclusions. Your task is to provide evidence. In fact, you will probably produce more useful interviews if you cannot reach the finality of clear answers. Defining puzzles is the focus of your research.

The final guideline for the interviewer, although the shortest, occasions more ethical dilemmas than any of the others.

It is important that all interviews be conducted in a spirit of objectivity and scholarly integrity and in accordance with stipulations agreed upon.

This is partially an attempt to prevent the creation of oral history myths, innuendoes, and fictions not unlike those fashioned from unevaluated FBI files; its principal aim is to discourage tapes that are primarily entertainments which either fascinate with intrigue or tickle the funnybone, but which are unhampered by accuracy. Outside of collections for folklore, the quality of oral history suffers from such amusements.

Once in a while a single word expresses a coalition of meanings more adequately than a torrent of prose. *Heuristic*, "helping to discover and learn," "serving to guide, discover or reveal" is such a word.[4] Although not specifically stated in the guidelines, *be heuristic* is what this final guideline means to say. When, after reading an oral history interview, a researching historian can lay it down with the comment, "Now that's a solid, heuristic effort," he has paid the oral historian the highest possible compliment.

Even with the best preparation, however, you sometimes find yourself on the other side of the microphone from a skilled and witty raconteur who, although amusing and delightful, does not share your commitment for heuristic interviews. Actually, you can develop some techniques to discourage exaggerations and distortions by using your research to pin her down with specific names and facts. And you can show her you are simply turned off by the exaggerated story or the colorful scandal which she may be telling you for the immediate reward of the look of relish on your face. Or you can always say, "Well, we'd better leave that out. It might be slanderous, you know, unless you can document it." If she persists in going through with it and leaving it in the transcript, your remaining recourse is to point out in her introduction to the tape or transcript that her charges are worth noting as an example of the perceptions of persons who hold her point of view in that particular group.

The truly heuristic approach is to choose memoirists for a series of interviews designed around a central core of inquiry, so that when one interviewee makes a charge or tells an unlikely story, you have a chance to tape others on the same topic. The result will be a series of different views that explore ambiguities and offer counter-weights to each other. However, even with the series technique, difficulties may arise. Example:

You interview Mr. Wiley. He insists on taping a serious charge against Mrs. Goldfarb. In a series, the logical follow-up is to make a note to include a question on this charge when you interview Mrs. Goldfarb. However, both interviews are still in process, so you are not free to quote Mr. Wiley to her and disclose your source if she should ask you, since the final agreement has not been signed. Besides, by quoting him to her, you may be starting a new controversy with possible chain reactions.

So you have a responsibility both ways: Goldfarb can insist she has a right to know her accuser. But your prior source, Wiley, retains quoting privileges. So getting a balance and counterbalance in a series sometimes places you in a moral morass.

But that is the good news. The bad news is that a virtuous, heuristic attitude can lead you into even a more difficult situation. Are you game for another example?

Interview transcripts are continually coming and going out of your office—
being transcribed, being sent to the memoirists, being returned to the office with
their corrections and additions. In an interview, Interviewee A gives you a clear,
running account of an event that started with a corruption scandal, moved into
the state administration for investigation, and finally landed in the courts for
resolution. Her account is not detailed: it is the sequential outline with valuable
information on who acted as catalyst in each stage. Such a comprehensive picture
is not available in print, so it is important.

Armed wtih this scenario, you then tape Interviewee B on his recollection of the
administration investigation. He does not request your source because he sees
you have only the general idea of what happened, and he cooperatively fills in
part B for you. Then you go to Interviewee C, who fills in the litigation section and
wraps up the story. With all three interviews, you have the story put together
from first-hand informants.

Put together, that is, until about two weeks later, when Interviewee A calls and
says, "I've decided to cull that story out of the transcript because I want to run for
office this year. It might be too controversial."

What is right for you to do in such a case? Is it fair to keep *her* information in the other two interviews, where it appears as a major reference? It
is still her story, although Interviewees B and C have covered their respective chapters with more detail and much more vividly than she had done.

Should you protect her confidentiality by removing those sections in
B's and C's interviews too? This action could throw you in conflict with
Guideline Number One (the interviewee's wishes should govern the
conduct of the interview) because neither man wants that section disturbed. You are back in the conundrum mentioned earlier, when *you*
want something closed and *he* wants it left open.

It is unlikely that any additions to the present guides and goals can
protect the conscientious oral historian from perplexities like these. As
with other dilemmas in life, some just have to be negotiated and muddled
through. In the example above, you could wait to see if she loses the
election. If she does, she will likely open that story again and all is well; if
she does not, then you either negotiate to close all three, or you put all
three in that office drawer labeled "temporary limbo" and try to explain
the delay to B and C.

The third part of the trinity—Guidelines for Sponsoring
Institutions—is actually only one guideline as it stands now:

Subject to meeting the conditions as prescribed by interviewees, it will be the
obligation of sponsoring institutions to prepare easily usable tapes and/or accurate typed transcriptions, and properly to identify, index, and preserve such oral
history records for use by the scholarly community, and to state clearly the provisions that govern their use.

In practice this means that the sponsoring institution must serve as a vehicle for carrying out longterm obligations incurred through the other two parts of the trinity. And this requires continuity and longevity of the institution. A library or historical society whose permanence is not reasonably assured can investigate allying itself on a cooperative basis with another more permanent institution.

Since that guideline was written, the number of institutions sponsoring oral history projects has soared, and many of the older sponsoring institutions have developed oral history research specialties. Perhaps it is time to consider a second guideline here: one for *relations* between oral history offices. It has become increasingly important for institutions to cooperate so that their oral history offices develop specialties that compliment those in other institutions while reflecting their own particular strengths. This will help prevent overlap of effort, competition for outside funds, and redundancy in the total pool of oral history tapes and transcripts.

Before we leave the *Goals and Guidelines*, let us consider a few that are not touched upon at all and that do not logically fit under any of the three headings.

It appears now that we might add "Guidelines for the Relations Between Oral History Projects"—and thereby become the first in history to create a four-part Trinity. This guideline springs from the phenomenon that more than one project frequently interviews the same memoirists. Horace Albright, who spoke briefly at the 1974 colloquium, has been interviewed by many major oral history projects in this country because he was the number two man in creating the national parks and was around to run them through several presidential administrations. His popularity is also due to his excellent memory.

Such overkill of interviewees indicates the need for agreement among oral historians not to interview a big-name person with a short, low-research interview which contributes little more than the aggrandizement of a project. Such an interview can make it appear that this major figure has already done his memoir, and when another project applies for a grant to do a thorough biography, it can be turned down on the grounds he has already been interviewed. Second, short topical interviews should be carefully noted as such in an appropriate catalog, with a notation of the subjects covered if possible. It also means making clear to the interviewee that history still lacks a full memoir from him; otherwise he might refuse subsequent requests to be interviewed since he's already done that. Sometimes a second interview request is rejected because his first was so superficial that he wants none of that again.

This problem also implies that each project should give priority to disseminating regular reports on what it has produced, through mailing its catalog (as Columbia and a few others do), notifying relevant journals, and turning in its listing to NUCMUC and other centralized cataloging services.

Another problem: the Grand Tetons colloquium seemed to be marked by much discussion and questioning of ethics involved in the commercial use of oral history. Parts of the present code relate to this question, such as agreeing beforehand with the memoirist on who will hold prior use rights and the literary rights. Royalties should be a part of this agreement, also. (In a number of projects, if an interview is published, the interviewee gets royalties automatically once the expenses for the interview are reimbursed to the project.)

In England, the law requires that anyone be paid whose interview is aired on BBC, and most oral history produced in Great Britain is for this purpose. This has led to problems in paying interviewees because their whereabouts are not known: They are not public figures and many were taped five or ten years before.

Unlike England, our country has a tradition of writers and researchers "exploiting" public figures for interviews. Similar exploitation of private citizens who belong to a special group such as core city dwellers, women, Native Americans, and Chicanos is occurring with increasing frequency. The question repeatedly raised is, Should oral history be made available for commercial publication with no remuneration to such interviewees?

In the United States the legal answer is often yes. But we need to examine this question further, or research in the several fields of ethnic studies could be badly undercut. One consideration that often balances the researcher's exploitation of an interviewee is the non-monetary benefits of publication to the group being studied. If the researcher cooperates, for example, with a tribal council (or perhaps its opposition group) when planning the interviews, or with an urban coalition committee, the end product could be useful for them too, perhaps for textbook material or for community consciousness raising.

Similarly, today's public figure is generally loathe to keep a diary and rarely has time in her schedule, even when "retired," to approach her memoir without the help of a highly-paid researcher and ghost writer. An oral historian furnishes her with background research, organizes and outlines interview sessions, guides her through with questions, and finally presents her with her own copy of the transcript. For her, it is a fortuitous way to leave a memoir for posterity, a free service that could otherwise have cost her untold dollars and hours. With publishing rights and royalties clearly spelled out beforehand, perhaps there is a fair balance of "exploitation" between the person of distinction who gets her memoir and the interviewer who gets a career credit for a heuristic piece of research.

Those of you who have wrestled the angels down to this last paragraph probably see little relevance now between the taping of oral history *properly done* and the processes indulged in by the former president. Anguished objections to Nixon-as-historian are based on his violations of every tenent in *Goals and Guidelines*, with the exception of number one for the interviewer ". . . to gather information that will be of scholarly usefulness in the present and the future." As we reject any classification of the Nixon tapes as "oral history," do we base that rejection on the definition of oral history that was offered at the First Colloquium? (It has to be oral and it has to be history.) Surely the Nixon tapes meet both those qualifications. Try the definition in the first sentence in the preamble of *Goals and Guidelines*: "The OHA recognizes oral history for what it is—a method of gathering a body of historical information in oral form usually on tape." Nixon's efforts fit that description, too.

So we conclude with a larger question for our ethical code: Should we seek a less-inclusive definition of oral history, in an effort to disassociate ourselves from surreptitious, non-interview taping? This requires further thought because there are, to mention only one related aspect, those members of OHA who tape speeches, riots, and current happenings, without infringing on anyone's rights. That is a fitting dilemma on which to end this set of reflections.

Notes

1. This is, of course, one argument for oral history offices that interview for the entire scholarly community.

2. Saul Benison, *Tom Rivers: Reflections on a Life in Medicine and Science* (Cambridge, Mass.: M.I.T. Press, 1967). See chapter 12 of the present volume.

3. Forrest C. Pogue, *George C. Marshall*, 3 vols. (New York: Viking, 1963–73).

4. *The American Heritage Dictionary of the English Language* (New York and Boston: American Heritage and Houghton Mifflin, 1969). See also *Webster's Seventh New Collegiate Dictionary* (Springfield, Mass.: G. and C. Merriam, 1967).

PART THREE
Oral History Applied:
Local, Ethnic, Family, and Women's History

16

Preface to *The Saga of Coe Ridge*
Lynwood Montell

In part 3 we explore the ways in which oral documentation can be applied to the varieties of history: folk, local, regional; then ethnic, women's, and family history. Many of these overlapping fields can be viewed together as the emergent discipline of ethnohistory, the frame of historical reference that a community uses to understand its traditions.

Our introductory selection comes from a recognized classic, The Saga of Coe Ridge *by William Lynwood Montell of Western Kentucky University. The author compiled the history of an isolated Afro-American community in rural Kentucky; of necessity he found himself writing folk history, "a body of oral traditional narratives told by a people about themselves." His preface, which appears below, successfully resolves the confusion surrounding history based on local legends and tales.*

The subject here is not oral history, as it is commonly understood, as much as oral traditional *history, based not on interviews with witnesses of history but on accounts passed on among generations—the sort of materials which Vansina and Finnegan discuss in their essays earlier in this book. Montell's approach is, in effect, that which any oral historian might adopt if called upon to explore an event which happened a century before without benefit of written sources. The community Montell studied left few documents such as birth records or tax rolls, and most interviewees were two and three generations removed from the events they described. Thus the author worked from the community's storehouse of self-knowledge, and he concentrated as much on the legendary growth which surrounded century-old events as on the solid kernel of fact.*

William Lynwood Montell has written and lectured extensively on the use of oral materials in historical research. He has published Monroe County History *(1970),* Ghosts along the Cumberland *(1975), and* From Memory to History *(with Barbara Allen Montell) (1981).*

This selection first appeared as the preface to The Saga of Coe Ridge: A Study in Oral History *(Knoxville: University of Tennessee Press, 1970).*

165

C OE RIDGE is the name of a tiny Negro colony that was nestled in the foothills of the Cumberland Mountains in Cumberland County, Kentucky, near the Tennessee line. Placed on the ridge as a result of Negro emancipation following the Civil War, the settlement withstood for almost a century the attempts of neighboring whites to remove this "scar" from the culture landscape of an otherwise homogeneous white society. During its existence, the Coe colony, some-times called Coetown and Zeketown, produced a belligerent group of people who became a legend before the community died in the late 1950's. It became a place of refuge for white women rejected by their own society and the breeding ground for a race of mulattoes. Additionally, Coe Ridge had ranked first among the moonshiners of southern Kentucky and, consequently, became the chief concern of federal revenue agents. It was this occupation, this livelihood of the outcasts that eventually was to bring about their downfall. After years of raids, arrests, and skirmishes, the revenuers succeeded in driving the Negroes from Coe Ridge into the industrial centers north of the Ohio River. Thus the colony died.

Historical events in the life of this Negro colony provide the basis for this book. *The Saga of Coe Ridge* is not an ordinary reconstruction of local history, however, for only a very few written records pertaining to this settlement remain. The major source materials are the inveterate oral traditions collected from former members of the colony and their white neighbors. A work of this type is founded on the premise that the story of any local group, as viewed by its people, is worthy of being recorded, for it can serve as a historical record in those areas where written accounts have not been preserved. One must be prepared to defend a thesis which holds that folk history can complement historical literature. This study proposes such a defense.

The Controversy over Oral Traditions

The utilization of oral traditions as undertaken here represents an area of open controversy and is severely attacked by some scholars who are accustomed to more conventional methods of documentation. A less hos-tile attitude claims that oral traditions can be utilized in historical writ-ings, provided that these recollections are approached with proper cau-tion. Still another line of thought holds that folklore is a mirror of history. That is to say, history can be viewed through folklore. A fourth position contends that the tales and songs of a people are grounded in historical fact. Inasmuch as *The Saga of Coe Ridge* is patently built upon the utiliza-tion of oral tradition, these various positions are worth examining in some detail. Let us look, therefore, at the thinking behind all four posi-tions, beginning with the totally negative approach.

Folk Tradition as Historical Fallacy

Legends and traditions of the people should be avoided, according to Homer C. Hockett, who claimed in 1938 that "the historian can make nothing of them of any positive value, in the absence of corroboratory evidence of a documentary, archaeological, or other kind, for the simple reason that they cannot be traced to their origins. And without knowledge of origins the ordinary critical tests cannot be applied."[1] Hockett renewed his attack on oral tradition in 1955 when he defined history as "the written record of past or current events"; he gave some credence, however, to certain devices such as utensils, structures, weapons, and artifacts as items that the historian could use to supplement the absence of written records.[2] Hockett saw no potential in myths, legends, or traditions as informative channels which might be utilized as aids to the historian. Yet in a chapter on "New Trends," Hockett recognized a recent rapprochement between local history and folklore.

Allen Johnson, writing in 1926, also enumerated a list of "remains," some three dozen in number, which could be included as source materials for historical research. Oral tradition was not listed because it was "handed on from generation to generation by word of mouth without being committed to writing." Johnson immediately contradicted his attack on oral tradition, however, by attaching some weight to the Icelandic sagas. "Under certain conditions," he stated, "where the professional raconteur has a pride in keeping the conventional tradition intact, the tale may have a fixed content and a stereotyped form, and eventually may be set down in writing substantially unchanged. On these grounds, the essential historicity of the Icelandic sagas is defended."[3]

Robert H. Lowie, an anthropologist, criticized the veracity of oral tradition a few years earlier than either Hockett or Johnson. He made what has been termed "the strongest statement against traditional history on this side of the Atlantic."[4] In 1915, Lowie published a short comment in the *American Anthropologist* on "Oral Tradition and History," objecting to the prohistorical position taken in that journal the previous year by John R. Swanton and Roland B. Dixon. Lowie's most biting comments were issued two years later to the American Folklore Society on the occasion of his presidential address, which was published in the *Journal of American Folklore*. He illustrated his thesis by using the traditions of North American Indians. "Indian tradition is historically worthless," he charged, "because the occurrences, possibly real, which it retains, are of no historical significance; and because it fails to record, or to record accurately, the most momentous happenings."[5] He further stated that stories of war and quarrels are not records of actual occurrences but are folklore, as attested to by their geographical distribution. Lowie conceded the point that traditional narratives are significant in the understanding of psychological, social, and religious phenomena associated with a tribal culture, but he categorically refused to allow any historical credence to the details of the narratives.

Lord Raglan, a recent student of comparative folklore and a clamorous champion of the skeptics of oral traditional history, studied both the classical and medieval bodies of traditional narrative and concluded that the great folk epics, the cherished sagas, the heroic legends and ballads, even the Christ story itself were ultimately drawn from ritual drama, not from historical fact.[6] The heroes of tradition, Raglan contended, were originally not men but gods, and the whole body of folk legend is a detritus of mythical accounts connected with ritualistic rites. After the rites ceased, the narratives remained and entered the realm of folk tradition where they were perpetuated as accounts of historical experiences. Raglan felt that a nonliterate people could not orally preserve the record of a historical event for more than 150 years and that any belief in the historicity of tradition stemmed from the desire to believe rather than from a critical analysis of the facts.

Edwin Sidney Hartland and Alfred Nutt, both talented Victorian folklorists, displayed negative attitudes toward the authenticity of oral historical narratives at an earlier date than Lord Raglan. Hartland studied *The Legend of Perseus* and was able to contend persuasively that certain African traditions are basically void of trustworthy history. Like Raglan, Hartland could allow only a brief time span to the limits of historical reliability in oral tradition. Among African peoples, he would concede one hundred, or at the most, two hundred years. In an article, Nutt attacked Sir William Ridgeway's *The Early Age of Greece,* which contained a strong plea for the acceptance of the Homeric poems as history. Nutt posed the question whether historic myths ever existed among barbaric peoples living in an oral-traditional mythopoetic stage of culture.[7] To Nutt's credit he at least called for an accumulation of more evidence before the thorny problems on the relationships of heroic legend and historic fact could be properly attacked.

Folklore as Embellished History

Joan Wake, a British historian, deemed folklore to be embellished history. She noted that although the old English village traditions are "liable to fluctuations and variations without end . . . there is much that is valuable in them. . . ."[8] And Américo Paredes wrote that "folklore does not always make a complete wreck of historical facts." He further stated, "Where documents are available for comparison, one may actually trace the process—the reshaping of history to conform with the folk group's own world view, the embellishment of bare historical detail with universal motifs." At that point in the accumulation of historical data, the historian should be familiar with the research methods of the folklorist, Paredes continued, for "some knowledge of the frequency with which motifs of this kind occur in folk narratives would put the historian on guard."[9] Merle W. Wells, historian and archivist, similarly wrote, "Historians who are not interested in folklore ought to have their work examined regularly by good folklorists. . . . Only a skilled folklorist, thoroughly familiar with several hundred folklore types and several thousand folklore motifs, has the competence necessary to distinguish folklore from history in scholarly historical accounts."[10]

Louis R. Gottschalk conceded that oral tradition, when utilized with proper caution, can supplement the efforts of the formal historian. He wrote that the legendary stories of William Tell, the imaginary hero of the Swiss war for independence, and Dr. Faustus, the sixteenth-century necromancer, "are good examples of folklore that may tell about the aspirations, superstitions, and customs of the peoples among whom the stories developed, provided the historian (or folklorist) is able to distinguish between the legendary embroideries and their authentic foundations."[11]

Despite occasional deviations from fact, Russian historical songs have been excellent sources of history when approached by the discerning scholar. Y. M. Sokolov described how the tendency of the people to idealize Ivan the Terrible led to a departure from historical truth in one of their songs. In the year 1581 Ivan the Terrible, in a fit of wrath, murdered his son Ivan, but in the historical song describing the incident, the anger of Ivan was vented on another son who had been accused of treachery. Other than this one radical departure from reality, Sokolov contended, the song preserved a great many of the real circumstances surrounding the event.[12]

Folklore as a Mirror of History

Allan Nevins, the founder of Columbia University's oral history program in 1948,[13] is among those who feel that folklore mirrors history, and he points out that folksongs and legends should be considered in the study of American history. After first challenging historians to record systematically the personal reminiscences "from the lips and papers of living Americans who have led significant lives," Nevins notes that "in our more recent history the legends of pioneer settlements, mining camps, lumbermen, and the cowboys of the western range, whether in prose or ballad, are by no means devoid of light upon social and cultural history."[14] Nevins advocates oral history as a means of documenting decisions in recent history that otherwise would be unrecorded. He uses oral testimonies narrated by members of the Ford family and household servants in *Ford: The Man, The Times, and The Company,* and praises their testimonies as "pure gold for the historian."[15] M. Gorky, an authority on Russian literature, also writes that the oral creations of the people provide excellent material for ascertaining the popular historical opinions on the phenomena of history. "From remote antiquity," Gorky states, "folklore persistently and with originality attends upon history. It has its own opinion of the doings of Louis XI, of Ivan the Terrible, and this opinion differs sharply from the evaluation made by history, which is written by specialists who are not very much interested in the question of what the conflict between the monarchs and the feudal lords actually contributed to the life of the laboring people."[16]

Certain American historians have directed their efforts toward producing works that point out the need for genuine cultural histories as a background for historical syntheses. One historian holding this view is Theodore C. Blegen, who feels that in order to understand the American people, historians should utilize folk documents, such as letters and diaries, which are the genuine indicators of history. In the past, our failure to define the American culture has been caused by what Blegen called "inverted provincialism"—that is to say, historians have scorned the simple and steered clear of the near-at-hand.[17] Philip D. Jordan, another cultural historian, writes that unless social stimuli are investigated, the contributions of the common man to historical movements cannot be articulated. American history has been written, he continues, but the full story is not to be found by a study of population statistics and historical documents; such channels of research are available to anyone, but the folklorist can bring to the formal historian knowledge of deeplying cultural patterns. Folklore grows out of the national experience, Jordan states, and an understanding of oral traditions would greatly contribute to those who wish more clearly to understand the historical narrative.[18]

Research Opportunities in American Cultural History, a collection of twelve essays, sounded the clarion call to historians. Leading cultural historians and folklorists pointed out that too much stress can be placed on our nation's political and religious institutions, thus jeopardizing consideration of the human element in history. A more rounded approach, the contributors felt, would be to focus attention on the people who lived during the major movements in American history. Among the more common words used throughout the book were "grass roots," "everyday life," and "folkways."[19]

Folk Traditions as Historical Fact

The fourth view, that "traditions often have a basis in historical fact," is supported by an article which appeared in the *Journal of American*

Folklore. In reporting the investigations of a historical tradition among the Southern Paiute Indians of southern Utah, David M. Pendergast and Clement W. Meighan disclosed that casual comments made by the Paiute revealed history that was consistent with archaeological evidence some eight hundred years old.[20] The traditions, which dealt with a prehistoric people, the Puebloids, were specific and generally accurate concerning the Puebloids' economic institutions, physical appearance, material culture, and Paiute-Puebloid relationships. The authors concluded that "archaeologists in particular should explore the possibilities of correlating historical traditions with archaeological data, since the historical information may substantiate, and in some cases broaden, inferences based solely on archaeological materials."[21]

The Southern Paiute example of the persistency of oral traditions was one of many emphatic rejoinders against the anti-historical pronouncements of Lowie and others who held to his school of relentless dogmatism. Frederica de Laguna, for example, issued a strong positive statement in 1958, writing that when a 1957 geological survey team reported habitable periods of the Icy Yakutat Bay area, the team was thereby confirming by means of radiocarbon tests native traditions dating from 1400. De Laguna concluded by saying, "Other natives' statements about the stages in the retreat of the ice in the Yakutat Bay during the late 18th and 19th centuries are in complete accord with geological evidence."[22]

The English folklorist, George Laurence Gomme, approached the question of the validity of oral tradition with what can be termed the extreme approach. He asserted that every folk custom and belief has roots in a historical event.[23] Closely akin to this stand, but not as dogmatically so, were the positions taken by the Chadwicks and Knut Liestøl. Hector M. and Nora K. Chadwick totally differed with the Raglan thesis by maintaining that folk heroes are rooted in history. During the process of cultural evolution experienced by a people, there was a historical Heroic Age characterized by a semi-nomadic, warring, raiding type of existence. At this stage of phylogeny, a great hero rose up to assume the leadership of his people. In some instances, the hero's exploits then entered the printed page and were thus perpetuated, but prior to that a great deal of fiction had already crept into the oral recountal. The painstaking scholar can winnow the historical from the unhistorical elements in that event, and this was one of the tasks undertaken by the Chadwicks.[24] If, for some reason, the hero's feats did not reach print, then the legends about him devolved into a cycle of songs or tales carried on in oral tradition. But historical traditions, whether oral or written, are authentic records of history, and the recurrent thesis postulated by the Chadwicks looks upon many of the persons and events described in the Teutonic, British, and Irish Heroic Ages as historical actualities.

The folklorist Knut Liestøl studied the origin of the Icelandic sagas and persuasively argued that under favoring conditions oral history can preserve its core of reality over long periods of time.[25] By a close analysis of oral traditions that originated during the period 930 to 1030 and later were written down in the period from 1120 to 1230, he showed that oral traditions could serve as a form of record-keeping, distinct from written historical accounts. Liestøl tested the reliability of the episodes recorded in the sagas by (1) comparing variant examples of the same incident in different sagas, to ascertain the original content and form of the oral tradition; (2) analyzing stylistic devices of oral narration, to see which of the written pages reveal the marks of oral style; (3) evaluating the amount of recognizable folklore material in the sagas; and (4) assessing the social *milieu* and the common historical background from which the sagas stemmed. In a society of more advanced peoples unshaken by wanderings and uprootings, according to Liestøl, historical recollections and folklore elements mingle to a considerable extent, but these two channels can be positively identified. The more advanced peoples utilize oral traditional history as a form of historical record-keeping that is separate and distinct from written historical records. Students of history, Liestøl contended, should not apply the rules of evidence belonging to documentary history in their evaluation of oral history.[26]

This was virtually the same stand taken by many Folk-Lore Society members who could not agree with Hartland and Nutt. Lach-Szyrma felt that the basic historicity of oral traditions in the West of England could be ascribed to the selective process of folk memory; David MacRitchie pointed out that archaeological findings in Wigtownshire verified local traditions which claimed that a cave in the vicinity had been occupied fourteen centuries earlier by Saint Ninias; and John Myres gave much credence to folkmemory in such isolated, stable, homogeneous, and preliterate societies as the Icelandic and the Polynesian, where family, community, and even regional history were matters of practical concern and common knowledge.[27] When a people share a common historical experience, according to Myres, the events in this experience become a tenacious part of folkmemory and may be perpetuated for centuries.

The Nature of Oral Traditions

Through the years the American continent has witnessed the birth and flowering of an immense body of local historical legends arising in response to actual occurrences, usually of a sensational nature. These traditions may vex the historian of the articulate classes, and he may continue to have nothing to do with something as elusive as folk tradition. Yet, no historian who is aware of the ways of the people on a local level, especially in rural areas where ties with the land are strong, will question th importance played by oral traditions in the lives of the people. Accuracy of local historical legends is not the most important question to be faced by the person who gathers and analyzes them, but rather the essential fact is that these folk narratives are believed by the people who perpetuate them. Even in the more literate societies, folklore records the joy, humor, pathos, and indestructible spirit of the local group. In the preface to their book on Mormon folklore, Austin and Alta Fife state that "we have sought the authenticity not of history but of folklore. . . . We have tried to view the materials less as historical data than as legend—not as they actually were, but as they have been viewed by the folk."[28]

Richard M. Dorson made a similar point in his concluding comments on the trustworthiness of oral traditional history. He noted that blanket judgments regarding the historicity of oral traditions should be avoided, and added, "It is not a matter of fact versus fiction so much as the social acceptance of traditional history."[29] And in another article Dorson astutely wrote, "If the event is historically false, it is psyoohhologically true, and its incorporation into tribal histories is something for the American historian to note."[30]

Ethnohistorians specializing in African history have approached the idea of historical truth from a perspective which stresses a periodical or cyclical rhythm of eternal repetition within the life-cycle of the individual. They note a direct correlation between the time perspective recognized by the society and the social structure.[31] One ethnohistorian, Paul Bohannan, writes in "Concepts of Time Among the Tiv of Nigeria" that repetitive natural or social events recorded in Tiv myths and legends explain the social process, not the historical past. Specifically, he remarks that "The most common incidents all cluster about a standard situation which arises time and again in the dynamic Tiv social process: particularly fission and fusion of lineage territories, which are the modal points in Tiv political process."[32]

Jan Vansina, pursuing these ideas in a book-length historiographical outline on nonliterate African societies, examined in depth the processes and functions of oral traditions in African societies. He pointed out the contrast in attitudes toward historical knowledge displayed by societies even in the same culture area. Because of a coherent political structure, the Rwanda were rich in family and local historical traditions, Vansina explained, but the Burundi were restricted in their oral communication because of an incohesive political framework. In conclusion Vansina stated, "Each type of society has in fact chosen to preserve the kind of historical traditions suited to its particular type of structure, and the historical information to be obtained by studying these traditions is restricted by the framework of reference constructed by the society in question."[33] Vansina's statement may well summarize the case for African ethnohistory.[34]

American folklorists, on the other hand, are concerned with a literate people who have produced bodies of oral traditional narratives which may reflect social conditions but certainly not reflect political organization. By utilizing methods of research peculiar to his discipline, the comparative folklorist can study these narratives in societal context and thus function as a cultural historian. In addition, he can come to the aid of the formal historian, whose analysis of statistical data and historical documents seldom permits conclusions regarding the ways of life on a local level.

In the interests of formal history, therefore, a summary of the history of the immediate area surrounding Coe Ridge is presented in the Prologue of *The Saga of Coe Ridge* as a complement to the oral traditions of the people themselves. Data for this summary are drawn almost exclusively from the federal census and from other sources which in turn were based on generalized data. The use of data, however, does not make it possible to take a personal approach to history—that is, to consider the people as a living force. This is the critical distinction between folk history and history written by orthodox methods of research.

Folk history, as applied in this book, can be defined as a body of oral traditional narratives that are told by a people about themselves, and, therefore, the narratives articulate the feelings of a group toward the events and persons described.[35] Folk attitudes are included as a part of this definition because they are an integral part of almost every narrative recorded from the informants. In this account of Coe Ridge, these attitudes occasionally become the primary consideration, for local history is often intricately tied with the subjectivity of the people. . . .[36]

Notes

1. Homer C. Hockett, *Introduction to Research in American History* (New York: Macmillan, 1938), p. 90.

2. Homer C. Hockett, *The Critical Method in Historical Research and Writing*, 3d ed. (New York: Macmillan, 1955).

3. A. Johnson, *The Historian and Historical Evidence* (New York: Scribner's, 1926), p. 5.

4. Richard M. Dorson, "The Debate over the Trustworthiness of Oral Traditional History," *Volksüberlieferung: Festschrift für Kurt Ranke,* ed. Fritz Harkort (Göttingen: O. Schwartz, 1968), p. 21.

5. Robert H. Lowie, "Oral Tradition and History," *Journal of American Folklore* 30 (April–June 1917), p. 165.

6. F. R. Raglan, *The Hero: A Study in Tradition, Myth, and Drama* (New York: Vintage, 1956).

7. Alfred Nutt, "History, Tradition, and Historic Myth," *Fokl-Lore* 12 (1901), pp. 336–39.

8. Joan Wake, *How to Compile a History and Present-Day Record of Village Life,* cited in Donald D. Parker, *Local History: How to Gather It, Write It, and Publish It* (New York: Social Science Research Council, 1944), p. 25.

9. Américo Paredes, "Folklore and History," in *Singers and Storytellers,* ed. Mody C. Boatright (Dallas: Southern Methodist University Press, 1961), pp. 58, 61.

10. M. W. Wells, "History and Folklore: A Suggestion for Cooperation," *Journal of the West* 4 (January 1965), pp. 95–96.

11. L. Gottschalk, *Understanding History: A Primer of Historical Method* (New York: Knopf, 1950), p. 114.

12. J. M. Sokolov, *Russian Folklore,* trans. Catherine Ruth Smith (New York: Macmillan, 1950), pp. 350–51 and passim. The basic historicity of the Russian historical songs has commanded the attention of Carl Stief, *Studies in the Russian Historical Song* (1953; Reprint ed., Westport, Conn.: Hyperion Press, 1981).

13. The increasing popularity of both university and private oral history projects is especially pleasing to folklorists, for the private interview is thus recognized as the basic unit of transmission in oral history. And, again in the mold of the folklorist, the oral historian uses the same tools and methodologies in field collecting. Some typical methodological descriptions would include the following works: Elizabeth I. Dixon, "Oral History: A New Horizon," *Library Journal* 87 (April 1, 1962), pp. 1363–65; Charles T. Morrissey, "The Case for Oral History," *Vermont History* 21 (July 1963), pp. 145–55; and Helen McCann White, "Thoughts on Oral History," *American Archivist* 20 (January 1957), pp. 19–30. Charles T. Morrissey's "Oral History and the Mythmakers," *Historic Preservation* 16 (November–December 1964), pp. 232–37, contains a brief but workable bibliography of the subject.

14. Allan Nevins, *The Gateway to History* (Boston: Appleton-Century, 1938), pp. iv, 66; Wyman D. Walker, "Western Folklore and History," *American West* 1 (Winter 1964), pp. 45–51, noted the strong relationship between folklore and the history of the American West, especially in the beliefs held by the pioneers concerning water, weather, and animals and in their stories of Indian fighting and in the lore of miners, cowboys, and sheepherders.

15. Cited in Morrissey, "Case for Oral History," p. 151.

16. M. Gorky, *On Literature,* cited in Sokolov, *Russian Folklore,* p. 347.

17. Theodore Blegen, *Grass Roots History* (Minneapolis: University of Minnesota Press, 1947).

18. P. O. Jordan, "The Folkorist as Social Historian," *Western Folklore* 12 (July 1953), pp. 194–201.

19. John F. McDermott, ed., "Research Opportunities in American Cultural History" (Lexington: University of Kentucky Press, 1961).

20. D. M. Pendergast and C. W. Melghan, "Folk Traditions as Historical Fact: A Paiute Example," *Journal of American Folklore* 72 (April–June 1959), pp. 128–133.

21. Pendergast and Melghan, "Folk Traditions," p. 132.

22. F. de Laguna, "Geological Confirmation of Native Traditions, Yakutat, Alaska," *American Antiquity* 23 (1958), p. 434; also cited in Dorson, "The Debate," pp. 23–24.

23. G. C. Gomme, *Folklore as an Historical Science* (London: Methuen, 1908). See especially chapter 1, "History and Folklore," pp. 1–122.

24. H. M. Chadwick and N. K. Chadwick, *The Heroic Age* (Cambridge: Cambridge University Press, 1912). The comments about this work were drawn from Richard M. Dorson, *American Folklore* (Chicago: University of Chicago Press, 1958), p. 209; the Chadwicks' three-volume study of *The Growth of Literature* is summarized by Dorson in "The Debate," pp. 20–21.

25. Knut Liestøl, *Origin of the Icelandic Family Sagas* (Oslo: H. Aschebourg, 1930). Dorson presents a brief but succinct summary of Liestøl's work in "The Debate," pp. 26–30.

26. Liestøl's persuasive arguments met with strong opposition in the analyses of Sigurdur Nordal, *The Historical Element in the Icelandic Family Sagas* (Glasgow: Jackson, 1957); Peter Hallberg, *The Icelandic Saga*, trans. Paul Schach (Lincoln: University of Nebraska Press, 1962), and Theodore M. Andersson, *The Problem of Icelandic Saga Origins* (New Haven: Yale University Press, 1964).

27. W. S. Lach-Szyrma, "Folk-Lore Traditions of Historical Events," *Folk-Lore* 3 (1881), pp. 157–68; David MacRitchie, "The Historical Aspect of Folk-lore," in *The International Folk-Lore Congress 1891, Papers and Transactions*, ed. Joseph Jacobs and Alfred Nutt (London: D. Nutt, 1892), 105–106; and John L. Myres, "Folkmemory," *Folk-Lore* 37 (1926), pp. 12–34 but especially p. 28.

28. A. E. Fife and A. S. Fife, *Saints of Sage and Saddle: Folklore among the Mormons* (Bloomington: Indiana University Press, 1956), p. xi.

29. Dorson, "The Debate," p. 34.

30. R. M. Dorson, "Oral Tradition and Written History: The Case for the United States," *Journal of the Folklore Institute* 1 (December 1964), p. 230.

31. See, e.g., Meyer Fortes, *The Dynamics of Clanship among the Tallensi* (New York: Oxford University Press, 1945), p. xi; G. I. Jones, "Oral Tradition and History," *African Notes* 2 (January 1965), pp. 7–11, uses narratives from eastern Nigeria and, in particular, origin myths of the Kalabari of the eastern Delta to show how oral traditions change in response to different social requirements and attitudes.

32. Paul Bohannan, *Southwestern Journal of Anthropology* 9 (1953), pp. 260–61.

33. J. Vansina, *Oral Tradition: A Study in Historical Methodology*, trans. H. M. Wright (London: Routledge and Kegan Paul, 1965), pp. 170–71 (see chapter 9 of the present volume); also quoted by Dorson in "The Debate," p. 35.

34. The theme of a conference on oral history in Africa, held at Northwestern University in 1965, was methodology as attested by the papers published in the *African Studies Bulletin* 8 (September 1965): Aristide R. Zolberg, "A Preliminary Guide for Interviews," pp. 3–8; Jan Vansina, "The Documentary Interview," pp. 8–14; Ronald Cohen, "Quantification," pp. 16–19; and Raoul Naroul, "Data Quality Control," pp. 19–23.

35. Benjamin A. Botkin, *Lay My Burden Down: A Folk History of Slavery* (Chicago: University of Chicago Press, 1945), p. xiii, defines folk history as "history from the bottom up, in which the people become their own historians." From the study of folk history, Botkin contends, one is able to consider "the inarticulate many as well as the articulate few."

36. In chapter 1, for example, it is demonstrated that oral tradition offers rich insight into Negro attitudes toward the insecure status on the plantation experienced by slave ancestors. Additionally, these narratives provide ample documentation of the socio-economic aspects of plantations located along the upper Cumberland River.

17

The Folklorist, the Oral Historian, and Local History

Larry Danielson

Beginning where William Lynwood Montell left off, the author of the next selection discusses local history from the perspective of folklore. Because folklorists have specialized training, they can help explain how local legends, folk beliefs, and customs interrelate; how traditional motifs crop up in oral narratives; and how local history can be "personalized" by specialized collecting. Selections later in this volume, particularly that of Richard Dorson, also explore the relation between oral history and folklore. While researchers in the two fields have often speculated on their differences, few of their narrators debate such matters. One key difference, however, is whether material collected orally is used for historical reconstruction or to understand the role and weight of oral tradition within a community. Danielson's essay is a case study of cooperation between the two fields.

Larry Danielson is an associate professor at the University of Illinois at Urbana-Champaign specializing in traditional and supernatural narrative forms. Danielson has written articles on topics in American folklore as wide ranging as transmuted spirits and Swedish-American mothers. He is the author of a two-part series on folklore and film in Western Folklore *(1980, 1981).*

"The Folklorist, the Oral Historian, and Local History" originally appeared in the Oral History Review *8 (1980), pp. 62–72.*

RICHARD M. DORSON is one of the most vocal and active matchmakers in the courtship of folklore and oral history. Over a decade ago, in his presidential address to the American Folklore Society, he exhorted: "If the folklorist moves outside genre collecting and the oral historian moves beyond interviews with the political and business elite, the two can meet in the recording of folk prejudices, rumors, biases, awes, hatreds, loyalties, phobias, stereotypes, obsessions, and fantasies."[1] Since then many folklorists have made the journey beyond the boundaries of genre restriction and item collection. Simultaneously, oral historians have often defined their purposes with the commonplace and ordinary men and women in mind, in contrast to the elitist orientation of their earlier research. The courtship between the two groups is under way, although no marriage announcement is forthcoming. It cannot be denied, however, that one of the parties—folklore—sometimes sulks when academicians enthusiastically commend the advent of oral history into their scholarly circles, or harbors surly suspicions that the new companion does not adequately understand how to undertake the task at hand.

On occasion students of folk history and the oral record become so immersed in their research they forget that the truisms about their topic are not common knowledge in the outside world. I recently interviewed an insightful and eloquent Finnish-American who grew up on the Minnesota Iron Range, worked in the mines as a young man, and eventually became a Lutheran pastor on the Michigan Upper Peninsula and the Iron Range. We talked a full afternoon, mostly about his Finnish-American childhood, his experiences on the farmstead and in the underground mines, and his ministry to tradition-directed Finnish-Americans. As we parted, he said to me: "I guess I didn't understand what you wanted to know from me. I thought you were going to ask me about history." The puzzled comment forcefully reminded me that even though the folklorist and the oral historian are beginning to cooperate more fully in their mutual concerns about the local past and its expression in the oral testimony, we should not assume that what we have said to one another has been heard or understood by all those outside our academic communities. History for many continues to be spelled in capital letters and describes "important events" in the national past. The life history and community history, which most of us accept as legitimate historical topics, still bear explanation to many as important subject matter, in spite of Alex Haley's Roots and by the easy availability of genealogy handbooks on the paperback stands.

Complications in such explanations will arise, sometimes because we have not adequately conceptualized the terms we use so casually. For example, how have we distinguished folk history from oral history? A common definition of oral history among oral historians focuses on the reminiscence about direct personal experience. According to Willa Baum, oral history "involves the tape recording of an interview with a knowledgeable person, someone who knows whereof he or she speaks from personal participation or observation, about a subject of historical interest."[2] Cullom Davis stresses that oral history is no longer exclusively concerned with the elite and reflects "the trend toward 'people's history'

. . . evident throughout the historical profession." He distinguishes between "genuine oral history (first-hand recollections) and oral hearsay (second-hand [recollections])," and notes "this is not to say that [oral hearsay] is of no value. It also is important to acknowledge that human memory is a fragile historical source; it is subject to lapses, errors, fabrications, and distortions."[3] Charles Hudson separates folk history from ethnohistory in order, it appears, to distinguish what is studied from how it is studied. Folk history, according to this ethnohistorian, "denotes the historical beliefs of other societies and cultures," but the aim of ethnohistory is "to reconstruct, using all available materials, 'what really happened' in terms that agree with our sense of credibility and our sense of relevance. . . . In a folk history we attempt to find what people in another society believe 'really happened,' as judged by their sense of credibility and relevance." Finally he uses the magic words: "Thus, the methodology of ethnohistory is essentially 'etic,' while the methodology of folk history is essentially 'emic.' "[4]

Richard M. Dorson wishes to create a new designation that will once and for all separate the folklorist's interest in the oral record from that of the orthodox oral historian: "Oral traditional history . . . seeks out the topics and themes that the folk wish to talk about, the personal and immediate history with which they are concerned." He distinguishes the recollections of first-hand experience as oral personal history in contrast to oral traditional history ("hearsay" in Davis' terminology) and calls both types of accounts species of oral folk history.[5] The eavesdropper must regard these discriminations concerning what is and is not oral history and folk history as pointless hair-splitting. Edward D. Ives has solved the issue easily. He suggests that oral history is a technique that may be used for a variety of purposes. It involves collecting different types of oral material about the past. The data can be used in the reconstruction of historic occurrences, or it can be used in the analysis of popular conceptions of past event and behavior.[6] Therefore folk history, unlike the methodology of oral history, is a substantive, particular subject matter. If we are interested in folk history, we are interested in a native view of the past, whether it is in the form of a collective tradition or a personal reminiscence. In order to gather data necessary in describing and interpreting that perception of the past, we use the techniques of oral history, among others.

Personal history, indeed, may be more reliable than collective "hearsay" in historical reconstructions. The folklorist, however, has long been sensitized to recognize the possibilities of fabulation in first-person accounts and fact in third-person accounts.[7] Sometimes, I think, folklorists sell themselves short in communicating to non-folklorists this special sensitivity. Mody Boatright's discussion of the family saga, for example, deserves a wider recognition than it has thus far received. In it he examines the clusters of traditional narratives and motifs that appear and reappear as descriptions of actual occurrence in oral family history and printed accounts based on that oral record.[8] The folklorist does not ignore them as unwelcome falsities, even though the cooperating family member may resent the classification of the stories as versions of widespread folk traditions. Instead the folklorist wonders why and how such narratives were created and maintained over the generations. Boatright's observations are insightful, but historians are not often interested in examining such materials for what they indicate about a community's perception of the past. It is difficult to convince many critics that it is as important to analyze the "inaccurate" account as it is to reconstruct the "objective reality." Folklorists perhaps respond more empathetically than do historians to Pontius Pilate's existential query, "What is truth?"

In addition to reminding others that the investigation of subjective reality is an important goal in oral local history research, folklorists need to share their knowledge of traditional patterns of behavior in past contexts. Sometimes folk arts and actions of the past, although verifiable as realities, are interpreted as so much hokum, either grotesque fictions or conscious prevarications. I once discovered a curious nineteenth-century manuscript in the archive of a well-known ethnic community in the Midwest. The dozen or so handwritten pages were filled with detailed folk remedies, so I asked a resident authority about the manuscript. "It looks like a put-on to me," he replied, pointing to such remedy ingredients as urine and mouse droppings. The fragile document was irrelevant to the settlement's cultural history, in his opinion. It was a revelation to him that the bizarre prescriptions were indeed legitimate folk medicine practices, often described in ethnographic accounts of nineteenth-century European peasant life, but ignored by scholars more interested in kinship structure and patterns of religious dissent. Sensitivity to tradition and an understanding of its specific expression in behavior are important contributions to the descriptions of the local past. In such cases either the oral record or the printed document and artifact, or all three, may communicate confused messages that required specialized interpretation by the folklorist.

I will not belabor other justifications for the folklorist's involvement in historical research that relies on the oral testimony because they are so familiar. Acquaintance with certain tendencies and tropisms in oral literature, for instance traditional patterning and repetition devices, an understanding of oral transmission processes and their possible consequences in matters of continuity and change, recognition of the mercurial relocations and transpositions that float a traditional story from one vivid personality to another years and miles apart, and fieldwork experience that requires observation and passive listening as well as asking questions—these are other well-known contributions the folklorist can make in cooperation with the oral historian in local history studies. The folklorist recognizes the oral narrative as an art form and is sensitive to the ways in which it re-shapes the past. As history finds expression in story, the oral testimony communicates a variety of truths.

History is made up largely of stories and tradition, and the folklorist is, or should be, an expert on that relationship.[9]

At this point it would be helpful to describe a specific venture of the folklorist into local history research that makes use of the oral record and the analysis of artifacts and printed sources. In 1977 community leaders in Homer, Illinois, a rural community of some 1400 residents, became interested in renovating a turn-of-the-century opera house located in a Main Street commercial building, now used as a city services center. As the renovation movement developed, it became clear that information about the original appearance of the opera house and its uses in the past was not available in printed sources. Few state or county histories had paid much attention to Homer, and its newspaper, the reliable, standard source for many community historians, was represented in official state archives by but a few scattered issues. The oral record, along with family memorabilia—photographs and old programs stored in attic boxes— became major sources of information about the opera house and its role in community life.

Soon, however, the local historical society began to expand its research goal, and, with a grant from the state humanities and arts council and aid from an area community college, an organized effort to retrieve Homer's past took shape. I was asked to direct the local history workshop that would effect that retrieval. In it I attempted to consider the uses of the oral testimony and the different kinds of truth it can yield up to us. The first session dealt with the rationale of local history research and its worth; the second, with field interview methodology and the types of information that can be extracted from oral sources; the third, with gaps in the record of Homer's history and the use of artifacts, photographs, and memorabilia in filling those gaps; and the fourth, with the preservation of the materials collected by the historical society and their organization into a usable Homer history archive. By mid-winter a number of active society members were at work with their cassette tape-recorders, notebooks, and cameras. The participants hoped to gather information about the community's past unavailable in the few official histories of Homer, to make these new historical materials available to the public, and to use them in a community presentation, "The Living History of Homer." Mostly middle-aged and elderly, they embarked their efforts in a spring program on the opera house stage.

The project was a successful one. Workshop participants became experienced in the collection and analysis of local history narratives, photographs, and the ephemeral documents some people, fortunately, can not bear to consign to the trash can. Their research retrieved valuable information about public and private experience in Homer's past that is of interest to the serious student of small-town life in the turn-of-the-century Midwest. As their studies progressed, the work of the local historical society gained impetus. The group now plans to re-locate its materials from members' homes into an archive in the old city hall, which it is renovating with funds collected through an opera house series, a varied group of entertainments, including a recital of American parlor music and a Victorian melodrama, presented in the renovated opera house. Individual members continue their interviewing and data collection, even though the official project has concluded. (One enterprising fieldworker brought her elderly informant and her tape recorder out to a local cemetery in order to question him about the past generation as the two walked among the gravestones—an imaginative innovation in the field interview.) The culmination of the project, the "Living History of Homer" program, was lengthy, elaborate, and detailed, and it proved to be a satisfying community experience.

The project was certainly not flawless. There were problems with tape quality, both in terms of sound reproduction and, on occasion, interview responses. A historical society crisis occurred because a local resident withdrew his donation of early twentieth-century photographs, thereby denying a rich source of information about Homer's everyday life usable in the public program. The opera house presentation, a multi-media event using slides, tapes, and film, proved to be a difficult task. And, of course, there were frustrations about the organization of the tape materials for the program, "The Living History of Homer," and for classification and retrieval purposes in the new archive.

The positive consequences of the project, however, were persuasive in demonstrating that the folklorist's involvement in local oral history research is justified. A remarkable collection of data about significant events, social behavior, and personal concerns in Homer's past was amassed: traditional medical remedies, burial and funeral traditions, descriptions of butchering and smoking meat, putting up ice, and threshing, information about Ku Klux Klan activities in the community during the 1920s, the functions of the opera house in past decades, commercial and political life over the years, everyday and holiday foodways, attitudes toward Gypsies and itinerants, and even a few stories about the sledding of community homes over the snow in 1855 from a river location, Old Homer, to a railroad location, New Homer. It is apparent that a folklorist's interests are reflected in the array of information. The materials are strongest in their description of daily and customary activities that many historians have paid little attention to—what old Homerites ate, what they did when they got sick, how they celebrated important occasions, and what traditional methods they put to use in their daily labors. Here, then, we have an illustration of oral history methods used to locate information about the past that is difficult to obtain in other sources. It is information that is ignored in many historical studies, even though most people, today and years ago, probably spend more time wondering about their health or the chores at hand than contemplating abstract, intellectual issues. In future decades information about living in Homer in the early to mid-1900s, data easily lost with the death of each generation, will be available to students of small-town life, whether they are historians, folklorists, anthropologists, or sociologists.

Another kind of information is also present. The stories were collected by Homer residents from Homer residents and they often reflect their own historical concerns and satisfactions. An elderly woman recalled that her father feared the widespread use of tractors would ruin the rich Illinois farmland because of their weight. Several interviewees excitedly described a local parrot and its salty vocabulary. (The bird still lives, but its communication is impaired, though not so much as to discourage one fieldworker from taping its squawks.) A simple request for information about old-time washdays prompted a lengthy and detailed description of the lye-making and soap-making. The interviewee, enlivened by the memory, reminisced that once a farmyard turkey flew into the lye kettle and "just got eaten up." Ephemera perhaps, curious local-color footnotes to some, but for community members sharing such stories, they are satisfying narratives about the past that make it come alive in personal ways. The emic categories expressed in stories about the town drunk, how a family managed to eat well during the 1930's depression, and what grandma did when one of her children stepped on a barnyard nail, are more meaningful to community members than those etic categories we are tempted to use in local history research, "history" in capital letters. Many of the tapes are made up of conversations among the residents themselves in which they talk about their community and personal past. The outsider plays no direct role in the transaction and the folk history of Homer comes alive. The reconstruction of a meaningful past becomes less artificial and self-conscious when community members talk with one another rather than for an interested, though alien visitor.

As usual in reminiscences and anecdotes about the rural American past, snake stories, for example frightening encounters with poisonous snakes and serpentine visitors in unexpected places, were shared in some of the liveliest exchanges. One elderly woman recalled seeing black snakes attached to the cows' udders as the animals were herded home for

milking. And, sure enough, there appeared the story about a child inno-
cently sharing her bowl of milk with a backyard snake. In this case, the
informant herself recalled taking her bowl of milk to the well where she
fed it to a large black snake each evening. The secret was eventually
discovered by her father, who threatened to kill the serpent. A farmhand
intervened, however, warning that if the snake were killed the child
would also die.

What is the historian to make of such narratives? In many cases convincing details merge with bizarre motifs that confound the separation of
fact and fiction. According to zoological expertise it is impossible for a
snake to attach itself to a cow's udder, but the Homer interviewee asserts
that she witnessed such an odd union. Her anecdote expresses a common
folk belief concerning milk-sucking serpents. Harry M. Hyatt, for example, cites four instances of the belief and includes a third-person narrative
concerning the phenomenon in his detailed collection, *Folk-lore from
Adams County, Illinois*. The fact that snakes can lap liquid from a saucer or
cup does not necessarily validate the second traditional narrative as historical incident. "The Child and the Snake" is a widespread folktale plot,
categorized in *Types of the Folktale* as no. 285. It is found in the Grimm
Brothers' *Kinder-und Hausmärchen* as the first narrative in tale number
105 and has been collected in Northern Europe, England, France, Spain,
Hungary, Czechoslovakia, Russia, India, and the New World. It appears
in the WPA slave narrative collection, a number of American folktale
collections, and occasionally in publications of pioneer reminiscences.
The traditional tale is also the subject of an early nineteenth-century
literary poem for children, probably written by Charles Lamb. As might
be expected, the Hyatt collection of Adams County, Illinois lore includes
the full narrative (remarkably similar to the story collected as personal
reminiscence in Champaign County, Illinois) as well as a related folk
belief: "If you find a snake drinking milk from a cup out of which some of
the milk was previously drunk by a child, always let the snake escape; for
if the snake is killed, the child will not live long."[10]

The folklorist is delighted to find such traditional motifs imbedded in
talk about the past, but both the folklorist and the historian must be
perplexed about further evaluation of these stories, especially when they
are narrated as personal experiences. We can probably assume that the
Homer interviewee was not prevaricating, even though her anecdotes
can be classified as accounts of traditional belief and legend rather than as
descriptions of historical occurrence. The fusion of traditional motif and
personal experience is not unusual in reminiscence (just as dream and
reality occasionally become confused in recall). This incorporation of
legend and hearsay into one's personal history is a complex problem,
demanding the cooperative effort of folklorist and historian. Localized,

personalized versions of a widely diffused traditional narrative are not useless or unimportant. The fact that the snake stories cited here are compelling to both interviewee and interviewer is significant and indicates the potency of the quasi-historical narratives for raconteur and audience. That the tales have been transmuted into first-person experience stories suggests that they constitute a meaningful perception of the rural past, a view of the prairie world remarkable for a strange and sometimes dangerous fauna. To dismiss oral traditional narrative because it cannot be used in the reconstruction of objective history is to ignore the community's perception of its past and to disregard the complex interaction between human psychology, narrative function, and historicity in oral history research.

The opera house program, "The Living History of Homer," crystalized the importance of the project for its participants, interviewer and interviewee, performers and audience. Not only did it provide some answers to interesting questions about Homer's past; it also reminded townspeople of their unique as well as representative location in time and space, how their town's history is similar to, yet different from, the histories of countless Midwestern villages. A few years ago Sam Bass Warner, Jr., urged his colleagues to re-evaluate their roles as professional historians: ". . . history is a natural act, a universal behavior. . . . I see the key to the reform of our historical profession to be freeing it from its artificial university constraints so that it may be turned to its multiplicity of useful tasks. The proper role of the professional historian, thus, should be to act as the facilitator of others' historical consciousness."[11] The folklorist and the oral historian can play crucial roles in this facilitation. The Homer project expanded the historical consciousness of many, and I include myself in that number. It did so, in part, because it allowed the contemplation of the oral record on the community's terms. It also accepted a conception of history as nourished, like literature, in Constance Rourke's words, by "the slow accretions of folk elements . . . the humble influences of place and kinship and common emotion that accumulate through generations to shape and condition a distinctive native consciousness."[12]

It is easy at this point to slip into a sentimental golden-glow about the folk doing their own folk history: let them collect what they wish and let them be content and self-satisfied in their forays into historic consciousness-raising. Such a patronizing attitude allows no efforts in the more official, scholarly analysis and interpretation of the local past. It is my experience, both personally and in working with various community history projects, that pleasurable appreciation and critical evaluation are not mutually exclusive. Around the workshop table we can soberly piece together the outlines of a past event from a dozen different interviews, and we can suggest that all the stories we have collected about a colorful settler may be more important for what the narratives say about community response to the eccentric than about the individual in question. A few hours later, perhaps, we may exchange some of the same stories that both entertain us and communicate some sort of historical information. We may share the tales as "true" even though we half-consciously question their veracity. We share them as history, nevertheless, because they satisfy a complicated need to talk about the past and to do so with some verbal artistry.

Richard M. Dorson has suggested that in "literate civilizations the personal sense of history has all but vanished—save in the local community" and that it is at this level that folk history plays a paramount role in the historical record.[13] The need for cooperation between the folklorist and the oral historian in local history research is obvious. We may reach some agreement that the collective oral record and the personal oral testimony can provide us data with which to construct a quasi-objective past as well as valuable insights into the way in which that past is perceived by community members. And these materials amassed may be studied for a variety of purposes. They are a significant contribution to the understanding of the local past, historically, sociologically, even psychologically. The personalization of history—that complicated nexus of art, tradition, comprehension of the past, and human psychology—which is crucial in the maintenance of historic consciousness, is a more difficult matter to assess. That it can most easily be studied within the contexts of local oral history, whether community, neighborhood, or family, is clear. That the folklorist and the oral historian be involved in its consideration is a necessity. Our contributions to understanding that process of personalization may be more consequential than anything else we have to say about folklore–oral history relations.

Notes

1. "A Theory for American Folklore Reviewed," reprinted from the *Journal of American Folklore* 72 (1969), pp. 197–242, in Richard M. Dorson, *American Folklore and the Historian* (Chicago: University of Chicago Press, 1971), p. 58.

2. *Transcribing and Editing Oral History* (Nashville: American Association for State and Local History, 1977), p. 5. See also Willa Baum, *Oral History for the Local Historical Society* (Nashville: American Association for State and Local History, 1971), p. 7.

3. *History with a Tape Recorder: An Oral History Handbook* (Springfield, Ill.: Sangamon State University, Oral History Office, n.d.), inside cover.

4. Charles Hudson, "Folk History and Ethnohistory," *Ethnohistory* 13 (Winter-Spring 1966), pp. 53–54. The terms "etic" and "emic" often appear in contemporary folklore studies. In informal academic usage "etic" has come to designate an outsider's point of view

and system of classification and "emic" the insider's conception of cultural categories and their order. The terms were borrowed from Kenneth Pike's linguistic theory. Writes Pike, "An emic approach must deal with particular events as parts of larger wholes to which they are related and from which they obtain their ultimate significance, whereas an etic approach may abstract events, for particular purposes, from their context or local system of events, in order to group them on a world-wide scale without essential reference to the structure of any one language or culture," in *Language in Relation to a Unified Theory of the Structure of Human Behavior*, 3 pts. (Glendale, Calif.: Summer Institute of Linguistics, 1954–60), p. 10. Alan Dundes discusses the relevance of the terms to folk narrative analysis in "From Etic to Emic Units in the Structural Study of Folktales," reprinted from the *Journal of American Folklore* 75 (1962), pp. 92–105, in Alan Dundes, *Analytic Essays in Folklore* (The Hague: Mouton, 1975), pp. 61–72.

5. Richard M. Dorson, "The Oral Historian and the Folklorist," in *Selections from the Fifth and Sixth National Colloquia on Oral History*, ed. Peter D. Olch and Forrest C. Pogue (New York: Oral History Association, 1972), pp. 44–46, passim.

6. Personal conversation, October 11, 1978. Edward D. Ives edits *Northeast Folklore*, an annual publication of special interest to the folklorist-oral historian, and directs the Northeast Archives of Folklore and Oral History, Department of Anthropology, University of Maine, Orono, Maine.

7. See, for example, William Lynwood Montell, "The Oral Historian as Folklorist," in *Selections from the Fifth and Sixth National Colloquia on Oral History*, p. 52.

8. Mody C. Boatright, "The Family Saga as a Form of Folklore," in *The Family Saga and Other Phases of American Folklore*, ed. Mody C. Boatright, Robert B. Downs, and John T. Flanagan (Urbana: University of Illinois Press, 1958), pp. 1–19.

9. Specific studies by folklorists that address the historical event include Gladys-Marie Fry, *Night Riders in Black Folk History* (Knoxville: University of Tennessee Press, 1975); Edward D. Ives, "Argyle Boom," *Northeast Folklore* 17 (1976), pp. 24–100; William Ivey, " ' The 1913 Disaster': Michigan Local Legend," *Folklore Forum* 3 (1970), pp. 100–14; and William Lynwood Montell, *The Saga of Coe Ridge: A Study in Oral History* (Knoxville: University of Tennessee Press, 1970; see chapter 16 of the present volume). These studies are heavily indebted to the oral testimony. Bruce A. Rosenberg's *Custer and the Epic of Defeat* (University Park: Pennsylvania State University Press, 1974) is an intriguing analysis of the Custer legend in terms of traditional heroic epic patterns.

10. See items 1567, 1568, 1569, 1570, 1571, 1572, and 1578 in Harry Middleton Hyatt, *Folk-Lore from Adams County, Illinois* (Hannibal, Mo.: Western, 1965). See also George Lyman Kittredge, *Witchcraft in Old and New England* (New York: Russell and Russell, 1956), p. 166, for a brief discussion of the belief in milk-sucking snakes.

The distribution of the tale type is found under no. 285, "The Child and the Snake," in Antti Aarne and Stith Thompson, *The Types of the Folktale: A Classification and Bibliography*, FF Communications No. 184 (Helsinki: Academia Scientiarum Fennica, 1964). See also Butler Waugh, "The Child and the Snake, A Comparative Folktale Study" (Ph.D. diss., Indiana University, 1959), and "The Child and the Snake," *Norveg* 7 (1958) pp. 153ff., and the bibliographic citations under tale type 285, "The Child and the Snake," in Ernest W. Baughman, *Type and Motif-Index of the Folktales of England and North America*, Indiana University Folklore Series No. 20 (The Hague: Mouton, 1966).

Easily available versions of the story appear in B. A. Botkin, ed., *Lay My Burden Down: A Folk History of Slavery* (Chicago: University of Chicago Press, 1965), p. 128; "The Little Girl Who Fed the Snake," in the *Frank C. Brown Collection of North Carolina Folklore*, vol. 1, *Games, Speech, Customs, Proverbs, Riddles, Tales*, ed. Paul G. Brewster, Archer Taylor, Bartlett Jere Whiting, George P. Wilson, and Stith Thompson (Durham: Duke University Press, 1952), p. 638. "The Snake and the Baby" (three texts), in Richard M. Dorson, *American*

Negro Folktales (Greenwich: Fawcett, 1967), pp. 174–75; "The Little Boy and the Snake," in Vance Randolph, *Who Blowed Up the Church House? and Other Ozark Folk Tales* (New York: Columbia University Press, 1952), pp. 87–89; and the *Foxfire Book*, ed. Eliot Wigginton (Garden City, N.Y.: Doubleday, 1972), p. 290 (see chapter 34 of the present volume). It appears as part of a Swedish-American pioneer's reminiscence in an unidentified newspaper story by Karolina Falk Miller in the *Salina Journal* (Salina, Kansas), 1932, reprinted in *The Smoky Valley in the After Years*, ed. Ruth Bergin Billdt and Elizabeth Jaderborg (Lindsborg, Kans.: Lindsborg News-Record, 1969), pp. 191–92. The children's poem, "The Child and the Snake," appears in Charles and Mary Lamb, *Poetry for Children* (Freeport, N.Y.: Books for Libraries Press, 1970), pp. 21–23.

11. Sam Bass Warner, Jr., "An Urban Historian's Agenda for the Profession," *Indiana Historical Society Lectures, 1971–1972: History and the Role of the City in American Life* (Indianapolis: Indiana Historical Society, 1972), pp. 52–53.

12. Constance Rourke, "The Significance of Sections," *New Republic*, September 20, 1933, p. 149, quoted in Benjamin Botkin, "Folklore as a Neglected Source of Social History," in *The Cultural Approach to History*, ed. Carolina F. Ware (Port Washington, N.Y.: Kennikat Press, 1940), pp. 314–15.

13. Richard M. Dorson, "Local History and Folklore," reprinted from the *Detroit Historical Society Bulletin* 18 (1961), in Dorson, *American Folklore and the Historian*, p. 148.

18

Documenting Diversity:
The Southern Experience

Jacquelyn Dowd Hall

*Moving from folk to local and regional history, we see in the next selec-
tions how available resources play an important part in determining how
and what history is written. In regions where oral tradition is strong and
the written historical record meager, oral history will necessarily play an
important role in the armory of historians.*

*One area exemplifying this tendency is the South, a geographic and emo-
tional cluster of communities which are particularly place and tradition
oriented—and therefore especially interested in oral historical techniques.
The use of oral history is only one of the techniques available to the workers who are fueling the growing interest in regional studies. In the following essay Jacquelyn Hall, director of the Southern Oral History Program,
draws on her experience to suggest ties between the regional studies movement and oral history. Her remarks apply equally to Afro- and Hispanic-
and Asian-American programs which use oral sources in social science and
humanistic research.*

*Jacquelyn Hall teaches oral history and directs the Southern Oral His-
tory Project at the University of North Carolina. She is the author of the
award-winning* Revolt against Chivalry: Jessie Daniel Ames and the
Women's Campaign against Lynching *(1979).*

*This excerpt from "Documenting Diversity: The Southern Experience"
first appeared in the* Oral History Review *4 (1976), pp. 19–28.*

THE USE OF personal recollections as historical evidence is
scarcely a recent or startling innovation. On the contrary, history
itself is—in its broadest definition—our collective memory of the
past. Interviews provide a means of conveying the uniqueness and integrity of individual lives, while at the same time broadening the research

base upon which our understanding of general patterns is predicated. Nevertheless, only recently have professional historians begun systematically to compile and use oral sources.

There are several reasons for the evolving interest in oral history. First, and perhaps most obvious, is the impact of technology on the historian's customary source materials. As the diary and confidential letter have declined as modes of reflection and communication, historians have been forced to turn to personal testimony for an understanding of political dynamics and individual motives.

Second, the rise of social history has engendered a creative search for evidence which reflects the consciousness and experience of those whom historians have considered the "inarticulate." Historians investigating such social phenomena as mobility, family structure, and black and white working-class community life are turning for quantitative evidence to court records, census returns, and demographic data. As they seek *qualitative* sources for writing the history of the total society, the utility of oral techniques becomes obvious. Neither individuals who have led essentially private lives, nor grass roots politicians, nor those who have built the infrastructure of institutions and communications networks which sustain both female and ethnic subcultures ordinarily leave behind written records. Records which *are* created are seldom preserved. Interviews, then, may often serve as an indispensable avenue into the lives of those who are otherwise hidden from history.

Moreover, this new commitment to social history has led historians to supplement their traditional modes of research with the concepts and methods of other disciplines. In doing so, they have encountered an established and sophisticated practice of information-gathering through interviews. For example, in African history Jan Vansina has pioneered in the use of oral evidence to reveal the structure and evolution of traditional societies.[1] Anthropological studies of Indian cultures have drawn on an oral tradition still very much alive despite centuries of assault and assimilation. John G. Neihardt's *Black Elk Speaks* (N.Y., 1932) and Nancy O. Lurie's *Mountain Wolf Woman: the Autobiography of a Winnebago Indian* (Ann Arbor, 1961), are two of the more well-known of these oral renditions of the native American experience. One of the earliest and most extensive oral history projects in the country was the nationwide program of Indian interviews sponsored by the Donner Foundation, the full importance of which is yet to be realized. Folklorists too have developed field techniques and gathered sources of clear relevance to social historians. An early and provocative mating of these two disciplines is William Lynwood Montell's *The Saga of Coe Ridge* (Knoxville, Tenn., 1970), a study of an isolated black community in the Cumberland foothills in Kentucky.

Sociologists, of course, have long based community studies and investigations of ethnic and family life on interview sources. Lee Rainwater's studies of working-class families and Mirra Komorovsky's book on working-class marriage provide important texts for the emerging field of women's history.[2] Impressive older works like Robert and Helen Lynd's *Middletown* (N.Y., 1929) and Florian Znaniecki and William I. Thomas' *The Polish Peasant in Europe and America* (N.Y., 1958) still offer the historian rare insights into cultural change. Richard Sennett and Jonathan Cobb's *The Hidden Injuries of Class* (N.Y., 1972) speaks to the problem of inequality in American society. Carol Stack's anthropological work, *All Our Kin*,[3] provides a new level of conceptualization for the historical debate on the nature of the black family. From a wide range of disciplines, then, have come studies drawing on oral evidence which provide material for social historians and encourage emulation.

Finally, I think oral history—as a methodological approach to historical problems—has gained converts because of a sense of crisis within the historical profession itself. As enrollments have dropped, taking with them faculty positions and financial resources, historians have looked with new concern at teaching methods and student attitudes. Oral history offers one means of bridging the gap between historical abstractions and the student's life experience. Eliot Wigginton's success in engaging disaffected high school students in the study of local traditions and folk culture has spawned *Foxfire* imitators across the country. In college courses, students are combining family history and oral sources in studies of generational change and continuity and are thus learning to see themselves and their society in historical perspective.[4] Graduate seminars represent an effort to imbue a new generation of scholars with a critical stance toward the biases of written documents and with the self-consciousness and skill necessary to create and use spoken sources. On all of these levels, oral history is becoming an important teaching tool and a means of reasserting the relevance and validity of the historical enterprise itself.

These, then, are some of the forces generating interest in oral history: the erosion of written forms of evidence; the growth of social history; the multi-disciplinary nature of modern scholarship; and the search for teaching methods appropriate to changing times.

But what about performance and prospects? How is oral history actually being used and what are the trends of the future? The 1975 Oral History Association Colloquium was entitled "Oral History Comes of Age." I would say the title was a bit premature. Oral history has "come of age" in the Eriksonian sense that it has acquired certain motor skills and has successfully survived the crisis of infancy and childhood. It now perches on the edge of adult life. There are at least 400 oral history projects in the country, and more spring up every day. The utility of oral evidence in studying the recent past has gained acceptance among professional historians. Tape recorders proliferate and interviews accrue. But the test of tapes and techniques will come as written works based on them emerge.

The Southern Experience

In the South, I believe, the prospects for oral history are especially bright. I'd like to suggest some of the reasons I think this is so. Then I want to describe the ways in which the Southern Oral History Program at Chapel Hill is seeking to contribute to a better understanding of the Southern region.

The sociologist John Shelton Reed, in a pathbreaking study called *The Enduring South* (Lexington, Mass., 1972), and George B. Tindall, in his 1973 Presidential Address to the Southern Historical Association,[5] pointed out that, despite perennial reports on the decline of Southern distinctiveness, the South is with us still: a state of mind, a burden of history, and a set of measurable social-psychological differences which give Southerners a group identity and a persistent sub-culture. This is not to resurrect the myth of the solid South. On the contrary, the direction of Southern studies is, and must be, away from constructions of "the mind" of the white male minority of the population.[6] The recognition of multicultural diversity, the affirmation that Southern culture is, most profoundly, a joint creation of black and white, the incorporation of the female experience into generalizations about Southern life—these are the tasks that will continue to invigorate and expand the field of Southern studies. Oral history can, I believe, speak directly both to the question of distinctiveness and to the documentation of diversity.

As John Reed has pointed out, Southerners are distinguished from Americans in other regions by an intense sense of place, a tendency to derive their individual identity from a particular piece of ground, a network of kin, a set of personal, rather than functional relationships. I would suggest that a corollary to this consciousness of place is a sense of family history and family culture. It is a truism that mobility, mass communications and mass culture vitiate oral tradition and break the links between generations. But historians are also discovering the power of the family to maintain and transmit traditional values and assumptions in the face of greatly changed external circumstances. They are taking notice of the remarkable resiliency of ethnic cultural forms beyond the melting pot. In the South, where modernization is least advanced and is superimposed upon a sharply divergent historical heritage, these continuities and traditions perhaps retain their greatest vitality. Rural blacks, whites in the piedmont cities, textile workers, mountaineers—all carry with them in their minds and memories the stuff of which social history is made. The tape recorder, handled sensitively by a researcher concerned about the pattern and rhythms of daily life, about culture in its broadest sense, should provide historians with the tools for writing a more comprehensive history of the South than has yet been possible.

In fact, scholars interested in the use of oral sources can look to a long tradition in Southern intellectual life. Motivated by a belief in the existence and desirability of regional differences, by a perception of folk culture as a key to Southern distinctiveness, and by a humane vision of scholars and planners working together for social change, Howard Odum made North Carolina the center for the intellectual movement known as "regionalism." The massive studies of Odum, Rubert Vance, Guy Johnson, and other gifted Southern scholars sought not only to provide documentation of social and economic forces but also to bring to life the dry statistics of poverty and progress in the region. By using oral testimony and folk tradition they gave voice to the ordinary men and women of the farms, hamlets, and industrial communities of the emerging New South.

During the Depression decade, Southern regionalism combined with a more general impulse toward documentary realism to inspire two of the earliest oral history projects in the country. One consisted of a series of Southern life histories, gathered under the supervision of University of North Carolina Press director W. T. Couch. The other was the Slave Narrative Collection of the Works Progress Administration. Both reflect a popular front ideology, characteristic of the times, which sought the basis for a social democracy in the common humanity of ordinary people.

As regional director of the Federal Writers Project, Couch proposed an ambitious effort to provide a complete picture of Southern life and culture through interviews which allowed individual Southerners to "speak for themselves." Between 1938 and 1939, writers collected over 900 biographical interviews with Southerners from all walks of life. Thirty-five of these stories were published in the critically acclaimed These Are Our Lives (Chapel Hill, 1939). But the unpublished majority of this collection, held by the Southern Historical Collection in Chapel Hill, has remained unused by scholars and unknown to the general public. The recent renaissance of oral history, however, has given impetus to the publication of another volume of these life histories. Hopefully its appearance will generate scholarly interest in the use of this rich vein of oral source material.

Because slavery and race relations have engaged the imaginations of Southern scholars to a greater degree than has the history of the white working class, the Slave Narrative Collection has emerged more quickly from obscurity. Yet it too has received the attention it deserves only in recent years. Originated by black scholars at Fisk University and at Southern University, the Collection grew into an archive of personal recollections of 2000 ex-slaves from 17 states. Although no effort was made at random sampling, the interviews as a whole provide the most representative first-hand accounts we have of the slave experience. Nevertheless, the bias of historians toward written documents and white sources meant that parts of this project were lost, and surviving materials were relegated to the shelves of the Library of Congress. Finally, in 1972, the contemporary search for clues to slave consciousness and culture brought about the publication of the Slave Narrative Collection in its entirety.[7] Such recent books as Eugene Genovese's *Roll, Jordan, Roll: The World the Slaves Made* (N.Y., 1974) have drawn fruitfully upon the collection for their portrait of the culture of slavery.

In addition to the work of regional sociologists and the oral history projects carried out by New Deal agencies, other studies of the South, from a variety of disciplines, have relied primarily on interview sources. Charles S. Johnson's *In the Shadow of the Plantation* (Chicago, 1934), Hortense Powdermaker's *After Slavery* (N.Y., 1939), Liston Pope's *Millhands and Preachers* (New Haven, 1942), John Dollard's *Caste and Class in A Southern Town* (New Haven, 1937), and John K. Morland's *Millways of Kent* (Chapel Hill, 1958)—all have provided historians with invaluable insights into Southern culture and community life. Folklorists have looked more closely at rural blacks and whites in the Appalachian Highlands than at any other ethnic or sub-cultural group. From political science has come V. O. Key's classic *Southern Politics in State and Nation* (N.Y., 1949), which was based in large part on a vast interviewing project which included 538 politicians and political observers in eleven Southern states. More recently, through the quarterly journal *Southern Exposure*, a group of regional journalists has begun to make available oral sources on labor history, civil rights struggles, and folk culture. . . .

Notes

1. Jan Vansina, *Oral Tradition: A Study in Historical Methodology* (London: Routledge and Kegan Paul, 1965; see chapter 9 of the present volume).

2. Lee Rainwater, *Working Man's Wife: Her Personality, World, and Life Style* (New York: Oceana Press, 1959); Mirra Komorovsky, *Blue-Collar Marriage* (New York: Vintage, 1967).

3. Carol B. Stack, *All Our Kin: Strategies for Survival in a Black Community* (New York: Harper and Row, 1974).

4. For an illuminating discussion of field work in a college English course, see R. C. Townsend, "The Possibilities of Field Work," *College English* 34 (January 1973), pp. 481–99.

5. G. B. Tindall, "Beyond the Mainstream: The Ethnic Southerners," *Journal of Southern History* 40 (1974), pp. 3–18.

6. W. J. Cash, *The Mind of the South* (New York: Vintage, 1941).

7. George P. Rawick, ed., *The American Slave: A Composite Autobiography* 19 vols. (Westport, Conn.: Greenwood, 1972).

19

Oral History and the Writing
of Ethnic History

Gary Okihiro

When the methods of oral history are applied to research on ethnic and minority groups, the history which emerges frequently has a populist or self-consciously democratic cast. Ethnic communities tell their history among themselves, and textbook writers have rarely listened. As a result such groups have lacked a nationally recognized identity. Efforts to redress the balance suggest a key problem in doing oral history: the impact of differences in world view between the interviewer and the interviewee—differences in setting, communication styles, dress, even in the reasons why narrators respond.

In our next selection, a professor of ethnic studies, Gary Okihiro, traces the place of ethnic history in the mainstream of the historical profession. Okihiro advocates oral sources as a means of enfranchising and empowering people whose lives have previously been shaped by "colonized history" written from the standpoint of outsiders, not cultural insiders. In this assertion, he parallels Paul Thompson, the English social historian whose essay appeared in chapter 3.

Okihiro foresees an oral-based ethnic history which could help ethnic groups understand their true condition and could help devise the means for their liberation from economic and social constraints. His essay reflects a recent trend toward increasingly theoretical and introspective writings on oral history.

Gary Y. Okihiro teaches at the University of Santa Clara in California, where he directs the Ethnic Studies Program. He has done field work in Africa and among Japanese-Americans; he is editing a collection of essays, Resistance in America's Concentration Camps.

"Oral History and the Writing of Ethnic History" first appeared in the Oral History Review 9 (1981), pp. 27–46.

WHILE ETHNIC historians have utilized oral history for a number of years, in varying degrees of sophistication, few have addressed themselves to the methodological problem of oral history as a tool for recovering history or the theoretical problem of what constitutes history which oral history proposes to answer. The intent of this paper is a modest one. It synthesizes the scattered body of literature on oral history method and seeks to show that oral history is not only method, but also is theory, in the loose sense of the word, and a way of conceptualizing history. The paper, therefore, is mainly concerned with the writing of history—particularly ethnic history—and is neither a primer on how to set up an ethnic oral history program nor a critical analysis of existing ones or the extant literature in ethnic studies. It is an essay on the writing of history and oral history as method and theory and is a reminder of oral history's significance to ethnic history.

The Writing of History

History is the knowledge of human beings in time. Marc Bloch argued that even if history were indifferent to political man/woman and were unable to promote social change, it would be justified by its necessity for the full development of human beings.[1] Still, history would be incomplete if it did not eventually help us to lead better lives. Historical explanation derives, in the first instance, from our need for explanation but thereafter enables us to act reasonably. Accordingly, this humanistic history advocated by Bloch springs from a desire to satisfy human intellectual needs/curiosity through an explanation of human lives—the human condition—for the guidance of human action.

Both of these aims in history—the needs for explanation and human guidance—require that historians reconstruct and explicate historical reality freed from the oppression of myths and lies. That objective reality, however, is independent of the historian's consciousness and may not even be approached. In his well-known 1932 presidential address to the American Historical Association, Carl Becker expressed an extreme position on that subject. According to Becker, history which is past reality complete and unchanging is distinct from our knowledge of history which is merely our conception of that historical reality incomplete and subject to change. Thus, he concluded, every man was his own historian.[2]

Two decades later, C. Vann Woodward objected to Becker's relativism. While conceding that myths may influence human activity and constitute a part of intellectual history, Woodward nonetheless maintained that they must be separated from historical reality, the object toward which historians strive.[3] As his own work on segregation in the South underscored,[4] individuals may well behave on the basis of misconceptions or myths; these may constitute reality for them, but it was Woodward's contention that the historian must distinguish between those subjective perceptions and objective reality.

While in accord with Woodward's strictures on the subject, I share the sentiments voiced by those like Arthur Schlesinger, Jr.; Jan Vansina; Studs Terkel; and Staughton Lynd to the effect that the historian must shed intellectual arrogance which presumes that s/he knows better than the historical actors themselves or that nonliterate people have no conception of history.[5]

Still, a revival of the old extreme relativism in the form of what Gene Wise has labeled as "perspectivist history" is ill-conceived if the distinction is blurred between historical reality and individual reality.[6] Stanley Elkins's Sambo might have been reality to some southern whites who only saw that profile of black people,[7] but it was not historical reality to blacks in their accounts of plantation life. What blacks emphasize are the subjects of slave rebellions and the deceptions played on white masters. Sambo was not, then, an internalized image, as proposed by Elkins, but was merely a mask for survival.[8] The contract here is elucidating. Elkins's thesis was derived from the traditional plantation sources—records, diaries, letters, et cetera—while the refutation came from the people themselves, the oral traditions or black folk. Further, the distinction between individual or group reality and historical reality is a necessary and liberating one.

Historians generally agree that historical explanations are really only propositions placed within a general interpretive framework postulated by the historian. "The history of societies," observed E.J. Hobsbawm, "requires us to apply, if not a formalized and elaborate model of such structures, then at least an approximate order of research priorities and a working assumption about what constitutes the central nexus or complex of connections of our subject, though of course these things imply a model. Every social historian does in fact make such assumptions and holds such priorities."[9] At the very first, therefore, historical research presumes that there is direction and purpose and that it is not value free.

The apparent paradox is that historians argue for the reconstruction of historical reality while, at the same time, they also admit that historical research begins with assumptions; and, in fact, they advocate the construction of models and theories to explain reality. If, however, one agrees that historical reality behaves in a systematic fashion, then theory which most closely resembles that reality best explains it; this is because theory provides boundaries for the system; identifies its elements, structure, and function; proposes explanations; poses questions; and provides a test of logical consistency for explanations. Even if the theory is divorced from reality, it at least provides expectations, things for the historian to look for; and if these are not found, the model can be modified accordingly.[10] The historian must, therefore, be sensitive and receptive to whatever the historical evidence may reveal.

A diagram of the process by which history is written is displayed in figure 19.1.

The Nature of Historical Evidence

While maintaining a receptive mind, the historians must also view the historical evidence critically. Apart from cultural and physical artifacts such as pottery, bones, and so forth, there are two broad categories of historical evidence—written documents and oral documents. Both of these varieties share common elements which are of concern to the historian. Historical documents derive from humans who have biases and prejudices, selective perceptions and memories, incomplete and limited powers of observation, and fallible memories. Further, people undergo changes over time and are subject to external influences and manipulation and, as such, are mirrors of their time and environment.

Besides these common human qualities which pervade historical documents, there is the question of audience to which the document is addressed. This assumes that historical documents are purposeful and that those purposes may determine, in a deliberate or unconscious way, the final shape of the document in which facts may be altered, emphases misplaced, or information suppressed. The historian must, therefore, distinguish between the behavioral or apparent meaning of the document and the ideational or internal, and thus hidden, meaning.[11]

Because of these characteristics of historical documents, they cannot stand alone nor can they "speak for themselves." They are, in fact, parts of a human-communications system which consists of a network of ele-

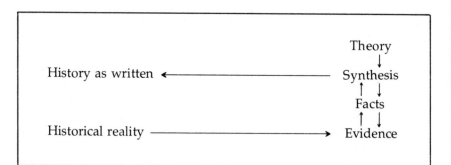

Figure 19.1. The writing of history. *Source:* Robert F. Berkhofer, Jr., *A Behavioral Approach to Historical Analysis* (New York: Macmillan, 1969), pp. 20–23.

ments within a pervasive environment over time. Thus, in historical documents, the critical historian must identify the author of the document in an identified position or vantage point at an identified moment.[12] The task, therefore, is a mapping of the terrain through a sociology of the systems or network to identify its elements and determine their relationships at a particular moment in time. That process, termed internal textual criticism, enables the historian to make a more valid evaluation of the reliability of the historical evidence.

When several historical documents are compared with each other, we say that the historian is engaged in external textual criticism. The comparative method of documentary evaluation is indispensable in reconstructing historical reality; for by comparing several texts, one is able to see variation, contradictions, and similarities. From that comparison, then, and through internal textual criticism and theory, the historian is better able to approach historical reality.

The reliance on theory increases as the quantity of historical documents diminishes because the less the number of witnesses to support, contradict, or modify a particular version, the greater the degree of uncertainty. Besides quantity, the quality or nature of the evidence may determine the extent for the need for theory. Thus, for example, one objective and perceptive witness is usually more valuable than three witnesses who had a particular ax to grind although that in itself could be illuminating;[13] and if the weight of the evidence supports a point of view which does not correspond with the historian's view of reality, the evidence may be used selectively to make it conform to the historian's theory of historical reality.

The end product of that process, history as written, may in an extreme case not even resemble the documents from which it was drawn; but the historian may claim that the interpretation is a closer approximation of historical reality because the theory more closely conforms to that reality. Some may see that claim as intellectual arrogance while others may view it as a breakthrough in interpretation; it depends on their world view or theory of history. Historical debate is fueled by the scarcity of reliable evidence—the lesser the amount of reliable evidence, the greater the dependence on theory and the greater the dependence on theory, the greater the opportunity for debate.

Types of Oral Documents

While sharing certain common features, oral documents are not identical to written ones. There is an important distinction which is of concern to the oral historian. The author of a written document is usually no longer living when the document is used by a historian—a feature of

various privacy and ethical codes. In contrast, oral documents are derived from living persons; at least the initial recording of any such document on tape or paper is a product of living persons in conversation.
Thus, whereas written documents are often referred to as dead letters,
oral documents are generally styled living testimonies.

The difference here can be an important one if, as is commonly the
case, a historian generates oral documents which s/he subsequently uses
for historical interpretation. This is because the archival historian is limited to the written word and cannot go beyond what the author of a given
document thought, what s/he thought happened or ought to happen, or
what s/he wanted others to think happened; in other words, the distinction between the behavioral and ideational is blurred; and the historian is
uncertain of the historicity of the evidence. On the other hand, the oral
historian who employs a document which s/he has created with an interviewee is able to observe human behavior firsthand in all its complexity
and under varying circumstances; and s/he is able to engage in dialogue
with the historical actor.

Of course, this interaction between historian and historical actor can
both illuminate and obscure historical reality. While a greater degree of
precision may be obtained by direct observation and communication,
greater uncertainty may also arise from the historian's role in altering
behavior or in predetermining the responses by the nature of the questions or from the historian's diminished capacity to be objective because
of any friendship so cultivated.[14]

There are several varieties of oral documents. Personal reminiscence or
oral history is the most elemental of these. Oral history is the recollections
of a single individual who participated in or was an observer of the events
to which s/he testifies. The document, therefore, derives from the historical actor him/herself or from an eyewitness. When oral history is passed
on to another person, usually of a succeeding generation in that family
or lineage, it becomes oral tradition.[15] Thus, oral tradition is derived from
a transmission of testimony vertically. If that tradition spreads horizon-
tally to a wider, definable group of people, it is referred to as folklore or
elitelore, depending on the social class of the group.[16]

As indicated at the outset, this paper is limited to a discussion of oral
history, and the distinction between that type of oral evidence and the
other varieties such as oral tradition, folklore/elitelore, legend, epic, fable,
and myth should be kept in mind.[17]

Oral History

Despite the claim that oral history is history, no more, no less, the
distinctions remain between individual perceptions of historical reality

and historical reality and between the process by which archival history is written and by which history derived from oral documents is written. The latter process is more complex than archival history, as is evident by contrasting figure 19.2 with figure 19.1.

The program director is the person who conceptualizes the oral history program, its purposes and direction. The director's world view or idea of history helps determine the linguistic community selected. ("Linguistic community" herein refers to those who share linguistic symbols and patterns of articulation, and a common world view and experiences.) Thus, for example, Joe Grant Masaoka, the director of the oral history collection of the Japanese American Research Project housed at the University of California, Los Angeles, generally chose to interview those who reflected his point of view about such controversial issues as the causes and conduct of the World War II evacuation and incarceration of West Coast Japanese Americans.[18] In that way, the collection to a large extent mirrored Masaoka's perceptions.

The selected individuals, however, need not be comprehensive nor statistically representative of the wider linguistic community from which they originate. Oral historians realize that the interview is a limited document. At the same time, they maintain that a given individual has as much right to be heard as anyone else and that his/her history is worthy of being recorded.[19] The difference is in one's conception of what constitutes history.

On the other hand, the oral historian (i.e., one who is a consumer of the interviews s/he has conducted) does not merely regurgitate the contents

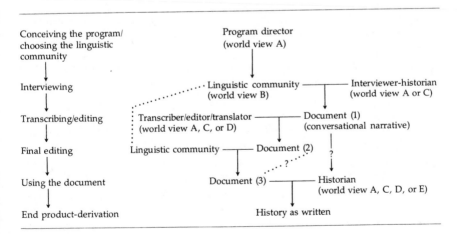

Figure 19.2. Steps in oral history

of the interview. As noted above, the historian must examine the oral document critically, both internally and externally and place that document within his/her theoretical framework. Thus, the oral historian must keep clearly in mind the distinction between an individual's right to be heard and the writing of history. The individual's perception of history need not necessarily coincide with historical reality. The oral historian is not a mere publicist of individual perceptions; the ultimate goal is the reconstruction of historical reality.

The second step in oral history, the interview, involves at least two different world views, that of the linguistic community and that of the interviewer or oral historian. A concern, therefore, is with these world views. Are they parallel, or do they clash, and what are the implications if they do not correspond? These questions are of particular relevance in cross-cultural situations in which the conceptions of what constitutes history differ.

When I did my fieldwork in Botswana, Africa, in 1974–75, at first, hoping not to bias the response, I invariably began with an open-ended question like "Tell me about the history of the Bakwena (the people I was studying)." The responses to that question were always very general and vague and indicated that the interviewees had little knowledge of Bakwena history. After numerous such disappointing interviews, I became discouraged and began to think that no one in the community had a deep and clear understanding of history. Because I was getting nowhere with that question, I began to pursue a different tack by asking more localized questions about the interviewee, his/her family, lineage, and clan. And as the information gushed forth, it became apparent to me that our conceptions of what constituted history did not correspond. The people's view was limited to one's family, lineage, and kin while my conception was one of nation or "tribe"; and because of our different world views, there was a restricted flow of information, and I labored under false impressions.

A second concern arising from the interview situation is the extent to which external factors influence the responses. It is a recognized fact that the setting in which the interview is held, the nature of the questions, and even the appearance of the interviewer may bias responses and restrict the flow of information. Various authors have noted how a setting unfamiliar to the interviewee or a highly formalized list of questions tends to inhibit communication and how class- or culture-bound assumptions, mode of speech, or dress has a similarly stultifying effect.[20] In addition, the oral historian must concern him/herself with the motives of the interviewee in agreeing to be interviewed. Studs Terkel, for instance, pays his interviewees; the question then arises, to what extent does reimbursement or the promise of publication influence the nature of the responses?

Certain bands of Bushmen (San) in southern Africa, frequently sought out by anthropologists, have grown astute in handling their visitors, giving them answers which the anthropologists want to hear in return for gifts.

One proposed solution to the problems of cross-cultural research has been participant observation. Oscar Lewis, in his studies of poverty and families, proposes that to understand the culture of the poor it is necessary to live with them, learn the language and customs, and identify oneself with their frustrations and aspirations.[21] That method stands in marked contrast to those studies done by Nathan Glazer and Daniel P. Moynihan, who relied on census data rather than engaging in ethnographic field research among the people themselves.[22] Then, too, there is the case of Victor and Brett Nee whose 1972 publication *Longtime Californ'* represents the most notable Asian American book to date using oral history. While claiming that it was an advantage to be outsiders because they could stand above local partisan conflict, the Nees nonetheless found that not being residents of Chinatown and not knowing Cantonese or other dialects restricted their full entry into the community and, no doubt, resulted in a less-than-complete picture of San Francisco Chinatown.[23]

Because of the many opportunities for distortions to arise in the interview, oral historians are cautioned to familiarize themselves with the extensive literature on interviewing techniques and to be aware of the various external factors which may influence the responses.[24] Further, they are urged to make thorough research preparations concerning the interviewee and subject matter before each session to provide the basis for a productive and meaningful conversation.[25] Oral historians maintain that the knowledge derived from those background researches coupled with the empathy and sensitivity developed through participant observation enables them to elicit significant and valid historical documents and to reconstruct historical reality.

As noted by Ronald Grele, the primary theoretical concern in writings on oral history has been the possibility for distortion in the interview while little discussion has focused on the exact nature of the oral document which is the end product of that interview. The document, observed Grele, is not simply a transcript or tape; nor is it an autobiography, biography, or memory; rather, it is a conversational narrative—conversational because it is a dialogue between interviewer and interviewee and narrative because it is a form of exposition. There are three sets of relationships in this conversational narrative: (1) internal to the interview, consisting of its linguistic and literary structure; (2) external to the text, the relationship created by interaction of interviewer and interviewee; and (3) external to the text, the relationship between the interviewee and the wider community which is both his/her audience and molder of his/her historical consciousness.[26]

All three relationships are enormously complex, but by untangling them invaluable insights can be gained. A linguistic analysis of the text, for example, may contribute toward a cultural definition of class; for, as demonstrated by William Labov, among ethnic groups and social classes there is a tendency of speakers to conform to certain unique patterns of speech.[27] In that way, those groups maintain their ethnic and class identity.

The relationship between interviewer and interviewee involves a reflexive process by which the interviewee's view of history is developed in relation to the historian's view, while the historian's questions, in turn, are developed in response to the interviewee's answers. Thus, *The Autobiography of Malcolm X* is not an autobiography; rather it is the mutual creation of two men, Malcolm X and Alex Haley.[28] The task of the oral historian is to analyze carefully that relationship between interviewer and interviewee to understand what kind of communication is taking place, what meaning is being conveyed, and what mutual influences are at work in the shaping of the conversation.

The relationship between the interviewee and the wider community involves the ideological or theoretical context within which words or phrases are placed, the presence or absence of concepts, and the individual's vision of history. To extricate the interviewee from both the interviewer and his/her wider community, then, is an exceedingly complex and comanding task. But by being able to direct questions at the interviewee's conceptions of history and historical change, the oral historian, unlike the archival historian, is able to arrive at a deeper understanding of the people and their history.[29]

The end product of the interaction between interviewer-historian and linguistic community–interviewee is oral document (1) (see figure 19.2) defined as a conversational narrative and normally in the form of a tape recording. Next comes the transcription, editing, and sometimes translating of that recording onto paper.

When Allan Nevins, considered to be the founder of oral history in the United States, set up the Oral History Research Office at Columbia University in 1948, he at first conceived his task to be a simple one. He interviewed well-known individuals about significant events, had the tapes transcribed onto paper, and saw the transcription as the raw stuff of which history would be written. The tapes were then erased, keeping only a small segment to give the flavor of the interview. During the transcription phase, there was free editing of the text which included the striking out of words and phrases.[30]

Later, on reflection, Nevins's procedure was seen to have posed serious methodological problems. The historian's intervention in transcribing and editing effectively altered the text so that entire meanings could be lost or changed. Thus, oral historians were cautioned to make certain that the transcriber faithfully recorded what was on the tape, including pauses, laughter, and coughs. In addition, the interviewer must be sure that everything which took place during the interview was recorded because oftentimes in the course of the interview the participants took a break, the duration for which the recorder was turned off. But a number of important things may transpire or be said during that period of relaxation. Thus, the interviewer was advised to keep the recorder on at all times.[31] And finally, the original tape recording must be kept intact for future reference.

Despite these cautions, there still remains the possibility of distortions in the transcribed text which may be the result of fatigue, hearing impairment, or misperceptions caused by divergent world views. This last factor is even more pronounced if the text is being translated as well as transcribed; translation, of course, introduces a whole new set of opportunities for distortion.

The end result of this interaction between transcriber and document (1) (see figure 19.2) is document (2) which is, ideally, an exact replica of the voices on the tape recording in written form. The usual procedure is then to give document (2) back to the interviewee for final editing. This is normally done because of the interviewee's ethical right to see the text before final release and out of courtesy to him/her who can if s/he so wishes delete or retract words, phrases, or expressions made during the interview. In effect, the interviewee acts as his/her own censor. Document (3) (see figure 19.2) is the end product of this interaction between interviewee and document (2), and the documents may or may not be the same.

Document (3) is used by the historian in the same way as other historical documents are used, as diagrammed in figure 19.1; the text is critically examined both internally and externally, and the final outcome of that interaction is history as written.[32] There is little doubt, from the process outlined above, that oral documents are qualitatively different from written ones; there exist more possibilities for distortions to arise, and they are more complex and hazardous to use. At the same time, however, oral history provides a unique opportunity for the writing of Bloch's humanistic vision of history, a people's history.

Oral History and the Writing of Ethnic History

This work is an impression and the search for a silenced voice, a crucial part in the chorus of American voices.

Black woman, silent, almost invisible in America, has been speaking for three hundred years in pantomime or at least in a borrowed voice. She has moved silently through the mythological roles forced upon her—from chattel to Mammy to Matriarch. She has solaced and fortified the entire South of the United States, black and white, male and female, a South which reveres and heeds her in secret, which confides in her and trusts her to rear its children, black and white, yet which—like the rest of America—has never asked her to speak, to reveal her private history, her knowledge, her imaginings, never asked her participation in anything but maintenance of humanity by way of the back door.[33]

The writing of ethnic history is both necessary and possible. It need neither be justified nor defended. The collective voice of the people, once silenced, has a right to be heard. Oral history is not only a tool or method for recovering history; it also is a theory of history which maintains that the common folk and the dispossessed have a history and that this history must be written. At the same time, however, this is not to ignore the importance of elitelore and the history of the ruling class, nor does it intend to equate oral history with the working class and written documents with the ruling class. Instead, the point is that there has been an overemphasis on the elite at the expense of the masses and that this imbalance has resulted in the writing of mythical histories.

Ethnic history does not deny the political importance of focusing on the dominant (oppressor) group in society and those institutions through which the majority represses and exploits the minority. Rather, ethnic history is the first step toward ultimate emancipation; for by freeing themselves from the bonds of a colonized history, they will be able to see their true condition, their own history. From that realization and from an understanding of the majority group and their institutions, minorities can proceed to devise means for their total liberation.

Oral history has been shown to be an invaluable means by which to recover the past of the inarticulate—women, the working class, ethnic and racial minorities, and people in nonliterate societies[34]—because these groups rarely leave written records of their lives; the meager documentary evidence about them is usually biased against them and rarely penetrates to the ideational, and they have largely been ignored by historians who view history in terms of "big men" and "important" events.[35] Besides being a tool for recovering history, oral history forges a link between the academy and the community through ethnographic field techniques and participant observation; and it has a potential for raising social consciousness and can provide strategies for social change.[36]

Terkel noted that the absence of knowledge about the past perpetuates myths about it and contributes to maintaining of the status quo.[37] A graphic illustration of that is the Republic of South Africa, where the official version of history is used to justify the repressive system of apartheid. Staughton Lynd, in his studies of American labor history, observed that rank-and-file unionists wanted to know the history of the 1930s so they could respond to the present upsurge of labor militancy in the CIO.[38] That knowledge was obtained by interviewing old-time activists; and, armed with those insights, the militants were able to understand how CIO unions had so rapidly grown bureaucratic and conservative and thereupon to devise effective tactics in seeking change. Socialist historians, though, like historians and intellectuals in general, must strive for maximum objectivity. Myths, both ideologically and radically inspired, must not be permitted to distort the historical landscape.[39]

The historiographical development in African history is of particular significance and relevance.[40] African history was first written by Europeans who saw Africans, in the words of the distinguished British historian Sir Reginald Coupland, as having no history and as having "stayed, for untold centuries, sunk in barbarism . . . [so that] the heart of Africa was scarcely beating."[41] African history, accordingly, was derived exclusively from European archives and the reminiscences and accounts of white colonialists, missionaries, and travelers. This variety of history portrayed Africa as being dark and peopled by primitive, faceless hordes; African history began with the arrival of the European who brought Christianity, enlightenment, and civilization. The focus, therefore, was on the white man who was the historical actor; and the African was merely a docile object to be manipulated.

During the 1950s, a new generation of historians broke away from that European tradition, pointing out that, besides its mythical qualities, the interpretation was not truly African history but merely the history of Europeans in Africa. Further, the offical version was used to justify the colonization of Africa by Europeans. The revisionist historians sought to rewrite the history of Africa by seeing Africans as historical actors and as human beings; but the traditional archival and published sources provided only brief, superficial, and biased glimpses of African society. That impasse was finally broken when the historians went into the field to record the oral traditions of the African people themselves; new insights were gained and a more humane variety of African history was written.

The primary characteristic of "colonized" history is that it is the view of outsiders and not the people themselves. The historical evidence upon which that variety of history draws is from the colonizer. Usually this is in the form of written documents—letters, diaries, and reminiscences of visitors—which describe the author's position among the people and his/her perceptions of that people. For various reasons, from the resumption of the primacy of written documents over oral ones to the assumption that the elite are the only ones who matter historically, the people themselves are ignored and are not asked about their perceptions of history. As a consequence, the actions of the colonizers are magnified so they become the central figures in the narrative; they are portrayed as the historical actors while the people are rendered as passive, powerless objects.

What, then, are the implications for American ethnic history? To varying degrees, the written history of ethnic minorities in our country has suffered under the yoke of colonial oppression. Our collective histories have long been colonized, and our self-perceptions have been distorted by historical documents written by strangers who have sojourned among us but who have little knowledge of us. Oral history offers an alternative way of conceptualizing history and a means by which to recover that past. And while oral history does not maintain that each individual's view of history is equally legitimate or that every voice must be heard, it does argue that by going directly to the people for historical documents, a more valid variety of history can be written. Oral history proposes that we rewrite our history to capture the human spirit of the people, to see how ethnic minorities solved or failed to solve particular problems, how they advanced or resisted change, and how they made or failed to make better lives for themselves and their children. In short, oral history proposes nothing less than the writing of a people's history, liberated from myths and imbued with humanity.

Notes

1. Marc Bloch, *The Historian's Craft* (New York: Vintage, 1953), pp. 9–10. See also Karl R. Popper, *The Poverty of Historicism* (London: Routledge and Kegan Paul, 1957). Cf. Staughton Lynd, "Guerilla History in Gary," *Liberation* 14 (October 1969), pp. 17–20, who argues that the reason for "guerilla history," or history from the bottom up, is to raise political consciousness and to promote action.

2. Carl Becker, "Everyman His Own Historian," *American Historical Review* 37 (January 1932), pp. 221–36.

3. C. Vann Woodward, *American Attitudes toward History* (London: Oxford University Press, 1955).

4. C. Vann Woodward, *The Strange Career of Jim Crow* (London: Oxford University Press, 1955), demonstrates that point by showing how widely believed lies of the past have shaped Southern opinions of the future.

5. Arthur Schlesinger, Jr., "The Historian as Participant," in *Historical Studies Today*, ed. Felix Gilbert and Stephen R. Graubard (New York: Norton, 1972), pp. 393–412; Jan Vansina, "Once upon a Time: Oral Traditions as History in Africa," *Daedalus* 100 (Spring 1971), pp. 442–68; Studs Terkel, *Hard Times: An Oral History of the Great Depression* (New York: Pantheon, 1970); and Staughton Lynd, ed., "Personal Histories of the Early CIO," *Radical America* 5 (May–June 1971), pp. 49–76.

6. Gene Wise, *American Historical Explanations: A Strategy for Grounded Inquiry*

(Homewood, Ill.: Dorsey Press, 1973); Arthur A. Hansen and David A. Hacker, "The Manzanar Riot: An Ethnic Perspective," *Amerasia Journal* 2 (Fall 1974), pp. 112–57.

7. Stanley M. Elkins, *Slavery: A Problem in American Institutional and Intellectual Life* (Chicago: University of Chicago Press, 1959).

8. Gladys-Marie Fry, *Night Riders in Black Folk History* (Knoxville: University of Tennessee Press, 1975), pp. 5–6; Ann Lane, ed., *The Debate over Slavery* (Urbana: University of Illinois Press, 1971).

9. E. J. Hobsbawm, "From Social History to the History of Society," *Daedalus* 100 (Winter 1971), p. 31.

10. John Habakkuk, "Economic History and Economic Theory," in *Historical Studies*, ed. Gilbert and Graubard, pp. 42–43; and Robert P. Baker, "Labor History, Social Science, and the Concept of Working Class," *Labor History* 14 (Winter 1973), pp. 98–105.

11. Robert F. Berkhofer, Jr., *A Behavioral Approach to Historical Analysis* (New York: Macmillan, 1969), pp. 9–10.

12. Jurgen Ruesch, "The Observer and the Observed: Human Communication Theory," in *Toward a Unified Theory of Human Behavior*, ed. Roy R. Grinker (New York: Basic, 1956), pp. 36–54.

13. James W. Wilkie and Edna Monzon de Wilkie, "Dimensions of Elitelore: An Oral History Questionnaire," *Journal of Latin American Lore* 1 (Summer 1975), p. 83; Saul Benison, "Oral History and Manuscript Collecting," *Isis* 53 (1963), pp. 113–17.

14. Berkhofer, *Behavioral Approach*, pp. 10–11, 14–17; Daniel Aaron, "The Treachery of Recollection: The Inner and Outer History," in *Essays on History and Literature*, ed. Robert H. Bremner (Columbus: Ohio State University Press, 1966), pp. 7–10, 16–17.

15. For definitions of oral tradition, see Jan Vansina, *Oral Tradition: A Study in Historical Methodology*, trans. H. M. Wright (London: Routledge and Kegan Paul, 1965; also see chapter 9 of the present volume).

16. Wilkie and Monzon de Wilkie, "Dimensions of Elitelore," pp. 82–83; Richard M. Dorson, "Oral Tradition and Written History," in *American Folklore and the Historian*, ed. Richard M. Dorson (Chicago: University of Chicago Press, 1971), pp. 129–44.

17. See Vansina, *Oral Tradition*, pp. 157–60, for definitions of legend, epic, fable, and myth.

18. Gary Y. Okihiro, *The Oral History Tapes of the Japanese American Research Project, Tapes 1–112: A Survey* (Los Angeles: Asian American Studies Center, 1974), pp. iv–vi. The collection reflects a point of view characterized as a JACL-WRA interpretation. See Gary Y. Okihiro, "Japanese Resistance in America's Concentration Camps: A Reevaluation," *Amerasia Journal* 2 (Fall 1973), pp. 20–34; and Hansen and Hacker, "Manzanar Riot."

19. See, for example, Studs Terkel, *Working: People Talk about What They Do All Day and How They Feel about What They Do* (New York: Pantheon, 1974); and Louis Starr, "Studs Terkel and Oral History," *Chicago History* 3 (Fall 1974), pp. 123–26.

20. Donald C. Swain, "Problems for Practitioners of Oral History," *American Archivist* 28 (January 1965), pp. 66–67; William W. Cutler III, "Accuracy in Oral History Interviewing," *Historical Methods Newsletter* 3 (June 1970), pp. 3–4 (see chapter 7 of the present volume); Alice Kessler-Harris, Introduction, *Envelopes of Sound*, ed. Ronald J. Grele (Chicago: Precedent Publishing, 1975), pp. 2–3; and Victor Nee and Brett Nee, *Longtime Californ': A Documentary Study of an American Chinatown* (New York: Pantheon, 1972), p. xiv.

21. Oscar Lewis, *Five Families: Mexican Case Studies in the Culture of Poverty* (New York: Basic, 1959); Lewis, *The Children of Sanchez: Autobiography of a Mexican Family* (New York: Random House, 1961); and *La Vida: A Puerto-Rican Family in the Culture of Poverty—San Juan and New York* (New York: Random House, 1966). Still, there are obvious limits to the efficacy of participant observation. For instance, it can never transform the researcher into the observed.

22. Charles A. Valentine, *Culture and Poverty: Critique and Counter-Proposals* (Chicago: University of Chicago Press, 1968), p. 101.

23. Nee and Nee, *Longtime Californ'*, pp. xiv–xv, xx.

24. See, for example, Lewis Anthony Dexter, *Elite and Specialized Interviewing* (Evanston: Northwestern University Press, 1970); William H. Banaka, *Training in Depth Interviewing* (New York: Harper and Row, 1970); Alfred Benjamin, *The Helping Interview* (Boston: Houghton Mifflin, 1969); and Robert K. Merton, Patricia Kendall, and Marjorie Fiske, *The Focused Interview* (Glencoe, Ill.: Free Press, 1956).

25. Saul Benison, "Reflections on Oral History," *American Archivist* 28 (January 1965), p. 73; Cutler, "Accuracy in Oral History," p. 4; and Ronald J. Grele, "Movement without Aim: Methodological and Theoretical Problems in Oral History," in *Envelopes of Sound*, ed. Grele, pp. 130–31.

26. Grele, "Movement without Aim," pp. 131–33, 135–37; Cutler, "Accuracy in Oral History," p. 7; Saul Benison, "Oral History: A Personal View," in *Modern Methods in the History of Medicine*, ed. Edwin Clark (London: Athlone Press, 1971), p. 291; and Lynd, "Personal Histories," pp. 50–51, all touch upon this subject; but they do not deal with its theoretical implications.

27. William Labov, "Phonological Correlates of Social Stratification," *American Anthropologist* 66 (December 1964), pp. 164–76; and *The Social Stratification of English in New York City* (Washington, D.C.: Center for Applied Linguistics, 1966). See also, Baker, "Labor History," pp. 98–105.

28. Malcolm X, *The Autobiography of Malcolm X*, with the assistance of Alex Haley (New York: Grove Press, 1965).

29. Grele, "Movement without Aim," pp. 135–42.

30. Kessler-Harris, Introduction, pp. 1–2.

31. Gould P. Colman, "Oral History—An Appeal for More Systematic Procedures," *American Archivist* 28 (January 1965), pp. 79–83.

32. See Hansen and Hacker, "Manzanar Riot"; Charles T. Morrissey, "Truman and the Presidency—Records and Oral Recollections," *American Archivist* 28 (January 1965), pp. 53–61; and Gould Colman, "Theoretical Models and Oral History Interviews," *Agricultural History* 41 (July 1967), pp. 255–56, for examples of how oral documents can complement written documents in the writing of history.

33. Joseph Carson, *Silent Voices: The Southern Negro Woman Today* (New York: Delacorte Press, 1969), p. 1.

34. Richard M. Dorson, "Ethnohistory and Ethnic Folklore," *Ethnohistory* 8 (Winter 1961), pp. 12–30; Gerda Lerner, ed., *Black Women in White America: A Documentary History* (New York: Pantheon, 1972); Lee Rainwater, Richard P. Coleman, and Gerald Handel, *Workingman's Wife: Her Personality, World, and Life Style* (New York: Oceana, 1959); Lynd, "Guerilla History"; Ronald Blythe, *Akenfield: Portrait of an English Village* (New York: Pantheon, 1969); William Lynwood Montell, *The Saga of Coe Ridge: A Study in Oral History* (Knoxville: University of Tennessee Press, 1970; and see chapter 16 of the present volume); Theodore Rosengarten, *All God's Dangers: The Life of Nate Shaw* (New York: Knopf, 1974; and see chapter 20 of the present volume); Fry, *Night Riders*; John Stands in Timber and Margot Liberty, *Cheyenne Memories* (New Haven: Yale University Press, 1967); and Daniel Francis McCall, *Africa in Time Perspective: A Discussion of Historical Reconstruction from Unwritten Sources* (Boston: Boston University Press, 1964).

35. Alice M. Hoffman, "Who Are the Elite, and What is a Non-Elitist?" *Oral History Review* 4 (1976), pp. 1–5.

36. Arthur J. Vidich, Joseph Bensman, and Maurice R. Stein, eds., *Reflections on Community studies* (New York: Wiley, 1964); Lynd, "Guerilla History"; Kessler-Harris, Introduction,

p. 4; and Willa K. Baum, "Building Community Identity Through Oral History—A New Role for the Local Library," *California Librarian* 31 (October 1970), pp. 271–84.

37. Kessler-Harris, Introduction, p. 4.

38. Lynd, "Guerilla History," pp. 17–29.

39. Eugene D. Genovese, *In Red and Black: Marxian Explorations in Southern and Afro-American History* (New York: Vintage, 1971).

40. For a similar development in Afro-American historiography, see Fry, *Night Riders*, pp. 3–29.

41. Basil Davidson, *The African Past* (Boston: Little, Brown, 1964).

20

Preface to *All God's Dangers: The Life of Nate Shaw*

Theodore Rosengarten

Ethnic history is an abstraction which Ned Cobb, the southern black narrator of All God's Dangers: The Life of Nate Shaw *lived. In this excerpt, biographer Theodore Rosengarten describes some of the difficulties and rewards associated with collecting life stories in the so-called everyman tradition, when the subject is neither famous nor wealthy. Rosengarten points out the value of flexibility in research when a particularly excellent narrator appears, and he provides an insider's account of how a professional writer-historian works. At the end, Rosengarten considers questions that relate to editing: the treatment of retellings of the same story and the arrangement of stories told out of chronological order.*

Clearly the preparation of an oral autobiography mutual engages interviewer and interviewee, as this account shows. The resulting memoir benefited not only Rosengarten, who received widespread critical acclaim for the book, but also Ned Cobb, the memoirist, for whom the telling of his life was a strengthening experience.

This preface may be compared with Saul Benison's reprinted earlier in this book: each is in its way a model interview history, though the two reflect very different interview techniques and narrators. Both document the place, context, and interaction which lies behind a printed interview; both show how it is possible to work with a narrator over an extended period of interviews.

Theodore Rosengarten is currently at work on a biography of Thomas Chaplin, an antebellum cotton planter from St. Helena Island, South Carolina; he is also writing a novel about the collapse of slavery along the Carolina seaboard.

All God's Dangers: The Life of Nate Shaw *appeared in 1974 (New York, Knopf).*

THIS BIG BOOK is the autobiography of an illiterate man. It is the story of a black tenant farmer from east-central Alabama who grew up in the society of former slaves and slaveholders and reached maturity during the advent of segregation law. For years he labored "under many rulins, just like the other Negro, that I knowed was injurious to man and displeasin to God and still I had to fall back." One morning in December, 1932, Nate Shaw faced a crowd of deputy sheriffs sent to confiscate a neighbor's livestock. He knew they would be after his, next. Burdened by the indignities he had suffered in the past and awed by the prospect of overturning "this southern way of life," Shaw stood his ground.

I met Nate Shaw in January, 1969. He had just turned eighty-four years old. I had come to Tukabahchee County with a friend, Dale Rosen, who was investigating a defunct organization called the Alabama Sharecroppers Union. Earlier in her research, Dale had read "In Egypt Land," a powerful narrative poem written by John Beecher, in 1940, which tells one version of a Sharecroppers Union confrontation with the law. We visited Beecher and he told us that he had recently met a survivor of the union who was a character in his poem; that the man was living near Pottstown, some twenty miles from Beaufort, the Tukabahchee County seat. Dale and I spent a week in Beaufort sifting through trial dossiers and newspaper files in the courthouse basement. Then, one icy morning we set out to meet the man I came to call Nate Shaw.

The road from Beaufort to Pottstown rolls and winds through piney woods country. Nate Shaw lives just below the foothills where the lowlands begin. We hunted for his house along the asphalt byroads until we came across a mailbox with the name Shaw in bold letters. A woman stepped out onto the porch of a tin-roofed cabin and, seeing us hesitate, called us to come in.

Her name is Winnie Shaw and she is the wife of Nate's half-brother TJ. She is a spare-built, walnut-colored woman with wide-set eyes and a girlish face. She said she was seventy-three years old but she looked much younger. We were already into the front room of her house before we introduced ourselves. We explained that we were students from Massachusetts and that we'd come to Alabama to study this union.

TJ walked in. He had been overhauling one of his machines—winter work—when he heard our car drive up in his yard. Winnie told him, "They want to see Nate." TJ walked out again and across the road to Nate's house. TJ completely filled the doorway walking in and out. He is six and a half feet tall when he stands straight. But sixty-five seasons of picking cotton have given him a stoop from the hips, so that standing still he resembles a man leaning on a long-handled hoe.

He came back with Nate, who had been feeding his mule—one of the last mules in the settlement. Nate is six inches shorter than TJ and a shade lighter, though both are dark men. He is trim and square-shouldered; he has a small, fine head and high Indian cheekbones and brow. We shook hands and he announced that he was always glad to welcome "his people." He knew why we had come by our appearance: young, white, polite, frightened, northern. People who looked like us had worked on voter registration drives, marched in Selma and Montgomery, rode those freedom buses across the Mason-Dixon line. He had seen "us" on television and it didn't surprise him to see us now because this was his movement and he knew a lot about it; he had been active in it before we were born. Raising his right hand to God, he swore there was no "get-back" in him: he was standing where he stood in '32.

Nate took off his hat and sat down with us by the fireplace. We asked him right off why he joined the union. He didn't respond directly; rather, he "interpreted" the question and began, "I was haulin a load of hay out of Apafalya one day—" and continued uninterrupted for eight hours. He recounted dealings with landlords, bankers, fertilizer agents, mule traders, gin operators, sheriffs, and judges—stories of the social relations of the cotton system. By evening, the fire had risen and died and risen again and our question was answered.

TJ turned on the electric light, a single high-watt bulb suspended in the center of the room. We talked some more with the Shaws about how we planned to use the information Nate had just given us. They were glad to help us, they said, and if our "report" reached other people who found their lives instructive, they would be gratified. We thanked them for being so kind and for taking us into their confidence and, promising to return, we left.

Driving north, we felt something slipping out of our grasp. We could remember the details of Nate's stories but no reconstruction could capture the power of his performance. His stories built upon one another so that the sequence expressed the sense of a man "becoming." Although Nate Shaw and the Sharecroppers Union had intersected only for a moment, everything that came before had prepared him for it. Nate had apparently put his whole life into stories and what he told us was just one chapter.

We had come to study a union, and we had stumbled on a storyteller. Nate must have told his stories—at least the ones we heard—many times before. TJ and Winnie, who listened as closely as we did, would stir whenever he digressed and remind him where his story was going. Nate would roll his tongue over the lone yellow spearlike tooth at the corner of his mouth and say, "I'm comin to that, I just have to tell this first."

Over the next two years I visited the Shaws twice. Each time I met other members of the family who, if more wary of my intentions, were no less hospitable. . . .

Each time I visited Nate Shaw, he told me a little more about them: how they support themselves, how they hold their heads up in the world. Shaw prides himself on the social standing of his children. . . .

Shaw revealed less about his first wife, Hannah. He praised her for her strengths and virtues and chided himself for not having acknowledged her sufficiently during her life. His remarks were brief and I had no cause to press him at the time. Later I learned from him and his children what a great-hearted woman she was.

Nothing so aroused Shaw as his recollections of his father. Shaw is still in conflict with a man who was a boy during President Lincoln's administration. While it is not unusual for a child to have unresolved feelings about a parent, it is disarming to see a struggle so open and honest. Shaw demonstrates that a person is, at every moment, everything he always was; his current role can eclipse his past but not deny it. Shaw remains his father's child though he is in his eighties and his father has been dead over forty years.

In March, 1971, I went back to Alabama with a proposal to record Shaw's life. He agreed that the experience would be good for both of us and the results might prove useful to people interested in the history of his region, class, and race. To appreciate his part in that history it is helpful to know something about his setting.

East of the Black Belt and south of the Appalachians the Alabama countryside descends slowly to a plain. Young piney woods stretch methodically between pastures and farms. Off both sides of the roads derelict chimneys stand like watchkeepers on the sites of tenant farmer shacks. These are the tangible signs of the tenant system's collapse.

Upland, the population is predominantly white and poor. Lumber camps and textile mills offer the steadiest employment in the region. Some small farms produce cotton for the mills, and fruit—mostly peaches—for roadside and out-of-state markets. But the soil is not particularly suited to cotton and the fruit is vulnerable to the great rains and late frosts that distress hill country agriculture.

The people of the lowlands still grow cotton, along with corn, sugar cane, peanuts, watermelons, and other table foods. The land is smooth and fit for extensive cultivation. This was plantation country and the population today is largely black. After the Civil War, owners of the plantations divided their lands into tenant plots. To their surprise and uneasiness, poor whites came down from the hills to compete with the freed slaves for land. For about twenty-five years, or until the 1890's, whites and blacks worked adjacent farms as sharecroppers and tenants. Then, hoping to counter falling cotton prices by exploiting a more submissive class, landlords pushed the poor whites back into the hills and filled their places with blacks.

Cotton prices reached new highs during the First World War, but farmers at the bottom of the tenant system shared little in the profits; for the system that encumbered them with mandatory debts also deprived them of authority to sell their crops. Thus, poor black farmers lived under twin yoke of race oppression and economic peonage. Taking advantage of new openings in wartime industry, many fled to the cities. This great movement north intensified during the early years of the boll weevil's devastation through about 1920, and again during the Great Depression and the Second World War. The migration continues at a regular pace today.

Nate Shaw stayed in Alabama because he believed his labor gave him a claim to the land. He watched his neighbors pick up and leave but *"that never come in my mind."* Though he loathed his situation, he thought, "Somehow, some way, I'd overcome it. . . . I was determined to try." I was hoping Shaw's autobiography would be a first installment in an intensive study of the family. I had no idea what shape it would take, or if I would have the means to do it, or if the children would cooperate. I did know that the Shaw family's experience was typical of many southern black families: the voyage from farm to factory, from country to city, from south to north. These relocations had profound effects on family life, class situation, and consciousness. There was much here to lure the historian.

I returned in June with a hundred pages of questions to ask Shaw. It became clear during our first session that I'd never get to a fraction of them. It would have taken years; moreover, my prepared questions distracted Shaw from his course. Since it was my aim to preserve his stories, I learned how to listen and not to resist his method of withholding facts for the sake of suspense. Everything came out in time, everything.

We would sit under the eave of his tool shed and talk for two to six hours per session. Shaw would whittle or make baskets as he spoke. He would quarter and peel a six-foot section of a young trunk, weave the strips into the desired shape, then put a handle on it. A large laundry basket would take him half a day to make, working steadily with wood cut the day before.

When it rained we would move our chairs inside the shed. There, in near dark, camped among baskets, broken-bottomed chairs, sacks of feed and fertilizer, worn harnesses and tools, Shaw enacted his most fiery stories. I am thankful for all the rain we had, for it moved us to a natural theater and pounded the tin roof like a delirious crowd inciting an actor to the peak of his energy.

To start, I asked Shaw if he knew how he got his name. This tapped an important source of his earliest knowledge—the stories of old people. Shaw announced a ground rule for himself: he would always distinguish between what was told for the truth and what was told to entertain, between direct experience and hearsay. He went on to recollect the content and flavor of his childhood. In sum, he described how a black boy growing up in rural Alabama at the turn of the century acquired a practical education. At the death of his mother and his first barefoot days behind a plow—events separated by two months—he learned what sort of hard life lay ahead.

Beginning with his recollections of the first time his father hired him out to work for a white man, in 1904, Shaw recalled events and relationships according to the year, as though he had kept a mental journal. Thus we would spend one session covering 1904 and 1905, pick up at 1906 and so on. Once he married and left his father's house and had his own crop, each harvest completed both his work cycle and the perimeter of his experiences for that year.

For each place he farmed I asked about the quality and extent of the land, changes in the technology of farming, the size of his crops and the prices they brought him, his contracts and relationships with white people at every stage of the crop, the growth of his family and the division of labor within it, and how he felt about all that. Shaw told me how he moved from farm to farm seeking good land and the freedom to work it to its potential. By raising all his foodstuffs and hauling lumber while his older boys worked the farm, he became self-sufficient. At every step along the way he faced a challenge to his independence. Landlords tried to swindle him, merchants turned him out, neighbors despised his success. In spite of their schemes and in spite of the perils inherent to cotton farming, he prevailed.

When we came up to the crucial events of the thirties the sessions turned into heated dialogues. I pressed Shaw for his motivations and challenged him to justify himself. Here, I want to make my sympathies clear. Nate Shaw was—and is—a hero to me. I think he did the right thing when he joined the Sharecroppers Union and fought off the deputy sheriffs, though, of course, I had nothing to lose by his actions. My questions must unavoidably have expressed this judgment but they did not, I believe, change the substance of his responses.

Our sessions dealing with the prison years were more even-tempered, just as Shaw had had to keep cool to live out his sentence. I asked him about conditions at each of the three prison camps in which he served. He answered with stories about his work life and his relations with prison officials and fellow convicts. During these years, his wife Hannah and son Vernon presided over his family and property. His mules died, his automobile ran down, but he forced himself not to think about it.

Shaw was fifty-nine years old when he came home from prison. The years following his release were the most painful for him to talk about. For in his struggle to reclaim a portion of his former status he faced insuperable barriers—his age, poverty, and obsolete skills. Again, my questions pursued him from farm to farm. I asked about the issues foremost in his mind—his new relationships with his children and, after the death of Hannah, with his second wife, Josie; the social and economic changes that directly affected him, his family, and his race; and still, his stand that morning in December, 1932, against the forces of injustice.

After sixty hours spread over sixteen sessions we completed the first round. Shaw had given me the outlines of his life and many representative stories. I hadn't asked the questions I'd come with and I had to choose between doing that and going over the same ground with a finer-toothed comb. Shaw wanted to add details and whole stories he had remembered after we passed their places in the narrative. Taking his lead and working from notes I had written while playing back the tapes, we began again. We lasted fifteen more sessions and another sixty hours. As our talks drew to a close the sessions grew longer. The initiative was his. Our work strengthened him and sustained his belief that his struggles had been worth the effort, although he had only his recollections to show for them. These filled his days with a reality more powerful than the present. . . .

Seeking a better judgment from God and his race, and aiming to leave his trace on the world, Shaw proceeded to narrate the "life" of a black tenant farmer. The result is an intimate portrait that reproduces the tempo of a life unfolding. Shaw has the storyteller's gift to suspend his age while reciting. Thus his childhood stories ring with the astonishment and romance of a boy discovering the universe. Similarly, stories of his old age are tinged by the bittersweet feelings of a passionate man who has lost his illusions.

Nate Shate belongs to the tradition of farmer-storytellers. These people appear in all civilizations and are only beginning to disappear in the most advanced ones. Their survival is bound up with the fate of communities of small farmers. When these communities disperse and farms become larger, fewer in number, and owned more and more by absentee investors, the sources of story material and audiences dry up.

But the decline of storytelling is more complicated than this. It has to do with the passing of craft activities, like basketmaking, which generate the rhythms at which stories flow; with the appeal of competing voices of culture, such as television; and with the unfortunate popular assumption that history is something that takes place in books and books are to be read in school.

What happens to the history of a people not accustomed to writing things down? To whom poverty and illiteracy make wills, diaries, and letters superfluous? Birth and death certificates, tax receipts—these occasional records punctuate but do not describe everyday life. In this setting, Nate Shaw is a precious resource. For his stories are grounded in the ordinary occurrences of the tenant farmer's world. Furthermore, they display as few records could an awesome intellectual life.

Shaw's working years span approximately the same years as the Snopes family odyssey in William Faulkner's trilogy. I mention Shaw and Faulkner in the same sentence not to invite comparison—each man's work ought to be appreciated within its own narrative tradition—but because they tell complementary stories. Both focus on the impact of history on the family. Faulkner, heir to a line of southern statesmen, pursues the decay and decline of white landed families and the rise of their former tenants. Nate Shaw records the progress of a black tenant family through three generations.

Both are steeped in genealogies. With the rigor of an Old Testament scribe, Shaw names the parents and foreparents of many of his characters. In fact, he names over four hundred people. Shaw creates a human topography through which he travels with the assurance of a man who knows the forest because he witnessed the planting of the trees. The act of recalling names is also a demonstration of how long he had been living in one place. Thus, his family chronicles express both the bonds among people and a man's attachment to the land.

In editing the transcripts of our recordings I sometimes had to choose among multiple versions of the same story; other times, I combined parts of one version with another for the sake of clarity and completeness. Stories that seemed remote from Shaw's personal development I left out entirely. By giving precedence to stories with historical interest or literary merit I trust I haven't misrepresented him.

Besides this hazardous selection process, my editing consisted of arranging Shaw's stories in a way that does justice both to their occurrence in time and his sequence of recollection. I tried, within the limits of a general chronology, to preserve the affinities between stories. For memory recalls kindred events and people and is not constrained by the calendar.

I have not reproduced a southern or black dialect because I did not hear it. I did hear the English language as I know it, spoken with regional inflection and grammar. In the case of present participles and other words ending in "ing," the common idiom usually drops the "g," such as in "meetin" for meeting, "haulin" for hauling, etc. Where the "g" is pronounced, often for exclamatory effect, I have kept it.

Shaw's vocabulary is remarkably broad and inventive, enriched here and there by words not found in the dictionary. The meanings of these words are usually clear from their contexts. In some cases I have offered definitions.

As a measure of protection and privacy I have had to change the names of all the people and most of the places in the narrative. In devising aliases I tried to be faithful to the sources, sounds, and meanings of the original names. Generally, where blacks and whites shared the same surnames or first names, they share aliases here.

There is something lost and something gained in the transformation of these oral stories to written literature. Their publication marks the end of a long process of creation and re-creation and removes them from the orbit of the storyteller. His gestures, mimicries, and intonations—all the devices of his performance—are lost. No exclamation point can take the place of a thunderous slap on the knee. The stories, however, are saved, and Nate Shaw's "life" will get a hearing beyond his settlement and century.

21

What's So Special about Women? Women's Oral History

Sherna Gluck

In this next essay, we review the efforts of feminists to apply oral historical methods to the history of women. The approach of Sherna Gluck, researcher and social activist, is to seek out "everywoman," whose story can illustrate the "common threads that link all women"; the writing of history thus becomes a validation of women's experiences and "a feminist encounter."

Gluck explores the problems of a mismatch between interviewer and interviewee and suggests that race (and particularly sex) differences can inhibit the success of interviews. She also discusses the practicalities of interviews that deal with women's-only issues, such as sex, contraception, and menstruation. The author writes with great sympathy about the difficulty of interviewing women unaccustomed to expressing themselves publicly, particularly members of the working class. When it was originally published in the women's studies journal of the University of Colorado, this article was a landmark survey of women's oral history. In describing her methods, Gluck touches on one of the by-products of oral history, the increase in self-esteem of the interviewee, and on one of its crucial functions in uniting social groups, the search for a collective memory and identity.

Sherna Gluck teaches women's studies at California State University, Long Beach, and directs the oral history program there. She has worked on several oral history projects on women, including one on women who worked in the Los Angeles aircraft industry during World War II. She is the editor of From Parlor to Prison: Five American Suffragists Talk about Their Lives *(1976) and the author of numerous articles which utilize oral history.*

An expanded version of "What's So Special about Women? Women's Oral History" was first published in FRONTIERS: A Journal of Women Studies 2 *(Summer 1977), pp. 3–13. The original article served as an introduction to a special issue of* FRONTIERS *that focused on women's oral history.*

REFUSING TO BE rendered historically voiceless any longer, women are creating a new history—using our own voices and experiences. We are challenging the traditional concepts of history, of what is "historically important," and we are affirming that our everyday lives *are* history. Using an oral tradition, as old as human memory, we are reconstructing our own past.

When women historians first began the task of creating and expanding the field of women's history, we relied on traditional historical concepts and methods. We busily searched for hidden clues to direct us to "lost heroines," and, whenever possible, we sought out those who were still alive in order to record their past experiences. Because so little documentation was available on the lives and activities of these women, we found ourselves in a situation similar to that of Allan Nevins, who "developed" the method of oral history in 1948.[1] With the advent of the telephone and the decline in the practice of journal writing and lengthy correspondence, historians were faced with a "drying up" of many of the sources on which they traditionally depended. Oral history, emerging then as the sound recording of the reminiscences of public figures, was hailed as a method which could create alternative sources.

Fitting women into this new scheme of things was essential and not very difficult. There were and are women who have been "important" figures in public life, both those who have functioned in the public eye and those who have worked behind the scenes. Some women achieved recognition as a result of their struggle for women's rights, while others who participated in that struggle remain unrecognized. But the majority of women did not lead public lives. Most women were not women's rights activists or union leaders or public participants in social movements. Until relatively recently, most women in the United States did not engage in wage-earning labor. By virtue of acculturation and socialization in a sexist society, women's lives were and are different from most men's. Whether women have played out public roles or adopted the traditional female role in the private realm, their lives have been governed by what Gerda Lerner has called a special rhythm.[2] In tracing this rhythm, it is important to document the lives and experiences of all of these women: to pore over newspaper accounts and organization papers, to seek out their living associates, to research fully their lives and activities, and to record their stories, for only then can we see the whole picture of women's lives, and how their rhythm has affected our lives.

Women all over the country have been using oral history to explore this rhythm of women's lives. In doing so, we are harking back to an oral tradition much older than that developed by white male historians in the United States in the 1940's. We are part of the tradition in which the life and experiences of "everywoman/man" was considered worthy of remembering and passing on to others—because it was history. It was this tradition, brought from Africa, which black historians tapped in the 1920's when they started to record the stories of former slaves.[3] It was this same tradition that both inspired Alex Haley to trace his roots and helped him to reconstruct the kidnap of his ancestors from West Africa.[4]

For women, using this model of oral history not only leads us to "any-woman," but it also raises a different set of questions to be explored. We thus ask about clothing and physical activity, menstruation, knowledge and attitudes about sex and birth control, childbirth, economic functions in the household, household work, the nature of relationships among women, the magazines and books they read, and menopausal experience, and the relationship of the private life to the public life. Thus, not only is the political base of women's oral history different from the Nevins model, but also, and, just as important, the content is special. No matter what women we choose to interview, regardless of how typical or atypical their life experiences have been, there are certain common threads that link all women.

It is the recognition that women's oral history is so special, and significantly, that it has developed as a field unto itself—primarily through the work of women outside the major university oral history centers—that inspired us to devote an entire issue of a women studies journal to the subject. . . .

The [oral history] process is a significant experience not only for the interviewer or those who might use the product, but also for the interviewee. As those of us collecting oral histories from women well know, there is invariably a reciprocal affirmation between interviewer and interviewee of the worth of the women being interviewed. The fact that someone is interested in learning about her life—a life the interviewee may see as "unexciting" and "uninteresting"—increases her self-esteem. . . . In fact, the oral history process can serve a positive function in the aging process by helping to integrate past life experiences, cope with reduced life activity and loss of close relationships, and ultimately, prepare for death.

Women's oral history, then, is a feminist encounter, even if the interviewee is not herself a feminist. It is the creation of a new type of material on women; it is the validation of women's experiences; it is the communication among women of different generations; it is the discovery of our own roots and the development of a continuity which has been denied us in traditional historical accounts.

II

Oral history, the creation of a new "document" through the tape-recorded interview, traditionally has been divided into three types: topical, biographical, and autobiographical. Each type is represented in this issue. The topical interview is, in many ways, most akin to the open-ended sociological interview; the interviewer brings in a specific focus in order to gather information about a particular event. It might center on something which applies to both women and men, like Yung's interviews with Chinese immigrants about their detention on Angel Island, or it might focus on those epxeriences particular to women only, such as hys-terectomy.[5] The biographical oral history is characterized by this same kind of specificity, but the focus is, instead, on a specific individual—usually a public figure. . . .

In the autobiographical interview, the course of the individual *inter-viewee's* life is what determines both the form and content of the oral history. Even when one interviews a group of women who participated in the same kind of activity, the questions will be tailor-made to each individual's experience and the information will be recorded as part of a total memoir. In other words, in biographical and topical interviews, a slice of the interviewee's life is explored; in the autobiographical inter-view, the total life history is recorded.

In reality, there is a great deal of overlapping among the three forms. In both the topical and biographical interview, enough autobiographical material must be recorded to establish the specific relationships of the interviewee to the event of the individual being researched. On the other hand, when autobiographical interviews are collected from a group of women who shared a similar activity, for example, participation in the labor movement, some common questions would be explored with all. . . . Further, in our efforts to revise women's historiography, there are certain areas which should be explored with all women as part of their autobiographical accounts, such as their reactions to the onset of menses.

The distinction between the autobiographical and topical interviews is further blurred by the fact that ultimately, specific materials might be extracted from several different autobiographical interviews and clus-tered together around a specific topic. . . .

In fact, the so-called autobiographical oral history should be as com-plete a document as possible so that a variety of uses can be made of it. Much like the anthropological life history, it should reflect the experi-ences, values, attitudes, and relationships of the interviewee—the pat-terns and rhythms of her life and times. It can stand on its own, as an autobiography of an individual, or sections can be extracted from it for analysis or use in documentation.

As with any source, questions about the validity of the material must be raised. Despite their awareness of the obvious bias of contemporary newspaper reports, historians traditionally have relied on journalistic accounts as primary sources. The same criteria should be used to assess the validity of *any* source, written or oral: how does it "fit" with what we know about the subject? The usual questions about the reliability of memory and the problem of retrospective interpretation must also be raised, as they would be for any autobiographical account.

The autobiographical oral history, however, is a rather strange hybrid, not like conventional autobiography, which is usually characterized by a certain amount of studied reconsideration by the "author" and by her self-selection of both form and content. The so-called autobiographical oral history is a collaborative effort of the interviewer (archivist/historian) and the interviewee (source/history). This very collaboration makes the oral history memoir unique. Based on face-to-face interaction, during which the source can be both questioned and evaluated, it becomes more than the sound of one voice.

Based on the background research and the historical perspective which the interviewer brings to the process, the life of the interviewee is reconstructed within a broader social context—a context not ordinarily provided by the self-recorded memoirist. An understanding of this context guides the interviewer in deciding which spontaneous material should be elaborated on more fully. Though the best interviewer will encourage spontaneity and self-direction, it is intellectually dishonest to discount the interviewer's role in creating the oral history. The advantages derived from her knowledge and perspective can, ideally, sensitize her to personal and cultural inconsistencies in the perspective can, ideally, sensitize her to personal and cultural inconsistencies in the content of the interview. Such inconsistencies might be indicative of a highly idiosyncratic woman; they might be an important source of information about the complex patterns in women's lives; or they might raise questions about memory and candor.

Besides subtle nuances in the content of the interview and voice inflections—which are captured on tape—there are nonverbal gestures which only the sensitive interviewer (or—if the interview is being filmed or video taped—the sensitive photographer) will observe. These nonverbal cues reveal the emotional tone of the interview and should be carefully noted afterwards; they will become part of the record used by both the interviewee and others to evaluate the validity and reliability of the material recorded.

Despite the obvious advantages of the collaborative reconstruction of the interviewee's life, there are, of course, drawbacks. The perspective of the interviewer cannot help but influence, even subtly, the content of the material—particularly what the interviewee will judge as "important." After we completed an interview, one woman commented that she could tell by the way my eyes sparkled at various times that I was particularly interested in the problems she faced as a woman in the male world of science. Although we can console ourselves with the knowledge that there is no such thing as "objective" reporting, we must recognize our own influence in the interview process and make a concerted effort to maintain a balance between what we, as feminist historians, think is important and what the women we are interviewing think was important about their own lives.

The collaboration between interviewer and interviewee results in more than new "historical" documents. It allows for the creation of a new literature, a literature which can tap the language and experiences of those who do not ordinarily have access to such public expression except perhaps through the more anonymous form of folk culture.

III

Oral history is not, nor should it be, the province of experts. On the contrary, some of the best work today is being done by individuals and groups outside "the groves of academe" and often by those without any formal training in history or journalism. Anyone who can listen to the women who are speaking can do oral history. It is not enough, however, to rush off to the nearest Senior Citizen Center with a tape recorder. It is important to be prepared.

Reading about interviewing technique is a helpful first step. Discretion and common sense must be used in evaluating recommendations for interviewing technique. Patently absurd suggestions are sometimes made, for example, the edict not to laugh when the interviewee says something funny. The oral history interview is a human interaction and the same kind of warm, human responses expected in other interactions should govern our behavior. Reading the instructional articles will heighten awareness of the interview process, but nothing will contribute to this awareness more than the actual interview experience. The best training for conducting an oral history interview is actual practice; practice interviews which are carefully listened to and evaluated and analyzed. These "mock" interviews should be conducted with persons other than the intended subject.

The more practice the interviewer has, and the more experience she gains, the more partisan she becomes to her own methods. Although there is widespread agreement among oral history practitioners on some points, there is also disagreement. The oral history interview, above all, is specialized, and therefore highly variable; it is tailored to the experiences and style of the individual interviewee. Keeping in mind the proviso that there is no *one* perfect method of collecting oral histories, I offer the following ideas based on my own experiences over the past five years in personally interviewing an enormous number and wide range of women, and in training students to gather in-depth women's oral history. The methods of making contact, choosing equipment, adopting an interview style, and processing the interviews have all worked successfully for me. Although these suggestions are based on autobiographical oral history interviews with women in their seventies, eighties, nineties, and even one-hundreds, many of the points are equally valid for the topical and biographical interviews and for women of almost any age group.

Making Contact

Whom we select to interview obviously will be governed by our own specific interest. In my classes for the past three years, randomly selected women have been contacted and "everywoman" interviews were conducted. Fully exploring the life of each individual woman became the basis for a study of women's lives in the early twentieth century. To locate women who have had a particular kind of experience, such as involvement in the labor movement, or defense industry work during World War II, different methods might be used. I have successfully located union women through the retiree groups of various unions, through widespread advertisement of my work among older radicals, and through public speaking. Other oral historians and interviewers have placed ads in local and national newspapers.

In selecting the women to interview, the question of cultural likeness—including gender, race, class, ethnic, and even regional identification—immediately arises. The combined forces of racism and sexism have also limited the number of "minority" women in the United States who have had access to the skills and equipment which would enable them to record their own past. Until these skills are learned—and each of us must do everything in her power to share these skills—the role of the "outsider" will remain crucial. Otherwise, the history of Black, Hispanic, Asian, and Native American women will be lost, not only to them, but also to us.

Besides being governed by necessity, the outsider can sometimes delve into certain kinds of experiences that insiders cannot.[6] There might be specific topics that are more easily discussed with "outsiders." Also, because outsiders are less conversant with the culture or subculture, they may take less for granted and ask for more clarification than insiders. On the whole, though, my experience has been that cultural likeness can greatly promote trust and openness, whereas dissimilarity reinforces cultural and social distance.

Because of my own light complexion and hair, the Jewish immigrant women I have interviewed have assumed that I was not Jewish. As soon as I dropped a clue for them, both the content of the interview (particularly about their childhood in the shtetls of Europe or the ghettos of

America) and the nature of our relationship changed. On the other hand, because of my appearance and my socialization into the larger Anglo culture I have "passed" when I have conducted interviews with Anglo-Saxon women. A very light-skinned black student of mine from Texas was politely treated and her interview with a black ninety-two-year-old woman and her seventy-year-old daughter progressed uneventfully until, during the third session, the interviewees realized that she was "one of us." The nature of the interview changed dramatically. Similarly, the few male students I have had in my women's oral history classes, despite their efforts, never overcame the barriers of gender difference.

It is not only a matter of trust; the subtle cues to which culturally similar women can respond might mean the difference between a good and bad interview. Though these nuances cannot be thoroughly learned by an outsider, the interviewer must prepare as best she can so that she can understand the attitudes, vocabulary, and body language of the group or subgroup with which the interviewee identifies.

No matter whom we choose to interview or how we have located her, the first contact with our interviewee is crucial, particularly since she might be subtly influenced by the way in which we located her. One of the activists whom I found through her union was convinced, despite all my explanations and protestations, that I was from the "union office." She was, therefore, guarded in her description of the difficulties she had faced as a woman in her union. On the other hand, when a particularly respected or loved friend was the source of my contact, the door was opened wide and the interviews were quite candid.

It is important in contacting the person to make clear how her name was obtained and to explain to her, in advance, what the interest in her is. For most women, especially those who did not participate in "important" events or in organizations outside of the home, there is tremendous initial reluctance to being interviewed; it is the reluctance which comes from being socialized female in this society. It is important to establish for her, at the very outset, why we feel her life and experiences are important. This might mean not only an explanation about our specific project, but also a discussion of how we view the daily life experiences of all women to be a part of history.

The interviewer's own credibility must also be established; this can be accomplished by reference to a relationship with someone the interviewer knows and/or by the use of letterhead stationery or a brochure which describes her work. (Though a letter from the instructor might be helpful for students, I have found that the "grandmother role" which the elderly so often adopt towards the student makes their entree relatively easy.)

Because it is often difficult for the elderly to hear well on the telephone, it is best to try to communicate this essential introductory material first by mail. Then, when contact is made, she will be clear about who is calling and what is wanted, and an appointment can be made. It is important to determine what time of day is best for her; her stamina and memory will vary. All the women I have interviewed have been sufficiently in tune with their own body rhythms to tell me *exactly* what was the best time to interview; then I adjusted *my* schedule accordingly.

It is still that initial face-to-face meeting which will make or break the oral history. Rather personal and intimate details about the woman's life will be openly discussed, and to do so means that there must be an attitude of trust. She will, rightfully, want to know how the material will be used. Although it is important to be open about both the purpose of the interview and the use of the material, I usually wait until after some sort of trusting relationship has developed before asking her to sign any releases or agreements; there is no subterfuge here, but even the simplest agreement forms can raise specters and create suspicions. . . . I have had only two woman refuse to sign an agreement once the interviews were completed; in both cases their oral histories were made anonymous and all identifiable references were deleted.

Open communication is crucial to establishing trust with an interviewee. Since we are asking a stranger to be self-revealing, we, in turn, must be willing to divulge information about ourselves. I have had some interviewees question me at length about my own background and life, whereas others have asked nothing. It is with the former that I have developed the most intimate mutual relationships and with whom I have probably created the richest oral histories. I do not mean to imply that the interviewer should insert her own life story into the actual interview. However, before beginning the first interview or while chatting over coffee, tea, or juice after the interview, the interviewer may talk about herself—to whatever extent is natural and the interviewee seems to expect. The interviewer's sharing her own feelings about the interview (her nervousness, for example), encourages the interviewee to talk about *her* feelings, and both parties can be placed at ease.

The first interview is not "just to get acquainted." The expectations and relationship which develop during the first encounter can determine the course of the other interviews. For this reason, the practice interviews, during training, should be done with others than those to be actually interviewed for a project. That first interview might be the only one conducted with a woman or, on the other hand, it might represent the first of some twenty sessions. The decision about how many interviews will be recorded can best be made on the basis of the outline developed and the research undertaken *after* the initial interview. Though it is best not to make a definite commitment to the interviewee until you can be more precise, she should be prepared for the eventuality that more than one interview may be recorded.

How much preparation is done before the first interview will depend largely on who the woman is. For a prominent individual, a "local figure," or someone involved in a well-documented activity, it is possible to research existing sources such as newspapers, organization records, and histories ahead of time. However, many of those we will interview are women about whom a great deal is not recorded; they are the "voiceless" unknown women who worked in the home, the women who worked at office jobs pushing the huge carriages of old typewriters, the women who rose at five in the morning to chop cotton, the women who bore three, four, five, and more children, the women who panicked at their frequent pregnancies and performed abortions on themselves. The best preparation for a first interview with these women is a familiarity with the time period, especially the living conditions and tenor of life in both rural and urban settings.

Familiarity with the texture of life allows us to explore fully her family history and her early years. The same principles will guide us as in later interviews; her own experiences and style of reminiscing provide the framework, while our general topical outline sensitizes us to certain areas and provides suggestions for probing. . . . After covering the early years, usually to adolescence (which might require more than one interview), a general biographical sketch is recorded in roughly chronological sequence. It is this sketch which will then be used as the basis for both structuring the subsequent interviews and directing us to the areas which should be researched.

Though most of the women whom we will interview probably do not have "papers," almost all do have photographs and various objects which they have kept from their past. Looking over these helps to inform the interviewer and to jog the memory of the interviewee.

I thought I had fully exhausted the recollections of a union woman about the various strikes in which she had participated until we looked over her photographs, late in the interview series. A picture of an ILGWU (International Ladies Garment Workers Union) picnic reminded her that this was a victory celebration; she was then able to recount her activities in yet another strike. It is best to look over these records early in the project, ideally during the first interview. Furthermore, it is a good idea to let the tape recorder run as she comments on her photo album or a newspaper clipping or displays her yellowed wedding dress. Although the material should be recorded again later, in the context of the period in which it took place, the second version of the story might be quite different from that first rendition—which could become a lost gem were we not to record it when the memory spontaneously surfaced.

The Interview Process

The interview is a transaction between the interviewer and the inter-viewee, and their responses to each other form the basis for the creation of the oral history. Each woman has her own style of recollecting, as well as her own specific experiences. As sensitive interviewers, we respond to each individually, and the interview process will therefore vary. This variability is one of the most distinctive features of the oral history inter-view and is what makes it different from the standardized interviews used by social scientists.

Despite experience and careful planning by the interviewer, there are several common tendencies which can mar any interview. These are a function of our own impatience and (in our eagerness to use our back-ground research) a dependency on our prepared outlines or guides. We fear lapses of silence. We squirm at what appear to be long, irrelevant digressions. We become impatient at the chaotic manner in which mem-ory divulges the past. In our fear and impatience, and also in our en-thusiasm for the material we are uncovering, we succumb to talking too much, asking too many questions too soon.

The best oral history is a quasi-monologue on the part of the inter-viewee which is encouraged by approving nods, appreciative smiles, and enraptured listening and stimulated by understanding comments and intelligent questions. Though the ideal interviewer is there primarily to provide a broad leeway in which to help the interviewee structure her recollections, sensitivity to both individual idiosyncrasies and class or culturally determined characteristics, might lead to more direct question-ing in some cases and total silence in others.

For example, despite her protestations that she would not be able to talk without a lot of questions, an old Jewish immigrant woman whom I interviewed would embark on an hour-long monologue at the beginning of each session. She had self-selected that material which was important to her, or which she thought was of general interest. I quickly learned that asking questions—except for points of clarification—was an intrusion. She demanded total eye contact at all times! During her spontaneous reminiscing, I remained virtually silent. Then, towards the end of the session, or at the beginning of the next one, I would ask some additional questions relating to the material she had provided or to my own outline.

In planning for the interview, I review the types of questions I wish to ask, and the order in which I want to ask them, but I also try to avoid too much "preordering" of the material. The principle which I generally use is to ask the most general question first, waiting to see where that ques-tion leads. It might lead to a detailed description, to what appears to be a digression, or to a blank. My own reaction, then, is tailored to the woman's response. If the general question, for example about living conditions during her childhood, yields detailed information, I can sit back, keeping a sharp ear for unexpected information, new directions to explore, and confusing material. If, on the other hand, the general question leads to a vague or general response, then the questions can be re-cast or phrased more specifically. If we are clear in our own minds what it is we are looking for, this is not difficult to do. For instance, when I ask about living conditions during the woman's youth, what I am seeking is sufficient information to re-create the basic social setting as well as the financial circumstances of the family. A general response such as "we were very poor," or "we lived in a tenement" does not tell me much. Asking more specific questions (for example, how many slept in a room, a bed; was there water/ plumbing in the living space, in the corridor, outside) can yield sufficiently rich descriptions so that no further questioning is necessary.

A general or vague response might indicate that the interviewee did not consider the subject very important. If we have touched upon an area that is not part of her basic self-definition, but is important to us as feminist archivists, then we must devise a way to get the information without letting our questions over-determine the interview. It might mean that we wait until the very end of the oral history recording sessions to ask some of our questions, even though they may be out of context. Otherwise, we can easily end up with an oral history that is defined not by the values and rhythm of the individual's life, but by the perspective that *we* bring about women, about class, about race.

If our general questions lead to a lengthy digression, then we must be prepared to follow that line until it is exhausted. It is imperative that we learn to let the train of memory association run its course; that we be able to scrap totally the direction in which we were originally headed; that we know when to ignore our outlines and pick up new avenues of inquiry. If, at the end of this new track, we still do not have the information we were initially seeking, then we can return to our original line of inquiry, perhaps asking for the same content in a different way.

Sometimes, though, the interviewee truly cannot recall the information we are seeking. As little as we know about memory function, we do know that it is related to blood flow and that it will vary at different times of the day and on different occasions during the week. Thus, sensitivity to the health and stamina of the interviewee is important; it is also a basic sign of human respect. This generally means determining what time of day is best to interview her; being prepared to cancel an interview if, when you arrive, she seems tired, upset, or "under the weather"; and, knowing when to cut the session short. During the course of the interview, as she tires, there will be noticeable memory loss and increased difficulty in remembering words. That should signal that it is time to end the interview for the day. (I have found that the ninety-minute interview is about the right length for most elderly women, though for some, one hour is the maximum. I openly discuss this with the interviewee.) When a question draws a blank or a line of inquiry is not productive, we have to be willing to give up. If it is important, we might want to make a mental note of it and try again on another occasion.

How do we keep track of our own line of thought during the various passages into the by-ways of memory? With attentive listening we can easily forget our own questions. How do we quickly note a new line of inquiry that was triggered by a comment of the interviewee; how do we keep some chronological sense when an interviewee's style is to rush headlong from one anecdote to another? There is as much diversity of opinion on note-taking during the interview as there is on sharing the outline or guide with the interviewee. My own experiences vary from one interviewee to the next, though invariably I do not share with her my outline or specific questions. My fear is that this outline, which is really just a guide for myself, will determine the course of the interview too much. I will suggest at the end of each session the *general areas* we might want to cover at the following session.

As for note-taking during the interviews, I usually try to avoid making notations of more than a single word or phrase—just enough to keep *my* memory intact. Stopping to take notes signifies to her either that what she is saying is not very important and that you do not have to listen, or that it is *very* important and you are taking notes in order to ask her more about it. In any event, the loss of eye contact, even for a brief moment, the break in the pattern of concentrated listening, can be very disruptive. In reviewing the tape later, the interviewer can note names, places, and dates, and can then ask for clarification of confusing material at the next session.

Perhaps the most difficult and frustrating task is to keep clear in our own minds some sense of chronology and the order of events. Some women, particularly less educated working-class women, are not accustomed to reflecting about themselves, to viewing their lives as important. The stories they are used to repeating are those which recount a courageous act, a funny episode, or a tragic event in their families. Consequently, the interview might be a string of anecdotes with little connecting material or insufficient descriptions to place these anecdotes in a context adequately understandable to outsiders. This is her style and rather than interfere (which would be useless anyway) the interviewer has to develop some systematic way of keeping time references clear and to ask questions *in relation to* the anecdote which helps to provide the total context. I have found it helpful to actually develop a chronological chart, based on the first contact interview, which clearly outlines the various stages in the woman's life. In this way, it becomes easier to keep straight which anecdote fits where.

The interview with the more educated, middle-class woman usually is quite a different process. She is more accustomed to reflecting about life, and also to articulating ideas. As a result the interview is more "orderly"; thoughts are more often completed, and sentences hang together. This is not to say that one interview is better or worse than another, but rather that we have to be aware of the ways in which class, particularly, affect thought processes and speaking patterns, and to adapt ourselves to these variations.

In addition to those differences related to class origins there are certain cultural characteristics which are a function of both ethnicity and generation. Though older and/or immigrant women might talk without much hesitation about "female concerns," they often find it difficult to be very explicit. For instances, most women will freely talk about the onset of menses. However, they might find it more difficult to describe the "pads" they used, where they were collected, washed, and so on. By the same token, though women might be willing to talk about birth control, they might be embarrassed to describe specific techniques and might speak in euphemisms, such as, "My husband took precautions." She might be referring to his using condoms, or to coitus interruptus. It will be up to the interviewer to then phrase questions which elicit the information without requiring the interviewee to use words with which she has difficulty or which embarrass her. Faced with the timidity of some older women, the interviewer must have sufficient knowledge about birth control practices in the earlier part of the century to step in and provide words as well as to ask for more details. This is part of the preparation that any good interviewer will have done, and these cultural differences may have important implications for the editing process.

Processing the Interview

Once we have successfully recorded one or a series of interviews, the initial product (and perhaps, the final one) is the raw tape recording. Since an important primary document has been created, it is important to take measures both to protect it and, at the same time, to make it accessible to others.[7] Minimally, this requires some summarizing and indexing of the contents of the tapes and either depositing them in archives or making their existence known to those who would have an interest in the materials. By using either extensive funding or a willingness to put in countless unpaid hours, we can next transcribe and edit the interviews, perhaps ultimately into a continuous narrative. The way in which the recordings are further processed depends on both the resources available and the use to which the material will be put.

The easiest and least expensive method is to develop a running summary of *each* tape. As a matter of course, if more than one interview is recorded with a single individual, it is a good idea to listen and to take notes on each interview before proceeding with the next. This is both to make sure that nothing has been missed—particularly new avenues hinted at—and to continually appraise our methods and sharpen our skills. Since the tapes should be reviewed anyway, it does not require much more time to keep a running summary while listening to them. Properly done, this summary can then be used as a basis for indexing the entire group of interviews with a single individual. . . .

This simple system allows the use of the material for any of several purposes, including extraction of specific segments for presentation as evidence, and development of audio or audio-visual presentations. In other words, this system allows for easy retrieval of the material which can then be selectively transcribed as needed. Though it might take a bit longer to locate the material on a tape and listen to it than it would to scan quickly the printed page the material *is available* for scholarly use, nevertheless. Furthermore, beucase of subtle communication patterns that cannot be captured on the printed page, listening to the segments might be considerably more revealing than merely reading a passage.

This is not to argue against transcribing the tapes if it is possible to do so, and if the resources are available. However, we should bear in mind that the enormous amounts of time and money required to transcribe an interview (an average of five to eight hours per interview hour) might be better utilized in collecting more oral histories from those older women whose numbers are rapidly diminishing.

If the tapes are transcribed, there are then several different methods of treating the literal transcription. Minimally, it is edited for clarity, punctuation, and correct spelling of names and places. The resulting "edited transcript" is usually placed on a library shelf, to be used primarily by scholars. More extensive editing of the transcripts might be done, when sufficient funds are available, as is the practice of the Regional Oral History Office of the Bancroft Library (University of California, Berkeley). The transcript is edited for smooth flow and continuity, which means that similar material from different portions of the interview is pulled together and organized into coherent sections with headings and subheadings. After a review of the transcript by the interviewee, the interviewer/editor writes an introduction and indexes the volume. Photographs and other documents might be included selectively in the final bound volume, which is deposited at Berkeley and UCLA and is available for purchase by other libraries. The resulting volume is more readable and certainly more accessible and usable than a simple, minimally edited transcript. However, it is quite costly to produce.

Another form of editing, usually in preparation for wider publication, involves all the other prior steps discussed above *and* editing the question/answer format into a continuous narrative, removing the interviewer's questions and comments. Once the questions are removed, transitional passages might be missing. We don't want to put words into the interviewee's mouth, yet we want the materials to flow smoothly and to preserve her unique syntax. We must work the material in ways that will render the written form the most authentic rendition of her oral account. This does not necessarily mean the most literal. When the spoken word is translated into the printed word, a great deal is lost—particularly when we are interviewing women unaccustomed to articulating their ideas or to revealing themselves publicly, especially working-class women. The subtle nuances of the spoken word, or the posturing and gesturing which accompany it often more effectively communicate emotional tone than do the words themselves. The sensitivity of the interviewer to the interviewee will largely determine many of the editorial choices that will be made. Ultimately, this kind of editing entails what can only be described as literary judgment, though it certainly does not require a writer to make these judgments.

No matter how we process the recorded interview, we must remember that we have created a unique "document," one which above all is oral/aural. There is no one method for best creating this new source or for best processing the raw materials. Each of us must develop the style that best suits her and the women she interviews. With our foremothers we are creating a new kind of women's history, a new kind of women's literature. To this task we should bring the sensitivity, respect, tremendous joy and excitement that come from the awareness that we are not only creating new materials, but that we are also validating the lives of the women who preceded us and are forging direct links with our own past.

Notes

1. Allan Nevins, "Oral History: How and Why It Was Born," *Wilson Library Bulletin* 40 (March 1966), pp. 600–601 (see chapter 2 of the presetn volume).

2. Gerda Lerner, *The Female Experience: An American Documentary* (Indianapolis: Bobbs-Merrill, 1977), pp. xvi–xviii.

3. A good account of the use of oral history in the study of slavery, beginning with the work at Southern and Fisk universities in the 1920s, is to be found in Ken Lawrence, "Oral History of Slavery," *Southern Exposure* 1 (Winter 1974), pp. 84–86.

4. Alex Haley, "Black History, Oral History, and Genealogy," *Oral History Review* 2 (1973), pp. 1–25.

5. Judy Yung, "A Bowlfull of Tears: Chinese Women Immigrants on Angel Island," *Frontiers* 2 (Summer 1977), pp. 52–55.

6. Yvonne Tixier y Vigil and Nan Elsasser (contributors to "Grandmother's Stories" in this issue [*Frontiers* 2 (1977)]) found that in interviews with Hispanic women there was a greater willingness to discuss sex with the Anglo interviewer than with the Chicana interviewer. On the other hand, topics associated with discrimination were more likely to be discussed openly with the Chicana than with Anglo. See Tixier y Vigil and Elsasser, "The Effects of the Ethnicity of the Interviewer on Conversation: A Study of Chicana Women," in *Sociology of the Language of American Women*, ed. Betty L. DuBois and Isabel Crouch (San Antonio: Trinity University Press, 1976), pp. 161–70.

7. There are several free booklets on the care of tapes which are available from 3M Company, St. Paul, Minnesota 55101. Generally it is a good idea to make duplicate copies of your tapes, preferably on a high-speed copier (which is available at the audio-visual centers of most schools). To avoid accidentally recording over your taped interview, the tabs at the back of the cassette should be punched out. Should you, for some reason, later wish to record on the tape, it is possible to do so by taping over the empty space created where the tab was punched out. For storage of tapes, a moderate temperature is recommended. Some sources recommend rewinding and winding the tapes at least once a year.

22

Using Oral History for a Family History Project

Linda Shopes

*Our section on the applications of oral history concludes with three arti-
cles that consider the growing field of family history. In the first, Linda
Shopes, a community historian, describes the basic oral historical techniques used by the family researcher. The approach that she advocates
helps develop a comprehensive context to an individual's life, a sense of
where one stands among generations on the road of life. Without a historical frame of reference, an individual family's record hangs suspended, out
of time and place.*

*Shopes offers useful advice on searching family records before interview-
ing and on creating a historical setting from personal and public documents. The author insists on the value—often overlooked among those researching their family's history—of indexing and organizing the project's results with an eye to adding information to the public record.*

*Linda Shopes teaches American Studies at the University of Maryland,
Baltimore County. Her interests lie in labor, community, and family history,
and she has done extensive research in the Baltimore area.*

*"Using Oral History for a Family History Project" was originally pub-
lished as Technical Leaflet 123 (Nashville: American Association for State
and Local History, 1980).*

Introduction

IMAGINE LISTENING to an elderly relative tell of her journey to
America as an immigrant, her arrival at Ellis Island, and her first job
in a clothing factory. Or imagine another family member describing
how he worked on the family farm, learned to read in a one-room school
house, and courted his wife at church socials. Such are the opportunities
available to the family historian who draws upon the method of oral
history.

Traditionally, family history has been equated with genealogy, the reconstruction of a person's lineage through the use of written records. However, the stories family members tell about their past are also a rich source of information on a family's history. In particular, they can yield information about motives and attitudes and the "feeling tone" of life that even the most extensive genealogical reconstruction lacks. Enlarging the notion of family history to include information gathered from oral sources also encourages people to investigate their pasts even though extensive genealogical records are not available.

The personal benefits of such an investigation are numerous. For subsequent generations of the family, who frequently lack significant contact with extended relatives and so have little knowledge of "where they came from," a collection of taped interviews is a rich inheritance. For people who are interviewed, particularly older people, reviewing their life experiences and trying to order them and articulate their significance can be a rewarding experience.

But it is for the family researcher that such a project perhaps has the greatest value. It can be the impetus for developing or deepening relationships with other family members. Even more important, it can enhance one's own sense of identity. By tying together the strands of the family history and trying to understand the meaning of individual lives in relation to the social and historical context within which they were lived, family historians can gain perspective on the context of their own lives.

This notion of family history as moving beyond the domain of the genealogist is supported by several recent developments in historical study. Since the 1960s, historians increasingly have sought to understand the daily life experiences of ordinary people. They have paid particular attention to the history of the family since it is so fundamental a social institution and shapes so much of people's daily lives. Oral history, too, has emerged in recent years as a method of historical research. Though by no means limited to the study of ordinary people, oral history interviews are especially valuable as a source of information about those individuals and groups for whom the written record is both scant and misleading.

Doing Background Research

Although oral history interviews may lie at the heart of a family history research project, they must be preceded by careful preparation if they are to be of much value. Before doing any interviewing, the family historian needs to assemble basic data on individual family members and then locate those individual lives within their broader historical context. This background information will give the researcher some idea what to interview family members about and will enable the interviewer to ask more thoughtful and searching questions during the interview itself.

Though the researcher may know some of this information already, especially about immediate family members, a good deal more can be gathered by research into both primary and secondary written sources. A good place to begin this research is the family Bible. In addition, in almost every family there is someone who has an old shoe box full of miscellaneous family papers such as school diplomas, old letters, and tax records. These need to be located and examined for information. Family photographs and material objects are especially interesting. Sensitively interpreted, they can suggest much about "what life was like" years ago. Also available to the family researcher are the kinds of public documents used by genealogists—birth, marriage, and death records, wills, censuses, immigrant passenger lists.

By drawing upon a number of these personal and public documents, the family researcher can begin to understand the basic pattern of events in family members' lives—when and where they were born, educated, and married, residential and occupational histories, the children born to them. It is useful to assemble this data on a single form for each family member being researched; a sample form is illustrated (figure 22.1). It also should be noted that background data might fruitfully be gathered for deceased relatives. Not only will it make the family history more complete, but also it can help stimulate recollections about these people during interviews with their relatives and close friends.

Once some background information about family members has been gathered, the next step for the family researcher is to try to understand these individual lives in relation to the social circumstances that affected them. This kind of understanding will add depth to the interview and may help the researcher perceive the family's history as something more than a collection of individual biographies. Thus, an afternoon spent in the local historical society or the local history section of the library might yield not only specific information about individual ancestors, but also a clearer sense of the historical setting within which these ancestors lived. Also useful are general accounts of American history and specific studies of historical events and processes like immigration or the Depression that may have affected family members. Biographies, particularly some of the more recent biographies of ordinary Americans based largely on oral sources, are yet another possible source of insight. The number of such works is enormous, but a local librarian or college history instructor might be able to make some useful suggestions for background reading relevant to individual families.

Determining a Focus

After gathering biographical data on family members and researching the general background of the family history, the family historian then

Name: _____

Date of Birth: _____ Place of Birth: _____

Mother's Name (include maiden name): _____

Father's Name: _____

Siblings' Names (include birthdates if known): _____

_____

_____

Spouse's Name (include wife's maiden name): _____

Date of Marriage: _____ Place of Marriage: _____

Children's Names (include dates and places of birth): _____

_____

Date of Death: _____ Place of Death and Burial: _____

Religion and Church Membership: _____

Schooling and/or Other Training (list all schools attended, the dates of attendance, and the level of education completed at each): _____

_____

Residential History (list all residences chronologically, noting the dates lived at each): ___

_____

Occupational History (list all occupations chronologically, noting the place of work, the type of work done there, and the approximate salary): _____

Membership in Clubs and Organizations (note dates of memberships and offices held): ____

_____

Figure 22.1. A sample form for recording family data. A separate form should be completed for each member of the family.

needs to decide what direction the interviews will take. Possible areas of inquiry fall within three broad categories: the impact of major historical events and trends such as racial segregation, technological developments, or the post World War II housing boom on the family; the relationship of various aspects of social life such as work, religion, community life, or class status and mobility to individuals within the family; and the structure and dynamics of family life itself, including household membership, relationships among family members, and family values. A fourth area of inquiry is suggested by family folklorists who are concerned not so much with the content of a family's history as with the forms a family uses to preserve its experiences. Thus, the family researcher also might collect family stories, traditions, customs, and beliefs.

Since the number of possible topics and subtopics within each of these broad categories is enormous, it is advisable to focus on a few main themes that seem most relevant to the family's experience; otherwise, the information gathered will be a random collection of unrelated facts, anecdotes, and insights. These themes, however, should only be tentative. The family historian needs to be aware that interviewees themselves may open up new areas of inquiry, new ways of understanding the family history.

Conducting the Interviews

Once some background research is done and a general focus for the investigation is determined, the family researcher is ready to begin interviewing. Choose for first interviews those family members with whom you feel most comfortable and who seem to enjoy talking about the past. If these interviews are successful, less enthusiastic family members might be encouraged to participate. In addition, the interviewer will have acquired skill in interview techniques before dealing with more difficult situations. Of course, common sense dictates that the oldest family members be interviewed first.

After selecting persons to interview, the family historian needs to consider very carefully how to encourage extensive and thoughtful recall from the interviewees. An interview is above all a social interaction; if it is awkward and tense, no matter how carefully researched, it will be intellectually and personally unrewarding.

The interviewer needs to contact the interviewees and explain the purpose of the interview, acquire additional biographical data if necessary, explore possible topics for the interviews, and in general encourage the subjects to begin thinking about their own and the family's history. A good technique is to review old photographs and documents with the interviewees for they are often valuable memory jogs. It also might be interesting to take the people back to scenes from their earlier years— former homes, schools, churches, places of employment—as a way of stimulating additional memories.

Based on this pre-interview conversation, as well as the background research and the general focus determined for the project, the family historian next needs to prepare an outline of topics to pursue during the interviews. Interviews can be structured autobiographically, so that the interviewees are guided into giving a chronological account of their lives, or topically, so that only certain aspects of their experiences are probed. The best family history interviews are probably a combination of autobiographical and topical narratives, though the individual researcher needs to decide which method best suits the previously established purposes.

The outline for the interviews should facilitate recall, not inhibit it. It is not a list of "twenty questions" to which the interviewer rigidly adheres, but a list of topics and subtopics to give direction to the interviews. It is important to emphasize, however, that the interviewer needs to have a clear sense of the categories of information to be sought; otherwise, it is easy to become overwhelmed by a welter of disparate facts and wandering recollections. Trying to compress the highlights of some fifty, seventy, or even ninety years of living into a few hours of a taped interview is, after all, a difficult task and demands considerable forethought.

During the interviews, the interviewer needs to encourage a mood of expansiveness in the subjects so that they are stimulated to recount life experiences openly and on their own terms. The best way to do this is to ask open-ended questions that can be developed at length by the interviewees. However, questions should not be so broad or complex that the interviewees do not know where to begin an answer. For example, suppose the interviewer wants to learn about the interviewee's childhood. A closed question like "When and where were you born?" does not allow room for elaboration upon experiences. Yet a too open statement like "Tell me about your childhood—your family, your school experiences, what your community was like—anything that you can remember" might simply elicit a few bits and pieces of information with no real focus. A better way to probe childhood experiences would be to say, "I understand you were born in Baltimore in 1905 to parents who had recently immigrated to this country [all this information having been learned from the background research done before the interview]. Tell me something about this family that you were born into."

Follow-up questions on what an interviewee has just said can encourage yet additional recall. Thus, to refer to the example above, depending upon how the interviewee has answered the question about the family, the interviewer can dig for details about the economic circumstances, emotional climate, the roles and responsibilities of each parent, the children's place in the family, and so forth. Then the researcher can go on to ask questions about other aspects of the interviewee's childhood such as school experiences and the community lived in. In all cases, each topic should be explored as completely as possible before moving on to another. If the interviewee wanders off the track, the interviewer can simply return to the subject by saying something like, "Before getting into the subject of your school experiences, I'd like to learn some more about your family. Tell me something about what your mother did in the home."

Throughout the interviews, the interviewer should play the role of "active listener," gently guiding and encouraging the interviewees' recollections but never intruding upon them. Thus, questions should be unbiased; they should be phrased in such a way that no particular answer seems expected. "Tell me more about . . . ," "Why do you think that . . . ," and "Give me an example of . . . ," are all good ways to draw out an interviewee even on fairly sensitive or controversial topics. On the other hand, phrases like "Don't you agree that . . . " or "Isn't it true that . . . " are likely to inhibit all but the most assertive interviewees. Interviewers also should refrain from commenting favorably or unfavorably on what the interviewees say. Good rapport can be maintained nonverbally by eye contact, nods and smiles, an intent expression, and a relaxed body position and verbally by an occasional non-committal "I understand" or "I see."

It is important also not to inhibit interviewees by interrupting once they have started to answer questions. Let them unfold the logic of their lives as they choose. Clarification and examples can be elicited after the original question is answered. It is a good idea to have a pad and pencil handy during interviews to jot down notes for these follow-up questions.

The interviewer should also be certain that the interviewees actually have finished answering a question before asking another. Pauses in narration, though uncomfortable for an eager interviewer, often signal efforts to gather additional thoughts on a topic, not the end of thought on it. The interviewer should keep in mind that generally the best interviews are those in which the interviewer says the least.

The setting of interviews can help nurture recall, and the interviewer should pay attention to this detail of the interview process also. Interviews should take place where those being questioned are most comfortable and used to talking informally; usually this means their own home—perhaps in the living room, but more often in the den, kitchen, or back yard. Wherever the interviews take place, they should be free of interruptions and distractions that might break the interviewees' concentration. They should also be free of background noise—nothing makes a tape harder to understand than the regular creaking of a rocking chair or the steady hum of an air condition. Interviewer and interviewee should sit close enough to one another to maintain eye contact easily. The tape recorder microphone should be directed toward the interviewee, and the recorder itself, which the interviewer is completely at ease with operating, should be near the interviewer so that tapes can be changed unobtrusively as necessary.

Though oral historians generally agree that maximum rapport is gained by interviewing only one person at a time, sometimes talking with a small group of family members about old times is an especially enjoyable and valuable experience that provides considerable information as individuals trigger each other's memories and spur one another on. A group interview also may provide insight into patterns of interaction among family members and may highlight differences and similarities among family members' individual experiences. A group session is perhaps best used in conjunction with more extensive individual interviews.

Because interviews are often exhilarating experiences for both interviewer and interviewee, the interviewer should take care not to end abruptly, but rather ask one or two deflationary questions at the end of the interview and then spend a few minutes visiting with the interviewee once it is over. They are also tiring, and two hours generally seems to be the limit for a single productive session.

A Word of Caution

Although interviewing family members is usually a mutually rewarding experience, sometimes certain problems arise. Some potential interviewees, schooled in the great-men-and-events version of history, have difficulty understanding that the story of their life experiences is of particular interest to anyone and so have little enthusiasm for a family history project. Others are simply unwilling to speak candidly about what they feel is personal and, therefore, private. Other difficulties can arise. Pain over a deceased relative, embarrassment at a youthful indiscretion, efforts by estanged relatives to get the interviewer "on their side," and attempts by an interviewee to present only "the good side" of the family history have all been encountered by family historians. There is no single solution to handling any of these problems, but tact, persistence, and a sensitivity to this human dimension of family history research are the best guides.

The very human quality of oral testimony raises particularly complex questions about its validity as a historical document. Memories do fade over the years, and it is difficult for most people to be objective about their own experiences. However, the mood the interviewer creates during the interview itself and the creativity of questions can affect significantly the candor of the interviewee's recollections. It is also important for the interviewer to do background research and interview several family members about the family history in order to judge the veracity of any single account. But what is most important is to accept all interviewees' interpretations of their lives as their interpretation. Oral testimony, like any other historical source, needs to be evaluated both for its factual accuracy and for what it reveals about the attitudes and values of the interviewee.

After the Interview

The family historian may well feel that a collection of documents and taped interviews is an adequate record of the family history. This material, however, should be organized in some way to facilitate access. A filing system, with individual files containing all pertinent information for each relative, coupled with a carefully labeled set of tapes, is perhaps the simplest way to organize a collection. A more complex filing system, by theme or by time period, may be necessary for more ambitious projects. It should be noted, however, that transcribing the tapes or making a running index of what is discussed on each tape makes retrieval of information considerably easier.

The family historian also may wish to organize and interpret more completely the data collected, write up a family history, and circulate it among family members. It might be well also to consider placing a copy of the completed paper in the local historical society or library so that future researchers may have the benefit of the work. If a written family history goes outside the hands of the immediate family, the family historian is advised to secure written permission from the interviewees for researchers to draw upon information contained in their tapes.

Conclusion

A family history project may seem to be enormously ambitious. Certainly, the methods outlined in this pamphlet can be adapted to fit specific situations. Considerable background research and a pre-interview conversation may not always be possible before each interview. Interviewing itself becomes easier as the interviewer gains experience. Careful organization of data, too, can wait for a later date. In the end, perhaps the best advice is simply to START.

Bibliography

Baum, Willa K. *Oral History for the Local Historical Society*. 2d ed. Nashville: American Association for State and Local History, 1974. (An excellent introduction to the hows and whys of an oral history project)

———. *Transcribing and Editing Oral History*. Nashville: American Association for State and Local History, 1977.

Blyth, Ronald. *Akenfield: Portrait of an English Village*. New York: Grove Press, 1969. (An eloquent description of the hardness of a rural way of life in the words of the people who have lived it)

Doane, Gilbert H. *Searching for Your Ancestors: The How and Why of Genealogy*. 4th ed. Minneapolis: University of Minnesota Press, 1973. (An excellent introduction to the methods and sources of genealogical research)

Epstein, Ellen Robinson, and Rona Mendelsohn. *Record and Remember: Tracing Your Roots through Oral History*. New York: Monarch, 1978. (A guide to the use of oral history techniques for personal family history research; emphasizes the mechanics of conducting and processing interviews)

Gordon, Michael, ed. *The American Family in Social-Historical Perspective*. 2d ed. New York: St. Martin's Press, 1978. (A collection of scholarly articles on various aspects of the history of the American family)

Hartley, William G. *Preparing a Personal History*. Salt Lake City: Primer, 1976. (A brief guide to preparing an autobiography; includes a list of hundreds of interview topics)

Hoopes, James. *Oral History: An Introduction for Students*. Chapel Hill: University of North Carolina Press, 1979. (A comprehensive guide to oral history as a research technique; includes an excellent bibliography; see chapter 31 of the present volume)

Jeffrey, Kirk. "Varieties of Family History." *American Archivist* 38 (october 1975), pp. 521–32. (An overview of recent scholarship in the field of family history)

Kramer, Sydelle, and Jenny Masur. *Jewish Grandmothers*. Boston: Beacon Press, 1975. (An oral history of the immigrant experience of twelve Jewish women)

Kyvig, David E., and Myron A. Marty. *Your Family History: A Handbook for Research and Writing*. Arlington Heights, Ill.: AHM, 1978. (Another guide to doing a personal family history; includes many excerpts from student-written family histories)

Lichtman, Allan J. *Your Family History*. New York: Vintage, 1978. (The best available guide to the kind of family history research described in this article; includes chapters on oral history, written records, photographs, and methods of research, also an excellent bibligraphy)

Rosengarten, Theodore. *All God's Dangers: The Life of Nate Shaw*. New York: Knopf, 1974. (The oral biography of a black Alabama sharecropper; see chapter 20 of the present volume)

Shumway, Gary L., and William G. Hartley. *An Oral History Primer*. Salt Lake City: Deseret, 1974. A brief guide to oral history with particular emphasis on biographical interviews.

Starr, Louis. s.v. "Oral History." Vol. 20. 1st ed. *Encyclopedia of Library and Information Science*. New York: Marcel Dekker, 1977. (A brief overview of developments in oral history over the last three decades; see chapter 1 of the present volume)

Tyrrell, William G. *Tape-Recording Local History*. Technical Leaflet 35. rev. ed. Nashville: American Association for State and Local History, 1978.

Watts, Jim, and Allen F. Davis. *Generations: Your Family in Modern American History*. 2d ed. New York: Knopf, 1978. (A manual for doing a family history project that stresses locating one's individual history in its broader social context; includes several essays on aspects of twentieth-century American history)

Zeitlin, Steven, et al., eds. *Family Folklore*. Washington, D.C.: Smithsonian Institution, 1976. (An explanation of family folklore with many examples culled from visitors to the Smithsonian's Festival of American Folklife)

23

The Search for Generational Memory

Tamara Hareven

Of the many possible explanations for the current interest in oral and family history, our next selection offers one of the most thoughtful: the widespread need to link our individual existences to a place in time—to understand where we came from and where we may be going.

Tamara Hareven, one of the best-known researchers in family history, here analyzes oral history as it can fire a collective historical consciousness through discovery of a common past. She traces the present movement to New Deal efforts to collect "living history" and to the vast popularity of Alex Haley's epic Roots. *Hareven's work has shown how people previously involved in organized social or political activity can overcome their feelings of powerlessness through participation in a community history project.*

The rising interest in ethnic identity and nationalism, Hareven suggests, can be attributed to the increasing assimilation of ethnic subcultures within America. At times when a group's unique customs, traditions, and history falter, a drive for preservation and celebration often surfaces. The author presents her arguments in the context of family history and generational memory, which she defines as "memories which individuals have of their own families' history, as well as more general collective memories about the past."

Tamara Hareven is professor of history at Clark University and research associate at the Center for Population Studies at Harvard University. She is the author, with Randolph Langenbach, of Amoskeag: Life and Work in an American Factory City *(1978) and* Family Time and Industrial Time *(1982). She has edited two volumes on family history research,* Transitions: The Family and the Life Course in Historical Perspective *and* Aging and Family Transitions in Interdisciplinary Perspective *(1982).*

"The Search for Generational Memory" appeared originally in Daedalus *106 (Fall 1978), pp. 137–49.*

248

IN 1958 CLAUDE COCKBURN recalled a meeting with three Ladino-speaking Jews in Sofia shortly after the Second World War. They explained that they were not Spaniards, but one of them added, "Our family used to live in Spain before they moved to Turkey. Now we are moving to Bulgaria." When Cockburn asked him how long it had been since his family lived in Spain, he responded that it had been approximately five hundred years. The man spoke of these events as though they had occurred "a couple of years ago."[1] This famous incident has been cited frequently as an example of the relativity of historical memory. It also suggests the lengthy time over which individuals associate themselves with events which occurred generations earlier.

By comparison to other cultures, for most Americans generational memory spans a relatively brief period. The term generational memory is employed here broadly to encompass the memories which individuals have of their own families' history, as well as more general collective memories about the past. Most people do not even remember, or never knew, their grandfathers' occupation or place of birth. For a small proportion of the American population memory reaches back to the American Revolution, or to pre-Mayflower England or Europe. For descendants of later immigrations, memory extends mostly to the first generation in America, or, in fewer instances, to the last generation in the "old country." A sense of history does not depend on the depth of generational memory, but identity and consciousness do, because they rest on the linkage of the individual's life history and family history with specific historical moments.

Recently, efforts in American society to stretch generational memory, namely, the search for roots, through the tracing of genealogies and through oral history, have gained considerable popularity. A touch of magic has been attached to the process since the Bicentennial, and, in the aftermath of *Roots*,[2] a number of efforts to commercialize the search have emerged as well. More traditional scholars and foundations have also begun to encourage oral history, both as a means of retrieving or salvaging vanishing historical information and as a way to spark community identity. The success of *Roots* has publically dramatized the symbolic significance of such efforts.

Genealogies originally functioned to provide pedigrees and legitimization for status, claims for property, inheritance, or access to skills or political positions. Such real and symbolic functions of genealogies have survived in American society, especially in the South, despite an increasing democratization of society. Even the Daughters of the American Revolution, whose genealogical efforts were initially directed towards the inclusion of common people into the nation's ancestry (providing they were present in America in the colonial and revolutionary period), eventually turned their pedigree into an exclusive status grouping justified by a genealogy.

When it was founded in 1890, the DAR was reacting against the heraldic genealogical movements of the earlier period, which tried to link Americans with the English nobility. Applicants for membership were required to have an ancestor who was alive during the American Revolution, regardless of rank or status. "Lineage tracing," writes Margaret Gibbs, "was as much the rage in this decade—and in the early 1900's as Mah-Jong and crossword puzzles in the 'roaring twenties.' "[3] Along with numerous other patriotic societies which were founded in that period, the DAR was dedicated to the preservation and protection of patriotic ideals. Partly, the movement developed as an expression of anxiety in face of expansive foreign immigration, a fear of "race suicide" and a fear of loss of status for native born middle and upper classes.

On the other hand, the recent genealogical movements, especially the search for roots and the reconstruction of family histories, involve a different constituency and fulfill an entirely different function. They encourage individuals to locate their own life histories in the context of activities and historical settings of family members in earlier generations. Rather than concentrating on lineages as such, they encourage detailed knowledge of those relatives and of the historical events and the social context surrounding their activities. In this respect, family histories represent a recent popular version of an older generation of autobiographies or traditional biographies of great families. Whereas, in the past, formal family histories were limited primarily to the upper classes, the uniqueness of our time lies in the democratization of the process and in the inclusion of large segments of the population in the search. The tapestry has thus broadened from those claiming descent from the Mayflower or from Southern aristocrats, to include the descendants of African slaves and immigrants.

The emphasis on individual identification with genealogy has thus shifted from the search for legitimization of exclusive status to a concern with emergent identity. Erikson defines "identity" as the meeting between individual life history and the historical movement.[4] The process involved in the current reconstruction of individual family histories goes beyond individual identity in Eriksonian terms. It encompasses the linkage of one's family background with the larger historical experience, which is recognized and accepted as part of a collective heritage. Earlier, and even today in some circles, the search for a genealogy was considered successful only if it led to high-status ancestry, but the current populist mood encourages the search for one's origin, regardless of the social status of one's ancestry. The discovery of ancestors who were mere commoners, poor immigrants, or slaves is now considered as legitimate as linkage to nobility and great heroes. The recent acceptance of slavery as part of America's heritage by whites as well as blacks is indicative of this change.

This is precisely why *Roots* had the impact on the American public which is did. Its most compelling aspect was not the book's rendition of the story of slavery in a humane and moving way, but rather, the successful trace of the connection between a contemporary man and the origins of slavery through an individual line of descent. In itself *Roots* offers few new insights into the history of slavery. Its key message is the resilience and survival of African traditions, demonstrated in the effort of Chicken George and his descendants to transmit their family history from generation to generation. Its uniqueness lies in the *process* of search and trace of the history of one family, whose odyssey fits closely the contours of the collective experience of American slavery. Although most reviews have praised Haley's book as a great epic of slavery, they underestimated the significance of the final chapter recounting Haley's journey into the past in his effort to trace his family history back to its African origin, prompted by several fragments of an aging grandmother's narrative.

Significant here are both the process of the historical search itself and its successful outcome, which offered thousands of people the opportunity of a vicarious linkage with the historical group experience. (This is one of the rare occasions when the painstaking and tedious process of historical research has been acclaimed in the popular culture as a heroic act.) To understand fully the role which *Roots* has fulfilled in American culture it is important to realize that Haley's search *had* to be successful. The process of search would not have been recognized as important in its own right.

What if Haley had failed? Consider two hypothetical alternative outcomes. The first alternative could have been a break in the chain of evidence. This is, in fact, what happens to the majority of people attempting to trace their family histories beyond two generations. Most people embarking on such efforts without Haley's ingenuity, commitment of time, networks of scholarly support, and financial resources, could never dream to travel a similar road. Had he failed, Haley's story of the search itself, without the final linkage to Africa, would not have electrified the public. Alternatively, suppose Haley had been successful in tracing his ancestry, but the tracks did not lead back to the kind of ancestor he found. Suppose the story diverged, and Haley discovered an ancestor, who, rather than being an innocent victim captured and sold as a slave, had himself been a collaborator in the buying and selling of slaves. The search itself would still have been historically meaningful and personally satisfying, but it would not have had the same impact on the American public, because it would have lacked the direct link with collective experience of slavery. In short, the significance of Haley's book for American culture of the seventies lies not merely in the successful tracing of a line of ancestry back to Africa, but rather in the fact that this ancestor's history was characteristic of the mainstream of the slave route to North America and of the slave experience.

It is no coincidence that Haley is also the author of the *Autobiography of Malcolm X.*[5] Both the *Autobiography* and *Roots* are American success stories. In both, the hero follows a progression which he views as destined to culminate in the ultimate triumph. Earlier life events lead in an almost linear sequence to the moment of triumph and redemption. In Malcolm X's biography, as in the *Confessions of St. Augustine*, the entire life sequence leading to the moment of conversion is viewed as providential. Even Malcolm's devastating life experiences, his "sins" and suffering, were justified as steps toward the final redemption. Similarly, in Haley's story, the memory of the suffering of Kinte and that of his descendants in slavery were redeemed in the historical moment of rediscovery and linkage between past and present.

Both individual stories fulfilled significant public functions: at the height of the Black Power movement, Malcolm X's story and conversion performed a symbolic function, purging Black Americans from repressed anger reaching back into several generations. Haley's story provided a symbolic route for rediscovery of a past and, with it, a historic identity for Black Americans. The two had to occur in this sequence. First, the anger had to be purged in order to reverse a negative into a positive identity. Then came the search for roots, the discovery of a past, and the acceptance of this past as a significant part of America's heritage. Appropriately, the subtitle of Haley's book is *The Saga of an American Family*.

Roots also represents another important historical linkage, namely, that of the informal family narrative transmitted from generation to generation, which is not intended as a formal source of history, with the formal oral tradition of Gambian society—the official chronicle recited by the Griot. In Africa and in other nonliterate societies both types of oral traditions coexist, each performing a different function. The oral history genre which has survived in the United States, especially in black culture, is personal and informal. One of the most remarkable of Haley's discoveries was the survival of fragments of an oral tradition in his grandmother's memory in 1950s America. By that time, these fragments had lost their specific significance, but they were still being transmitted with a purpose; so that one's children and children's children would remember.

In modern American society, archives and formal histories have long replaced oral chronicles as official history. As the rich collection of folklore in Appalachia, or the very moving account of *All God's Dangers* suggests, generational memory and real traditions have persisted as historical sources in islands of local folk culture throughout the United States, though most prominently in black culture.[6] There is, however, a significant difference between the informal oral tradition which has survived in the United States and the official oral tradition in nonliterate societies. In such societies, the oral tradition has an institutionally recognized place and purpose in the culture, and whether it constitutes an official chronicle, a family narrative, a fable, or other types of memories, it is structured and presented in specific formulae. The function of oral testimony may range from myths aimed at providing an explanation of the creation of the world and of society as it exists, to those providing a pedigree for tribal rulers or to a justification of the political structure. The oral testimony can be legalistic, didactic, or explanatory, and its structure and mode of presentation may vary accordingly. Whatever its function, its social purpose is officially valued in these cultures.

In modern American society, although, in the absence of such a well-defined tradition as in nonliterate societies, it is difficult to find a formal place for oral history, informal oral history as a historical source is not a new phenomenon. It has been utilized systematically as an archival and research tool especially to record the memories of public figures who have been active in political and social life, as evidenced in projects of Columbia University and the Kennedy Library. Such projects have been carried out with historical scrupulousness, where the process of interviewing itself was preceded by research in written documents. Informal oral history has been employed effectively also in more modest historical projects, where the oral evidence was linked with written records and interpreted in conjunction with them.

Oral history also has an important social science heritage, which has developed since the 1930s, namely, the use of the individual life history for the "study of lives," which Dollard and subsequently Allport and White had developed as a major research method in psychology.[7] More recently, Oscar Lewis and Robert Coles have demonstrated the power of this method when applied to the urban poor, to Puerto Ricans and Mexicans, and the children of migrant workers and sharecroppers.[8] Inspired by this approach, radical historians have utilized oral history as a means to record the experiences of workers, activists, and participants in social protest movements, not only to retrieve and record information, but also as a way to form group consciousness through the process of interviewing itself.

More recently, oral history has been used on the community level for a similar purpose, namely, that of firing collective historical consciousness through the discovery of a common past. Some oral history efforts which emerged in recent years are filiopietistic and attach a mystique to the process because of the encounter with the living past which it represents.

The Bicentennial, in particular, gave an impetus to oral history projects which are intended to stimulate "community awareness" and "identity." Such undefined slogans, which have been used rather indiscriminately, do not explain how community consciousness would be raised through such projects and *whose* history is actually being recovered. The widespread use of the cassette tape recording machine over the past decade has contributed considerably to the popularization of oral history interviewing. Like the computer, the recorder has not only facilitated the gathering and preservation of data; it has also generated a mystique of authenticity which is conveyed through the magic of technology. Oscar Lewis somewhat glorified its role: "The tape recorder used in taking down the life stories in this book has made possible the beginning of a new kind of literature of social realism. With the aid of the tape recorder, unskilled, uneducated and even illiterate persons can talk about themselves and relate their observations and experiences in an uninhibited, spontaneous and natural manner."[9] People using the tape recorder, like those using the computer, discover quickly, however, that it does not have intrinsic magic. Without the historical and sociological imagination shaping the interview, one can end up recording miles of meaningless information.

Little attention has been paid to two aspects of oral history which are central to its role, namely, the nature of the interview process itself and the function of oral traditions in a modern, literate society.

First, the interview process. During an extensive oral history project in a large New England industrial community,[10] we became acutely aware of the fact that oral history is not strictly a means of retrieval of information, but rather one involving the *generation* of knowledge. Essentially, an oral history narrative is the product of an interaction between interviewer and interviewee. By its very nature such a process determines what is going to be recalled and how it will be recalled. The interviewer is like a medium, whose own presence, interests, and questions conjure corresponding memories. Even if the interviewer tries to remain inconspicuous, the very process is intrusive.

Oral history is therefore a subjective process. It provides insight into how people think about certain events and what they perceive their own role to have been in the historical process. "A testimony is no more than a mirage of the reality it describes," writes Jan Vansina, the leading scholar of oral tradition in Africa. "The initial informant in an oral tradition gives either consciously or unconsciously a distorted account of what has really happened, because he sees only what he has seen."[11]

Oral history is an expression of the personality of the interviewees, of their cultural values, and of the particular historical circumstances which shaped their point of view. This is precisely its great value, rather than its limitation. Similar arguments could be made about written documents; diaries and personal letters are also highly subjective, though their subjectivity is of a different origin. A diary reflects a person's individual experiences or observations, whereas an oral history is the individual's experience as evoked by an interviewer who has an intentional or unintentional influence on what is remembered and the way in which it is remembered. Oral histories are also distinguished from diaries or letters in their retrospective construction of reality. Like autobiographies, oral histories are past experiences presented from the perspective of the present.

The dynamic interplay between past and present in an individual's reminiscences can take different forms. At times, interviewees temporarily immerse themselves into a past episode as they recount it. This is especially true for childhood memories. On such occasions, the individual reminiscing slips back into the past, and recounts vibrant memories without any consciousness of the present. The interviewee becomes like an actor fully playing the role in his or her own past. On most occasions, the person remembering maintains a conscious separation between the account of the past and the present, though hindsight provides a contemporary perspective on past experience.

On many other occasions, interviewees find it difficult to distinguish past from present, or earlier from subsequent events. Interviewees also misrepresent or reinterpret actual events or situations through faulty memory or repression of difficult experiences. Traumatic experiences also lead to the reinterpretation of events. For example, when we interviewed former workers of the Amoskeag Mills, some of them said they had finished working in the Amoskeag in 1922. When we pointed out to them that their work records in the corporation files indicated they had worked until 1930 or later, the typical reply was "Oh yes, but that was after the strike. Things were not the same anymore." The strike of 1922 represented to the majority of the people who worked there at the time the destruction of the world to which they had become accustomed. Even though they returned to work after the strike, they associated the strike with the end of their career.

Sometimes people just forget experiences; other times they *care* to forget, or, if they remember them, they do not want to talk about them. As Gunhild Hagestadt points out, in many families there are prohibited zones, which most family members choose not to tread in, as if by unspoken agreement. An interviewer can sense the invisible electrified fences when approaching such areas, but can do very little about them.

Oral history is a record of perceptions, rather than a re-creation of historical events. It can be employed as a factual source only if corroborated. The difficulty of cross-checking information does not detract, however, from its value for understanding perceptions and recovering levels of experiences which are not normally available to historians. It offers almost the only feasible route for the retrieval of perceptions and experiences of whole groups who did not normally leave a written record. The major contribution of *Akenfield* and of *Hard Times* is not in their historical accuracy, but rather in their contribution to an understanding of human experiences and social conditions.[12] As long as one understands this, rather than assumes, as some do, that oral history is the closest to "unadulterated human memory" we can approach, it can be valued for what it is and utilized creatively.[13]

The second major feature of oral history involves its very significance in modern industrial society. In the absence of an established oral history tradition in American society, it is difficult to define its place and to justify its meaning to individual interviewees. It is almost impossible to stimulate *spontaneous reminiscing* as many community identity projects suggests one should. To make oral history meaningful, one has to find a link between an individual life and a broader historical context. Such links are exceedingly difficult to identify unless the individuals participated in a common distinct cultural activity, organization, or group with a shared interest or if their lives were affected directly by a common dramatic event.

Even in the black community, where the oral tradition is alive, particularly in the South, it is often difficult to link informal experiences and memories to a larger picture, unless the interviewees themselves are aware of a common focus.

Without such linkages, in most instances in the United States, oral history interviewing remains a private exercise. In Africa, by contrast, Vansina points out, "Every testimony and every tradition has a purpose and fulfills a function. It is because of this function that they exist at all."[14] In nonliterate societies the functions of an oral tradition are socially defined and are recognized by all members. In modern America there is no such established tradition, except in regional oral traditions which survive in isolated localities. Within the larger community, the public role and social significance of oral history are not automatically understood.

People who have not been "famous" or who have not participated jointly in a specific movement, such as a labor movement, or a strike, or in an organized political or social activity, would find it difficult to achieve such an identification. Such people experience great difficulty in making the connection between their own lives and the historial process. Community organizers who expect the emergence of "instant identity" through the interview process face an instant disappointment.

In societies where the oral narrative is part of the formal culture, no explanation is needed as to why a certain story is significant. The very time-honored practice and the setting within which the oral tradition takes place lend it strength and meaning. In modern America, except for historically conscious individuals or groups and unusually articulate and interested individuals, most people do not see an immediate significance in being interviewed. Although they might be inclined to reminiscence privately, telling stories to their own grandchildren or sharing memories of past experiences, most people are rather bewildered when requested to tell their life histories to strangers.

When approaching the former workers of the Amoskeag Mills in Manchester, New Hampshire, for interviews, we frequently encountered the questions: "Why ask me? My story is not special," or "What is so important about my life?" Except for a few people, those who consented to be interviewed did so, not because of their understanding of the importance of this process, but because, prompted by their own work ethic, they wanted to help us do "our job."

Attitudes changed drastically after the exhibit "Amoskeag: A Sense of Place, A Way Of Life" opened in Manchester. [15] Although this exhibit was primarily architectural and was aimed at professionals and preservationists rather than at the larger public, it evoked an unexpected response from former and current textile workers in the community. It provided the setting for the former workers' public and collective identification with their old work place and it symbolized the historical significance of their work lives. Thousands of people, mostly former mill workers and their families, came to see the exhibit. Most striking were recurring scenes where old former workers searched for their relatives in huge historic group portraits of the workers, and where grandparents led their grandchildren through the exhibit, often describing their work process of thirty to forty years earlier. Even though they had privately cherished many memories associated with their work experience, they felt that industrial work, especially textile work, was generally looked down upon. The sudden opportunity to view their own lives as part of a significant historical experience provided a setting for collective identification. Under these circumstances, interviewing ceased to be an isolated individual experience. It turned, instead, into a common community event. Former mill workers recognized each other at the exhibit, some not having seen each other for thirty years. Although the exhibit was not designed to serve this purpose, it turned into a catalyst.

The oral histories which followed were of an entirely different character from the earlier ones: people we approached were willing to be interviewed. They related their work and life histories with a sense of pride. Many individuals who had heard about the project volunteered to be interviewed. Identification with the work place and with the buildings thus provided a more direct and immediate stimulation of memory and interest in the process than isolated interviewing. The exhibit established our credibility as interviewers and laid the foundation for a continuing series of interviews with the same individuals. This is not to suggest that every successful oral history requires an exhibit or some other external device to engender identification. It suggests, however, how tenuous oral history is among those elements of the population who do not have an oral tradition. It is also becoming clear that, except for the search for roots through the reconstruction of one's own family history, the quest for oral history is more common among the educated, the professional, and the semiprofessional, especially among second- or third-generation ethnics, than as a "folk movement."

Why this exercise of "tribal rites" in an advanced technological society? Today, when the printing and circulation of information have reached an all-time peak, and when computers generate and objectify knowledge, scholars, foundations and cultural organizations, and the general public are reviving genealogy and the oral tradition—the tools of transmission of collective memory in nontechnological societies. Among scholars, this revival represents a revolt against "objective" social science and a shift from an emphasis on strictly formal knowledge to existential process. Oral history and the search for roots also fit into the effort of recent scholarship to integrate the experience of large segments of the population into the historical and sociological record. On a more popular level, the oral history revival is connected with an effort to authenticate the experiences of different ethnic groups in American culture. It thus represents a commitment to pluralism and expresses the reemergence of ethnicity and its acceptance as a vital aspect of American culture.

The current search is also prompted by a realization that the traditions which one is trying to record are about to become extinct. *The World of Our Fathers, The Godfather,* and many other ethnic monuments were generated at the moment when the last living links with the world are about to disappear. [16] Most of these efforts to capture ethnic traditions do not bring back the heritage from the old country, but rather the experience of the first generation of immigrants in America.

The search for roots in our time is not entirely new. An earlier centralized effort of this sort took place in the 1930s in the midst of the Great Depression. Current popular oral history projects are miniscule by comparison to the undertakings of the Works Progress Administration's Federal Writer's Project in most American communities. Some of its achievements include the American Guide Project, which generated a massive collection of local guides, the recording of over two thousand narratives of former slaves, the compilation of numerous volumes of local oral histories, and the assembling of a number of major collections of folklore. The national folklore project under the direction of John Lomax was intended to capture the surviving oral traditions and folkways. It produced a national volume entitled *American Folk Stuff,* designed as a collection of readable tales. "All stories must be narrated as told by an informant or as they might be told orally with all the flavor of talk and all the native art of casual narrative belonging to the natural story-teller," read the instructions of the national program director to all state directors.[17]

The folklore project stressed the collection of materials from *oral* sources with reference to the life of the community and the background of the informant. It captured urban and ethnic folklore as well as rural. "All types of forms of folk and story-telling and all minority groups—ethnic, regional and occupational are to be represented for two reasons: first to give a comprehensive picture of the composite America—how it lives and works and plays as seen through its folk storytellers; second, by the richness of material and the variety of forms to prove that the art of story-telling is still alive and that story-telling is an art."[18] Under the auspices of the Farm Security Administration, some of that generation's master photographers, such as Dorothea Lange, James Agee, and Walker Evans, recorded the words and faces of sharecroppers, "Okies," migrants, and Appalachians, bringing the faces of rural America into the center of the nation's consciousness. Thus, through a concerted government effort, rural roots were exposed and recorded for posterity.

Much of the social documentation of rural life resulted from the recognition that that world was fast disappearing, and from the fear that some of its wholesome values would be swept out by a new industrialism. To a large extent, this passion to document rural life was stimulated by the discovery of chronic poverty and deprivation in the rural South and Midwest, which had been ignored while the "pathology" of cities had occupied the limelight during the first three decades of the twentieth century. While they conveyed the suffering and deprivation of their subjects, the photographs and narratives in *Let Us Now Praise Famous Men* and in other kindred documentaries also conveyed the resilience and wholesomeness of this group.[19] The faces of the "Sharecropper Madonna" and of the Okies also had a sobering effect on those who idealized the myth of self-reliance and frontier life. In addition to the strong humanistic empathy for the subjects and their ways of life, these projects also expressed the period's longing for a lost mythical past of innocence and wholesomeness. The very launching of these projects in the midst of a catastrophic depression resulting from the "industrial plant being overbuilt" was a reaction against "progress" and with it, the destructive pace of modern, industrial life.

The 1930s was the era of the discovery of rural native American and black roots. The day of the immigrant was still to come. The WPA writers' project also attempted to record urban folklore. The New York City folklore project, for example, was intended to reveal "the epic of construction, excavation and wrecking, transportation . . . and the symphony of New York night life. . . ." Similarly, the social ethnic project which the WPA launched was intended to shift the emphasis from "the contribution of ethnic groups to American culture" to their participation in various aspects of community life. However, the definition of ethnicity which the WPA introduced was one very different from the ethnic revival today: "Immigrants and the children of immigrants are American people. Their culture is American culture."[20] Generally, the images and experiences which captured the imagination of the thirties were the documentaries of rural life. The earlier documentation of life and poverty in immigrant slums in New York, Chicago, and Baltimore, which was carried out in the late nineteenth and early twentieth centuries by Jacob Riis, the Russell Sage Foundation and the *Survey*,[21] and Lewis Hine's prolific photographic record of child labor, was documenting the plight of urban immigrants and the deterioration of social and economic life as part of a social protest movement, not in order to capture ethnic "roots." Immigrants who had flooded American cities between the 1880s and World War I were still too recent and still represent undigested alien masses.

The current quest for roots holds in common with that of the 1930s a genuine concern for recovering the historical experience as it was viewed and perceived by participants. As in the thirties, the search emerged from a crisis in values, and from a questioning of the very foundations of American society. Both in the 1930s and in the 1960s, the search for roots came in response to a disillusionment with technology, industrialism, and materialism. In the thirties the effort led to a reaffirmation of the qualities and strengths of American folk culture. Alfred Kazin, one of the unemployed writers in the WPA project, described the interview experience as "A significant experience in national self-discovery—a living record of contemporary American experience."[22] The current search is aimed more specifically at the recovery of ethnic group identities. In the 1960s and 1970s the search for roots has been individual as well as group oriented. Unlike in the 1930s when the effort was organized and supported by the government, in the current decade it represents a more spontaneous movement. Its very emergence is part of an aftermath of the Civil Rights and Black Power movements and as part of the recent acceptance of ethnicity as part of American culture.

Ironically, we are now engaged in recovering generational memory, after much of it had been wiped out in a century-long effort to assimilate immigrants. As Lloyd Warner pointed out, the symbols which dominated the historical rituals and pageants of Yankee City's Tricentenary were those of the colonial period and the era of the American Revolution. [23] An entire century of Yankee City's history had been almost completely ignored. Despite the fact that they already comprised a significant element of the city's population, the ethnic groups were expected to choose themes from the colonial and revolutionary era for the floats which they sponsored in the historical pageant (the Jews choosing an episode in the life of Benedict Arnold). Even in 1976, during the Bicentennial celebration in one of the historic mill buildings in Lowell, Massachusetts, the majority of the participants from the community (who were of different ethnic origins) were wearing revolutionary era costume, though Lowell was founded in 1820 and symbolized the beginning of the new industrial order. Similarly, a recent follow-up study on Yankee City in the 1970s find that the new owners of the Federalist houses in Newburyport are reconstructing the genealogies of these houses, rather than their own family histories. [24]

The current return to ethnicity in American culture is possible precisely because so much has been forgotten already and because of the distance in time between the current generation and the two generations of immigrants who came to the United States between 1880 and 1920. Before ethnicity could be recognized as a permanent feature in American culture, the different ethnic subcultures had to go the full cycle of assimilation and come close to extinction.

In some ways we are now witnessing the final consequences of the closing of the gates in the 1920s. The end of immigration at that point facilitated the absorption of immigrants who had arrived earlier into the United States. Had there been a continuous influx of new immigrants, it is doubtful whether ethnic diversity would have been accepted today as a genuine part of American culture. The current search for ethnic roots is in itself a rebellion against the concept of the melting pot; it is an effort to salvage what has survived homogenization. In the process, it is also likely to create new identities, new heritages, and new myths. Part of this process represents an effort to counteract alienation and to seek comfort and reassurance in memories of close family ties and community solidarity which are generally attributed to the lost ethnic past. For most ethnic groups this past represents the world of the first generation of immigrants in the United States, rather than the old country. The search for an ethnic past becomes especially significant for our times because of the generational watershed which we are currently experiencing: the two generations of European immigrants which had come here from the old country in the late nineteenth and early twentieth centuries are now dying out, while the generation which is now reaching the prime of its adulthood has no personal memory of World War II. What this would mean for the generational memory of the children of this age group is an interesting question in itself.

In assessing the significance of the current search for roots from a historical point of view, we must ask where this all leads. In 1911, confronting the DAR, Jane Addams warned them: "We know full well that the patriotism of common descent is the mere patriotism of the clan—the early patriotism of the tribe—and that, while the possession of like territory is an advance upon that first conception, both of them are unworthy to be the patriotism of a great cosmopolitan nation. . . . To seek our patriotism in some age rather than our own is to accept a code that is totally inadequate to help us through the problems which current life develops."[25]

It would be a historical irony, of course, if the groups which had been excluded for so long from the official cultural record, would fall into a similar trap of exclusiveness and separatism when recreating their own history. Some of that danger would be present if the reclamation is particularistic and parochial. Is the current individualism and ethnocentrism going to result in a retreat and withdrawal from a common culture and common social goals? Will it eventually lead to fragmentation rather than a balanced pluralism? Whatever the outcome might be, the current search inevitably has to take place first within the subcultural compartments, since until very recently, the larger society has tried to mold the identity of different ethnic groups in its own image.

Notes

In the process of writing this essay, I have benefited from a number of enlightened conversations and from the insights of the following people: Randolph Langenbach, Richard Brown, Ronald Grele, Nancy Chudacoff, John Modell, Frank Fustenberg, and Carol Stack and Robert LeVine. I am indebted to Stephen Graubard for valuable comments, to Howard Litwak for editorial assistance, and to Bernice Neugarten and Gunhild Hagestadt for their insights.

1. Quoted in M. I. Finley, "Myth, Memory, and History," in *History and Theory*, ed. George H. Nadel (New York: Harper, 1965), pp. 281–302.

2. Alex Haley, *Roots* (Garden City, N.Y.: Doubleday, 1976).

3. Margaret Gibbs, *The DAR* (New York: Holt, Rinehart and Winston, 1969), p. 21.

4. Erik Erikson, *Identity: Youth and Crisis* (New York: Norton, 1968); Erickson, *Life History and the Historical Moment* (New York: Norton, 1975).

5. Malcolm X, *Autobiography of Malcolm X*, with the assistance of Alex Haley (New York: Grove Press, 1965).

6. Theodore Rosengarten, *All God's Dangers: The Life of Nate Shaw* (New York: Knopf, 1974; also see chapter 20 of the present volume).

7. John Dollard, *Criteria for the Life History* (New Haven: Yale University Press, 1935); Gordon Allport, *The Use of Personal Documents in Psychological Science* (New York: Social Science Research Council, 1942); Robert White, *Lives in Progress* (New York: Dryden Press, 1952).

8. See Robert Coles, *Children of Crisis*, particularly *Migrants, Sharecroppers, Mountaineers* (Boston: Little, Brown, 1967); Oscar Lewis, *Five Families: Mexican Case Studies in the Culture*

of *Poverty* (New York: Basic, 1959); Lewis, *La Vida: A Puerto Rican Family in the Culture of Poverty—San Juan and New York* (New York: Random House, 1966).

9. Lewis, *La Vida*, p. 2.

10. This project involved extensive and repeated interviews of approximately three hundred former workers in the Amoskeag Mills in Manchester, New Hampshire (once the world's largest textile company). The people we interviewed represented all levels of skills and came from different ethnic groups. In addition to the workers, we also interviewed people from management, as well as people from different programs, including the clergy, and in the community. This oral history project grew out of extensive research in historical records. The reconstruction of most of each interviewee's work history and family history preceded the interview itself. Edited selections from this project were published in Tamara K. Hareven and Randolph Langenbach, *Amoskeag: Life and Work in an American Factory City* (New York: Pantheon, 1978).

11. Jan Vansina, *The Oral Tradition: A Study in Historical Methodology* (Chicago: Aldine, 1965; also see chapter 9 of the present volume).

12. Ronald Blythe, *Akenfield: Portrait of an English Village* (London: Allen Lane, 1969); Studs Terkel, *Hard Times: An Oral History of the Great Depression* (New York: Pantheon, 1970).

13. Cullom Davis et al., *Oral History: From Tape to Type* (Chicago: American Library Association, 1977).

14. Vansina, *Oral Tradition*, p. 77.

15. The exhibit, funded by the National Endowment for the Arts and by local foundations, was created and produced by Randolph Langenbach at the Currier Gallery of Art in Manchester, New Hampshire. It documented the development of the architectural design and the urban plan of Manchester, New Hampshire, by the corporation which founded the city and continued to control it until the corporation's shutdown in 1936. Through eighty mural-size photographic panels by Langenbach, as well as historic photographs, the exhibit documented the connection between the architectural environment, corporate paternalism, and the experience of work. Unexpectedly, 12,000 people came to see the exhibit during its five weeks. Most of them were former mill workers.

16. Irving Howe, *The World of Our Fathers* (New York: Harcourt Brace Jovanovich, 1976).

17. Instructions from Henry Alsberg, director of the writer's project to all state directors, quoted in William F. McDonald, *Federal Relief Administration and the Arts* (Columbus: Ohio State University Press, 1969), p. 7.

18. McDonald, *Federal Relief Administration*, p. 11.

19. James Agee and Walker Evans, *Let Us Now Praise Famous Men* (Boston: Houghton Mifflin, 1941). For slave narratives see George P. Rawick, ed., *The American Slave: A Composite Autobiography*, 19 vols. (Westport, Conn.: Greenwood, 1972). On local oral history projects, see, for example: *These Are Our Lives: As Told by the People and Written by Members of the Federal Writers' Project of the Works Progress Administration in North Carolina, Tennessee, and Georgia* (Chapel Hill, N.C., 1939).

20. On the ethnic program see McDonald, *Federal Relief Administration*, p. 725.

21. Jacob Riis, *How the Other Half Lives* (New York: Scribner's, 1890); *The Children of the Poor* (New York: Scribner's, 1892). The Russell Sage Foundation sponsored and published studies of poor and working people; its most notable publication was Paul Kellogg, ed., *The Pittsburgh Survey*, 6 vols. (New York: Charities Publication Committee, 1909–14). The *Survey* was the best of a number of social reform journals.

22. Alfred Kazin, *On Native Grounds: An Interpretation of Modern Literature* (New York: Reynal and Hitchcock, 1942), p. 378.

23. Lloyd Warner, *The Living and the Dead* (New Haven: Yale University Press, 1959).

24. Personal communication, Prof. Milton Singer, Department of Anthropology, University of Chicago.

25. Jane Addams, quoted in Gibbs, *The DAR*, p. 2.

24

Black History, Oral History, and Genealogy

Alex Haley

Our final article on applying oral sources to family history describes a re-markable adventure in historical writing: Alex Haley's Roots. *Four years before the record-breaking broadcast of the televised film—now seen by hundreds of millions of people around the world—Haley gave the following account of his research during a colloquium of the Oral History Association.*

While this is no ordinary how-to story of family history, his article illus-trates the excitement of research with living oral sources. Haley investi-gated oral traditional history, the historical narratives that passed from generation to generation by word of mouth. The final links in the historical saga uniting the author with his African ancestors of two centuries earlier was the Griot, or local history reciter, at one time common in tribal cul-tures.

Critics of Haley's research have charged that the documentation he pro-vides to link his African and American families is more emotional than sci-entifically sound. Yet for the study—and inspiration—of black and ethnic history based on oral sources, this piece remains a classic. Alex Haley is the coauthor of The Autobiography of Malcolm X *(1965) and* Roots: The Saga of an American Family *(1976).*

"Black History, Oral History, and Genealogy" was first published in the Oral History Review *1 (1973), pp. 1–25.*

WHEN I WAS a little boy I lived in a little town which you probably never heard of called Henning, Tennessee, about 50 miles north of Memphis. And I lived there with my parents in the home of my mother's mother. And my grandmother and I were very, very close. Every summer that I can remember growing up there in Hen-ning, my grandmother would have, as visitors, members of the family who were always women, always of her general age range, the late forties, early fifties. They came from places that sounded pretty exotic to me—Dyersburg, Tennessee; Inkster, Michigan—places like that, St. Louis, Kansas City. They were like Cousin Georgia, Aunt Plus, Aunt Liz, so forth. And every evening, after the supper dishes were washed, they would go out on the front porch and sit in cane-bottomed rocking chairs, and I would always sit behind grandma's chair. And every single evening of those summers, unless there was some particular hot gossip that would overrule it, they would talk about otherwise the self same thing. It was bits and pieces and patches of what I later would learn was a long narrative history of the family which had been passed down literally across generations.

As a little boy I didn't have the orientation to understand most of what they talked about. Sometimes they would talk about individuals, and I didn't know what these individuals were often; I didn't know what an old massa was, I didn't know what an old missus was. They would talk about locales; I didn't know what a plantation was. And then at other times, interspersed with these, they'd talk about anecdotes, incidents which had happened to these people or these places. The furthest-back person that they ever talked about was someone whom they would call "The African". And I know that the first time I ever heard the word Africa or African was from their mouths, there on the front porch in Henning.

I think that my first impression that these things they spoke of went a long way back, came from the fact that they were wrinkled, greying, or completely grey in some cases, and I was a little boy, three, four, five, and now and then when some of them would get animatedly talking about something, they would fling their finger or hand down toward me and say something like "I wasn't any bigger than this young 'un here". And the very idea that someone as old and wrinkled as she had at one time been no older than I was just blew my mind. I knew it must be way, way back that they were talking about.

When they were speaking of this African, the furthest-back person of all, they would tell how he was brought on a ship to this country to a place they pronounced as "Naplis". And he was bought off this ship by a man whose name was John Waller, who had a plantation in a place called Spotsylvania County, Virginia. And then they would tell how he was on this plantation and he kept trying to escape. The first three times he escaped he was caught and given a worse beating than previously as his punishment. And then the fourth time he escaped he had the misfortune to be caught by a professional slave catcher. And I grew up hearing how this slave catcher decided to make an example of him. And I grew up hearing how he gave the African the choice either to be castrated or to have a foot cut off. And the African chose the foot. And I grew up hearing how his foot was put against a stump, and with an ax was cut off across the arch. It was a very hideous act. But as it turned out that act was to play a very major role in the keeping of a narrative down across a family for a long time.

The reasons were two. One of them was that in the middle 1700's in Virginia, almost all slaves were sold at auction. A male slave in good condition would bring on the average about $750. At the end of every slave auction they would have what they called the scrap sale, and those who were incapacitated, ill, or otherwise not so valuable for market, would be sold generally for amounts of $100 or less in cash. And this particular African managed to survive and then to convalesce, and he posed then to his master an economic question. And his master decided that he was crippled and he hobbled about, but he still could do limited work. And the master decided that he would be worth more kept on that plantation than he would be worth sold away for cash of less than $100. And that was how it happened that this particular African was kept on one plantation for quite a long period of time.

Now that came at a time when, if there was any single thing that probably characterizes slaves, it was that they had almost no sense of what we today know and value and revere as family continuity. And the reason simply was that slaves were sold back and forth so much. Characteristically slave children would grow up without an awareness of who their parents were, and particularly male parents. This African, now kept on the plantation by his master's decision, hobbling about and doing the limited work he could, finally met and mated with another slave on that plantation, and her name (in the stories told by my grandmother and the others on the front porch in Henning) was Bell the big house cook. And of that union was born a little girl who was given the name Kizzy. As Kizzy got to be four or five or so, this African would take that little girl by the hand, and he would take her around and point out to her various natural objects, and he would tell her the name for that thing—tree, rock, cow, sky, so forth. The names that he told her were instinctively in his native tongue, and to the girl they were strange phonetic sounds which in time, with repetitive hearing, the girl could repeat. He would point at a guitar and he would make a single sound as if it were spelled *ko*. And she came in time to know that *ko* was guitar in his terms. There were other strange phonetic sounds for other objects. Perhaps the most involved of them was that contiguous to the plantation there was a river, and whenever this African would point out this river to his daughter Kizzy he would say to her *"Kamby Bolongo"*. And she came to know that *Kamby Bolongo* in his terms meant river.

There was another thing about this African which is in the background of all the Black people in this country, and that was that whoever bought them off the slave ship, when they got them to a plantation, about their first act was giving them an Anglicized name. For all practical purposes that was the first step in the psychic dehumanization of an individual or collectively of a people. And in the case of this particular African his master gave him the name Toby. But whenever any of the other adult slaves would address him as Toby, this African would strenuously rebuff and reject it and he would tell them his name was *"Kin-tay"*, a sharp, angular two-syllabic sound that the little girl Kizzy came to know her father said was his name.

And there was yet another thing about this African characteristic of all those original Africans in our background, and that was that they had been brought from a place where they spoke whatever was their native tongue, and brought to this place where it became necessary to learn English for sheer survival's sake. And gradually, haltingly, all those original Africans learned a word here, a phrase there, of the new tongue—English. As this process began to happen with this African, and he began to be able to express himself in more detailed ways, he began to tell his little daughter Kizzy little vignettes about himself. He told her, for instance, how he had been captured. He said that he had been not far away from his village chopping wood to make himself a drum when he had been set upon by four men, overwhelmed, and taken thusly into slavery. And she came to know along with many other stories the story of how he was chopping wood when he was captured.

To compress what would happen over the next decade, the girl Kizzy stayed on the plantation in Spotsylvania County directly exposed to her father who had come directly from Africa, and to his stories, until she had a considerable repertoire of knowledge about him from his own mouth. When the girl Kizzy was 16 years of age, she was sold away to a new master whose name was Tom Lea and he had a much smaller plantation in North Carolina. And it was on this plantation that after a while the girl Kizzy gave birth to her first child, a boy who was given the name George. The father was the new master Tom Lea. And as George got to be four or five or so, now it was his mother Kizzy who began to tell him the stories that she heard from her father. And the boy began to discover the rather common phenomenon that slave children rarely knew who their fathers were, let alone a grandfather. He had something which made him rather singular. And so it was with considerable pride the boy began to tell his peers the story of his grandfather; this African who said his name was *Kin-tay*, who called a river *Kamby Bolongo*, and called a guitar *ko* and other sounds for other things, and who said that he had been chopping wood when he was set upon and captured and brought into slavery.

When the boy George got to be about 12, he was apprenticed to an old slave to learn handling the master's fighting gamecocks. And this boy had innate, green thumb ability for fighting gamecocks. By the time he was in his mid-teens he had been given (for his local and regional renown as an expert slave handler and pitter of fighting gamecocks) the nickname he would take to his grave decades later—Chicken George.

When Chicken George was about 18 he met and mated with a slave girl. And her name was Matilda, and in time Matilda gave birth to seven children. Now for the first time that story which had come down from this African began to fan out within the breadth of a family. The stories as they would be told on the front porch in Henning by grandma and the others were those of the winter evenings after the harvest when families would entertain themselves by sitting together and the elders would talk and the young would listen. Now Chicken George would sit with his seven children around the hearth. The story was that they would roast sweet potatoes in the hot ashes, and night after night after night across the winters, Chicken George would tell his seven children a story unusual among slaves, and that was direct knowledge of a great-grandfather; this same African who said his name was *Kin-tay*, who called the river *Kamby Bolongo*, and a guitar *ko*, and who said that he was chopping wood when he was captured.

Those children grew up, took mates and had children. One of them was named Tom. And Tom became an apprenticed blacksmith. He was sold in his mid-teens to a man named Murray who had a tobacco plantation in Alamance County, North Carolina. And it was on this plantation that Tom, who became that plantation's blacksmith, met and mated with a slave girl whose name was Irene and who was the plantation weaver. And Irene also in time bore seven children. Now it was yet another generation, another section of the state of North Carolina and another set of seven children who would sit in yet another cabin, around the hearth in the winter evenings with the sweet potatoes in the hot ashes. And now the father was Tom telling his children about something virtually unique in the knowledge of slaves, direct knowledge of a great-great-grandfather, this same African, who said his name was *Kin-tay*, who called the river *Kamby Bolongo*, who said he was chopping wood when he was captured, and the other parts of the story that had come down in that way.

Of that second set of seven children, in Alamance County, North Carolina, the youngest was a little girl whose name was Cynthia, and Cynthia was my maternal grandmother. And I grew up in her home in Henning, Tennessee, and grandma pumped that story into me as if it were plasma. It was by all odds the most precious thing in her life—the story which had come down across the generations about the family going back to that original African.

I stayed at grandma's home until I was in my mid-teens. By that time I had two younger brothers, George and Julius. Our father was a teacher at small black land grant colleges about the South and we began now to move around wherever he was teaching. And thus I went to school through two years of college. When World War II came along I was one of the many people who thought that if I could hurry and get into an organization of which I recently heard called the U.S. Coast Guard, that maybe I could spend the war walking the coast. And I got into the service and to my great shock rather suddenly found myself on an ammunition ship in the Southwest Pacific, which was not at all what I had in mind. But when I look back upon it now, it was the first of a series of what seemed to be accidental things, but now seem to be part of a pattern of many things that were just meant to be, to make a certain book possible, in time. On the ships in the Coast Guard, totally by accident, I stumbled into the long road to becoming a writer. It was something I had never have dreamed of.

I became a writer in the time when if you were black and you went into the naval services you automatically went into what was called the steward's department. And first you were a mess boy, and that meant that you would shine shoes and wait on tables, clean the toilets, make up the beds, things like that. And if you did these things sufficiently well and long, you would advance to cook. And I became a cook on this ammunition ship in the Southwest Pacific. My most precious possession on the ship was a portable typewriter. Every night, when I would finish my pots and pans, I would go down in the hold of the ship, and I'd type letters to everybody I could think of—ex-schoolmates, friends, even teachers, anybody that I could think of. Other ships would take mail ashore.

With us out there, far from home as we were and for as long at sea we would stay (sometimes two, three months before we would get ashore in places like Australia and New Zealand), mail call was a very epochal event for us. And when I got things going pretty well, I would get on the average 30 to 40 letters every mail call. And ships have swift grapevines, and it quickly circulated about this ship that I was the ship's most prolific writer and receiver of mail.

Concurrently, after we would be at sea two or three months and finally got ashore somewhere in Australia or New Zealand, our topmost priority was to fall in love with somebody as quick as possible. And we would do the best we could and then we'd go back out to sea. And now there would be maybe a hundred young guys on the ship as I was, 17 or so, who was just smitten with some girl he had left ashore, and girls have a way of getting prettier in your mind the longer you're at sea, and some of my buddies who were not as articulate on paper as they were verbally, began to come around and in a covert way they began to suggest that since I wrote so many letters that maybe I would be willing to help them compose a letter to some girl. And I began to do this. I would sit at a mess table with a stack of three by five index cards. And my clients would line up and as they got to me I would just interview them. I'd say, "now, what does she look like—hair, eyes, nose, so forth?" And they would tell me. And I'd say, "what did you want to tell her, where did you go, was there anything you want to say in the way of details?" And then I would take each card, put her name and his name on it, and then later as I got a chance, I'd write, for him to copy later in his own handwriting, a rather personalized love letter utilizing that specific information about that girl.

The girls in Australia and New Zealand were not used to these kinds of missives. And I will never forget one day and night that were to prove most motivational and pivotal in my becoming a writer by accident. We had been at sea for three months, during which time three batches of mail had been taken off our ship, so that each of my client's girls had these many letters. We got into Brisbane, Australia about noon. Liberty was declared at 6 in the afternoon and everyone who had liberty just flew ashore. Around midnight most of those came back wobbling and stumbling, having accomplished the most they'd been able, which was to get very drunk. And then it was almost as if a script had been written. Around 1 in the morning my "clients" started coming back, individually. Before a steadily enlarging and increasingly awestruck audience, they were describing, in the graphic way that only sailors can, how when they in person got to that girl behind these letters, they met just incredible results, sometimes practically on the spot. I became heroic on that ship that night and for the rest of World War II, I never fought a soul. All I did was write love letters.

Writing love letters led me secretly to begin trying to write stories for modern romances and true confessions. I would write these stories making out I was a girl and this lout had done this, that or another to me and I was trying to resolve my problem, and I would send out those manuscripts and they would come back just as fast as wartime mails would permit. I wrote every single day, 7 days a week for 8 years, before the first story was bought by a magazine. And I stayed on in the service, shipping on whenever my hitch was up, until lo and behold I was 37 years of age and I had 20 years of service and retired. I came out of the service in San Francisco determined, because I had sold by now to *Atlantic Monthly, Harper's, Reader's Digest,* and a good number of stories to men's adventure magazines, mostly sea adventure stories because that was the material I had accessible to me in the service, I was going to find for myself a career as a free-lance writer. My first assignment was from *Reader's Digest* to do an article about the then-newly emerging social phenomenon called the Nation of Islam, or colloquially, the Black Muslims. I now met Malcolm X, I worked with him in writing that article. Then I worked with him and another writer writing a piece for the *Saturday Evening Post,* and in the interim I had happened to begin the feature called *"Playboy* Interviews", and *Playboy* asked me if I would interview Malcolm X, which I did. The interviews are very in-depth and intensive. I worked now with Malcolm very, very intensively for about three weeks. And when that interview was published, Doubleday asked Malcolm if he would be willing to tell his life in book-length detail. After some demurring Malcolm finally agreed. Because I had happened to be the black writer who worked with him on most of the major magazine stories which had been done about him, he asked me if I would be willing to work with him on the book. I was, of course, pleased and honored and flattered to do so.

I had a place in Greenwich Village and Malcolm X, after his extremely busy days, would come to my place about 9 in the evening and stay generally until about 1 or 2 the following morning. And he would do this about 4 nights a week. And each of these nights I would just interview him, picking out of this man's memory every thread, every fiber of everything he could remember across the whole of his life. And that went across a calendar year. At the end of that time I had a great volume of notes of his memories. I spent a second year arranging those notes and vicariously, as if I were Malcolm, writing in the first person, putting onto paper, and with all the rewrites and the drafts, what hopefully would sound to a reader as if Malcolm X had just sat down and told that reader, from his memory, from earliest memory to the time he was talking. When the *Autobiography of Malcolm X* manuscript was finished I got in touch with Malcolm and we went into a hotel, and he went across the whole manuscript. I can see his red ball point pen, changing the name of someone whom he said he didn't wish to embarrass, and things of that nature. And finally when he was finished, he said: "Brother, I don't think I'm going to live to read this in print. So I'd like to read it again." And he spent three days in the New York Hilton Hotel, reading again that manuscript. And it was then sent to the publisher.

Malcolm proved very prophetic, because it was two weeks later he was shot to death on a Sunday afternoon in the Audubon Ballroom. And as much as Malcolm had talked matter-of-factly about the imminence of violent death, it just seemed to me impossible. And it was a very, very rocky, traumatic kind of night for me. The following morning I sat down at the typewriter, just dropping blank white sheets in that machine and drumming on the keyboard for the space of maybe 30 or 40 minutes, sit, stare at the keyboard, drum again. This is the only thing I've written in my life in that manner. And over a period of three days was written that part which appears now at the end of the book called "The Epilogue". And it was just a tumbling out of the memory of the reminiscence of having met and worked with this man, and anecdotes and insights into him. Then that was sent to the publisher.

Now there happened one of the things when I look back upon it, like the first of a series of miracles that were subsequently to make it possible for me to pull together a book that aspires to be the first of its kind in having to do with black history, black heritage, black pride, just blackness in general. The first thing that happened here in this series of miracles was *Playboy* magazine called and asked if I would fly over to England and interview the actress Julie Christie. So I flew over there. Julie Christie was involved in the making of a motion picture called *Far From the Madding Crowd*. The weather was terrible. They had to move the set from one side of England to the other and Julie Christie was so uptight she was scarcely speaking to the director, let alone some interviewer who had appeared from this country. I had to get in touch with *Playboy* and tell them this. And they sent me a cable and said, "Well, you're over there so stand by and see what develops." And that was how I, who always innately had loved history and had been steeped in history by grandma and others from the time I was a little boy, found myself plunked in one of the places on earth that had probably more history per square foot than anywhere I know—London. I was all over the place. There was scarcely a tour guide in London that didn't have me on the next several days.

One morning I was in the British Museum and I came upon something, I had vaguely heard of it, the Rosetta Stone. It just really entranced me. I read about it, and I found how, when this stone was discovered in 1799, it seemed to have three sets of texts chiseled into the stone: one of them in Greek characters, which Greek scholars could read, the second in a then-unknown set of characters, the third in the ancient hieroglyphics which it was assumed no one would ever translate. Then I read how a French scholar, Jean Champollion, had come along and had taken that second unknown set of script, character for character, matched it with the Greek and finally had come up with a thesis he could prove—that the text was the same as the Greek. And then in a superhuman feat of scholarship he had taken the terribly intricate characters of the hieroglyphics and cross matched them with the preceding two in almost geometric progression, and had proved that too was the same text. That was what opened up to the whole world of scholarship, all that hitherto had been hidden behind the mystery of the allegedly undecipherable hieroglyphics.

And that thing just fascinated me. I would find myself going around London doing all sorts of other things and at odd times I would see in my mind's eye, almost as if it were projected in my head, the Rosetta Stone. And to me, it just had some kind of special significance, but I couldn't make head or tail of what it might be. Finally I was on a plane coming back to this country, when an idea hit me. It was rough, raw, crude, but it got me to thinking. Now what this scholar worked with was language chiseled into the stone. And what he did was to take that which had been unknown and match it with that which was known, and thus found the meaning of what hitherto had been unknown. And then I got to thinking of an analogy; that story always told in our family that I had heard on the front porch in Henning. The unknown quotient was those strange phonetic sounds. And I got to thinking, now maybe I could find out where these sounds came from. Obviously these strange sounds are threads of some African tongue. And my whole thing was to see if maybe I could find out, just in curiosity, what tongue did they represent. It seemed obvious to me what I had to do was try to get in touch with as wide a range of Africans as I could, simply because there were many, many tongues spoken in Africa. I lived in New York, so I began doing what seemed to me logical. I began going up to the United Nations lobby about quitting time. I wasn't hard to spot Africans, and every time I could I'd stop one. And I would say to him my little sounds. In a couple of weeks I stopped a couple of dozen Africans, each and every one of which took a quick look, quick listen to me, and took off. Which I well understand; me with a Tennessee accent trying to tell them some African sounds, I wasn't going to get it.

I have a friend, a master researcher, George Sims, who knew what I was trying to do and he came to me with a listing of about a dozen people renowned for their knowledge of African linguistics. And one who intrigued me right off the bat was not an African at all, but a Belgian. Educated at England, much of it at the School of Oriental and African Studies, he had done his early work living in African villages, studying the language or the tongue as spoken in those villages. He had finally written a book called in French, *La Tradition Orale*.[1] His name: Dr. Jan Vansina, University of Wisconsin. I phoned Dr. Vansina. He very graciously said I could see him. I got on a plane and flew to Madison, Wisconsin, with no dream what was about to happen. In the living room of the Vansinas that evening I told Dr. Vansina every little bit I could remember of what I'd heard as a little boy on the front porch in Henning. And Dr. Vansina listened most intently. And then he began to question me. Being himself an oral historian, he was particularly interested in the physical transmission of the story down across the generations. And I would answer everything I could. I couldn't answer most of what he asked. Around midnight, Dr. Vansina said, "I wonder if you'd spend the night at our home," and I did stay there. The following morning, before breakfast, Dr. Vansina came down with a very serious expression on his face; I was later to learn that he had already been on the phone with colleagues, and he said to me: "The ramifications of what you have brought here could be enormous." He and his colleagues felt almost certain that the collective sounds that I had been able to bring there, which had been passed down across the family in the manner I had described to him, represented the Mandinka tongue. I'd never heard the word. He told me that that was the tongue spoken by the Mandingo people. He began then to guess translate certain of the sounds. There was a sound that probably meant cow or cattle; another probably meant the bow-bow tree, generic in West Africa. I had told him that from the time I was knee-high I'd heard about how this African would point to a guitar and say *ko*. Now he told me that almost surely this would refer to one of the oldest of the stringed instruments among the Mandingo people, an instrument made of a gourd covered with goat skin, a long neck, 21 strings, called the *kora*. He came finally to the most involved of the sounds that I had heard and had brought to him—*Kamby Bolongo*. He said without question in Mandinka, *bolongo* meant river; preceded by *Kamby* it probably would mean Gambia River. I'd never heard of that river.

It was Thursday morning when I heard those words; Monday morning I was in Africa. I just had to go. There was no sense in messing around. On Friday I found that of the numerous African students in this country, there were a few from that very, very small country called Gambia. And the one who physically was closest to me was a fellow in Hamilton College, Clinton, New York. And I hit that campus about 3:30 Friday afternoon and practically snatched Ebou Manga out of an economics class and got us on Pan American that night. We flew through the night to Dakar, Senegal, and there we got a light plane that flew over to a little airstrip called Yundum—they literally had to run monkeys off the runway to get in there. And then we got a van and we went into the small city of Bathurst, the capital of Gambia. Ebou Manga, his father Alhaji Manga (it's a predominantly Moslem culture there), assembled a group of about eight men, members of the government, who came into the patio of the Atlantic Hotel, and they sat in kind of a semi-circle as I told them the history that had come down across the family to my grandmother and thence to me; told them everything I could remember.

And when I finished, the Africans irritated me considerably because *Kamby Bolongo*, the sounds which had gotten me specifically to them, they tended almost to poo-poo. They said, "Well, of course *Kamby Bolongo* would mean Gambia River; anyone would know that." What these Africans reacted to was another sound: a mere two syllables that I had brought them without the slightest comprehension that it had any particular significance. They said, "There may be some significance in that your forefather stated his name was *Kin-tay*." I said, "Well, there was nothing more explicit in the story than the pronunciation of his name, *Kin-tay*." They said, "Our oldest villages tend to be named for those families which founded those villages centuries ago." And then they sent for a little map and they said, "Look, here is the village of Kinte-Kundah. And not too far from it is the village of Kinte-Kundah-Janneh-Ya." And then they told me about something I never had any concept existed in this world. They told me that in the back country, and particularly in the older villages of the back country, there were old men called *griots*, who are in effect walking, living archives of oral history. They are the old men who, from the time they had been in their teen-ages, have been part of a line of men who tell the stories as they have been told since the time of their forefathers, literally down across centuries. The incumbent *griot* will be a man usually in his late sixties, early seventies, and underneath him will be men separated by about decade intervals, sixty, fifty, forty, thirty, twenty, and a teen-age boy, and each line of *griots* will be the experts in the story of a major family clan; another line of *griots* another clan; and so on for dozens of major clans. Another line of *griots* would be the experts in the history of a group of villages. Another would go into the history of the empires which had preceded it, and so forth. And the stories were told in a narrative, oral history way, not verbatim, but the essential same way they had been told down across the time since the forefathers. And the way they were trained was that the teen-age boy was exposed to that story for forty or fifty years before he would become the oral historian incumbent.

It astounds us now to realize that men like these, in not only Africa but other cultures, can literally talk for days, telling a story and not repeating themselves, and telling the details in the most explicit detail. The reason it astounds us is because in our culture we have become so conditioned to the crush of print that most people in our culture have almost forgotten what the human memory is capable of if it is trained to keep things in it. These men, I was told, existed in the back country. And the men there told me that since my forefather had said his name was *Kin-tay* they would see what they could do to help me.

I came back to this country enormously bewildered. I didn't know what to do. It embarrasses me to say that up to that time I really hadn't thought all that much about Africa. I knew where it was and I had the standard cliche images of it, the Tarzan Africa and stuff like that. Well, now it was almost as if some religious zealotry came into me. I just began to devour everything I could lay eyes on about Africa, particularly slavery. I can remember after reading all day I'd sit on the edge of a bed at night with a map of Africa, studying the positions of the countries, one with relation with the other.

It was about six weeks later when an innocuous looking letter came to me which suggested that when it was possible I should come back. I was back over there as quickly as I possibly could make it. The same men, with whom I had previously talked rather matter-of-factly, told me that the word had been put out in the back country and that there had indeed been found a *griot* of the Kinte clan. His name, they said, was Kebba

Kanga Fofana. When I heard there was such a man I was ready to have a fit. Where is he? I figured from my experience as an American magazine writer, the government should have had him there with a public relations man for me to talk to. And they looked at me oddly and they said, he's in his village.

I discovered at that point that if I was to see this man, I was going to have to do something I'd never dreamed before: I would have to organize a safari. It took me three days to rent a launch to get up the river, lorry, Land-Rover to take supplies by the back route, to hire finally a total of 14 people, including 3 interpreters, 4 musicians (they told me in the back country these old oral historians would not talk without music in the background), bearers and so forth. And on the fourth day we went vibrating in this launch up the Gambia River. I was very uncomfortable. I had the feeling of being alien. I had the queezy feeling of what do they see me as, another pith-helmet? We got on up the river to a little village called Albreda on the left bank. And then we went ashore. And now our destination by foot was a village called Juffure where this man was said to live.

There's an expression called "the peak experience". It is that which emotionally nothing in your life ever can transcend. And I know I have had mine that first day in the back country in black West Africa. When we got up within sight of the village of Juffure the children who had inevitably been playing outside African villages, gave the word and the people came flocking out of their huts. It's a rather small village, only about 70 people. And villages in the back country are very much today as they were two hundred years ago, circular mud huts with conical thatched roofs. And from a distance I could see this small man with a pillbox hat and an off-white robe, and even from a distance there was an aura of "somebodiness" about him. I just knew that was the man we had come to see. And when we got closer the interpreters left our party and went straight to him. And I had stepped unwittingly into a sequence of emotional events that always I feel awkward trying to describe, simply because I never ever verbally could convey the power, the physical power, of emotional occurrences.

These people quickly filtered closely around me in kind of a horseshoe design with me at the base. If I had put up my hands I would have touched the nearest ones on either side. There were about 3, 4 deep all around. And the first thing that hit me was the intensity of the way they were staring at me. The eyes just raped. The foreheads were forward in the intensity of the staring. And it was an uncomfortable feeling. And while this was happening there began to occur inside me a kind of feeling as if something was turgid, rolling, surging around. And I had this eerie feeling that I knew inside me why it was happening and what it was about, but consciously I could not identify what had me so upset inside.

And after a while it began to roll in: it was rather like a galeforce wind that you couldn't see but it just rolled in and hit you—bam! It was enough to knock you down. I suddenly realized what so upset me was that I was looking at a crowd of people and for the first time in my life every one of them was jet black. And I was standing there rather rocked by that, and in the way that we tend to do if we are discomforted we drop our glance. And I remember dropping my glance, and my glance falling on my own hand, my own complexion, in context with their complexion. And now there came rolling in another surging galeforce thing that hit me perhaps harder than the first one. A feeling of guilt, a feeling rather of being hybrid, a feeling of being the impure among the pure.

And the old man suddenly left the interpreters, walked away, and the people as quickly filtered away from me and to the old man. And they began a very animated talking, high metallic Mandinka tongue. One of the interpreters, his name was A. B. C. Salla, whispered in my ear and the significance of what he whispered probably got me as much as all the rest of it collectively. He said, "They stare at you so because they have never seen a black American." And what hit me was they were not looking at Alex Haley, writer, they didn't know who he was, they could care less. But what they saw me as was a symbol of 25 millions of us over here whom they had never seen. And it was just an awesome thing to realize that someone had thrust that kind of symbolism upon me. And there's a language that's universal. It's a language of gestures, noises, inflections, expressions. Somehow looking at them, hearing them, though I couldn't understand a syllable, I knew what they were talking about. I somehow knew they were trying to arrive at a consensus of how did they collectively feel about me as a symbol for them of all the millions of us over here whom they never had seen. And there came a time when the old man quickly turned. He walked right through the people, he walked right past three interpreters, he walked right up to me, looked piercingly into my eyes and spoke in Mandinka, as instinctively he felt I should be able to understand it. And the translation came from the side. And the way they collectively saw me, the symbol of all the millions of us black people here whom they never had seen was, "Yes, we have been told by the forefathers that there are many of us from this place who are in exile in that place called America and in other places." And that was the way they saw it.

The old man, the *griot*, the oral historian, Kebba Kanga Fofana, 73 rains of age (their way of saying 73 years, one rainy season a year), began now to tell me the ancestral history of the Kinte clan as it had been told down across the centuries, from the times of the forefathers. It was as if a scroll was being read. It wasn't just talk as we talk. It was a very formal occasion. The people became mouse quiet, rigid. The old man sat in a chair and when he would speak he would come up forward, his body would grow rigid, the cords in his neck stood out and he spoke words as though they were physical objects coming out of his mouth. He'd speak a sentence or so, he would go limp, relax, and the translation would come. Out of this man's head came spilling lineage details incredible to behold. Two, three centuries back. Who married whom, who had what children, what children married whom and their children, and so forth, just unbelievable. I was struck not only by the profusion of details, but also by the biblical pattern of the way they expressed it. It would be something like: "and so and so took as a wife so and so and begat and begat and begat," and he'd name their mates and their children, and so forth. When they would date things it was not with calendar dates, but they would date things with physical events, such as, "in the year of the big water he slew a water buffalo," the year of the big water referring to a flood. And if you wanted to know the date calendar-wise you had to find when that flood occurred.

I can strip out of the hours that I heard of the history of the Kinte clan (my forefather had said his name was *Kin-tay*), the immediate vertical essence of it, leaving out all the details of the brothers and the cousins and the other marriages and so forth. The *griot* Kebba Kanga Fofana said that the Kinte clan had been begun in a country called Old Mali. Traditionally the Kinte men were blacksmiths who had conquered fire. The women were potters and weavers. A branch of the clan had moved into the country called Mauretania. It was from the country of Mauretania that a son of the clan, whose name was Kairaba Kunta Kinte (he was a *Marabout*, which is to say a holy man of the Moslem faith), came down into the country called the Gambia. He went first to a village called Pakali n'Ding. He stayed there for a while. He went next to a village called Jiffarong; thence he went to a village called Juffure. In the village of Juffure the young *Marabout* Kairaba Kunta Kinte took his first wife, a Mandinka maiden whose name was Sireng. And by her he begot two sons whose names were Janneh and Saloum. Then he took a second wife; her name, Yaisa. And by Yaisa he begot a son whose name was Omoro. Those three sons grew up in the village of Juffure until they came of age. The elder two, Janneh and Saloum, went away and started a new village called Kinte-Kundah Janneh-Ya. It is there today. Literally translated it means "The Home of Janneh Kinte". The youngest son, Omoro, stayed in the village until he had 30 rains, and then he took a wife, a Mandinka maiden, her name Binta Kebba. And by Binta Kebba, roughly between 1750 and 1760, Omoro Kinte begat four sons, whose names were Kunta, Lamin, Suwadu and Madi.

By the time he got down to that level of the family, the *griot* had talked for probably 5 hours. He had stopped maybe 50 times in the course of that narrative and a translation came into me. And then a translation came as all the others had come, calmly, and it began, "About the time the king's soldiers came." That was one of those time-fixing references. Later in England, in British Parliamentary records, I went feverishly searching to find out what he was talking about, because I had to have the calendar date. But now in back country Africa, the *griot* Kebba Kanga Fofana, the oral historian, was telling the story as it had come down for centuries from the time of the forefathers of the Kinte clan. "About the time the king's soldiers came, the eldest of these four sons, Kunta, went away from this village to chop wood and was seen never again." And he went on with his story.

I sat there as if I was carved of rock. Goose-pimples came out on me I guess the size of marbles. He just had no way in the world to know that he had told me that which meshed with what I'd heard on the front porch in Henning, Tennessee, from grandma, from Cousin Georgia, from Aunt Liz, from Cousin Plus, all the other old ladies who sat there on that porch. I managed to get myself together enough to pull out my notebook, which had in it what grandma had always said. And I got the interpreter Salla and showed it to him and he got rather agitated, and he went to the old man, and he got agitated, and the old man went to the people and they got agitated.

I don't remember it actually happening. I don't remember anyone giving an order, but those 70 people formed a ring around me, moving counter-clockwise, chanting, loudly, softly, loudly, softly, their bodies were so close together, the physical action was like drum majorettes with their high knee action. You got the feeling they were an undulating mass of people moving around. I'm standing in the middle like an Adam in the desert. I don't know how I felt; how could you feel a thing like that? And I remember looking at the first lady who broke from that circle (there were about a dozen ladies who had little infant children slung across their backs), and she with a scowl on this jet black face, broke from that circle, her bare feet slapping against the hard earth, came charging in towards me. And she took her baby and roughly thrust it out. The gesture said, "Take it!" and I took the baby and I clasped it, at which point she snatched it away and another lady, another baby, and I guess I had clasped about a dozen babies in about two minutes. I would be almost two years later at Harvard when Dr. Jerome Bruner told me, you were participating in one of the oldest ceremonies of human kind called "the laying on of hands"; that in their way they were saying to you, "through this flesh which is us, we are you, and you are us." There were many, many other things that happened in that village that day, but I was particularly struck with the enormity of the fact that they were dealing with me and seeing me in the perspective of, for them, the symbol of 25 millions of us black people in this country whom they never had seen. They took me into their mosque. They prayed in Arabic which I couldn't understand. Later the crux of the prayer was translated, "Praise be to Allah for one long lost from us whom Allah has returned." And that was the way they saw that.

When it was possible to leave, since we'd come by water, I wanted to go out over the land. My five senses had become muted, truncated. They didn't work right. If I wanted to feel something I would have to squeeze to register the sense of feeling. Things were misty. I didn't hear well. I would become aware the driver sitting right by me was almost shouting something and I just hadn't heard him up to that point. I began now, as we drove out over the back country road, with drums distantly heard around, to see in my mind's eye, as if it were being projected somehow on a film, a screen almost, rough, ragged, out of focus, almost a portrayal of what I had studied so, so much about: the background of us as a people, the way that ancestrally we who are in this country were brought out of Africa.

The impression prevails that most of the slaves were taken from coastal Africa. Not so. Coastal Africa's population never could have begun to satisfy the voracious maw of two centuries of slavery. By far most of us came from those interior villages. And I was seeing the way so many, many times I'd read about it, many, many different accounts, that the people would come screaming awake at night in the villages with the thatched roofs aflame falling in on them. And they'd dash out into the dark, into the very arms of the people who fired the villages, and the element of surprise and the arms were on one side and the slaughter was relatively brief, and the people who survived, those who were left whole enough, were linked neck by neck with thongs into what were called "coffles". It is said that some of the coffles were a mile long. And then there would come the torturous march, down towards the sea where the ships were. Many, many died hideously along the way, or were left to die when they were too weak to go on. And finally those who survived would get to the beach area, and down on the beaches were what they would call "barracoons", low structures of bamboo lashed together with thongs. And it would be in here that they would be put, rested, washed, fed better for a period of time, greased, their heads would be shaved, and so forth, and when it was felt that they were in condition, they would be sent out into the small yards in front of the barracoons for inspection by those who came from the ships for the purpose of purchase. And those who were finally selected for purchase after the most incredible examinations of every orifice in the human body would be branded and marched out to the ships.

It seemed to me, seeing all this riding along there, that the Africans really hadn't up to this time comprehended the enormity of what was about to happen to them. And the reason being that there was precedent up to now for everything that had happened. Cruelty was nothing new to them. The Africans were hideously cruel one to the other. Slavery, as such, was nothing new to Africans. Over half the people in Africa were slaves of other Africans. The difference being that there was no concept in Africa of what western type slavery would be. Slavery in Africa would equate with what we call share-cropping. It was only when, it seemed to me, these Africans were being moved from barracoon, freshly branded, across that strip of sandy beach, and they could see for the first time those cockle shell canoes at the water's edge and out further on the water the larger things that they thought were flying houses. I had read, and now was seeing it in my mind's eye, how when the Africans were being moved across that beach, many of them would scream, they would go into paroxisms of shouting, fall flat, go clawing as deep as they could with their heads down into the sand, and taking great gulping choking mouthfuls of sand trying to get one last hold on the land which had been their home. And they were beaten up from that and taken into the canoes and thus they went into the holds of those ships which are utterly undescribable. And it was in that manner that every single one of our forebears came over, with no exceptions. And I was full of this.

When we got to the first village, it was with a great, great shock I realized that the drums I'd been dimly hearing were the talking drums that still work in back country Africa. They told what had happened behind us in the village of Juffure. Now as the driver slowed down, I could see the people in the village ahead of us packed on either side of the road and they were waving and there was this cacophany of sound coming out of them, growing louder as we came closer. And when we got to the edge of the village, I stood up in the Land Rover and looking down on these people, jet black people waving up, dimly I could see them. And I heard the noise coming from them. And the first thought, that just overwhelmed me, was that they were down there having never left Africa and I-we (symbolic of we here in this country) were standing up there in the Land Rover, and it was only caprice, which of our forefathers had been taken out. That was the only thing that made the difference of where we were, one place or the other. And I was just full of the realization of that. And I guess we'd gotten about a third of the way in the village when it finally registered upon my brain what it was they were all crying out. I hadn't understood it, I think, because they were all crying out the same thing, tightly packed, tightly massed, wizened old black elders, little naked tar black children all crying out in mass, "Mister Kinte, Mister Kinte". And let me tell you. I'm a man, but a sob hit me at ankle level and just rolled up. I just began crying as I have never cried in my life. It just seemed to me that if you really knew the ancestral history of blacks, we blacks, if you really knew the way every single one of us had come here, that no matter what ever else might later be your reaction, that you first had to weep. And that's all I could do. I remember being aware of people staring as if to say, "What's wrong?" And I didn't care. That was all I could do.

We got out of the village, we got to where I could get a taxi to Dakar. I got there, I got a plane, got back to this country. It took me about a week to get myself emotionally together enough to go back to the publisher. I went to Doubleday and I told them what had happened. I told them it isn't the story of a family; it's the saga of a people passed down in this oral history way. And the reason it was a saga of people is because we black people—probably more than any other people on the face of earth in as large a number—have the most common generic background; that every single one of us without exception ancestrally goes back to some one of those villages, belonged to some one of those tribes, was captured in some way, was put on some one of those slave ships, across the same ocean into some succession of plantations up to the Civil War, the emancipation, and ever since then a struggle for freedom. So this book had to be the saga of a people. And since it was such, it was up to me to give it every possible thing that I, as a symbol of us, who happened to be a writer, could bring to that book. I had to do everything, to find every thread that could have any bearing on the history, the saga, of us as a people. They said they understood, and they gave me time to go.

When I look back over the whole of my life it seems so many things happened from the time I was a little boy that would prepare me for something that this book would demand. By accident I had gone to the Coast Guard. By accident I had become a writer in the Coast Guard. When I began to write seriously the material available to me had been old maritime records. I had spent years combing in old records of the old U.S. Maritime Service, of the old Lighthouse Service. Not a lot of people generally know a lot about old maritime records and in particular few black people happen to have been exposed to this simply because it's not something in our average background. But I did know a great deal about them.

From the time I was a little boy grandma always said that ship came to what they call "Naplis". Now I knew they had to be talking about Annapolis, Maryland. Now also I knew specifically where that slave came from; so obviously some ship had come from that area of the Gambia River and sailed to Annapolis, Maryland. And what I wanted now was the symbolic ship that brought over, it is said, 15 million of our forebears alive to this country, and in order to be the proper symbolic ship it had to be the specific ship that had brought Kunta Kinte. And I went now on a search for that ship. The *griot* had set a time reference in his oral history dating way: "About the time the king's soldiers came." And it was now when I found that he was talking about this group called Colonel O'Hare's forces who had come to the Gambia River in 1767 to guard the Fort James slave fort. So that gave me a calendar date. Now I went to work to find that ship. This was still colonies at the time; the mother country was England. So I got on a plane now and went to London. I began to search in records. I went to Lloyd's of London and got to a man named Mr. R. C. E. Landers. And I got in his office and I just poured out what I was trying to do, and after a while he said to me, "Young man, Lloyd's of London will do all we can to help you." And it was Lloyd's of London who began to open doors for me to get to the source of the records in England.

I began to search for the records of ships that had moved from Africa to this country. There are cartons of records of slave ships, of ships in general, but also of slave ships, that moved two centuries ago that have never been opened, nobody ever had occasion to go in them since. There are just stacks of records. Slavery was an industry; it was not viewed as anything pejorative at all. It was just a business at the time. In the seventh week of an almost traumatizing searching, one afternoon about 2:30 I was in the 1,023rd set of slave ship records and pulled up a sheet that had the movements of 30 ships on it, and my eye ran down it and I saw number 18, and my eyes went out to the right and something just said to me, that might be the ship. The essential things were there. My reaction was a very dull one. I wrote down on an envelope the information, turned it in at the desk and walked out. Around the corner from there on Castle Lane was a little tea shop. I went in there and I had tea and a cruller, and I'm sitting up there and sipping the tea, and swinging my foot like it's all in a day's work, when it suddenly did hit me that maybe I'd found that ship. I still owe that lady for that tea and cruller.

I got a taxi; I didn't even stop at the hotel to get a toothbrush. I told that taxi, "Heathrow!" In my mind's eye I was seeing the book I had to get my hands on. I'd had the book in my hands. The taxi got me to Heathrow in time to get the 6:00 Pan American to New York, and I flew that ocean that night and didn't sleep a wink. I could see that book, it had a dark brown leather cover, *Shipping in the Port of Annapolis* by Vaughan W. Brown. I got to New York, shuttled to Washington, the Library of Congress, got the book. One line in agate type tended to support that it was indeed the ship, and I just about went berserk. I got on the phone, got finally to the author Vaughan Brown, a broker in Baltimore. I got to that man's office, went by his secretary, just as if she wasn't there, and went in his office. Here was a man who probably had never exchanged a social syllable with a black person in his life. He was raised in Virginia, Maryland, and so forth, his background was that. But when I could, man to man, communicate the fervor, the drive, the passion of trying to pull together the history of a people based on an oral history, married by now with documented history, people would literally quit what they were doing, quit their jobs, temporarily, to help me. That man left his brokerage office, drove to Annapolis, to help me pin down that that was the ship.

I crossed the Atlantic Ocean round trip three times in the next ten days. In the next several weeks I was all over New England, Peabody Museum, the Widener at Harvard, various other places, looking for every thread, everything of any kind I could find about this ship, the symbolic ship that brought the 15 million, the specific ship that brought Kunta Kinte.

Finally, from one or another source, I knew that she was by name the ship the *Lord Ligonier*. She was built in 1765; this was her maiden voyage. Her captain was Captain Thomas Davies. She had sailed in 1765 with a cargo of run to Gravesend, England. She had sold the rum, used the proceeds to buy the slaving hardware (the chains, the shackles, the other restraining objects) to put on the extra food stuffs a slave ship needed, to put on the extra crew a slave ship needed, and then she had set out up the English Channel. There were look-out points at intervals along the waterways. And the records are still there for those look-out points. I would get the records from this one and sift wildly through them until I found the *Lord Ligonier* had passed and I'd run to these records, sift through them until she passed. It became almost like running along the beach looking at her. I knew what that ship looked like. I knew her timbers. She was made of loblolly pine planking. I knew that her beams were made of hackmatack cedar. I knew the nails that held her together were not really nails, they were "treenails". They were made of black locust split in the top with a wedge of oak. I knew the flax that made her sails had been grown in New Jersey. I knew everything about her. I knew the rig of her sails. And visually I could see her. I could read the captain's mind. I knew he had a new ship, maiden voyage, and everything in him was driving to get as fast as he could to the source of the black gold, to load and get back by the quickest passage which would make him look good to the owners. And I followed her from look-out point to look-out point and then she came along to a place called the Downs, and for God's sakes I found she dropped her anchor. And I nearly had a fit. Why in the world would she drop the anchor? I knew he was driving to make a great trip, and it just flipped me. I couldn't bear not to know why she stopped. And I began to think and it finally arrived upon me that ships then had no engines. The only thing that moved the ship was wind in the sails, so if I was going to find out why this ship moved or stopped, obviously what I had to know was more than I knew about weather. And I dropped everything. I found out the British meteorological headquarters was in a city called Bracknell. I got on a train, went over there, and told some people, look, I have got to have the weather for the fall of 1766. And they looked at me as if I was crazy.

And I went back that night to London as near suicide as I have ever been in my life. I was obviously just a total failure if I couldn't find that. It was three days before I was functioning again. And I came out of that stupor thinking there had to be a way. And now again the previous training came into play. I hadn't been 20 years in the U.S. Coast Guard for nothing. I went and got me a big blank meteorological chart. I got my little dividers and tools and figured the band of ocean through which any ship would have to sail to get from the mouth of the English Channel to the Gambia River on the mid-West African coast. Then I figured that what I had to do by any means I could possibly do it was to collect all possible documented weather data that I could for that particular band of ocean between the months of April and September, 1766. I began to go to every city in England that had in the 1760's been a major sea port—Liverpool, Hull, the others. And every time I'd get to one of these towns I'd go to everything that looked like a library.

And I knew one thing as an old sailor from the Coast Guard, that every time a sailing ship has the watch changed they record the weather and the longitude and latitude in the log. And whenever I'd find any ship that had been anywhere in any direction in that band of ocean between April and September, 1766, I would pluck out the weather readings and take the longitude-latitude figures to pin point where she was when she made that weather reading and date it.

I went back to Bracknell about three weeks later with four hundred and eleven weather readings scattered over that band of ocean. I found two lieutenant-commanders, Royal Navy, professional meteorological people and they called in colleagues, and for them it was like a double acrostic puzzle. It took them about two days to recreate the weather in which the *Lord Ligonier* had sailed. I found out why at first she stopped: the wind had shifted on her. She had been coming around the Channel and in a place where she had to have easterly winds to keep progressing she'd met southwesterly winds, and all she could do was tack back and forth between the English and French coasts. So she had dropped the anchor in a place called the Downs, not too far from where Caesar's oared galleys had brought Britain into the Empire. She had had to lay in anchor there in about 8 fathoms for about 2 weeks until the wind changed southeasterly. That was Tuesday morning, May 15th, 1766. The physical weather was about 66° temperature, the millibar reading was 10-10, the weather was a drizzle becoming fair. And that was the day she ran up the sails. She went out down past the white cliffs of Dover, Shakespeare Cliffs, Dungeness, Berry Head on down the Channel to Lizard Head. She went into the open sea southeast of the Bay of Biscay, southerly down past the Cape Verdes, the Canaries, and finally into the mouth of the Gambia River. She would spend the next ten months slaving in the Gambia River area. At the end of ten months she got a cargo: 3,265 elephants' teeth as they called tusks, 3,700 pounds of beeswax, 800 pounds of raw cotton, 32 ounces of gold, 140 slaves. And with that cargo she set sail July 5, 1767. It was a Sunday.

One of the most perverse things I was to run across was that the people who might be described as a hierarchy of slaving, the owners, the agents, the captains of those ships, strove in every possible way to manifest that they were functioning in a Christian context. If at all possible a slave ship when loaded would leave, as this one did, on the Sabbath. There was a popular saying at the time, "God will bless the journey." The *Lord Ligonier* sailed directly from the Gambia River to Annapolis, Maryland. She arrived the morning of September 29, 1767. September 29, 1967 I was standing on the pier at Annapolis drenched with tears.

I went to the Maryland Hall of Records (in the one set of records you can generally find back to the time of Christ: tax records) to find out what had she come in with and declared for tax. And I found she declared for tax the same cargo she declared leaving Africa, except that the original 140 slaves had become 98 who had survived that crossing. She crossed from the Gambia in two months, 3 weeks and 2 days, a voyage of about 5,000 miles.

I knew that when you had a cargo as valuable as slaves that then, as today, they advertised. And I went to the records of the *Maryland Gazette*. In the issue of October 1st, 1767, page 3, far left column, third head down was the *Lord Ligonier*'s ad. She had just arrived from the River Gambia "with fresh slaves for sale" to be sold the following Wednesday at Meg's Wharf. I trusted oral history now better than I trusted the printed page and I knew Grandma always said that Mas' John Waller had bought that slave, had named him Toby but later Mas' John had sold him to Mas' William, his brother. And I knew that most transactions involving slaves, even among families, were legal matters. And I went to Richmond, Virginia, searching the legal deeds, and found a deed dated September 5, 1768, between the two brothers John and William Waller, Spotsylvania County, Virginia, transferring goods between them. And on the second page in this fairly long deed were the words "and also one Negro man slave named Toby."

I could stand up here six hours and talk about this. I'm obviously obsessed with it. I've been almost 8 years now working on it. One of the spin-offs is that my brothers and I have begun a Kinte Foundation with numerous purposes. One of them is to establish this country's first black genealogical library. Wendell [Wray] and Courtney [Brown] and others of us have begun this work. There will be a staff of about 15 all told in time, of people who are beginning the early work of collecting the documentation for the creation of the Kinte Black Genealogical Library which will projectively open its doors in Washington, D.C. in bi-centennial 1976. The library will collect everything that we can lay hands on that documents slaves, free blacks, any blacks, preceding 1900.

Since so much of our material is derivative, which is to say that you can find many of the black records in what are surfacely white records, it is most important that we try and communicate this to you. You in your work may come upon things that we would love to have that you would, I know, be happy to let us have. I feel that, hopefully, the book, the motion picture (motion picture rights have already been negotiated), the library, the foundation, the whole thing will project a tremendous new emphasis and public awareness of and public image—worldwide—of oral history. We also hope to be able to project worldwide a correction of something that plagues not just black history, but all history for everybody, and that is that history had predominantly been written by the winners, which messes it up from the very beginning. Here now is a vehicle that I hope will be able to spread an awareness that black history is not just some euphemistic cry on the part of a people trying to make some spurious case for themselves, but that it does happen to be a matter of disciplined documented dedicated truth.

Note

1. *De la traditional orale: Essai de méthode historique* (Tervuren, Belgique, 1961). The English translation is *Oral Tradition: A Study in Historical Methodology* (Chicago: Aldine, 1965; see chapter 9 of the present volume).

PART FOUR
Oral History and Related Disciplines:
Folklore, Anthropology, and Gerontology

25

The Oral Historian
and the Folklorist

Richard Dorson

Oral historians sometimes consider themselves pioneers, working with nontraditional sources, outside the mainstream of the historical profession. But this view overlooks our kinship with other researchers who rely on oral sources in their work, including folklorists, anthropologists, and gerontologists. In part 4 of our book we present important writings which have attempted to bridge the boundaries separating some other disciplines from oral history.

It is fitting that we begin with the writing of the late Richard Dorson, the Harvard-educated folklorist whose training included the disciplines of history and American studies. In this, Dorson's address to the Sixth Colloquium on Oral History, he suggests some fundamental differences between the oral historian, who interviews on the basis of prior research, and the folklorist, who collects often from chance encounters. The historian primarily researches national structures, in Dorson's view: laws, politics, battles, social trends; the folklorist seeks out traditions and what Dorson calls "people's history." The author suggests that oral historians widen their scope to include "oral folk history," which includes oral personal history (first-person narratives) and oral traditional history (sagas and local legends).

Richard Dorson, professor of folklore and history at the University of Indiana, was one of the most influential folklore scholars of the twentieth century. His publications comprised two dozen books, some two hundred articles, and countless reviews and introductions. He was awarded numerous fellowships and grants, including an unusual third renewal of his Guggenheim Fellowship. Some of his other essays on oral history and folklore appear in Folklore and the American Historian *(1971).*

"The Oral Historian and the Folklorist" was first published in the Selections of the Fifth and Sixth National Colloquia on Oral History *(New York: Oral History Association, 1972).*

IN THE UNITED STATES students of history and students of folklore have shared little common ground. This is less true in Europe, where history lies enshrouded in a traditional past and folkloristics is recognized as an authoritative branch of learning. If American history has not yet been extended back in time to embrace a mythical Indian past, its boundaries are being stretched to include large sectors—blacks, ethnics, mountain whites, city folk—whose stories must be sought through oral and traditional rather than through printed and written sources. And folklore as a scholarly discipline has made spectacular gains in American universities in the 1960's. Consequently the old rigid polarization between history as scrupulously documented fact, and folklore as unverified rumor, falsehood, hearsay, old wives' tale—often equated with myth and legend in similar senses—is beginning to break down. Historians are moving closer to the methods of the folklorist through the new departure of oral history, and folklorists are becoming more history-minded as their discipline solidifies. . . .

Folklorists by and large have not been very history-minded. Most of them lean toward literature on the humanities side and toward anthropology on the social science side. Since my own doctorate was in History of American Civilization, I have always supported the synthesis of folklore and history, and have found some response among our graduate students, notably Lynwood Montell, who in the dissertation eventually published as *The Saga of Coe Ridge* combined the two methodologies. . . .

A few historians could in turn be cited as having sympathy toward the folklore approach, notably Theodore Blegen in his too neglected *Grass Roots History*, but only with the advent of oral history is the historical profession making a turn toward the methods of the folklorist. Up until the new oral history, a sharp line always divided the documentary record that served the historian from the oral flotsam that he scorned but which, for some curious reason, the folklorist devoured. Wresting himself from the library and archives, the retooled oral historian now marches forth with tape recorder to interview live people face to face. And to his astonishment he discovers, at some point, that this technique of obtaining information is the particular speciality of the folklorist. Some of my history colleagues, bent on establishing an oral history archives on campus, were surprised when I told them that there already existed at the university an extensive folklore archives for the depositing of tape-recorded interviews. These tapes, as well as separately housed manuscript collections, contained chiefly songs, tales, and other folkloric genres, but they held their share of oral history.

Before the oral historian and the folklorist can compare notes over the tape recorder about interview techniques and archival systems, they need to consider large divergences in their concepts and methods.

In respect to method, the oral historian *interviews* while the folklorist in the field *collects*. It would never occur to a practitioner of oral history to set out in the morning toting his Sony or Wollensak or Uher with little or no idea as to whom he will meet and record. Such action would appear to be not historical research but some species of madness. Yet this is exactly the way the folklorist operates. He follows up one lead after another, frequently stumbling down blind alleys and reaching dead ends, in his search for articulate bearers of verbal traditions or savvy expositors of traditional life styles. On locating a good informant—the technical term for the folk narrator or folk singer—he may of course revisit him frequently. Yet he must continually be ferreting out new informants in the [effort] to cast his net as widely as possible, in his search for a broad tradition.

Collecting techniques vary according to the personality of the collector. Two of the most successful fieldworkers in the United States used quite opposite techniques. Cecil Sharp, the Englishman prospecting for old English and Scottish ballads in the southern Appalachians, employed the pointblank approach; climbing to the mountain cabin, he asked the surprised family if they knew old songs and if they did promptly wrote down words and music. Vance Randolph, lifelong resident of the Ozard hills, adopted the participant-observer strategy on his home grounds, never posed the frontal question, but hung around a likely informant waiting till he uttered items of folklore, then excused himself and surreptitiously wrote them down in his notebook. Recently a retired Episcopal clergyman, Harry M. Hyatt, had produced an extraordinary two-volume tape-recorded collection of esoteric Negro magical beliefs, *Hoodoo, Witchcraft, Rootwork, Conjuration,* which he obtained by chasing down and directly interrogating Negro hoodoo doctors and their clients throughout the southeast.

As a compromise between the two field strategies, some folklorists are now proposing what they call the "induced natural context" to create so far as possible a spontaneous storytelling or folksinging situation without waiting indefinitely for it to arise. All this is far removed from the interview situation in which the oral historian poses questions in the living room to a political or business or labor leader about his personal career.

Besides the schism in their methodology, the oral historian and the folklorist differ appreciably on their basic concepts. The one seeks personal data of contemporary history, the other hunts for folk traditions. The small number of history-minded folklorists will keep their ears open for folk history, that is, the versions of past events that have remained in folk memory and folk tradition. This folk history has little in common with the elitist history that prevails in professional historical circles. The guild of American historians operates within the conceptual framework of a national political structure, which determines the chronology, the cast of characters, the issues and topics that bore history students from primary school through graduate school. Students run on a treadmill that never takes them beyond the federal government, presidents and senators, the national economy, international diplomacy, reform legislation. Of the people's history, they hear nothing.

In an essay oft-cited but never followed, "Everyman His Own Historian" (1931), Carl Becker spoke for a personal rather than a national view of history. The guild praised it, but anyone looking at the flood of historiographical works on American history over the past decade—by Higham, Garraty, Cunliffe and Winks, Noble, Hofstadter, Eisenstadt, Schlatter, Skotheim, and others—can very quickly recognize the overwhelming force of national, elitist history as practiced by all leading American historians. While revisionism is much in evidence, it is revisionism of the research methods, interpretations, and judgments of Frederick Jackson Turner, Charles Beard, Carl Becker (who never pursued the injunctions of his own essay) and other giants of the profession, national historians all. Revision of their subject matter is not broached. Oral history faithfully follows the elitist emphases of the guild, naturally enough, for the broad outlines of nationalist, federal government-structured history are clear and familiar, and those of folk history are fuzzy and obscure. For until someone records folk history, we do not even know its shape and content.

One encouraging sign for the development of interest in oral folk history can be seen in occasional expressions by the professional historians of disaffection with elitist history. A. S. Eisenstadt comments on the concentration of American history writing on a narrative of well-known events in political history dominated by major American presidents, as in Allan Nevins' *Ordeal of the Union* and Arthur Schlesinger's *The Age of Franklin D. Roosevelt*. Yet Nevins himself declares that the most fascinating part of history, and the most difficult to obtain, is the story of how plain men and women lived and were affected by the economic, social, and cultural changes of their times. Samuel P. Hays asks for a shift from "presidential history" and "top-level affairs" to "grass-roots happenings." Speaking on the colonial period, Jack P. Greene rues that historians have spent so much time studying the elite and thereby ignoring other elements.

One school of American historians has in the past few years expressly called for a rejection of elite history and a revolution in historiographical attitudes that will bring about concern with the inarticulate mass of the people. These are the historians of the New Left—Staughton Lynd, Eugene Genovese, Jesse Lemisch, Barton J. Bernstein—and they scoff at pretended revisionists who merely swap heroes of business for heroes of politics. Yet they themselves fall into the same nationalist trap and attempt to write about history from the bottom up using the same old tired categories of the American Revolution, Jacksonian democracy, the Civil War, the rise of industrialism, and so down to the New Deal and the New Frontier. Valiantly attempting to make dead men who have left no records tell their stories, they bemoan the difficulty of getting at ordinary folk. Now here is where the folklorist can aid, for he does make dead men tell their tales—through the lips of their living descendants, who relay family and local history passed orally across the generations.

One New Left historian, John J. Williams, did discover the folklorists and presented a paper in the radical historians panel at the December 1970 meeting of the American Historical Association, on "The Establishment and the Tape Recorder: Radicalism and Professionalism in Folklore Studies, 1933–1968." Looking into the folklore scholarship of the past three decades, Williams perceived a watershed dividing the nonacademic Old Left folklorists of the 1930's and '40's, notably represented by the Almanac Singers, and the academic establishment folklorists of the 1950's and '60's, ignobly epitomized by myself, and he quoted various statements of mine to illustrate my establishment tendencies. Now the New Left historians and folklorists in general do share a common premise, that the folk, the mass of the people, possess a culture and a history well worthy of study. But as a folklorist I do not correlate my interest in the folk with a radical ideology—or with a liberal or conservative or any other ideology. The folk fall into all these camps, and outside them, and I listen to what they have to say without prejudgment. In Negro folklore you can find bitterness against whites, certainly, but you can also find tales preferring the southern white man to the northern white man, and you can find traditions a-plenty that are shared by both blacks and whites.

How then is the oral historian to benefit from the techniques and concepts of the folklorist? The view of *oral history* must be enlarged to embrace *oral folk history*. Oral history as currently practiced is still elitist history, and so misses the opportunity to document the lives of anonymous Americans. Writing in the Oral History Association *Newsletter* of July, 1971, on the Texas Oral History Project devoted to the life and times of Lyndon B. Johnson, Paige Mulhollan stated that "oral history testimony . . . is intended to supplement, not to replace, traditional documentary research." This is indeed the case. Oral traditional history, on the other hand, seeks out the topics and themes that the folk wish to

talk about, the personal and immediate history with which they are concerned. We have no way of knowing in advance what are the contours of
this history, except that they will bear no resemblance to federal
government-structured elitist history. Local personalities are the actors,
local events form the chapters, but this is not state history following state
political boundaries, nor local history embalmed in township records, but
folk history preserved in tradition. The incident that engages the attention of the folk may appear ludicrous, trivial, bizarre, and grotesque to the
documentary historian. The anthropologist Robert Lowie roundly asserted that Indians possessed no ability to distinguish the sublime from
the ridiculous in their historical records. Near the top of their list of
memorable events, for example, they placed titanic drinking orgies.
Scarcely of the same noteworthy character as the Wilson-Gorman Tariff
or the Webster-Ashburton Treaty!

But it is not for the historian of the people to prejudge what the people
consider important. On a field trip to the Upper Peninsula of Michigan I
heard talk of several events celebrated in community remembrance: the
lynching of the McDonald boys at Memoninee; the "stealing" of the
courthouse at Iron River by the men of Crystal Falls; the highfalutin
speech Pat Sheridan delivered to the iron ore trimmers of Escanaba; the
incendiary Italian Hall fire in Calumet (about which William Ivey will be
commenting).

Each one of these episodes has a base in historical fact thickly coated
over with legendary accretions, but otherwise they possess little in common. One involved a scene in a brothel, a killing, and a grisly lynch party;
another is a comic saga of political rivalry between townships competing
for the county seat; a third centers on a piece of unintentionally humorous
rhetoric; a fourth deals with a disaster that led to charges and counter-
charges between striking copper miners and mine operators. The folk
historian is as keenly interested in the legendary growth surrounding
these happenings of six to nine decades ago as in the solid nub of fact,
could he establish it, for the play of tradition upon the events leads us into
the folk mind and the folk conception of the meaningful past.

Any folklorist engaged in fieldwork will stumble upon this folk history,
whether he is looking for it or not—and most often he is not. While
collecting Negro folktales I continually encountered historical traditions,
usually obscure to me and removed from any familiar context. James D.
Suggs told in close detail of the Ku Klux Klan killing a Negro brakemen on
southern railroads in 1914, and of the public burning in Mississippi in 1904
of a colored man who confessed to killing two white men. E. L. Smith
recounted exploits of his slave grandfather, Romey Howard, who outwit-
ted and outran "patterollers" and bloodhounds. Mary Richardson re-

lated brutalities she had observed on a "colored prisoner farm" near Clarksdale, Mississippi where she worked as cook's helper.

I seen them whip one man to death. He was a slim, skinny man, and they whipped him 'cause he couldn't pick two hundred pounds—that was his task and he couldn't never get it. So they whipped him morning and night until he couldn't work at all, just lay in his cage. The prisoners all slept in one room with double-deck beds 'side the walls. He couldn't even get out of bed to get his food. The feeder wasn't allowed to unlock the door, and each man had to come and get his pan; so he'd leave the sick man's in the window. I'd take the bread and roll it up in a piece of paper and throw it to his bunk, like a puppy. They told me I'd get prison for life if they found that out.

He died and they buried him in the farm cemetery, just like he was; didn't wash or change him. 'Cause the hole was too short they stomped on him, mashed, tramped, bent him down in there, and threw dirt on him.

Here is black experience from a black source, and because so few black sources are written, this and many sources equally informative are oral. Suggs, Smith, and Mary Richardson were all deft storytellers of traditional tales, but they were also all expert transmitters of oral history, precise with names, dates, places, settings, fluent and yet unemotional in their narratives, telling their grim narratives factually and without editorializing. The recollections at first-hand of Suggs and Mary Richardson we can call *oral personal history* of the non-elite, or the folk; the saga of Romey Howard as told across the generations by Smith, as well as accounts I was given of slave escapes on the Underground Railroad, fall under *oral traditional history.* Together they comprise *oral folk history.*

The oral folk historian will search out articulate members of the folk community and interview them for their personal and traditional history. Rewards obtainable from this kind of quest can be seen in the books of the skillful radio and television interviewer, Studs Terkel, who in *Division Street America* and *Hard Times, an Oral History of the Great Depression,* printed his taped interrogations of a number of people from different backgrounds concerning their own lives and outlooks. In the first work he confined himself to Chicago and eschewed celebrities, while in the second he cast a broader net, geographically and socially, for his speakers, and directed his questions more specifically to their recollections of the depression and its impact on them personally. *Hard Times* is consciously history-oriented, but in the national sense, so that *Division Street America,* centered on a Chicago neighborhood, conveys more the sense of personal folk history. While each Chicagoan possesses his own *gestalt,* he often shares certain common, traditional attitudes with his fellow residents on Division Street: one theme that echoes throughout the confessionals in the nostalgia for the good old days, when people walked, a true neighborhood existed, and the races interacted peaceably.

There are also sharp conflicts of attitude disclosed in these retrospective statements, and here lies a key aspect of oral folk history: the traditions collide. Or to put it another way, more than one folk exists, and each folk group regards events and personalities of the past through its own particular lens. Jesse James and Billy the Kid are hero-villains, depending on whether you talk with midwestern farmers or southwestern cowpunchers. As a Robin Hood, Jesse held up banks and trains, the agencies of big business, and gave their tainted money to widows and the impoverished. As a desperado, he shot helpless cashiers and trainmen in cold blood and stole the widows' money they guarded. Billy the Kid as Sir Galahad protected the open range and the freedom of the grazing cattle from encroachers who would fence in nature's bounty, but as a badman he slaughtered in the manner of a sadistic gunman and moronic punk.

Examine local-history traditions and see how often they splinter into two or three reenactments. Legends of Beanie Short, a guerrilla leader in the Cumberland Mountains of northern Tennessee during the Civil War, portray him both as a rebel renegade and as a freedom fighter, with a blending of the two roles; some Cumberland families boast that Beanie stole supplies from their grandparents. Did the McDonald Boys kill their man only in self-defense, and were the lynch leaders who denied them a fair trial the real murderers, as the ballad made out? And whose blood permanently stained the jail cell wall from which they were removed by the mob, the blood of a McDonald or the blood of a lyncher? Or was there ever any bloodstain? Folklore consistently notes an ineradicable blood stain where murder has occurred. Men and women in Crystal Falls and Iron River agree that residents in the first town "stole" the courthouse (i.e., its blueprints, or building fund, or the county papers) from the second town, but where a native of Crystal Falls regards the deed as high derring-do, the property owner in Iron River thinks of it as the worst skullduggery. Was Pat Sheridan who defied the ore-boat owners for his nascent ore-trimmers union an heroic workman finding his voice or an inept buffoon tongue-tied when he tried to rise above his station? These ambiguities permeate folk history.

If there are such differences of opinion in the folk memory, how then can the folk memory ever be trusted to transmit a consistent historical record? The question of the trustworthiness of oral traditional history has been endlessly debated in a variety of scholarly disciplines, with judgments ranging the whole spectrum from complete rejection of verbally relayed testimony to its acceptance as gospel. Every folklorist knows how floating motifs creep into any orally repeated report, no matter how firmly grounded in historical fact—the Icelandic sagas are a case in point.

Yet, under given conditions, the historic kernels endure and are identifiable. These conditions, in brief, involve such matters as continuity of residence in the area of the tradition; reinforcement of the tradition with reference to surrounding landmarks; and the training, formal or informal, of oral chroniclers within the society.

Folk memory may prove surprisingly reliable. In collecting oral accounts of the lynching of the McDonald Boys I was puzzled by two variant descriptions as to where the bodies were strung up, one saying on a railroad crossing sign, the other on a pine tree; but ultimately I learned they had been lowered from the railroad sign, dragged to the tree, and hoisted up again. What the oral folk historian wishes to record is not the plain unvarnished fact but all the motions, biases, and reactions aroused by the supposed fact, for in them lie the historical perspectives of the folk.

A word should be said about the divisions or classifications of oral folk history. The commonest terms here, as employed by the folklorist, are legend, anecdote, memorat, family saga. *Legend* signifies a tradition of an historical happening shared by a group of people. *Anecdote* refers to an historical incident befalling an individual, whether a local eccentric or a popular hero. *Memorat* is the term introduced by the Swedish folklorist Carl von Sydow to describe a remarkable or unusual personal experience related by the person to whom it happened. *Family saga* covers the miscellany of reminiscences about pioneer times, immigrant crossings and culture shock, black sheep characters, and ancestral ups and downs that the family unit treasures as its own unwritten—and hitherto unsought—history. These are some of the kinds of spoken narratives for which the oral folk historian will cast his net.

In so doing, he will be recording fresh and valuable information for what now becomes his oral folk history archives. Into such an archives will go tape recordings of community, neighborhood, ethnic, black, Indian, occupational and other orally transmitted history. The interviewer will become a collector, or will add a collector to his staff, and he will plan ways of tuning in on the folk history of his area. An anthropologist on the American Universities Field Staff who spends much of his time in Afghanistan, Louis Dupree, became interested in planning an oral folk history project after visiting our Folklore Institute one year, and on returning to the field retraced the route of the British army's retreat in 1848 from Kabul to Jalalabad, carrying his tape recorder with him and collecting traditions of the battle all along the way. His findings, published in an article in the *Journal of the Folklore Institute*, and to be developed into a book, present the Afghan folk view of the war previously known almost entirely from British documentary sources. In the United States we have plenty of our own Kabuls and Jalalabads to keep us occupied.

26

Oral History as Communicative Event

Charles Joyner

Our second article on folklore and oral history is from Charles Joyner, who holds doctoral degrees in both history and folklore. On the basis of his readings in these fields, Joyner suggests that folklorists should emulate historians' concern with time and change, and oral historians should explore folklorists' emphasis on the telling of a story (or history) as a communicative event in a context of social interaction.

Joyner further urges oral historians to include in their interview histories the performance and sociolinguistic elements of the interview situation—"a full description of the context in which the testimony was taken, including the mannerisms and gestures of the informant and the reactions of the audience." A narrator's way of telling his history itself reveals a truth, one at times truer than the historical facts described. Joyner's extensive notes suggest readings in folklore of interest to historians. His article is an invitation to oral historians to view their work from the standpoint of its basic unit: the words used to communicate.

Charles Joyner is professor of history and anthropology at the University of South Carolina, Coastal Carolina College. His writings include Folk Song in South Carolina *(1971) and* Slave Folklife: Cultural Change in a South Carolina Slave Community *(in press). He had done extensive folklore field work in Scotland, Northern Ireland, Newfoundland, and the United States.*

"Oral History as Communicative Event" originally appeared in the Oral History Review *7 (1979), pp. 47–52.*

HOW DO WE honestly and carefully study the large proportion of the population who left behind few if any written records? At least part of the reason for the long neglect of Afro-American history, Native American history, the history of women and of various ethnic groups was an historical methodology which failed to provide us with sufficient usable data on such subjects. The great challenge is to develop a more adequate methodology for studying history "from the bottom up."[1] I believe that folkloristics (a term folklorists use to distinguish the discipline from the material studied) has much to contribute to the development of that methodology and the theory upon which it must stand. Because oral history makes possible the gathering of historical evidence on people who would otherwise be left out of historical study (or treated only statistically), and because oral communication reveals more than written documents, I believe oral history is the most important single method of historical reserach and should be part of the methodological training of every historian. The historian who is ignorant of oral history, like the historian who still does not comprehend quantification, is only partly trained.

But note that I refer to oral history as a method, not as a separate field of history. Oral history should be used in conjunction with other methods of historical inquiry, appropriate to the historical problem under consideration. Studies in oral history, like all historical studies, should begin with statement and analysis of the historical problem to determine what are the relevant data and what are the most effective means of obtaining them.[2] Not all historical problems are susceptible to oral research, but more of them are than many historians might think. It is not a sign of health in our discipline that most historians do not "do" oral history, and that most oral historians do not "do" any other kind of history.

I think we oral historians must accept an important part of the blame for this lack of health in the discipline. Oral history, as practiced by far too many of us, is stuck back at the stage where the study of folklore was fifty years ago, when so-called folklorists collected and published lore and made little or no attempt to comprehend the life of the "folk" who supplied it. Too many oral historians are content to interview and transcribe, making little effort to comprehend more than the literal referential meaning of the words.

It is not enough to proceed directly from problem statement to interview. To enter an interview without analyzing the problem is to invite a simple-minded and arbitrary collection of data. It is not enough to publish raw collections of testimonies. What is necessary is a full description of the context in which the testimony was taken, including the mannerisms and gestures of the informant and the reactions of the audience. What is necessary, and long overdue, is that publication be based upon meaningful interpretation of what those testimonies mean to the people who transmitted them.

The oral historian who would undertake to interpret the history of the folk is confronted with numerous problems. We must begin with careful ethnographic description. Anthony F. C. Wallace's dictum that "all of the comparative and theoretical work of cultural anthropology depends upon a thorough and precise ethnographic description" would seem to be no less true for the oral history of the folk.[3]

Merely to recognize the importance of careful ethnographic description, however, does not guarantee its attainment. The first problem is cultural comprehension. Too often historians interpreted their subject only in terms of their own customs and interests.

The riddle for us is how much our perceptions convey an accurate picture of the culture we are trying to interpret. The nearer we are culturally to the group we are trying to interpret, the more difficult it is for us to explain it to others; the nearer we are culturally to our audience, the greater our difficulty in understanding the subject.[4]

In the study of folk history, not only must the usual historical standards of internal and external criticism of sources be rigorously applied, but we need to be proficient in semiotics, structural analysis, sociolinguistics, and functional analysis as well. Since most historical training does not include work in these areas, historians have understandably shied away from the history of the folk.[5]

If we have shied away from oral folk history, we have shunned folklore proper like the plague. Folklore materials are not readily susceptible to the kinds of analysis with which we are most comfortable. Internal criticism seems irrelevant to a folktale which does not even purport to be true. And what is the historian to make of a proverb, or a riddle? And songs—even if the historian can find some semblance of meaning in the words, what is the historical meaning of the tunes? Those few historians who have tried to use folklore materials, such as John Blassingame and Eugene Genovese, have not plowed very deeply because their modes of analysis were irrelevant to the materials, and they were unable or unwilling to make use of folkloristic analysis.[6]

Furthermore, many of the large folklore collections of the past are so divorced from their social and cultural context as to be inadequate for our purposes. As an historian interested in folk culture, I have been led to fieldwork as much by necessity as by choice. Linda Degh states that collectors of folktales "should consider the close relationship between the text and the individual and should record the general atmosphere in which the text is transmitted."[7] Her injunction would seem to be applicable to all forms of oral tradition if they are to be of any value to the cultural historian.

I have not hesitated to complain about the historian's neglect of folk culture. I have elsewhere complained to folklorists of their neglect of history. A considerable sociological richness has been achieved in contemporary folklore studies through borrowings from the social sciences, but that achievement has been at the expense of historical richness. The pervasively static quality of much current folklore scholarship is the result of what M. G. Smith calls "the fallacy of the ethnographic present." Stephan Thernstrom observes, "Ahistorical social science is as often narrow and superficial as sociologically primitive history, and it is certainly no less common."[8]

Folklorists would do well to emulate the historian's concern with change and time, but oral historians have much to learn from folklorists as well, especially from their emphasis on folklore as a communicative process in a context of social interaction. An oral history interview is a communicative event, not comprehensible apart from social interaction, and intimately bound up with the changing values and institutions of a changing society.[9] Analysis of the interview as a communicative event offers oral historians who are willing to adopt folkloristic means an unusual opportunity to achieve unprecedented historical ends.

Such an analysis depends upon a conception of language as a part of social life and a deeper sense of the social patterning of language use. The concept of "performance" has come into increasing prominence in recent folklore scholarship. In particular three folklorists, Dan Ben-Amos, Roger Abrahams, and Alan Dundes, offer theories of performance which challenge us to integrate the communicative elements and the historical elements of oral history. Ben-Amos emphasizes that "the performance situation, in the final analysis, is the crucial context for the available text." Dundes distinguishes between knowing folklore and knowing how to use folklore, thus pointing toward analysis of communicative events in terms of cultural rules of communication—what is communicated to whom at what times and at what places. Abrahams links the concept of performance as a structured event and the concept of performance as stylized behavior. The communicative event involves reciprocity between performer and audience. The common element in their approaches is the emphasis on the communicative event, not the text, as the analytical focus.[10]

Such elements of an oral history testimony as the degree of explicitness, the use of conventional phrases and formulations, the use of direct vs. indirect speech, modes of addressing and referring to other persons, the means of issuing commands and requests, means of indicating politeness or rudeness, and the means of opening and closing conversations are not accidental. They have both linguistic and social meaning and are analyzable for historical meaning in ways that written documents are not.[11]

Thus the folkloristic analysis of the interview as a communicative event offers an approach to historical truth not previously available to scholars. I want to emphasize that the approach I am recommending is not limited to studies of the history of the folk. It is as applicable to the politician, the business executive, and the scientist as it is to the migrant farmer, the factory worker, the suffragette, or the ex-slave.

Seen from this perspective, the familiar complaint of orthodox historians that oral history is unreliable (because interviewees will attempt to present themselves in as favorable a light as possible) is irrelevant.[12] Of course they attempt to put themselves in a favorable light in interviews, as well as in correspondence, memoranda, and other written artifacts. Therefore what? I contend that informants *never* lie to a good historian (although they may try to); they just reveal the truth in some unique ways. Even if the informant consciously attempts to lie to the interviewer, he cannot help but reveal evidence of his deepest value system—that elusive "why?" of his motivation that historians have so long sought. The "lie" may reveal more truth than the mere fact.[13]

Truth, after all, is not precisely the same thing as a collection of facts, as any comparison of historical interpretations of the same event demonstrates. But what is an historical "event?" When people share an historical experience, did they remember or experience the "same" event? And if a society's perceived truth is "known" to the investigator to be an error, is it any less influential upon that society's behavior? Lies and errors may be a society's motivation for otherwise inexplicable actions.

The testimony that emerges from an interview may be fact or fantasy. We need not apologize for the method if we discover, not merely the straightforward truth of history, but also some of the more subtle truths of fiction and poetry. It is our responsibility as historians to ascertain which is which.

Notes

1. The idea of studying history "from the bottom up" seems to have been first advanced by folklorist Benjamin A. Botkin, in his *Lay My Burden Down: A Folk History of Slavery* (Chicago: University of Chicago Press, 1945), p. ix. It has been popularized in recent years, without attribution to Botkin, by Jesse Lemisch, in "The American Revolution Seen from the Bottom Up," *Towards A New Past: Dissenting Essays in American History*, ed. Barton J. Bernstein (New York: Pantheon, 1968), pp. 3–45.

2. See F. S. C. Northrop, *The Logic of the Sciences and the Humanities* (New York: Meriden, 1959).

3. Anthony F. C. Wallace, "Culture and Cognition," *Science* 135 (1962), p. 351. See also Herbert Halpert, "American Regional Folklore," *Journal of American Folklore* 60 (1947), pp. 355–56; Herbert Halpert, "The Functional Approach," *Journal of American Folklore* 54 (1946), pp. 510–12; Richard M. Dorson, "Standards of Collecting and Publishing American Folktales," *Journal of American Folklore* 80 (1957), p. 54; Kenneth S. Goldstein, *A Guide for Field Workers in Folklore* (1964; Reprint ed., Detroit: Gale, 1974), p. 7.

4. Alfred Kroeber and Clyde Kluckhohn, *Culture: A Critical Review of Concepts and Definitions* (Cambridge, Mass.: Harvard University Press, 1952), p. 182; William P. McEwen, *The*

Problem of Social Scientific Knowledge (Totowa, N.J.: Bedminster Press, 1963), pp. 34–35; Benjamin N. Colby, "Ethnographic Semantics: A Preliminary Survey," *Current Anthropologist* 7 (1966), pp. 3–32.

5. There are two notable exceptions to this generalization, both written by folklorists. W. Lynwood Montell's *The Saga of Coe Ridge: A Study in Oral History* (Knoxville: University of Tennessee Press, 1970; see chapter 16 of the present volume) reconstructs ninety years in the life of a black community in the foothills of the Cumberland mountains through extensive tape-recorded interviews with former residents, their descendants, and their neighbors. As a folklorist, Montell is able to identify with unusual accuracy the universal folklore motifs in his informants' testimonies and to penetrate the embellishments of his sources. Gladys-Marie Fry's *Night Riders in Black Folk History* (Knoxville: University of Tennessee Press, 1975) focuses on the theme of how whites used black folk as a means of social control of blacks during and after slavery. Fry combines analysis of interviews from the W.P.A. Slave Narratives Project with numerous interviews of her own.

6. John W. Blassingame, *The Slave Community: Plantation Life in the Ante-Bellum South* (New York: Oxford University Press, 1972); Eugene D. Genovese, *Roll, Jordan, Roll: The World the Slaves Made* (New York: Pantheon, 1974). A more satisfactory treatment is Lawrence W. Levine, *Black Culture and Black Consciousness: Afro-American Folk Thought from Slavery to Freedom* (New York: Oxford University Press, 1977). None of these studies, however, involves fieldwork, or folkloristic analysis of the kind I am calling for.

7. Linda Degh, *Folktales and Society: Storytelling in a Hungarian Peasant Community* (Bloomington: University of Indiana Press, 1969), p. vii.

8. Charles W. Joyner, "A Model for the Analysis of Folklore Performance in Historical Context," *Journal of American Folklore* 88 (1975), pp. 254–65; M. G. Smith, "History and Social Anthropology," *Journal of the Royal Anthropological Institute* 92 (1962), p. 77; Stephan Thernstrom, *Poverty and Progress: Social Mobility in a Nineteenth Century City* (Cambridge, Mass.: Harvard University Press, 1964), pp. 225–26.

9. Roger D. Abrahams, "Introductory Remarks to a Rhetorical Theory of Folklore," *Journal of American Folklore* 81 (1968), p. 157; Clyde Kluckhohn, "Parts and Wholes in Cultural Analysis," in *Parts and Wholes*, ed. Daniel Lerner (New York: Free Press of Glencoe, 1963), p. 121; John Gumperz, Introduction, *Directions in Sociolinguistics: The Ethnography of Communication*, ed. John J. Gumperz and Dell Hymes (New York: Holt, Rinehart and Winston, 1972), p. 26; Pier Paolo Giglioli, *Language and Social Context* (Harmondsworth, Middlesex, England: Penguin, 1972), p. 13.

10. Dell Hymes, *Foundations in Sociolinguistics: An Ethnographic Approach* (Philedelphia: University of Pennsylvania Press, 1974), pp. 3–66; Dan Ben-Amos, "Towards a Definition of Folklore in Context," *Journal of American Folklore* 84 (1971), pp. 3–15; Alan Dundes, "Texture, Text, and Context," *Southern Folklore Quarterly* 28 (1964), pp. 251–65; Roger D. Abrahams, "Introductory Remarks to a Rhetorical Theory of Folklore," pp. 144–45; Roger D. Abrahams, "Rapping and Capping: Black Talk as Art," in *Black America*, ed. John F. Szwed (New York: Basic, 1970), pp. 132–42; Roger D. Abrahams, "The Training of the Man of Words in Talking Sweet," *Language in Society* 1 (1972), pp. 15–30.

11. Dell Hymes, "Models of the Interaction of Language and Social Life," in *Directions in Sociolinguistics*, ed. Gumperz and Hymes, pp. 35–71. See also Joel Sherzer and Regna Darnell, "Outline Guide for the Ethnographic Study of Speech Use," in *Directions in Sociolinguistics*, ed. Gumperz and Hymes, pp. 548–54.

12. For a review of the long-standing controversy over the historical reliability of oral traditions, see Charles W. Joyner, *Folklore and History: The Tangled Relationship*, Newberry Papers in Family and Community History No. 78–2 (Chicago: University of Chicago Press, 1978).

13. Kay Cothran, "The Truth as a Lie—The Lie as Truth: A View of Oral History," *Journal of the Folklore Society of Greater Washington* 3 (Summer 1972), pp. 3–6.

27

The Anthropological Interview and the Life History

Sidney Mintz

Turning now to the interface of anthropology and oral history, we note that anthropologists and ethnographers share techniques with their colleagues in history, though they search out different information. In the anthropological "life history," the researcher "must have a conception of how people are at once products and makers of the social and cultural systems within which they are lodged," according to experienced field worker Sidney Mintz.

The anthropologist, unlike the oral historian, records interviews to learn the structure and patterns of a society as exhibited by a representative individual's world view, cultural traits, and traditions. The culture's internal perceptions of a specific activity's meaning are thus more useful than an external appraisal. This discussion of the ethnographic interview provides useful insights in interviewing individuals not as historical witnesses but as culture bearers.

Sidney Mintz is professor of anthropology at Johns Hopkins University; he has taught at Columbia and Yale universities and has conducted field work in Puerto Rico, Jamaica, Haiti, Iran, and other countries. He has served as a fellow to the American Anthropological Association and the Guggenheim and Rockefeller foundations. His books include Worker in Cane: Plantation Systems of the New World *(1959),* Caribbean Transformations *(1974),* An Anthropological Approach to the Study of Afro-American History *(1976), and* Esclave—facteur de production *(1981).*

"The Anthropological Interview and the Life History" was first published in the Oral History Review 7 *(1979), pp. 18–26.*

I T IS NOT entirely certain that the anthropological interview differs significantly from interviews by specialists in other disciplines, but it may be useful to explore this possibility from the vantage-point of ethnography. There is probably no better place to start than a fine essay by Harold C. Conklin, entitled "Ethnography," which appeared in the *International Encyclopedia of the Social Sciences:*

The data of cultural anthropology derive ultimately from the direct observation of customary behavior in particular societies. Making, reporting, and evaluating such observations are the task of ethnography. . . . An ethnographer is an anthropologist who attempts—at least in part of his professional work—to record and describe the *culturally significant behaviors* of a particular society. Ideally, this description, an ethnography, requires a long period of intimate study and residence in a small, well-defined community, knowledge of the spoken language, and the employment of a wide range of observational techniques including prolonged face-to-face contacts with members of the local group, direct participation in some of that group's activities, and *a greater emphasis on intensive work with informants than on the use of documentary or survey data.*[2] (*Italics added.*)

Much of this concise statement would need discussion if we intended to examine the ethnographic undertaking in general, but I shall restrict my comments to the anthropological or ethnographic interview as used in collecting the life history. For this purpose, two of Conklin's emphases deserve special attention: the stress put upon "intensive work with informants," and the reference to "culturally significant behaviors."[2]

Even if fieldwork is confined at some point to dealing with a single informant, there is great benefit in being able at least to observe that informant interacting with other members of the group. Though there is no way of proving it, I suspect that a good deal of the confidence an anthropologist may feel in a particular informant arises from his or her judgments of how *others* regard that informant, as manifested in their interactive behavior. Even in confining my emphasis to interviewing for the life history, I would certainly not argue that verbal communication between informant and biographer can or should be the sole source of relevant information. Elsewhere, I have suggested the opposite, contending that many life histories lose some of their value because the fieldworker lacks sufficient knowledge of the community and culture within which the informant lives, and which he or she expresses, in one way or another, in nearly everything he or she says or does.[3] Thus, for the life history, while intensive work with one informant or several is of course absolutely essential, it must not preclude broader interviewing, or the study of the community within which the principal informant lives and works.

Conklin's reference to "culturally significant behaviors" addresses an important disciplinary premise. Anthropology is concerned with the range and variation of behavior in any given society, but it is also concerned with behaviors that are "culturally significant," which is to say other than random or unique. Thus, while a life history might be elicited precisely because the informant was so far from the apparent "norm" for his or her group in one or another regard, anthropology assumes that *any* individual, in some fundamental and inalterable ways, gives expression to, incarnates, the culture, and cannot do otherwise. David Aberle has argued:

The individual of the life-history is only one of many comparable members occupying the positions in a social system. Every individual in a society is oriented to a set of explanatory beliefs, most of which he shares with others, and to social norms, felt both as facilitations and as constraints. Every action of his—conforming, individualistic, or revolutionary—is oriented to the fact of those norms, the existence of which he recognizes and knows that other people recognize.[4]

Aberle goes even further, in clarifying the irreducible nature of culture as something much more than personality writ large:

Although it remains true that within a culture individuals differ because of biological inheritance, social positions and idiosyncratic experience, it is a central fact of social science . . . that experience is patterned and that the patterns are limited in any society. The reactions to culturally established situations, though varied, are also limited. The history of any individual's reactions affords considerable understanding of the relationship of motivation and institution. Were the individual grossly deviate—even to the point of being psychotic, deluded, and hallucinated—his experiences, interpreted with sufficient care against a background of the society, would still give us insights and valid knowledge.[5]

The relationship between culture and personality has never been articulated fully to the satisfaction of anyone. But I am sympathetic to those anthropologists who believe personality can only manifest itself in a cultural guise, and that no psychological interpretation, no matter how ambitious, can avoid dealing with the cultural encapsulation of personality. Coarse though such a view may seem in these days of psychohistory and sociobiology, it may at least keep us from trying to explain war as the consequence of aggressive drives, politics as the consequence of aggressive drives, politics as the consequence of an instinct for power, or good works as the inevitable outcome of the right genes.

If this viewpoint is accepted, then the ethnographic life history interview must deal with distinctions between the personal, unique or idiosyncratic, on the one hand, and the culturally typical or normative on the other. The distinction between these categories is not sharp; I tried elsewhere to specify the difficulty, when I wrote: "The goal of such an undertaking would not be to deemphasize individual uniqueness or to eliminate the significance of personality in the study of change, but rather to specify with more confidence the way individuality plays itself out against terms set by sociocultural forces."[6] When one seeks to interpret a radical change in individual world-view—the acceptance of a new religion, in this case—as reflecting the convergence of different and superindividual forces, how can one weigh the relative importance of individual character in affecting this outcome? Presumably, not everyone in the culture, exposed to precisely the same forces, would react in the same way. But who would? To attempt to find out, one might consider collecting a number of life histories of converts who share some of the fundamental class, age, sex, occupational and familial characteristics of the first informant, in order to try to weigh the possible significance of each of these features, as against the importance of distinctive individual traits.

Whlie the ethnographic interview as part of the life history can proceed primarily on the basis of simple question-and-answer exchanges, it will be profitable to return to Conklin's article once more, for the enumeration he provides of elicitation procedures:

. . . recording and using natural question-response sequences and implications; testing by intentional substitution of acceptable and incongruent references; testing by paraphrase; testing by reference to hypothetical situations; testing by experimental extensions of reference; and testing by switching styles, channels, code signals, message content, and roles (by reference or impersonation). . . .

Because ethnographers interact personally and socially with informants, they find themselves carrying on a unique type of natural history, in which the observer becomes a part of (and an active participant in) the observed universe. The extent of this involvement and its importance for ethnographic recording depend on many situational considerations, including the personalities of the ethnographer and his informants. In some types of field inquiry the ethnographer's practical success or failure may depend as much on those impressions he makes locally as on the cultural events being observed. . . . Especially where long-term investigation of intimate personal relationships is concerned, most anthropologists would agree with Condominas (1965: 35) in stressing the *"nécessité d'ethnographier les ethnographes."*[7]

Such assertions underline the highly personal nature of the ethnographic interview in which, for most purposes, the ethnographer and his or her informant are interrogating each other. It is of course absolutely true that such confrontations are most frequently not only between members of two different cultures, but between those whose access to wealth and power is radically different. While it is conceded that, until the interview relationship is firmly established, the ethnographer may be figuratively at the mercy of the informant, quite the opposite is likely to be the case thereafter. It is one thing for a reporter to request and be granted an interview with a Begin or a Sadat, and quite another for an ethnographer to record the life history of a Hopi, or a Puerto Rican cane worker. The prerogatives available to the ethnographer, while they must be used with some restraint, strengthen his or her investigative powers immensely. How those powers will be used is, of course, a different matter.

I have already implied that life history studies must grapple with the problem of typicality or representativeness. One may expect a life history to reveal to the reader what is typical in that culture, but not how representative that life is within it. Indeed, many who have recorded life histories have consciously rejected the use of the life history for this purpose. If anything, the stress is usually on trying to "make sense" of the life itself. I say "if anything" because many anthropological life histories are, for the most part, descriptive accounts intended to speak for themselves. But they would be much more useful if the recorder would try to say who he or she is, and why the life history was recorded in the first place. Some of what are intrinsically the most interesting anthropological life histories—those by Oscar Lewis, or Leo Simmons' *Sun Chief*, or Michael Smith's *Dark Puritan*, or Waler Dyk's *Son of Old Man Hat*—seem to be pushed out in front of the reader at the end of a long stick, while the character of the collector and the relationship between him or her and the collected remain largely obscure. In such instances, the issue of the possible representativeness of the protagonist is as dormant as the nature of the rapport.

These assertions are consistent with the fictitious Trapnel's complaints: "The biographer, even at his highest and best, can only be tentative, empirical. The autobiographer, for his part, is imprisoned in his own egotism." But while Trapnel is entitled to conclude that only a novel can "imply certain truths impossible to state by exact definition," historically-oriented scholars disposed to use the spoken word as data are not thereby obligated to become novelists—even if some have tried. The choice ought not to be between a disembodied individual who floats outside and above the culture and society, on the one hand, and a culture and society which imprison and make irrelevant the individuality of the informant, on the other. The biographer-ethnographer must have a conception of how people are at once products and makers of the social and cultural systems within which they are lodged. He or she must also make an honest effort, at least after the materials have been collected, to address the issue of how the informant and the fieldworker were interacting, why they were drawn together, what developing concerns for (or against) each other influenced the rhythm and nature of the enterprise. In short, he or she must respond to Conklin's observation that ethnographers carry on "a unique type of natural history, in which the observer becomes a part of (and an active participant in) the observed universe."

There are really two contentions here. The first is that the ethnographer try to define his or her place between the informant and the reader. The second is that the ethnographer help the reader to see the informant within the culture and society. Perhaps a little more can be said about this second assertion. Many social scientists have grappled with the supposed distinctions between the concepts of "society" and "culture," and some have even referred to "personality" as a kind of third or middle term. It may be useful to add to this view with particular reference to the life history. In his illuminating essay on the study of life history, Mandelbaum distinguishes between the cultural and social dimensions in a satisfactory fashion. The cultural dimension provides a scenario or chart, with the attendant understandings and behaviors, for the individual life; while the social dimension comprises the real-life interactions in which individuals make choices, and even shift cultural definitions. To these, Mandelbaum adds a psychosocial dimension; in general, his treatment corresponds to that offered by Parsons, Geertz, and Wolf.[8] Though such conceptual schemata are never entirely satisfying, they do enable us to think usefully about our research.

An institution, a cuisine, a complex of belief and behavior traditional within some society, can be traced backward in time, and its elements or features isolated and examined. Whether it be pants-wearing, handshaking, or choosing godparents, the social historian is often able to provide us with historical guidelines of a kind. Such materials are "cultural." But at any point in time, in any specific society, the particular ways people wear pants, shake hands, or choose godparents, and the ways they start doing them differently, will depend on numerous considerations that are immediately relevant, and that cannot be explained simply by reference to the past. Such maneuverings are "social." They are the reflections of both the composition and structure of the social group at that point in time, and the manifestations of individual variation within the group. It is in this sense that the elusive phenomenon we dub "personality" reveals itself at the boundary between social and cultural perspectives on behavior. To be specific about the life of an informant, in order to illustrate this assertion, would require too much narration. Perhaps it is sufficient to say that we make our decisions, as individuals, under conditions laid down by forces over which we have unspecified control, and that our perceptions of such conditions clearly influence our sense of autonomy. In getting at the life-profiles of others by collecting data on their experiences, we may examine, within limits, the extent to which such profiles are isomorphic with each other, or with some aggregate profile of the culture as a whole—if we know enough about the culture to make such comparisons possible. Differences among individuals are revealed not only by difference in the decisions made, but also by differential perceptions of alternatives.

But there are only two immediately apprehendable ways to get at the range of variation within one or more cultural norms or values. One must either find out from a large number of people, by observing their behavior or by asking them about it; or one must pose to one or more informants who have acted in accordance with such norms or values the possibility of alternatives, to which such informants may then respond with word or deed. Since the ability of people to explain their behavior *post hoc* appears to be very widely distributed, there are tangible benefits to be gained from studying decisions that are being made while one observes them, together with the collection of data on past decisions of a similar kind. For instance, while allowing for the many possible sources of difference, I found it useful to ask older informants about their first marital unions, and, at the same time, collect information on how their children were entering into comparable unions in the present. Among other things, such subject matters naturally provoke considerable discussion about how things are not what they used to be. Although a good deal of phony piety may enter, so do moral judgments, moral prescriptions, and active comparisons. It is within such terms that culture, conceived of as a repository of prescribed opportunities, and society, conceived of as an arena of maneuver, may be highlighted by the opinions of a single informant, silhouetting his or her distinctive experience against the backdrop of our knowledge of the group.

There is no high road to insights of this sort. But since there seems to be no way to learn about the culture without learning about the informant, or vice-versa, there are good reasons for making the life history interview the last kind of ethnographic undertaking, rather than the first. The questions we learn to ask may not be the better psychologically, but they should, at least, serve us well in coaxing the individual, the distinctive, and the idiosyncratic into clearer view.

Notes

1. Harold C. Conklin, s. v. "Ethnography," in *International Encyclopedia of the Social Sciences* (New York: Macmillan, 1968).

2. I will not deal with the question of the observation of behavior, except insofar as it concerns the immediate behavior of informants, even though, from the ethnographic perspective, this is rather like forsaking sight in order to benefit from the simplicity of reading Braille. Cf. Sidney Mintz, "Comments: Participant-Observation and the Collection of Data," in *Boston Studies in the Philosophy of Science, 1966–68*, vol. 4 (Dordrecht, Holland: D. Reidel, 1969), pp. 341–49.

3. I believe that this is true even for informants who have migrated elsewhere. Of course many factors can affect, reduce, trivialize, or romanticize the way the community and culture are expressed by an informant remote in space or time from his or her past. But past experience does continue to manifest itself in perception and articulation—only how much or how little is open to argument. Cf. Sidney W. Mintz, "Comments" on Mandelbaum: "The Study of Life History: Gandhi," *Current Anthropology* 14 (1973), p. 200.

4. David Aberle, *The Psychosocial Analysis of a Hopi Life-History*, Comparative Psychol-

ogy Monographs, Vol. 21, No. 1, Serial No. 107 (Berkeley: University of California Press, 1951), p. 2.

5. Aberle, *Psychosocial Analysis*, p. 4.

6. Mintz, "Comments," p. 200.

7. Conklin, "Ethnography," p. 172; George Condominas, *L'Exotique est quotidien: San Luk, Vietnam Central* (Paris: Plon, 1965), p. 35.

8. David G Mandelbaum, "The Study of Life History: Gandhi," *Current Anthropology* 14 (1973), pp. 177–206; Talcott Parsons, *The Social System* (Glencoe, Ill.: Free Press, 1951); Clifford Geertz, "Ritual and Social Change: A Javanese Example," *American Anthropologist* 55 (1957), pp. 32–54; Eric R. Wolf, "Specific Aspects of Plantation Systems in the New World: Community Sub-Cultures and Social Class," *Plantation Systems of the New World*, Social Science Monographs No. 7 (Washington, D.C.: Pan American Union, 1959), pp. 136–46.

28

Three Ways of Reminiscence in Theory and Practice

Marianne Lo Gerfo

Anthropologists are not alone in having developed a specialized interview format for their research; gerontologists, who study the aging process, have done so as well. And because the field of oral history depends in large part on the memories of elder informants, articles such as this one, which aids our understanding of reminiscence, make a valuable contribution to the profession.

Since the early seventies, gerontologists have shown increasing interest in the therapeutic value of reminiscence for the aging. One technique in common use, the life review, shares certain characteristics with oral history interviewing, though the focus is customarily on the benefit to the narrator rather than on the information obtained. In this selection, Marianne Lo Gerfo, a social work researcher, divides reminiscence into three varieties: informative, evaluative, and obsessive. Those working with older narrators might profit from understanding each type, she suggests. She briefly surveys the research on aging and life review, listing various studies; her notes and bibliography allow the reader to delve more deeply. Combining historical and geriatic processes is difficult but worthwhile; this article may be a valuable guide in developing future projects which combine the two fields.

Marianne Lo Gerfo is a social worker specializing in the problems of the aged. She was formerly associated with the Northshore MultiService Center in Woodinville, Washington.

"Three Ways of Reminiscence in Theory and Practice" originally appeared in the International Journal of Aging and Human Development, *12 (1980–81), pp. 39–48.*

WHEN WE invite older adults to delve into their personal past through oral history, we often assume that we will be providing a positive opportunity for them to share with us a cherished pastime: reminiscence. But, do the elderly really descend into memory more often than younger people? Is this voyage healthy and creative . . . or should it actually be discouraged? After two decades of research, the experimental literature offers no definitive answers. For example, while Cameron (1), Chiriboga and Gigy (2) and Giambra (3,4) reported only minor differences among age groups in the temporal setting of thoughts or daydreams, Lieberman and Falk (5) and Sherman and Havighurst (6) suggested that frequency of reminiscence increases markedly with age. Higher frequency of reminiscence was associated with good adjustment, ego integrity or stability of self-concept in the studies of McMahon and Rhudick (7), Havighurst and Glasser (8), Boylin, Gordon and Nehrke (9), and Lewis (10). However, Lieberman and Falk found no correlation between preoccupation with the past and subsequent adjustment (5). Reminiscence was unrelated to psychiatric diagnosis in the work of the Chiriboga and Gigy (2).

Why the discordance? Part of the answer lies in the fact that these researchers studied very different people in widely different ways. Elderly persons studied varied from the employed, to the retired, to the recently institutionalized, to those imminently facing death. Methodologies included single questions, elaborate questionnaires and unstructured interviews. Some of the studies were designed to ascertain the time orientation of conversation, while others dealt with mentation. There appears to have been no standard operational definition of reminiscence. Furthermore, with the exception of such researchers as Coleman (11). McMahon and Rhudick (7), and Lieberman and Falk (5), little systematic attention has been paid to the vast differences in content, function and effect of reminiscence behavior. Yet, an understanding of the basic types of reminiscence and their implications is a great advantage in helping people to use their memories of the past in the service of the present. Literature and practice suggest at least three distinct, though overlapping, categories of reminiscence: informative, evaluative and obsessive.

Informative Reminiscence

Informative reminiscing is focussed on the factual material reviewed instead of on its relevance for a re-evaluation of the personality or life-history. Its main functions are to provide pleasure and to enhance self-esteem through reliving and retelling past events. Gratification comes not only from the remembrance itself, but also from the tribute to longevity and mental soundness that memory of the distant past celebrates.

This essentially nonproblematic form of recollection is probably the most common among older people. The most frequent reason for reminiscing in the Lieberman and Falk study was personal satisfaction (5).

It appears that the studies describing a syndrome of good adjustment, positive affect of reminiscence and high frequency of reminiscence (7, 8, 10, 12) were dealing with people who were eager to enjoy and share an established sense of themselves and their past.

In their 1964 study of Spanish-American War Veterans, McMahon and Rhudick (7) have left us a vivid picture of the joy and pride of their story-tellers as they passed on some of their knowledge and experience to a new generation. In Jung's analysis of the stages of life, he postulated that this transmission of "culture" provides the meaning and purpose of the second half of life (13). Moreover, as these men returned to a time when they were in the same life stage as their listeners, they created a real sense of intimacy. The anthropologists' "affinity of alternate generations" can be observed in action, as elders reminisce more readily to those at least two generations younger.

This time parity was not created by the study's story-tellers. Another group, who tested as less well-adjusted than the first, emphasized instead the disparity between past and present. Glorifying the "good old days," they tended to be more defensive and to assert their superiority through fantasy or "pseudo-reminiscence." Such a stance is indicative of poor self-esteem and a need to maintain control over the relationship. As Pincus pointed out, it is important to recognize and accept the time frame presented, whether the reminiscer is attempting to negotiate differences of age and status by maintaining an egalitarian or an authoritarian footing (14).

Stimulating informative reminiscence may arouse the younger competent person who slumbers inside the seriously impaired elder. Two reports by a pair of social workers (15) and an art therapist (16) working with nursing home residents revealed that paternalism decreased, mental alertness increased, a higher level of functioning was achieved, a sense of identity was better maintained, and more emotions concerning present circumstances were expressed when the elderly were provided an opportunity to reminisce. Far from the losing the person in the past, recollection served as points of departure for the revival of old interests and the development of new ones.

Informative reminiscing is particularly amenable to group sharing, as Ebersole demonstrated in her nursing home work (17). Groups focussing on recollection have brought people together in the name of therapy, fellowship, education and artistic creation. Lewis and Butler's intergenerational life-cycle groups had a frankly psychotherapeutic goal (18): to help young and old to become more secure in their sense of identity, worth and perspective by re-experiencing the past through each other's lives. Poetry and art therapies work through unresolved problems by calling up long-buried thoughts and feelings in resonance with the reading of a poem or the creation of a picture or sculpture.

Recreational reminiscence groups may have a social or educational setting. Meyerhoff and Tufte conducted a weekly "Life History" class in which taped discussions of participant-chosen topics became a collective historical chronicle (19). Recollections were more deliberately shaped as personal history in Western's memoir-writing classes (20). These groups concentrated on the individual creation of accurate and vivid records, suitable for magazine publication, library and historical society archives or family legacy. In Kaminsky's groups, the dreams and images of the past were recorded as collaborative poems as they emerged from lively conversational interchanges. Songwriting groups set their poetry to music (21).

All of these groups exhibit a wide variety of format but a remarkable unanimity of result. Group leaders noted that their members increased their awareness of the richness of personal experience and their responsiveness to each other. Can these benefits be secured for participants in oral history projects, where the events of the past, rather than the informants themselves, are the chief objects of concern? Admittedly, the therapeutic benefits of participation are a by-product, not a purpose, of the interviews. However, new historical projects present the opportunity to build in consideration for the needs of the interviewee, which has often been left to chance.

As a start, studies should be done on the psychosocial impact of participation in an oral history project. Ideally, a follow-up interview should be made to assess any new needs created by the project, from a desire to continue reminiscing with a confidant, to a wish to contact other interviewees, to referral for help with disturbing memories evoked during testimony. More radical yet is Butler's call for a synthesis of research and therapy (22). Recognizing that reviewing part of one's life for an oral history project can be an insightful and therapeutic experience, he urges that such projects be done in collaboration with other disciplines, including psychoanalysis and gerontology. Such a comprehensive approach would make the experience richer and safer for the informant, while producing a broader spectrum of source materials.

Evaluative Reminiscence

Evaluative reminiscence, the second category, is based primarily on Butler's concept of life review (23). It is an attempt to come to terms with old guilt, conflicts and defeats, and to find meaning in one's accomplishments. Through life review, an individual may attain the final developmental stage posited by Erikson (24), ego integrity: the acceptance of one's life history as right and inevitable.

In the past few years, there has been more experimental evidence concerning evaluative reminiscence. Defining life review as "psychologizing" about life-long personality and motivational trends, Coleman found that it was correlated in his study of sheltered housing residents with good adjustment in the present and negative feelings about the past (11). That is, those who were uneasy about their former lives were more likely to spend time re-evaluating them, if they had the ego strength to do so.

Lieberman and Falk also uncovered a good deal of what they labelled "cognitive restructuring" of memories (5). In their study of community residents, institutionalized elderly, and those on nursing home waiting lists, signs of this dramatization and simplification of life history were separated from current reminiscing behavior. They were viewed as a possible end-product of evaluative reminiscence, a sign that it may have occurred. People within a year of their death exhibited a low frequency of reminiscing and significant evidence of cognitive restructuring, suggesting that the re-evaluation process had been accomplished earlier. Coleman cited a corroborating study by Gorney, which reported more introspective activity in the 60's and 70's than in the 80's (11).

It seems that the live sense of mortality as one ages may be a more frequent triggering factor than the real approach of death itself. Indeed, Neugarten has described the vital part that review and re-assessment play earlier yet, in middle age (25). It seems clear that some degree of evaluative reminiscence is a common response to any major life change or developmental crisis. Nevertheless, an awareness of the reality of one's own death presents a major threat and potentially the greatest hazard for panic or despair.

Hence the need for what Butler called a "participant-observer" to assist the older person in the review (23). A major task of the confidant might be to prevent the reviewer from becoming stuck at some painful point in the past. As Marshall indicated, biography was viewed most positively when it ranged freely over the entire life cycle (12). Genealogies, scrapbooks, pilgrimages to significant places may all be included in the creation of the extensive autobiography that Lewis and Butler called "life review therapy" (18). Such an enterprise can disarm a guilty or hurtful recollection by reducing it to one small incident in the larger perspective of a lifetime. It may recall the innumerable factors involved which were not under the individual's control. It can demonstrate the growth made beyond former limitations, or, by shifting viewpoints, make a blessing of a bane.

An interesting new technique for harnessing the power of the past for personal renewal is the Journal Workshop developed by Ira Progoff (26), a

Jungian analyst. The atmosphere of this enterprise is not cognitive and social, but one of deep meditation. One begins by sitting quietly and experiencing the past event. The history of the participant is explored by listing its landmarks or steppingstones, then becoming still again to experience these in depth. Life's crossroads are re-entered by projecting one's self along roads formerly taken and not taken, remaining alert for signs that a missed chance is now a live option. This technique promises not only to stimulate and deepen the life review process, but also to open new doors to the present and future.

Obsessive Reminiscence

Unfortunately, both informative and evaluative reminiscence can become obsessive and dysfunctional. As Butler warned, if older people, overwhelmed by guilt or despair, are not able to accept their past, they may well become seriously agitated, depressed or suicidal (23). Obsessive reminiscing about a particular situation may not yield to life review therapy. Instead of taking a broader view of the past, it may be necessary to concentrate completely on the problematic experience. Particularly if the reminiscence unfolds without apparent affect, it is helpful to involve the sense of touch, smell and sound, as well as the visual memory. Progoff's technique of relating to a piece of the past as if to a "person" with a process and life history of its own, can provide a route to its inner workings. Similarly, the methods of psychodrama are useful in providing reminiscers with the opportunity to say and feel what they never allowed themselves to express, rather than merely rehashing what they recall. Pouring out stored-up thoughts and feelings may finally set them at rest.

Obsessive reminiscence may be precipitated by stress. Pincus noted that excessive reminiscence may result fron an ungratifying present life situation (14). It is a defense which prevents the development of new possibilities, as the older person withdraws from his surroundings and other people become too bored or discouraged to intrude. These recollections can be used to diagnose the anxieties underlying the current source of stress and to identify characteristic strengths, values and coping mechanisms. They provide some direction for the essential efforts to relieve the stress, to find new outlets, and to provide feedback about the disruption obsessive reminiscence creates in relationships.

Mourning is another occasion in which prolonged, obsessive reminiscence can be maladaptive. Preoccupation with thoughts and images of the lost person or object is, of course, a central part of the grief process. However, mourning recollections which are intensely disruptive and long term signal a morbid grief reaction (27). Such a reaction may simply mean that the mourner has not been able to find any satisfactory replacement for the loss, a complication for which the elderly are certainly at high risk. On the other hand, any new attachments may be blocked by failure to resolve the grief. Full discharge of emotion may be prevented by insufficient opportunity to express feelings to an empathetic listener, the repression of negative emotions connected with the loss; or a life-long inability to really feel one's feelings so that one does not know how to mourn. Guilt over the anger felt at being abandoned or over any real or imagined trespass is especially troublesome, because the mourner may feel unworthy of recuperating and may resist help. Indeed, any change may be rejected as a betrayal of the former relationship.

Clearly, techniques which stimulate the full expression of emotion, like life review therapy, psychodrama and Progoff's journal, are indicated. A guided, in-depth re-experiencing of the entire relationship can be helpful in allowing the release of negative feelings in association with situations less threatening than the death itself. Again, the goal should not be to cut off the obsessive reminiscence completely, but rather to focus it so that it can be used in the healing process until it is no longer needed.

On the other end of the spectrum are those who cannot mourn. Delayed mourning may be part of a more general inability to reminisce. McMahon and Rhudick painted a dismal picture of those veterans in their study who did no reminiscing (7). Severely depressed, they had a much higher mortality rate than their better adjusted fellows. While it might be suspected that the lack of reminiscence among depressed people is just a function of symptomatic social withdrawal, Coleman's study reported no difference in the amount of conversation for his poorly adjusted non-reminiscers (11). He identified a definite syndrome of low satisfaction with both the past and present, and lack of reminiscing. Such pervasive joylessness indicates a profound alienation from characteristic sources of pleasure and direction.

The hope is always that a descent into memory will change and heal, and help the older adult to move toward the resurrected objectives that William Carlos Williams discovered. It may be that most older people do not reminisce significantly more. It is certainly true that all reminiscence is not healthy or functional. But, through creative attention to its content and function, reminiscence can become the fertile ground for a new growth in confidence and energy.

Reference Notes

1. P. Cameron, "The Generation Gap: Time Orientation," *Gerontologist* 12 (1972), pp. 117–19.

2. D. A. Chiriboga and L. Gigy, "Perspectives on Life Course," in *Four Stages of Life*, ed.

M. F. Lowenthal, M. Thurnber, and D. A. Chiriboga (San Francisco: Jossey-Bass, 1975), pp. 122–45.

3. L. M. Giambra, "Daydreaming across the Lifespan: Late Adolescent to Senior Citizen," *International Journal of Aging and Human Development* 5 (1974), pp. 115–40.

4. L. M. Giambra, "Daydreaming about the Past: The Time Setting of Spontaneous Thought Intrusion," *Gerontologist* 17 (1977), pp. 35–38.

5. M. A. Lieberman and J. M. Falk, "The Remembered Past as a Source of Data for Research on the Life Cycle," *Human Development* 14 (1971), pp. 132–41.

6. S. Sherman and R. J. Havighurst, "An Exploratory Study of Reminiscence, Abstract," *Gerontologist* 10 (1970), p. 42.

7. A. W. McMahon and P. J. Rhudick, "Reminiscing in the Aged: An Adaptational Response," in *Psychodynamic Studies on Aging*, ed. S. Levin and R. Kahana (New York: International Universities Press, 1967).

8. R. J. Havighurst and A. Glasser, "An Exploratory Study of Reminiscence," *Journal of Gerontology* 27 (1972), pp. 245–53.

9. W. Boylin, S. K. Gordon, and M. E. Nehrke, "Reminiscing and Ego Integrity in Institutionalized Males," *Gerontologist* 16 (1976), pp. 118–24.

10. C. N. Lewis, "Reminiscing and Self-Concept in Old Age," *Journal of Gerontology* 26 (1970), pp. 240–43.

11. P. G. Coleman, "Measuring Reminiscence Characteristics from Conversation as Adaptive Features of Old Age," *International Journal of Aging and Human Development* 5 (1974), pp. 281–94.

12. V. W. Marshall, "The Life Review as a Social Process, Abstract," *Gerontologist* 14 (1974), p. 69.

13. C. G. Jung, *Modern Man in Search of a Soul* (New York: Harcourt, Brace and World, 1933), p. 110.

14. A. Pincus, "Reminiscence in Aging and Its Implications for Social Work Practice," *Social Work* 15 (1970), pp. 47–53.

15. J. Liton and S. C. Olstein, "Therapeutic Aspects of Reminiscence," *Social Casework* 50 (1969), pp. 263–68.

16. I. Dewdney, "An Art Therapy Program for Geriatric Patients," in *Art Therapy*, ed. E. Uhlman and P. Dackinger (New York: Schocken, 1975).

17. P. Ebersole, "Reminiscing," *American Journal of Nursing* 79 (1976), pp. 1304–1305.

18. M. Lewis and R. N. Butler, "Life Review Therapy: Putting Memories to Work in Individual and Group Psychotherapy," *Geriatrics* 29 (1974), pp. 165–73.

19. B. Meyerhoff and V. Tufte, "Life History as Integration: An Essay on an Experiential Model," *Gerontologist* 15 (1975), pp. 541–43.

20. L. Western, "How to Write Your Memoirs," typescript (Port Angeles, Wash.: Port Angeles Senior Citizen Center).

21. M. Kaminsky, *What's Inside You—It Shines Out of You* (New York: Horizon Press, 1975).

22. R. N. Butler, "Studies of Creative People and the Creative Process after Middle Life," in *Psychodynamic Studies on Aging: Creativity, Reminiscing, and Dying*, ed. S. Levin and R. H. Kahana (New York: International Universities Press, 1967).

23. R. N. Butler, "The Life Review: An Interpretation of Reminiscence in the Aged," in *Middle Age and Aging*, ed. B. Neugarten (Chicago: University of Chicago Press, 1968), pp. 486–96.

24. E. Erikson, *Childhood and Society* (New York: Norton, 1950), pp. 268–69.

25. B. Neugarten, "The Awareness of Middle Age," in *Middle Age and Aging*, ed. Neugarten, pp. 93–98.

26. I. Progoff, *At a Journal Workshop* (New York: Dialogue House, 1975).

27. E. Lindeman, "Symptomatology and Management of Acute Grief," in *Crisis Intervention*, ed. H. J. Parad (New York: Family Service Association of America, 1965), pp. 7–17.

Bibliography

Boylin, W., S. K. Gordon, and M. E. Nehrke. "Reminiscing and Ego Integrity in Institution-alized Males." *Gerontologist* 16 (1976), pp. 118–24.

Butler, R. N. "The Life Review: An Interpretation of Reminiscence in the Aged." In *Middle Age and Aging*, ed. B. Neugarten. Chicago: University of Chicago Press, 1968.

———. "Looking Forward to What?" *American Behavioral Scientist* 14 (1970), pp. 121–28.

———. "Successful Aging and the Role of the Life Review." *Journal of the American Geriatric Society* 22 (1974), pp. 529–35.

Cameron, P. "The Generation Gap: Time Orientation." *Gerontologist* 12 (1972), pp. 117–19.

Chiriboga, D. A., and Gigy, L. "Perspectives on Life Course." In *Four Stages of Life*, ed. M. F. Lowenthal, M. Thurnber, and D. A. Ciriboga. San Francisco: Jossey-Bass, 1975.

Coleman, P. G. "Measuring Reminiscence Characteristics from Conversation as Adaptive Features of Old Age." *International Journal of Aging and Human Development* 5 (1974), pp. 281–94.

Dewdney, I. "An Art Therapy Program for Geriatric Patients." In *Art Therapy*, ed. E. Ulman and P. Dachinger. New York: Schocken, 1975.

Ebersole, P. "Reminiscing." *American Journal of Nursing* 79 (1976), pp. 1304–1305.

Erikson, E. *Childhood and Society*. New York: Norton, 1950.

Giambra, L. M. "Daydreaming across the Lifespan: Late Adolescent to Senior Citizen." *International Journal Aging and Human Development* 5 (1974), pp. 115–40.

———. "Daydreaming about the Past: The Time Setting of Spontaneous Thought Intrusion." *Gerontologist* 17 (1977), pp. 35–38.

Havighurst, R. J., and R. Glasser. "An Exploratory Study of Reminiscence." *Journal of Gerontology* 27 (1972), pp. 245–53.

Jung, C. G. *Modern Man in Search of a Soul*. New York: Harcourt, Brace and World, 1933.

Kaminsky, M. *What's Inside You, It Shines Out of You*. New York: Horizon Press, 1975.

Keen, S., and A. V. Fox. *Telling Your Story: A Guide to Who You Are and Who You Can Be*. New York: New American Library, 1973.

Levin, S., and R. Kahana, eds. *Psychodynamic Studies on Aging: Creativity, Reminiscing, and Dying*. New York: International Universities Press, 1967.

Lewis, C. N. "Reminiscing and Self-Concept in Old Age." *Journal of Gerontology* 26 (1971), pp. 240–43.

Lieberman, M. A., and J. M. Flak. "The Remembered Past as a Source of Data for Research on the Life Cycle." *Human Development* 14 (1971), pp. 132–41.

Lindeman, E. "Symptomatology and Management of Acute Grief." In *Crisis Intervention*, ed. H. J. Parad. New York: Family Service Association of America, 1965.

Liton, J., and S. C. Olstein. "Therapeutic Aspects of Reminiscence." *Social Casework* 50 (1969), pp. 263–68.

Marshall, V. W. "The Life Review as a Social Process, Abstract." *Gerontologist* 14 (1976), p. 69.

Meyerhoff, B., and V. Tufte. "Life History as Integration: An Essay on an Experiential Model." *Gerontologist* 15 (1975), pp. 541–43.

Neugarten, B. "The Awareness of Middle Age." In *Middle Age and Aging*, ed. B. Neugarten. Chicago: University of Chicago Press, 1968.

Pincus, A. "Reminiscence in Aging and Its Implications for Social Work Practice." *Social Work* 15:3 (1970), pp. 47–53.

Progoff, I. *At a Journal Workshop*. New York: Dialogue House, 1975.

Sherman, S., and R. J. Havighurst. "An Exploratory Study of Reminiscence, Abstract." *Gerontologist* 10 (1970), p. 42.

Vansina, J. *Oral Tradition: A Study in Historical Methodology.* Chicago: Aldine, 1965. (See chapter 9 of the present volume)

Western, L. "How to Write Your Memoirs." Typescript. Port Angeles, Wash.: Senior Citizen Center.

Zeigler, B. "Life Review in Art Therapy with the Aged." *American Journal of Art Therapy* 15:1 (1976), pp. 47–50.

29

Oral Historians
and Long-Term Memory

John Neuenschwander

*Our next reading further explores the psychological dimensions of memory.
The specific characteristics of long-term memory, like other aspects of the
context in which oral history is performed, frequently pass unexamined during researching, interviewing, and fund raising. Here John Neuenschwander, a writer on oral history and education, steps back from the profession's
everyday tasks to question its implicit beliefs regarding memory and historical reconstruction.*

*After summarizing various schools of psychological thought on remembrance, the author urges researchers to incorporate into their research design some tests of long-term memory and to interview participants about
their own views of their memory. A thorough documentation of the effects
(and structure) of memories held over long periods of time might radically
alter the ways in which oral historians interpret these sources.
Neuenschwander's brief guide to the various schools of thought on memory
may help encourage such documentation.*

*John Neuenschwander is a professor at Carthage College in Wisconsin,
where he directs the oral history project. In his book* Oral History as a
Teaching Approach *(1976), he offers teachers a practical approach to
using oral history in the classroom. In* Kenosha Retrospective *(1981) he
developed an award-winning biographical approach to local history.*

*"Remembrance of Things Past: Oral Historians and Long-Term
Memory" appeared originally in the* Oral History Review 6 *(1978),
pp. 45–53.*

AS A GROUP, oral historians have more interest in and contact with
human memory than any other professionals except psychiatrists and psychologists. Yet despite the centrality of memory to
their task, they have not considered it a suitable topic for study. A review
of Manfred Waserman's *Bibliography of Oral History*, for example, reveals

only a handful of articles on that subject.[1] This is not to say that oral historians do not worry or speculate about human memory. Whenever they gather at professional meetings their shop talk invariably turns to anecdote swapping about strong, weak, and unique memories. The purpose of this article is to examine some of the unstated assumptions that most oral historians share in light of the predominant theories of long-term memory among psychologists. Some suggestions as to how oral history methodology might be brought into closer congruence with these theories will also be offered.

The reasons oral historians have neglected the study of memory are not hard to locate. As participants in an academic growth industry, most oral historians so concentrate upon gathering interviews that there is little opportunity to embark on the study of anything so nebulous as long-term memory. And nebulous it can be, especially if one gets caught up in the ongoing debate among psychologists and other social scientists over the essence of memory. The quantity and complexity of that literature compose a thicket that few oral historians have wished to penetrate.[2] Thus when a prominent psychologist like Robert Menninger told an Oral History Colloquium that "memory is difficult to define and to study," it is no wonder that oral historians were quite content to go back to collecting memory claims rather than trying to study them.[3]

Although this state of affairs has persisted for almost two decades, the time has come for oral historians to begin to grapple directly with the essence of memory. For as William Moss of the John F. Kennedy Library noted several years ago in his provocative essay "The Future of Oral History":

. . . if oral history is to be respected, and if it is to justify a national association in its name, it would seem proper that scholars who use the product and institutions that fund projects have a means by which to judge the quality of what is being done. Oral historians should, out of sheer self respect, refuse to allow continued measure of their worth to be in terms of quantity and diversity of product and projects.[4]

Without a far deeper commitment to the study of long-term memory than most oral historians have today, it is difficult to imagine how quality control can be implemented.

All of this is not to say that most oral historians have no theoretical position on memory. The theory they hold to, however, is an implicit one, lying buried in oral history methodology. This methodology, in turn, has become virtually standardized. For what were once suggested or tentative guidelines on interviewing, have in recent years become codified and stand as the rules for success that are held out to the uninitiated.[5]

The theory of long-term memory that coats standard interview guidelines goes something like this: Human memory is a vast storehouse of life experiences. What and how much people remember will vary due to individual differences in such things as life style, personality and state of health. Whether an interviewee can or will share the contents of this storehouse is heavily dependent upon the interpersonal skill of the oral history interviewer. Ninety-nine per cent of what the interviewee does share should be accepted as an honest if not a wholly accurate account of what transpired. Experience has shown that the stronger the rapport between interviewer and interviewee, the richer the return in terms of source material.

While a thorough grounding in written materials is always one of the interview guidelines, oral historians are famous for being quite ambiguous about how much preparation is enough.[6] If one takes all of the commonly recommended interview guidelines into account, this is understandable since most of them have to do with building and maintaining rapport. Thus interpersonal skills rather than mastery of background materials and corroboration seemst o be the preferred method of stimulating memory. It can hardly be otherwise if the major result of rapport building is to convince an interviewee that through extra effort on his and the interviewer's parts, they can produce from memory an accurate and significant corpus of information. Once such terms have been set down, even if the interviewer has done a great deal of homework, to shift the memory stimulus from warm feelings to cold facts is unthinkable.

How does this theory of memory and memory stimulus compare to theories of long-term memory in psychology? While my determination of what are the most widely accepted theories or models may well be open to question, my purpose here is to offer some basis of comparison with the implicit theory found in the oral history methodology. Two distinct traditions or paradigms are discernible in the study of memory. Hermann Ebbinghaus, usually considered the first psychologist to study memory, in 1885 published a monograph appropriately entitled *Memory*. The work was based on carefully-controlled laboratory studies of short-term memory. He was most interested in those factors that aided or hindered the learning and retention of nonsense symbols like TAX, ZIN and VEC. Although Ebbinghaus' interest in memory was actually far broader, including exhaustive self study, his laboratory approach to the study of memory soon became the dominant method and still is today.[7]

In 1932, a British psychologist, Sir Frederick Bartlett, published a seminal work entitled *Remembering*. Unlike Ebbinghaus, whom he criticized for being too narrow and artificial in his approach, Bartlett conducted experiments using materials found in everyday life and dealing with longer memory spans. In his most famous experiment, he read a North American folk tale to a group and then studied the changes in structure and content in successive recall attempts. He found that while facts were dropped, added, and invented with each successive recall, the end product was not so much a distortion of the original as a simpler, more functional rendition. This led him to advance a schematic theory of long-term memory. According to his theory people remember by organizing things within the framework of their experiences. Thus for Bartlett the process of recalling an event or episode from the past is essentially one of reconstruction. Instead of drawing forth a holistic memory unit when the need arises, people energize the relevant schemata and recreate anew the event or incident they are attempting to revive.

This theory not only went beyond Ebbinghaus' work but diverged significantly from Sigmund Freud's view of memory. Although he never undertook the study of memory in its entirety, Freud placed great emphasis on forgetting as a means of repressing painful experiences. His assumption, which Bartlett's work challenged, was that painful memories were stored holistically. Retrieval through psychotherapy was thus a matter of convincing an individual to lower his or her defenses and let the memories surface.

Today, most psychiatrists no longer adhere to this rather simplistic theory of forgetting. In some respects they have moved into Bartlett's corner. For many have come to view long-term memory as an emotionally adaptive mechanism in which "recollection changes with the change in one's view of oneself and the world."[8]

Since the early 1950's a group of psychologists using a computer model have developed a theory of memory that incorporates both Bartlett's schemata and to a lesser extent psychiatrists' concern with the influence of affective behavior.[9] This theory is best known as information processing. Long-term memory from this vantage point is a vast storehouse of semantic and episodic traces. The former are verbal symbols that record non-affective information, such as, school busses are yellow. Episodic traces are thought to record events or actions and seem to be stored in a time-line fashion. According to proponents of the information processing theory, long-term recall is essentially a matter of reconstruction. A typical example of this process is as follows:

Interviewer: What was the CCC Camp like at Devil's Lake?
Interviewee: Gee, that was a long time ago. Well let's see, I was sent there in 1937 or was it 38? No, it was 37 because that was the year of the great drought. I remember that because my dad just up and left the farm in June when the crops all withered and died.

If we accept the ideas of Frederick Bartlett and the information processing theorists that long-term memory is basically a matter of reconstruction, what are the implications for oral history? At first glance there seem to be major areas of agreement between their theory and the implicit one that oral historians operate on. They both consider the information storage potential in long-term memory to be infinite and recognize that the nature of the recall stimulus has a great deal to do with the response. They diverge, however, most importantly on the accuracy of the information drawn from long-term memory. Whereas most oral historians tend to be generally sanguine about the trustworthiness of the material they extract (or they would be doing something else), most psychologists are deeply skeptical. They prefer to study short-term memory and have given scant attention to long-term reminiscence. Oral historians encounter it all the time, but their uncritical interest has precluded any serious study on their part. Thus the study of reminiscence as a factor of long-term memory has fallen beyond the reach of the psychologist and beneath the grasp of the oral historian.

The term reminiscence as used here refers to the practice of repeatedly recounting or thinking about particular events and incidents in one's life. Such things as favorite anecdotes, accounts and stories fit under this heading, as well as very private episodes that we frequently recall only to ourselves. Every interviewee has a store of such accounts that oral historians spend a good part of their time getting on tape. By virtue of the information and perspective that oral historians bring to interviews, they certainly tap unrehearsed memories as well. On balance, however, since most oral history interviews are with people over 60, and senescence or aging is known to accelerate reminiscence in long-term memory, I suspect that most oral history interviews contain far more rehearsed than unrehearsed memories.

The relationship between reminiscence and refabrication is not at all clear. One could argue that frequent reminiscence about major episodes might well serve to insulate them from the adaptive process of refabrication. Such accounts might almost be frozen in time rather than constantly changing as claimed by Bartlett and the information processing theorists. A contrary view would be that some episodes and incidents are recalled more frequently than others and thus may be more holistic but still continue to change in content and emphasis due to the nature of long-term memory. Whether this is a valid question for oral historians to consider will ultimately be determined by experimental interviewing.

But who will conduct such experimental interviews? The vast majority of oral historians, as already noted, simply move from one project to the next with little apparent theoretical concern about how they are practicing their craft. Yet oral historians could incorporate some experimental interviewing into many ongoing projects.

An example of how this could be done comes from a project I worked on during 1977 involving survivors of the American Expeditionary Force in

Siberia. This contingent originally numbered between ten and twelve thousand American soldiers who were stationed in Siberia from August 1918, until April 1920. Although recruited or drafted, for the most part, to fight in The Great War, they spent most of their time guarding and maintaining sections of the Trans-Siberian Railroad. Due to the extreme political ferment in Russia, President Woodrow Wilson determined that they should remain in Siberia after the Armistice was signed but that under no circumstances were they to intervene directly in Russian affairs. This decision soon placed the American troops in the inenviable position of being disliked and distrusted by all factions in Siberia. Although daily physical danger was not common (scores of Americans were, however, killed in ambushes and firefights) the harsh climate, difficult living conditions and their ambiguous role made their experience a trying one.

Given the lengthy passage of time and the unusual character of their military experience, I was interested in trying to determine whether repeated public reminiscence had created a stylized pattern of recall. In other words, would the Siberian veterans who enjoyed recounting their exploits at VFW posts and other social gatherings tend to emphasize similar aspects of the experience and perhaps be less reliable? What in turn would the veterans who rarely discussed the experience consider important?

My study from the start was plagued by both financial and time shortages. Since most of the survivors of the Siberian Expedition who live east of the Mississippi River are widely scattered, it was possible to conduct only a limited number of interviews. The results were far from conclusive. Noticeable structural similarities were found among the accounts provided by veterans who reminisced frequently. The relative accuracy of their accounts when compared with the official records of the American Expeditionary Force-Siberia at the National Archives was markedly lower than the accounts provided by veterans who rarely recounted their experience in public. While the results of this study were mixed at best, it at least points up the opportunity that oral historians have to engage in experimental interviewing.

The potential value of such efforts cannot be overemphasized. For the uncertainty that exists regarding the nature of long-term memory makes it imperative that oral historians employ the most effective and rigorous methodology. Ironically, it has often been the interviewees who have questioned standard interviewing procedure. In his representation to the Second Oral History Collquium, the noted publisher Alfred Knopf expressed considerable doubt about the memoir he had given: "My feeling is that people when they talk freely to a tape recorder depend much too much on the 'infallibility' of their memory, and I used to find myself interpolating now and then 'Please don't use this without checking it.' "[10] Another example of interviewee concern was General George C. Marshall's admonishment to his biographer, Forrest Pogue:

You must be very careful not to publish in any way or broadcast or arrange for later publication just out of hand what I say here—speaking off the cuff and at considerable length of course at times when I'm a little bit tired. I am covering a vast amount of ground in a short time.[11]

Finally, a comment by the world famous conductor and musician Pablo Casals to his oral historian points up another area of interviewee concern: "Reading your book has awakened many thoughts in my mind which would perhaps be out of place to record here: you would have to start a new chapter—discussions on our discussions—and where would that lead us?"[12]

It could lead to a healthier skepticism about the memory claims of interviewees and a different emphasis in interview techniques. A recent book by Peter Friedlander, *The Emergence of a UAW Local 1936–1939*, is a good example of an interviewer doing what Knopf, Marshall and Casals alluded to. Friedlander's book is about the formation of Local #229 (UAW) at the Detroit Parts Company. His research consisted of a thorough immersion in available written sources and extensive, in-depth interviews with Edmund Kord, the first President of the Local. From the beginning of their association, Friedlander made it clear that he wished not so much to gather rehearsed memory claims as to work with Kord in refabricating as many aspects as possible of the organizing years. The collaboration extended intermittently over several years and certainly exemplifies the friendly but decidedly interrogative and corroborative process that Allan Nevins originally thought oral history should be all about.

At this point, the most argumentative readers could raise a host of objections such as:

1) Most oral historians gather materials for archival rather than their own scholarly interest.

2) There are so many significant people to interview there is simply not enough time for the sort of preparation and depth interviewing advocated in this article.

3) What you advocate would scare most neophytes away and rather than have them do poor oral history on their own, we should at least give them the rudiments of how it should be done with the greatest emphasis on interpersonal skills.

On the surface such rejoinders seem perfectly sound and logical. Yet if oral historians knowingly settle for less rigor in their methodology than they know there can or should be—what will be the result? One very obvious one is the continuation of the stepchild status that oral history holds among historians and other social scientists. As Ronald Grele noted recently: "The dominant tendency [among historians] has been to be overly enthusiastic in public print and deeply suspicious in private conversation."[13] If one considers for a moment how most historians rank sources their attitude becomes more understandable. For nine out of ten historians would probably still subscribe today to the general rule that "reliability is always inversely proportional to time-lapse between event and recollection, the closer the document is to the event it narrates the better it is likely to be for historical purposes."[14]

The relatively low marks that autobiographies and memoirs receive from historians as sources is an example of how this rule is applied. Given the similarity of oral history materials to such personal documents as autobiographies, it is not surprising that historians do not accept oral sources more readily. A defense often heard from oral historians is that the interviewer's presence together with the relative spontaneity of the interview genreally inhibit an interviewee from whitewashing the past or twisting it to his advantage, as he so often does in written autobiographies and memoirs. But if most oral historians continue to exalt the memories of interviewees and allow them to record whatever happens to come to mind, the difference between a traditional autobiography and one induced by oral history seems minimal.

In conclusion I would like to suggest some ways that the major points in this article might be made operational:

1) Oral historians who are seriously engaged in the archival or scholarly use of oral history must reemphasize the importance of thorough preparation in written sources. Only when interviewers know the ground they are covering and seek to corroborate the interviewee's memory claims can they hope to avoid the currently prevalent "you were there and must know syndrome."

2) Oral historians can and must begin to seriously study long-term memory. What is needed are studies of how interviewee memory claims differ over time. Reinterviewing narrators after 5, 10 and 15 year intervals may provide helpful insights on long-term memory. Likewise, studies on differing responses to male/female interviewers are needed. Oral historians should also build into their interview format questions about memory. Explanations of how interviewees think their memories work could prove helpful.

3) Finally, oral historians need to make more interdisciplinary pilgrimages into psychology, anthropology and sociology to gain perspective on current methodology. Current members of the Oral History Association seem to have lost the interdisciplinary curiosity that was so prevalent during the early years.

What this article amounts to is an endorsement and plea for a dictum offered by William Moss in his previously mentioned "Future of Oral History": THERE WILL BE MORE ORAL HISTORY AND LESS TAPE RECORDING. [15]

Notes

1. See William W. Cutler III, "Accuracy in Oral History Interviewing," *Historical Methods Newsletter* 3 (June 1970), pp. 1–7 (see chapter 7 of the present volume); David F. Musto and Saul Benison, "Studies on the Accuracy of Oral Interviews," in Gould P. Colman, ed., *The Fourth National Colloquium on Oral History* (New York: Oral History Association, 1970), pp. 167–81; Alice M. Hoffman, "Reliability and Validity in Oral History," *Today's Speech* 22 (Winter 1974), pp. 23–27 (see chapter 5 of the present volume).

2. According to some psychologists it is impossible to separate memory from other key functions of the brain, such as learning, perception and thinking. See, for example, Michael J. A. Howe, *Introduction to Human Memory: A Psychological Approach* (New York: Harper and Row, 1970), pp. 3–4.

3. Robert Menninger, "Some Psychological Factors Involved in Oral History Interviewing," *Oral History Review* 3 (1975), p. 68.

4. William W. Moss, "The Future of Oral History," *Oral History Review* 3 (1975), p. 9.

5. While it can be argued that such factors as program resources, objectives and interviewer diversity still provide some variation in application, since Willa Baum's pioneering work the refrain from oral history manuals and national workshop panels has been largely the same. See Willa Baum, *Oral History for the Local History Society*, 2d ed. (Nashville: American Association for State and Local History, 1974); John A. Neuenschwander, *Oral History as a Teaching Approach* (Washington, D.C.: National Education Association, 1976); Gary L. Shumway and William G. Hartley, *An Oral History Primer* (Fullerton: California State University, 1973).

6. Saul Benison is one of the few who is not. He recommends thirty hours of preparation for each hour of interviewing. Saul Benison, "Oral History: A Personal View," in *Modern Methods in the History of Medicine*, ed. Edwin Clarke (London: Athlone Press, 1971), p. 287.

7. Alan D. Baddeley, *The Psychology of Memory* (New York: Basic, 1976), p. 7.

8. Leon Salzman, "Memory and Psychotherapy," in *Phenomenology of Memory*, ed. Erwin W. Strauss and Richard M. Griffith (Pittsburgh: Duquesne University Press, 1970), p. 134.

9. Two excellent books on information processing theory and memory are: Geoffrey R. Loftus and Elizabeth F. Loftus, *Human Memory: The Processing of Information* (Hillsdale, N.J.: Erlbaum, 1976), and Donald A. Norman, *Memory and Attention: An Introduction to Human Information Processing* (New York: Wiley, 1969).

10. Alfred A. Knopf, "A Contributor Reviews His Memoir," *The Second National Colloquium on Oral History* (New York: Oral History Association, 1968), p. 26.

11. Forrest C. Pogue, *George C. Marshall*, vol. 2, *Ordeal and Hope, 1939–1943* (New York: Viking, 1965), pp. 443–44.

12. J. Ma. Corredor, *Conversations with Casals* (New York: Dutton, 1956), p. i.

13. Ronald J. Grele, "Movement without Aim: Methodological and Theoretical Problems in Oral History," in *Envelopes of Sound*, ed. Ronald J. Grele (Chicago: Precedent Publishing, 1975), p. 127.

14. Louis Gottschalk, "The History and the Historical Document," in *The Use of Personal Documents in History, Anthropology, and Sociology* (New York: Social Science Research Council, 1945). p. 16.

15. Moss, "The Future of Oral History," p. 5.

30

Radio and the Public Use of Oral History

David Dunaway

Our final essay on fields related to oral history brings us to the subject of broadcast media, an area where professional oral historians are increasingly active.

As historians reach out to the public, they often find themselves involved in publishing and broadcasting their interviews. This article examines radio, one medium for bringing oral narratives to wide audiences. As the costs of film and television rise, and as the public's interest in oral history grows, the relatively inexpensive medium of radio offers continuing possibilities for public programs. With patience, the right equipment, and the right guidance, any oral or community history group can produce its own programs. David Dunaway, this volume's co-editor, explores the advantages and disadvantages of radio production based on oral sources.

David Dunaway teaches folklore and oral history at the University of New Mexico. The author of an award-winning biography based on oral interviews, How Can I Keep From Singing: Pete Seeger *(1981), he has spent the last decade working as a producer and consultant on two dozen radio and television documentaries, including "Pie in the Sky," a historical radio series funded by the National Endowment for the Arts.*

RADIO BROADCASTING and oral history interviewing seem, at first glance, made for one another. Radio producers search constantly for thoughtful, provocative interviews; oral historians seek an audience beyond library stacks, a public for their work. Documentarians, academic and public sector historians, community organizers, local history groups, educators, interested citizens—all could benefit from a marriage between history and radio.

Oral history archives can provide, when broadcast, an open window into history, one custom built for radio and rich with the color and pacing of real speech. Many interviews are of gem quality, though considerable mining and polishing may be required before the jewels are extracted. They carry greater depth than for-radio interviews; they are usually transcribed (and transcription makes for easy editing and assembling of programs); and they involve not certified experts but us regular folks, the narrators and the listeners, in the making and the transmission of history.

Why, then, aren't radio producers courting oral history archives? Before any wedding between the two fields can take place, radio and oral history producers must understand each other far better than they do today. Nevertheless, such an event will be worth waiting for, because radio broadcasting may be the medium of choice for public use of oral history.

To understand the relationship between oral history and radio, we will explore the advantages and disadvantages of combining the two fields, the differing aims of producers of radio and oral history, and the production of a radio program based on oral history interviews.

This survey is addressed to three audiences: oral historians who wish to make their tapes available for public use through media presentation; historians who wish to produce radio programs themselves, basing them on oral history interviews; and radio producers considering oral history archives as a source for programs on historical subjects. While our subject is radio, many of the observations apply to film or video use of oral historical sources and to the related fields in the humanities which rely on oral sources (folklore, anthropology, etc.).

History and Radio

Since the early days of radio broadcasting, theoreticians have realized the medium's power to use voices to connect a people with their past.[1] Pioneer radio productions such as "History Highlights" and "March of Time" used interviews and dramatic reconstructions to effect intimacy and create an understanding of an epoch.[2] The beginnings of radio drama employed actual interviews alongside researched and scripted historical treatments.[3] And since radio began, social scientists interested in cultural preservation have speculated on how the medium links isolated communities with their traditions.[4] Broadcasting has always relied on language and sound; thus the same words which individuals use to fashion history as they saw it can be recorded by either the oral historian or the radio producer. Old radio broadcasts have themselves become valuable documents for historians of the recent past, as English historian Paul Thompson has noted.[5]

Oral history has been used most effectively by radio in Europe and Canada, where sound archives are often associated with publicly supported broadcasting systems. Thus the British Broadcasting Corporation (BBC) produces some sixty programs per *week* which take material from archival sources, and the Foundation for Film Science in Utrecht is actively involved in media production using historical interviews. One of the leading groups in this effort has been the European Broadcast Union's Radio Programme Committee. Founded in 1967, this group takes as part of its mandate "the programme possibilities of sound archives." To this day, sound archivists have an edge over oral historians in using radio to promote public consciousness of the sound environment; this advantage to a great extent results from the work of professional organizations such as the International Association of Sound Archives and the U.S. Association for Recorded Sound Collections.[6]

In Canada, broadcasters interested in oral history have found a home in the Canadian Broadcasting Corporation (CBC).[7] Starting in the early 1960s, Imbert Orchard, the Cambridge-trained dramatist and radio producer, recorded almost 1000 interviews for the CBC, "drawing from them the basis of some 200 radio programs."[8] In his work and writings, Orchard has developed the most sophisticated analyses of radio's use of historical interviews; he coined the term "aural history," referring to historical recordings of sounds. Others in the CBC have helped make it a world center for radio use of history, particularly at the CBC Archives in Toronto and the Sound and Moving Image Division of the British Columbia's Provincial Archives.[9]

In the United States in the 1970s, the National Endowment for the Humanities and regional/state organizations have funded a number of award-winning radio series based on oral historical sources, though televised history programs have far outnumbered radio history projects.[10]

Advantages in Combining Radio and Oral History

Though radio and oral history involve distinct production operations, they can be joined, to their mutual benefit. As a medium of communication, radio has several inherent advantages for communicating the results and process of history.

Consider the nature of radio: the medium relies on sound, rather than on televised images, to achieve its effects. Listeners absorb the content without having to stop what they're doing; radio travels to where people are, in their cars, backyards, or kitchens. Listening does not disrupt the normal tempo of life. Americans already consume, on the average, three hours of radio daily. Using this popular medium avoids the difficulty of persuading the public to pick up a book and stop doing something else (much less read an unedited transcript). Furthermore radio, with its immediacy and speed, is a natural environment for sharing the voices of history. Unlike television or film, which require a suitable illustration for each sound, radio allows our minds to populate history from our own surroundings and to imagine the personalities behind the voices.

Radio production remains far less expensive than other broadcast media and also far less capital-intensive. Whereas professionally produced film or television documentaries cost from $1,500 to $5,000 per minute of finished product, radio's costs range around an eighth of that amount. This makes the medium particularly suitable for programs of less than national interest—local history and specialized topics. Instead of costly cameras, monitors, and editing bays (Super 8 and home video formats are more economical) radio can proceed with the equipment that an oral historian may already own: a microphone, two tape recorders, an inexpensive editing block, a razor blade. For sophisticated productions, more equipment will naturally be required, but it will still cost a fraction of the cost of equipment for television or film production.

Radio is also less complex to master, in part because the creative elements are limited to sound. Complete mastery of the process of radio production naturally demands a good deal of practice—as any art does. But the beginning oral historian, who already knows how to work a microphone and a recorder, could probably learn the elements and basic procedures of audio production in a matter of months or even weeks, if he or she was fiercely determined. With the assistance of a trained technician (and a consultant to supervise the balance between technical and content elements), an oral historian might assemble an informative documentary about a community's history in several months, using existing interviews. By comparison, a filmed documentary, involving costly and time-consuming laboratory work, can take years to finish. Funding sources understand these differences in cost and effort; state humanities councils, for example, are increasingly relying on radio grants to widen public understanding of the humanities.[11]

One of the spin-off advantages of using radio for oral history projects is that the broadcasting and production studios are widely distributed, and can be found even in the most rural locations. Commercial television, with its sizable capital investment, tends to produce air-quality material only in the largest communities, with smaller stations serving as broadcast outlets. Virtually every radio station now operating, on the other hand, could be used to produce oral history programs. And since radio stations have a legal obligation to produce local programs in the public interest, oral history project workers may discover that their local stations are enthusiastic about programs which beam a community's history back into that community. There are many precedents for locally produced, locally sponsored programs of public affairs; the oral historian with carefully recorded topical interviews might find a radio station willing to include them in a weekly hour-long slot. (One way to begin is to write the station's program director and propose selected topics.)

Radio producers would likewise benefit from the resources of oral history, for there is a chronic shortage of thoughtfully produced public affairs materials for radio. As large corporate chains control more and more broadcast outlets, they may need locally produced material to balance the networked feeds from Los Angeles or New York.

The Different Aims and Methods of History and Radio

To date, oral history and radio production have not melded in the United States; one obvious reason is that they represent entirely different disciplines, showing virtually no overlap in training, employment, and professional communities. (Interestingly enough, in countries with a national broadcasting service which customarily employs liberal arts graduates, such as the famed BBC, the ties between the two fields are stronger.)

Radio producers are trained most often as journalists in departments of journalism, communication, or speech. Their education emphasizes not content but technique: how to record, edit, conceptualize, and finally produce a radio program, regardless of subject. Even in areas where the training of radio professionals might be expected to overlap an oral historian's—such as the basic techniques of interviewing—different ends demand different procedures. The radio producer is taught to conduct an interview on a moment's notice, under adverse circumstances, and to ferret out a story, overcoming the reluctance of the subject with a combination of bravado, cunning, and persistence. He or she reaches the controversial points fast, evokes a show of emotion, and presents the material all in a short time frame.

The professional oral historian, on the other hand, is most likely educated in departments of history, literature, or a specialized field such as medicine or physics. As researchers, they regard the content as the whole; the complex and subtle requirements of media production sometimes prove intimidating or frustrating. No matter how anxious university-trained oral historians may be to have their inquiry reach a wide audience, most leave the academy with only a smattering of knowledge on the audio-technical side of their profession; few oral history classes, for instance, discuss microphone placement at any length. Rarer still is the technical education which would allow scholars to use up-to-date equipment and evaluate sound environments for extraneous noises.

Unlike the radio producer, the oral historian seeks historical detail in interviews, not emotional reactions; relying on the subject's cooperation and on lengthy research, the interview proceeds at a more gradual pace.

The historical interviewer gathers source materials, whose significance may be accurately determined only after years of further study.

In this context I will discuss some fundamental differences between radio and oral history, and I hope neither radio producer nor oral historian will take offense from the following general remarks. From the standpoint of a practitioner in both fields, the major differences concern time pressures, legal questions and authorship, and differing end products.

The production of radio works by deadline. Rarely, if ever, does time permit the producer to explore the nuances he or she sees, to find all their interview subjects at home or office, to take follow-up trips to the library to check and double-check facts. Historians, in contrast, proceed with extreme patience and caution. A single oral history project may continue for several years; by that time a radio producer or documentarian would have been sacked more than once.

There are several reasons for this different pace; one is the different legal considerations in each field. Radio producers are less concerned with questions of copyright, ownership, review, and storage of materials, matters over which full-time oral historians lose sleep. I do not mean to imply that radio producers are casual about their work—by no means! But a main concern of a media producer (and his boss) is not to violate laws of libel or invasion of privacy. The interviewer for radio assumes legal ownership (or at least broadcast privileges) for interviews and considers review of the interviewer by the subject not only impractical, but a violation of the producer's independence. By contrast, legal issues in oral history are sufficiently complex that few lawyers have had the patience even to survey the problems.[12]

Copyright and authorship may also be less complicated for the radio producer. While oral history is a joint, co-authored process, few radio producers would willingly share their byline with the government official interviewed for their program. Such sharing would open producers to charges of collusion with their sources, which challenges prevailing notions of an objective press and media. (In fact, in most productions sources "feed" information to the media in a state of mutual dependency.) Radio interviewing leans toward an adversary or investigative role, while oral history favors the collaborative, "as told to" approach. The for-radio interview relies on personalities to hold the audience's ear; some documentation may be lost in the press for entertainment.

These different approaches stem from differing end products and concerns. The final product of a thorough oral history session will be a narrator-approved transcript, deposited in a publicly accessible library or institution. This transcript and tape will be preserved whole, as a resource for future generations (though in the U.S., the transcript, rather than the tape, will circulate).

In radio the end product is also a tape, but one composed of a series of interviews, edited, encapsulated, rearranged, and mixed together with sound effects, music, and sound ambience. (It is not unusual to use only a minute of an hour's interview in the final production.) This highly crafted tape is often all that is preserved—the original recording may lie on the floor of the editing room or may be erased for recycling. The program is the fruit of the producer's labors, and it is judged by immediate audience response and by the production values demonstrated—not by its value to future generations of scholars. Thus different documents emerge from the differing goals of the historian and the producer—and each answers (or inspires) different questions. Radio producers work with action, sensation, emotion, and audio presence in their palette; the oral historian, with objectivity and verisimilitude. Both pursue truth, on different roads.

In recent years, these distinct approaches have begun to coalesce. Radio producers, particularly on the network level, spend increasing time on research and on clearing legal issues through counsel. Similarly the oral history profession may be shifting its attention from exclusively collecting raw data to analyzing, editing, and evaluating their sources—in short, to making history (based on transcripts as well as other sources).

For this confluence to become a collaboration, producers of oral history and radio can begin with a few simple steps. Oral historians, whatever their intentions for later use of their materials, should: (1) produce good quality recordings; (2) flag, in some fashion, the most striking statements in their interview; (3) use release forms which provide for the possibility of broadcast; (4) guide radio producers in the historical frame and main themes covered by the interview. They should encourage public use and access beyond print or tape circulation of interviews. This may require expanding the scope of collecting efforts to anticipate multiple use, such as collecting ambient sound during interviews—the sounds of a steel mill operation complementing an interview on steel working, for instance.

Ultimately, this process will involve the archivist in initiating contacts with the local broadcast community, as discussed earlier. Even where interviews were originally done on substandard equipment, an oral historian can guide a producer to the best narrators and the best questions so that the interview can be redone, where possible, quickly and effectively.

On the part of radio producers, a collaboration might involve: (1) duplicating interviews in their entirety *before* editing, and making arrangements to donate this copy to a local archive; (2) obtaining permissions from interviewees which would allow these tapes to be deposited; (3) learning about existing interviews already stored in archives (such interviews would only enhance the producer's own efforts); and (4) making more time available for historical programming.

Disadvantages of Combining Oral History and Radio

Before describing the assembly of a radio program from oral history interviews, we should consider the disadvantages and difficulties of combining radio and oral history from the standpoint of the historian. These might be summarized as getting permission, getting audiences, and getting quality.

Without a proper release from all narrators, no one should broadcast an interview; to do so invites legal and ethical dilemmas. The information confided in an interview might not be appropriate for public distribution; the speaker might harm or libel or embarrass. Oral historians are not investigative reporters, and as mentioned above, they work in different, more collaborative traditions. Radio broadcast constitutes "publication" in the legal sense of the term; information should not be published without the express consent of the interviewee.

Getting audiences for interviews involves publicizing the archives' holdings and making sure that use of the interviews will not present radio producers with headache-ridden, time-engulfing labor. Streamline the forms to be filled out, eliminate lengthy correspondence, routinely obtain clearance for broadcast. Provide high-quality duplications if at all possible (second- or third-generation copies are unacceptable for broadcast purposes). While some archivists may recoil at the thought of an edited interview, most realize that broadcasting a four-hour interview in its entirely would tax *any* listener.

Getting quality means obtaining, from the beginning, the very best recording which circumstances permit and handling and assembling the material with care and skill. Well-maintained equipment, skillfully manipulated, can add immeasurably to the potential of an oral history interview.

Bear in mind that not all oral history projects may be suited for adaptation to radio. Some historians may find, in the words of one archivist, that "the limitations of programme length, the producers' duty to entertain, the tendency of programme themes to become overly generalized or simplistic can be in contrast to the qualified or precise statements that historians are more accustomed to make."[13]

From the radio producer's standpoint, there may likewise be disadvantages to working with historians. Immersion in their subject may prevent historians from understanding how their findings would sound to an interested but uninitiated mass audience. Frequently the individualistic work patterns of historians make for a difficult transition into a collaborative production-team mode. And finally, using radio requires far more than rewriting an interview history so that it can be read aloud. Radio, like any medium of communication, has its own aesthetic boundaries which historians might profitably understand, even if they themselves do not intend to go into radio production.

Aesthetics of Radio Production

Radio, according to McLuhan's *Understanding Media*, "is that extension of the human nervous system which is matched only by human speech itself."[14] It is intimate and personal, carried from car to house to backyard. Ultimately, its aesthetic boundaries derive from its mimesis of speech and its ability to paint images and emotions in sound. Some characteristics which the oral historian will want to consider in using the medium are the ways in which radio portrays the presence, pacing, clarity, and unity of sound.

The precisely trained ear can listen to a few bars of music or a minute of interview and can guess the room in which it was recorded: its height, wall and floor coverings, the size of the space. This is because a tape recorder captures not only the sound source—a speaker or event—but the sound *environment* or soundscape: the collection of echoes, low-flying airplanes, refrigerator hums, and so forth. If you doubt this, try splicing together two interviews, one recorded in a large roomy hall, such as a church, and the other in a small book- and carpet-lined study. The first will sound boomy, hollow, and live; the second flat, more intimate. No sound environment is best for all purposes, and a producer may choose to enhance or neutralize background noise to suit his or her ends. An interview with a retired whaler might be effectively recorded outside, by the ocean. Imbert Orchard at the CBC successfully juxtaposed readings from the journals of early explorers with sounds recorded on a contemporary canoe trip down their route.[15]

Since all media production involves telescoping life, compressing into minutes events which might have taken years, pacing is critical in TV and radio. This constraint presents special problems for oral historians. Some interviewees, no matter how crucial their words, will not broadcast successfully. They may talk too slowly, "um" and "er" with distracting frequency, or vary their volume from one sentence to another. While editing can slice out pauses or digressions, there are limits to even the best sound surgery. Preparing a program for the general public involves a constant battle between historical content and its presentation in an effective, moving manner.

The clarity and fidelity of sound is of course maximally important in broadcasting recordings. Radio cannot portray the gestures which may make a point clear in the interview situation. Listeners depend on clear, crisp recordings to fill in the lost visual information. Thus high-quality microphones and recorders, intelligently positioned, should be used to catch the speech flow. Such equipment requires more funds and more training than many amateurs currently have for oral history recording, but much equipment can be borrowed or rented. Clarity comes from paying as close attention to the quality of the sound as to the content of the interview itself. The advice of folklorist Kenneth Goldstein is useful on this point:

Too many field workers treat their equipment as troublesome adjuncts to field work, and care little for the quality of their recordings as long as they are audible and transcriptions can be made from them. Yet these same collectors work extremely hard to insure the fidelity and exactness of their handwritten notes. Essentially there is no difference between the two forms of data-collecting. Both should be treated with equal care.[16]

While sound enhancement techniques can help improve existing recordings (equalization, filtering, and panning sounds from one channel to another) these are costly, time-consuming processes which should ideally be used with recordings which are already well made.

By "unity of sound," I mean the whole that the ear receives from a well-crafted radio program. The essence is montage, the superimposition of sounds, interviews, and narration to create an aural effect. The craft of radio production rises to art in the hands of someone fashioning a program from disparate interviews, ambient noise, and historical recordings such as speeches and old radio broadcasts. By juxtaposing these elements the expert producer creates a textured tapestry of sound, complete with the built-in punctuation of pauses and music.

How to Produce a Radio Program
from Oral History Interviews

The production of radio programs from oral history interviews can be long and demanding. The studio and editing time required for a short production (three to ten minutes) can vary from ten to twenty-five hours per minute. As we explore all the steps involved, the reason will become clear. It is impossible to outline in detail all the steps and techniques of radio production in a few pages; in my brief discussion, I will ignore more technical issues in order to break the process down into preproduction, production, and postproduction phases.

Two important terms in radio production are *actuality* and *continuity*. Actuality refers to the interviews and sounds (ambient noise and special effects) incorporated into a production. Continuity is the narration, scripted beforehand, which ties the voices, sounds, and music together. Obviously music and special effects are also needed to create a pleasing texture of sound, which winds effortlessly from one moment to another.

Preproduction

1. Reflect upon and plan your project. What is the overriding purpose of the program? Who is the audience? What special skills or knowledge do you bring—or must you obtain?

2. Survey existing materials on your subject. This includes previous broadcasts, interviews in your collection, interviews in other collections, holdings in national archives. Consider, in your survey, the success of other similar projects—who funded them, how were they received and distributed?

3. Design your project. What effect do you hope to produce? What will you include and omit? What will be the best length? How will it be distributed? Who will do the work, who will help? Where and when will the actual production take place?

4. Assemble your resources. Find funds and time to meet the objectives outlined above. Obtain the necessary hardware (such as microphones, tape recorders, an editing block, a studio for additional recording, if possible); software (reel-to-reel tape, cassettes, splicing tape, razor blades, equipment for labeling tapes, etc.) and technical assistance (consultants or colleagues to help review content and technical standards). Schedule production.

5. Practice using the microphones and recorder with a friend, paying particular attention to mike placement (ideally within one foot from the speaker, unless a clip-on or lavalier type is used). Make recordings at different levels to find the best recording volume.

6. Prepare a rough script. This should include the overall framework of the program and the production elements (continuity, actuality, music if desired, sound effects). Decide what your story is and how you will present it, keeping in mind your specific audience.

Production

1. Conduct your interviews. Listen attentively and take good notes. If the interviews are not yet transcribed, begin with selected passages which you are sure of using. Decide which supplemental interviews are needed to fill in the holes in what you already have. Check that you have all necessary permissions to broadcast materials.

2. Revise script.

3. Duplicate (dub) the interviews on a reel-to-reel recorder for editing; this should be done at high speed (seven and one-half or fifteen inches per second) to make editing easy. Never cut into an original recording. Make arrangements to deposit your original tape in an archive. Label everything clearly, reels and boxes. Edit the passages you would like to include, reducing them considerably in size and length. Remember that selection is the heart of art.

4. Assemble your other production elements (music for interludes or dramatic

effect, ambient noise, sound effects) on separate reels, with white leader separating the portions you will use.

5. Polish and record your continuity (narration); if possible, find a trained voice among the local broadcast or acting community. Divide the narration into numbered sections, so that each piece can be integrated later with interviews and effects in the final mix; record the names of your interviewees, so that these too can be intermixed. Include an introduction and an outroduction.

6. Mix the production elements into a smooth program—easier said than done. This can be the most complex and time-consuming process of the project and the one where craft is most evident and necessary.

7. Time your finished tape carefully.

Postproduction

1. Put your program aside for a period, then listen to it and begin cutting it to a distributable length.

2. Begin distribution; hire an assistant, if necessary, to handle the many phone calls and letters. Prepare a brochure or mailing to let the world know of your work. Be patient and persistent.

3. Duplicate several copies and circulate them to interested parties and authorities on your subject. (Note that high-speed tape duplication is usually inaccurate, and the best copies are made one-to-one, on the machines originally used for the program.)

Producing radio programs involves learning not only about radio production but about radio distribution—how to get programs aired once they are completed. (This is a long and complex process, and without including funds and time for distribution in a budget, no one may hear the results of your labor.) Professionals in radio production—like those in history—spend many hours in professional gatherings (such as the annual U.S. Public Radio Conference), read up on the latest equipment, carry on a professional correspondence, write proposals for funding and so forth. Above all they listen to work done by others under similar circumstances. Close attention to the finer productions heard on National Public Radio will ease many beginners into a new field.

Conclusion

The future of oral history radio programs depends to a great extent upon future funding. Professional historians interested in radio believed as early as 1934 that the medium could be put to great public service for relatively little cost. Instead of broadcasting university lectures, the History Committee of the National Advisory Council on Radio in Education suggested "reasons for broadcasting to the man in the street in order to develop 'historical mindedness' and plans for intriguing 'by starting with what is on his mind.' "[17] To extend this process to oral history, "to what is on his tongue," would be simple, mostly a matter of national and regional funding.

One comprehensive study of the public's understanding of humanities concluded that collaborations between scholarship and public TV and radio offered "a promising model for increasing understanding."[18] Organizations such as the National Endowment for the Humanities could set up summer sessions for historians, folklorists, and other humanists interested in working in radio and other media. Such training sessions could include not only the basics of production but the subtleties of media presentation (such as those mentioned above in connection with aesthetic concerns). State and regional humanities councils could set up residencies for scholars in radio and TV stations and could encourage the development of curricula and programs joining the production of oral history and radio.

Recent developments in oral history suggest an increasing professionalization of the field, though oral history continues to rely on dedicated volunteers at a grass-roots level. Perhaps training sessions for oral history volunteers could include a component on media production. Qualified consultants can be found among the few professionals trained in both fields. Local oral history projects might consider contacting their local media with an eye (or ear) to collaborating on a public affairs program of high community interest. Individual oral historians could participate in a summer seminar such as those outlined above or could themselves enroll in media production courses at local colleges.

From these steps could come not only more interesting and illuminating radio and television, but also the beginnings of a historically educated citizenry. In an electronic, media-laden culture, it may be too much to expect more than the smallest percentage of a population to read history. But by taking historical materials to the forms of media people use in these declining years of book reading, we can enfranchise and empower people with their own past.

Notes

1. See, for example, Frank Stanton, "Psychological Research in the Field of Radio Listening," *Educational Broadcasting 1936* (Chicago: University of Chicago Press, 1936), pp. 1–12; and Levering Tyson, ed., *Proceedings of the Fourth Annual Assembly of the National Advisory Council on Radio in Education: Report of the History Committee* (Chicago: University of Chicago Press, 1935).

2. Lawrence Lichty and Thomas Bohn, "Radio's 'March of Time': Dramatized News," *Journalism Quarterly* 51 (Autumn 1974), pp. 458–62, reprinted in *American Broadcasting*, ed. Lichty and Topping (New York: Hastings, 1975).

3. Max Wylie, *Radio Writing* (New York: Rinehart, 1939), pp. 297–308; most historical radio was at this time called educational or children's radio.

4. Stephen Reda, "Ramah Navajo Radio and Cultural Preservation," *Journal of Broadcasting* 22 (Summer 1978), pp. 361–71.

5. Paul Thompson, *The Voice of the Past: Oral History* (New York: Oxford University Press, 1978), pp. 12–14 (see chapter 3 of the present volume).

6. *Proceedings of International Association of Sound Archives in Lisbon, Portugal* (London, 1978); Rolf Schuursma, "The Sound Archive of the Film and Science Foundation and the Dutch Radio Organization" and Paul Thompson, "The B.B.C. Archives," *Oral History* 1 (Summer, 1971), pp. 23–26, 11–18.

7. Dennis Duffy and David Mitchell, *Bulletin of the Association for the Study of Canadian Radio and Television* 6 (November 1979), pp. 5–7. Another Canadian radio-historian is Barbara Diggins, author of "Designing Sound Documents," *Canadian Oral History Association Journal* 3 (1978), pp. 23–25.

8. Imbert Orchard, "Tape Recordings into Radio Documentaries," *Sound Heritage* 3 (1974), pp. 28–40; a more comprehensive draft is his unpublished "The Documentary in Sound." For the history of the coining of the term "aural history," see Orchard's interview with Dennis Duffy, July 6, 1978, Accession No. 990:6, pp. 11–12, Provincial Archives of British Columbia. Orchard told the author that his first public use of "aural history" came in 1968, in one of his pioneering "People in Landscape" series.

9. Robin Woods, *Canadian Oral History Association Journal* 5 (1980), pp. 41–42.

10. Some NEH-finded radio history productions are "Banks of Barre," "First Person America," and "Living Atlanta," referred to in *Medialog,* ed. L. Jimenez, M. Mayo, and V. Schofield (New York: Film Fund, 1982). See also the review of the Appalachian media production group, Appalshop, in *In These Times* (Chicago, Ill.) October 20, 1982.

11. See Richard Hinchcliffe, "The Sound of the Humanities," *Federation Reports* 4 (September 1981), pp. 12–15.

12. The best review-articles are Joseph Romney, "Oral History, Law and Libraries," *Drexel Library Quarterly* 15 (October 1979), pp. 40–49, and Truman Eustis III, "Get It in Writing: Oral History and the Law," *Oral History Review* 4 (1976), pp. 6–18.

13. David Lance, "Dissemination of Radio Resource Materials," *Journal of the International Association of Sound Archives* 7 (December 1978), pp. 29–34.

14. Marshall McLuhan, *Understanding Media* (New York: McGraw-Hill, 1964), p. 264.

15. Imbert Orchard, "Tape Recordings."

16. Kenneth Goldstein, *A Guide for Fieldworkers in Folklore* (1964; Reprint ed., Detroit: Gale, 1974), p. 45.

17. Levering, Tyson, ed., *Proceedings of the Fourth Annual Assembly of the National Advisory Council on Radio in Education* (Chicago: University of Chicago Press, 1935).

18. National Commission on the Humanities, *The Humanities in American Life* (Berkeley: University of California Press, 1981).

PART FIVE
Oral History and Schools

31

Oral History for the Student

James Hoopes

Oral history has found increasing acceptance both as a means of teaching history writing and as a gateway to the rich cultural resources outside the classrooms and textbooks. Part 5 explores ways of using oral history to promote learning in the schools. The first selection is directed to students and the subsequent articles to teachers.

James Hoopes, author of one of the student texts in oral history, outlines the sorts of roadblocks students can expect as they set out to collect oral history. He is frank about the prejudice against oral sources which students may encounter in the classroom but notes that despite this prejudice, the rewards of student interviewing are great, prompting students and teachers alike to rely on it to raise enthusiasms. Oral history offers students a way of situating themselves in the history of their community and teaches them a new respect for their elders and institutions. No wonder the use of oral historical techniques is finding a wide audience in schools.

James Hoopes is an associate professor of history at Babson College in Massachusetts. A scholar of New England puritanism, he used oral sources in his Van Wyck Brooks: In Search of American Culture *(1977). He has edited an edition of Perry Miller's classic* Sources for the New England Mind *(1981) and has written for* American Quarterly *(1982) and the* Journal of American History *(1983).*

"Oral History for the Student" is excerpted from Hoopes's Oral History: An Introduction for Students *(Chapel Hill, N.C.: University of North Carolina Press, 1979).*

EVERY GOOD history course includes work meant to give you the experience of *doing* history. This is often a research paper, and it should be the most interesting, stimulating aspect of the course. Too often, though, it is tedious, not because it is hard work, but because the challenge to human sympathy and imagination is neglected. In part

349

this may be because students sometimes feel that their efforts are repetitive, that they cannot do original research in documents that other historians and students have already researched. They are wrong to think so, because the test of originality, applied to history, is a test not only of the material's freshness or richness but also of the scholar's creativity. Still, this important point might be learned with more ease and interest if those of you who wished to work with new material could do so. One advantage of oral history interviewing as a teaching and learning technique is that the documents are always new, at least in the sense that no previous historian has examined them.

Some teachers, skeptical of the idea that students can profit from oral history research, might point out that history is an exercise not only of the imagination but also of the intellect. Oral history is so often thought of as merely the tape recording of interviews that it may seem a mindless activity to some. Actually, conducting a good interview requires hard intellectual as well as imaginative effort, just like other kinds of research. Yet an instructor who refuses to accept the raw tape or transcript of an interview is surely as much within his rights as he would be in refusing written research notes in place of a finished term paper. Though you are acting as a historian when doing research, your actions are not very visible. You are most clearly active as a historian when you can be seen thinking, rigorously and imaginatively, about your data. And a written research paper is usually the best way to reveal the quality of both your research and your thinking. This book is therefore designed around the idea that your oral history research will be incorporated into a more or less traditional term paper employing written documents as well.

At present, many students who have the opportunity to try oral history research do so in the context of a group oral history project. At their best, the student interviewers for these projects have a clear intellectual objective and use written documents as background material. The project at Duke University, for example, is focused on black history. Students participating in the project research written documents first and then use that research as a basis for conducting oral interviews, which become part of a permanent collection. In this way they have the satisfaction of knowing that they are contributing to a genuine scholarly purpose. I hope that this book will be useful to students in such projects.

But I have also designed this book for a larger audience by suggesting that those of you who do not have the opportunity to participate in an oral history project can still use oral history in the term papers often assigned in upper division courses and sometimes in broader surveys as well. Oral history may comprise a large part or only a small portion of your research, depending on its usefulness for your particular topic. It is assumed that you already have some experience in doing library research. If not, you may wish to consult one of the numerous guides to writing term papers. *Researching and Writing in History*, by F. N. McCoy, is especially good on the biggest hurdle for many students—choosing a topic.

The objective of this book is to keep the clear intellectual focus of the best *group* oral history projects but to adjust some of their procedures to the needs of *individual* students and scholars. Students who wish to work with oral as well as written documents can do so (enthusiastically, I have found) in the context of the term paper. At the same time, other students are free to pursue different research interests and techniques. Though some class time may be devoted to oral history, most of the course can still be spent on whatever is supposed to be its subject—the history of business, labor, politics, science, society, and so on. Such freedom and flexibility in accommodating individual interests of both students and teachers are the only conditions under which oral history is likely to find broad acceptance in the classroom, especially the college classroom.

This attention to the needs of the individual researcher is consistent with the fact that this is the first "how to" book on oral history where "you" readers are students rather than teachers or researchers.[1] I follow as well as argue "transactional" principles by acknowledging that students sometimes see teachers as destructively cautious in discouraging innovative research. But I also think that teachers are right to be skeptical of devoting an entire history course to *imitating* a group oral history project. It may be an excellent thing if the course is an *actual part* of an ongoing oral history project or if the course has a clear intellectual focus on a specific historical problem, with attention to background research and to preserving the interviews. But without that focus it is surely futile to import the conditions of a group project into the classroom by merely having students tape and transcribe interviews that, if the project is imitative, are unlikely ever to be used by anyone else. Taping and especially transcribing are too laborious to be done to no purpose.[2] You should be asked to engage in only the aspects of oral history that make sense for genuine historical or learning purposes. Otherwise, you will learn not history but the technique of oral history in a vacuum, and the result will be one more frustratingly sterile schoolroom exercise.

Addressing the needs of individual students engaged in individual projects is also consistent with an additional objective of this book—to address the problem of integrating oral history with other kinds of research and knowledge. Able students can and should make significant contributions to oral history, and I hope that this book, which I view as a contribution to greater rigor and sophistication in the field of oral history, will help them to do so. My own qualifications for writing the book do not include experience as a professional oral historian, collecting for a group project. But I have used oral history techniques in my own research and am one of the numerous but nonetheless isolated teachers who have experimented with oral history in the classroom. Perhaps these are just the right qualifications for the author of a book addressed to the needs of individuals and to the question of how oral history can be related to other kinds of history.

Judging by much of the "how-to" literature, the field of oral history is at present relatively unsophisticated, not only in the obviously crucial area of interviewing, but perhaps more importantly in its relations with other types of historical research.[3] If oral history becomes an isolated field, more interested in the oral than the historical, it will not fulfill its potential for humanistic research. One professional oral historian has warned of "danger signs" that "A quasi-professional group called 'oral historians' might well emerge who become method-mad pedagogues, claiming authority on every facet of oral history. . . . Oral historians must be historians first". . . .[4]

Oral history will obviously be most likely to be useful to you in recent and contemporary history courses. Your instructors in such courses will probably agree to oral history as part of your research efforts, provided that you can convince them that the oral research has historical significance. This requirement may seem a large obstacle, because of our almost automatic assumption that significant information can only be acquired from "important"—and therefore difficult to interview—people. Obviously, an ex-president or senator, famous philosopher, author, actor, military leader, industrialist, business person, or some other VIP can tell us things about important events, events of national significance. But is it possible to interview such people? Yes, it is, though it may require hard work, persistence, and luck. Peter Joseph, a Princeton undergraduate in the late 1960s and early 1970s, showed exemplary initiative in interviewing hundreds of people, many of them famous, for his senior thesis, which was later published under the title *Good Times: An Oral History of America in the 1960's.*[5] But most students will not interview nationally prominent figures. . . . Also, it is well to remember that "historical significance" is a relative term. Persons who are not nationally prominent may count for much on the regional, state, or local scene. Doctors, lawyers, judges, clergy, politicians, and newspaper editors may be excellent and important sources within a local context.

Furthermore, the best interviewee is quite likely to be someone who has never been interviewed before. Famous people are so experienced at separating public life from private that they may find it difficult to be not only honestly retrospective but also introspective in an interview. Tending to omit specific, personal details, they also leave out the "feel" for the facts. Jean Stein, in conducting interviews for *American Journey: The Times of Robert Kennedy*, found that "the freshest, most informative material seemed to come less from the public figures than from those for whom being interviewed must have been a novelty, the women particularly. . . ."[6] The wives had the vantage point of their famous husbands, but not being celebrities, they were not jaded interviewees.

It should also be possible to find ordinary people who have something to tell us about an important event. For example, in a course on the history of American labor you might decide that you want to write a paper on a strike that occurred in the last thirty or forty years. Many people involved in the strike, whether workers or managers, are likely to be still alive. Interviews with them could be an important supplement to information you would find in old newspapers, company and union records, and previously published studies. From interviews you might find out additional facts not only about what things happened but also about why they happened. The emotions that went into obstructing a public highway or hiring strikebreakers are the least likely things to be preserved in official records. Someone present at a union or company meeting is much more likely to be informative on emotions than a secretary's minutes. And you should consider the inner, human significance of the strike. How did it affect the people who lived through it? Did management harden or soften? Were workers more or less militant as a result of the strike? Were there any shifts in cultural values, say in the concept of the rights of private property?

But this last sort of research, on a cultural value, is the kind most likely to be resisted by your teacher, who may think that the question is vague and that you cannot make any significant generalizations on the basis of an interview or two. Actually, the representativeness of a small number of interviewees can be high, especially if they are articulate, introspective people.[7] If representativeness is a goal, try to balance your sample by interviewing, say, a worker and a manager. You should also try to explain that the interviews are to supplement traditional written sources by providing information in depth, information that gets its significance as much from its "thickness" as from its representativeness. None of these tactics availing, you have to decide whether or not to take the course, basing your decision, naturally, on all relevant factors—the quality of the course in other respects, degree requirements, and so on. Your teacher may also doubt that it is feasible or practical to attempt a specific research project, and it may be to your advantage to respect those doubts.

Although oral history usually involves interviewing older people, there is no reason why interviewees cannot be young. If you are writing a paper on some aspect of the Vietnam War, a thirty-year-old person might be a good source. For even more recent events, it is possible that a good interviewee might be in his teens or even younger, if he was in a time and place relevant to your topic.

No matter what topic you decide to work on, asking yourself some critical questions at the beginning can save wasted effort. Will interviewing be genuinely useful? If not, don't interview for the sake of interviewing. If you want the experience of doing oral history, find another topic where it will be useful. Consider practical problems. Will you have time to do the number of interviews you think are necessary? Two or three interviews are almost certainly the maximum you should plan for a term paper; you will find that preparing for, conducting, and using the results of just one interview can be very time-consuming. Also, will you have time and money enough to travel to the site of the interview? For many students, the ideal interviewee will be someone who lives near school or home.

But oral history research is not necessarily limited to American history courses. Travel overseas for a summer or an entire year is a reasonable hope for many students. If you do plan to visit another country, you may want to consider doing an oral history project there. But you should be aware that in many countries it is much harder than in the United States to get people to talk frankly to strangers.[8] Discuss the possible problems and complications in such a project with someone, perhaps a college faculty member, who has been to the country in question and knows its culture well. Despite the potential difficulties, oral history research may greatly enhance your understanding of another people. And the contact with local people it requires might be an excellent way to break through cultural and linguistic barriers, making your trip less lonely.

Finally, students who cannot undertake interviews for some reason— the resistance of a teacher, a topic so remote in time that potential interviewees are dead, lack of travel funds or time—may still be able to use oral history material. Many transcripts of interviews on file in oral history collections are available on microfilm or through interlibrary loan. Also, many history books are based in part on interviews. These documents can be useful, provided they are subjected to the same critical questions you should ask of oral documents you have gathered yourself. Therefore, the last chapter of this book discusses how to locate and use oral history documents collected by others.

Notes

1. John A. Neuenschwander, *Oral History as a Teaching Approach* (Washington, D.C.: National Education Association, 1975) and Van H. Garner, *Oral History: A New Experience in*

Learning, (Dayton: Pflaum, 1975), are addressed to teachers and follow the group approach. Cullom Davis et al., *Oral History: From Tape to Type* (Chicago: American Library Association, 1977), though designed for possible use as a textbook, is not written especially for students.

2. Thomas Charlton reports, on the basis of a survey of college teachers, that "almost all universities face problems in motivating students to transcribe the results of their interviews" ("Oral History in Graduate Instruction," *Oral History Review* 3 [1975], p. 66). In some cases the reluctance may be for good reason.

3. Charlton found that integrating oral history with written sources was one of the most common difficulties reported by instructors using oral history as a teaching technique ("Oral History," p. 66).

4. Joseph H. Cash, Ramon I. Harris, et al., *The Practice of Oral History* (Glen Rock, N.J.: Microfilming Corporation of America, 1975), pp. 76–77.

5. Unfortunately, Joseph's book suffers from the same weakness as Terkel's *Hard Times:* no interest in written documents or in establishing significant historical contexts (Peter Joseph, *Good Times: An Oral History of America in the 1960's* [New York: Charterhouse, 1973]; Studs Terkel, *Hard Times: An Oral History of the Great Depression* [New York: Pantheon, 1970]).

6. P. x.

7. Lewis A. Dexter, *Elite and Specialized Interviewing* (Evanston: Northwestern University Press, 1970), p. 8.

8. See, for instance, Daniel Lerner, "Interviewing Frenchmen," *American Journal of Sociology* 62 (September 1956), pp. 187–94.

32

Oral History in the Classroom

George Mehaffy, Thad Sitton, and O. L. Davis, Jr.

As our first essay suggested, oral history can be an exciting tool in the classroom. Our next readings help answer the questions most teachers ask about oral history: how do I get started? What kind of equipment is needed? How do I conduct an interview? What have others done?

Anyone who has read this far realizes that such questions demand sophisticated answers. Nevertheless, teachers often need practical working solutions—and here three educators working at the University of Texas offer one of the best outline guides to bringing oral history into the classroom. They provide model release and interview forms, specific suggestions on end products for students interviewing, and some brief but useful tips on interviewing.

George Mehaffy directs the College of Education at Eastern New Mexico University; he and the other authors of this guide have written Oral History: Projects for the Classroom *(1983). Thad Sitton, who trained with Mehaffy at the University of Texas and co-authored numerous articles with him, developed an oral history project for the Texas Sesquicentennial. O. L. Davis, Jr., directs the Oral History Program in Education at the University of Texas at Austin.*

"Oral History in Classroom" is excerpted from How To Do It 2 *(1979), pp. 1–7, published by the National Council for the Social Studies (Washington, D.C.).*

CROSS THE nation, increasing numbers of teachers and their students are using oral history techniques during portions of the school year. The oral history process has been used, in fact, in classrooms at every school level—elementary, secondary, college, and university. While some schools have developed full-blown projects including publications, most classroom efforts are smaller in scale. This . . . [article] is designed to help social studies teachers make practical decisions about using oral history with students. It is based on an understanding of the real constraints of real classrooms.

Two major commitments about oral history and classroom teaching are explicit in this guide. First, student learning is more productive *and more fun* when students are active rather than passive. Oral history is useful in helping students find that "the stuff" of history is everywhere around them. Engaging in a search for explanations and descriptions relating to important local matters is satisfying and increases personal meanings. Some of these meanings relate to substantive historical knowledge; for example, construction of a highway (and transportation system), communication of national election results before and after the development of television, and the effects of wartime on a particular family. Other meanings relate to the essential methodology of history; for example, the necessity of using incomplete data and the hazards of generalization. Of particular importance is that oral history can be stimulating, exciting, and fun for students. Their active participation takes them "into the field." They meet people they do not know. Their work "counts"; it is not just "checked."

Second, students can create useful documents as they learn about their past. Classroom oral history efforts continue to produce important, even impressive, documentation; for example, eyewitness accounts of a strike or of events during a presidential inauguration. These oral histories make available recollections, insights, and perceptions that others may use. Classroom oral history is not restricted to the individual classroom or a particular set of students. The accumulated oral histories ("memoirs") constitute an invaluable archival source about local communities and institutions, and they may well be useful in settings beyond the local scene. Documents produced by students, therefore, may be seen as legitimate historical documents. Classroom oral history involves students in the larger historical enterprise.

A few practical suggestions are presented here. They may serve as reminders as teachers plan to use oral history in their own classrooms.

• *Oral history is not just a person with a tape recorder.* A tape recorder and tape are important, but oral history emphasizes planning prior to interviewing. What is the purpose of this interview? Which person is likely to be an important informant? How reliable is memory and, especially, the memory of a specific individual? How can we secure the information the individual possesses? What questions will tap into memory and sustain reminiscences? Into what local or national (or international) context does the projected interview fit? The actual interview needs a tape recorder controlled by a knowledgeable interviewer.

• *Oral history need not be transcribed to be useful.* Ours is mainly a print culture. Consequently, most people will be most comfortable with oral histories transferred from tape to transcript. Transcription can be expensive and time-consuming. Trade-offs obviously must be anticipated when transcription is considered, whether as an entire recording or only as sections. One crucial advantage of the oral history record is that *it is oral*. It is part of the oral, not print, tradition; and reduction to print destroys much of the value, and accuracy, of the original recording. Many oral history programs, particularly those in Canada and the United Kingdom, do not transcribe. Clearly, oral history documents need not be transcribed to be useful.

• *Classroom oral history need not be a BIG project*. Several school projects in oral history or cultural journalism, particularly the widely published ones such as *Foxfire*, have been large-scale endeavors. Some have incorporated oral history into classwork throughout the year and have involved many, if not all, students enrolled. Most successful classroom oral history efforts have not been as large. Some emphasize oral history for only a short time, perhaps for only one period or several periods during the year. Some use oral history components for a special emphasis. Realistically, we recommend that teachers should consider gaining experience with oral history in a rather highly focused study extending over a relatively short time. With teachers who have experience, longer and/or more comprehensive projects may be undertaken with confidence.

• *Oral history is not the final product of history*. The oral history document (whether tape or manuscript) is a *source* for history, typically, not history itself. Oral history is subject to the same historiographic canons as are other documents. For example, how reliable is the information? To what extent does it have external and internal validity? How can this information be related to other information available through oral history and other procedures? The oral history document is "raw," albeit personal and quite valuable. It is likely that it will be a major source of historical inquiry in the classroom.

Getting Started and Continuing in Oral History

The next two sections contain numerous practical suggestions for beginning and continuing classroom oral history projects. The first section concentrates on *ideas* or *focus*. It describes examples of program elements that teachers have found to work. Further, it relates these to categories of oral history emphases. The second section attends to specific questions about equipment, planning, and procedures. . . .

(1) *The Life history*. Students might interview (and record) relatives or non-relatives about their lives, and transcribe these recordings. Many variations are possible here. These life histories might be focused chronologically (a grandmother's memories of her childhood, a grandfather's experiences in World War II), or topically (a grandmother's or a

grandfather's life as a farmer, from earliest experiences to the present day). The raw field-recordings could be submitted in their original state, or selectively edited tape-to-tape in a re-recording process utilizing a second tape recorder. The interviews could be fully or selectively transcribed, and the transcription could be edited into a coherent story by the student historian. In its most ambitious form, the life history might expand to incorporate documentary and photograhic sources about the informant's life, and might imbed the transcribed materials in a larger interpretive framework derived from a general study of United States history during that life span.

The life history has several advantages for an introductory student project. It has a natural focus in its concentration upon the individual life, and (as suggested above) it may be approached at a variety of levels of sophistication. If the student begins, as will most often be the case, with a relative or some other person well known to her, she eases her way through the initial anxieties that plague most would-be fieldworkers.

(2) *The Family History.* As in the case of the individual relative, the student's family is a natural focus for his or her field research, and again a wide range of projects is possible.

As their introduction to a larger family history assignment, or as a component in such an assignment, students might talk to the oldest members of their families and collect historical traditions of the greatest possible "time depth." This would be a sort of "Roots" assignment.

Materials collected would be the oldest obtainable traditions about the family and where it came from—the stories told to students' grandparents by *their* grandparents. The idea would be to explore the ultimate limits of each family's knowledge of its own oral histories—stories, personal anecdotes, songs, traditions. For Alex Haley, the author of *Roots*, these were words and phrases from a West African language and traditions about "an African."

Another possibility would be a limited family history that explored the family fortunes of *one* side of the student's family for two generations, and related this family experience to larger national developments during the period. Limiting himself or herself to one parent and that set of grandparents, the student might follow a sequence involving: (a) a review of general national developments ovcer the decades covered, (b) a study of family documents and photographs derived from that period, (c) interviews with the parents, grandparents (and other relatives—aunts, uncles, etc.), (d) transcription of the interviews, and (e) use of all these primary source materials for the compilation of a coherent family history covering these two generations.

There are, of course, many other possibilities for the classroom family history project. In a more unstructured assignment, the student might become the "family archivist," and create a historical inventory of family documents and photographs; then the student could go on to tape-record older family members for other data to include in the archives.

(3) *Special Oral History Projects.* Beyond the life history and the family history, there is a wide range of options for the classroom oral history project; some of these are briefly suggested below.

• *Examining the local effects of national and international events (hypotheses testing).* Students might generate testable hypotheses from their textbook study of national or international events and then go out into the local community to test the fit between that "big picture" history and the perceptions and experiences of local folks. In terms of the larger historical framework, the Great Depression was an era of hard times and social disorder, but what was the experience of *this* community? Such testing can assist students to determine the validity of descriptions of events.

• *Chronicling local events from oral sources.* Students might embark on the study of a variety of "significant events" in community history. Every community experiences its share of these historical turning points— events that most older persons remember as meaningful, vivid, and important. These might be a famous murder or murder trial, the day the community first voted "dry" (or "wet"), a natural (flood, tornado) or an economic disaster (the failure of cotton agriculture, the closing of the steel mill, etc.). Students would choose one of these events for study, interview older family members and others about it, and then attempt to reconcile the conflicting testimonies to arrive at an interpretation of "what really happened." Since, for most communities, community history still remains to be written, such research by students should be regarded (and conducted) with some seriousness. The findings may help the members of a community to understand better their own attitudes and their actions.

In a variation of the above, students might collect oral testimonies on a variety of recent events in the community, and compose from those taped materials the formal histories of these events. Student activities would thus merge the roles of historian and newspaper reporter.

• *Compiling histories of local institutions/organizations.* Using both documentary and oral sources, students might compile the history or histories of a variety of local institutions. These might include churches, schools, voluntary organizations, and neighborhoods. Such institutions form a natural focus for student fieldwork, and students might interview both past and present participants in them.

• *Exploring topics in community social history.* Students might choose to research any of an almost limitless number of topical alternatives in community social/cultural history. The various *Foxfire* books illustrate the range of possible options here: hunting stories, farming practices, technologies (skills, trades, occupations, processes), beliefs about ghosts, birth/coming-of-age/marriage/burial customs, recipes, food preservation, folk remedies, and "how to do it" subjects of many kinds. This is the "past culture of the community" in the anthropologist's sense; it is social history to a historian.

Again, many variations are possible. A single student could collect a variety of oral testimonies on a given topic (folk remedies), or the whole class could become involved in collecting materials on that topic. Telephone interviews can also be useful. Students might work on "then/now" essays ("courtship and marriage, then and now" or "roles or women and men, then and now"), which would take advantage of students' knowledge of how such things are presently being done, and then go on to explore how the same matters were handled in their parents' and grandparents' day. The students develop skills of research and "learn by doing," and their final products are of value to the community.

Finally, in the multicultural communities, such topical studies could focus upon ethnic variations in the patterns studied—ethnic differences in child-rearing practices, celebrations, burials, folk medicine, and others. In a multicultural community, the study of topics in local social history is also, by necessity, "ethnic studies," and a classroom project may choose to capitalize upon that fact. Students who live in more homogeneous communities should also be given opportunities to participate in projects in multicultural communities. . . .

(4) *Field Research in Community Folklore.* In an enterprise closely linked to the study of community social history, students in social studies or English classes might locate, record, transcribe, and analyze a variety of folkloric materials (stories, songs, sayings, jokes, riddles, legends, superstitions, etc.) from their peers, families, ethnic groups, and the community at large.

Folklore is the "verbal folk art" of the community, which is transmitted orally, person-to-person, and is not written down. It varies from ethnic group to ethnic group and from generation to generation (students, for example, have their own folklore). Students and teacher decide what kind of folklore project they wish to embark upon—the target group from which the materials will be collected, and the kinds of materials they wish to collect. The materials are then field-recorded, brought to class, and compiled.

Some general categories of folklore are: ghost stories, tall tales, riddles, jokes, skip-rope rhymes, weather signs, old sayings, folk remedies, "luck" superstitions, graffitti, songs, and animal lore. Project possibilities include: (a) students' research among their families to collect folklore from older (and younger) family members, especially the grandparents—a "family folklore" project; (b) an emphasis upon collecting folkloric materials from older (or younger) members of the different ethnic communities (for example, an examination of the differences and similarities in Black, Anglo and Mexican-American folklore); (c) students' collection of children's folklore (skip-rope rhymes, riddles, etc.) from their younger brothers or sisters; and (d) students' collection of the current folklore of the students' peer groups within the school. This might begin with what students in the class already know. For example, do students know the story about the "dude who grew claws" (on a date, no less), or the "devil's appearance in the roadhouse"? (These are common stories in the Texas public schools.) And this makes another point. Folklore is not just "old stuff"; living folklore is (at least) halfway believed in.

What Are the Products of Classroom Oral History?

At the beginning of this exploration of "program suggestions," several common denominators of the classroom oral history projects were examined. Common factors were identified which lay beneath the surface diversity of these real and suggested projects. Nearly all the projects involve students in field research enterprises within the local community, and, in so doing, involve these students in a "personalized history," a quest for personal roots in family, ethnic group, and community. A final common element of these projects—and, we believe, a critically important one—is that such projects are, in effect, "real." They actually do something. They can produce a tangible and socially valuable product, and this explains their unique potential for stimulating student enthusiasm and excitement.

In many communities, there is insufficient information about local history, folklore, and political life. Classroom oral history projects may be designed to do their part to remedy this situation, and thereby generate a product that is socially useful. Again, there are several possibilities.

(1) *Curriculum Materials.* One reason that "local history" is so often missing from the secondary school curriculum is the nearly complete lack of curriculum materials about local history. Many of the project ideas outlined above can produce materials of great usefulness to the teacher of social studies, materials that may serve to link textbook social studies to the face-to-fact reality of community social life, as students themselves know and experience it.

(2) *Community Oral History Archives.* Perhaps even more important, the classroom oral history projects could result in tapes, transcripts, photo archives, and other materials of great interest and usefulness to persons in the local community. In so doing, the classroom project would function within the area of "public history" to create a "usable past" for the local

community. There is evidently a widespread need at the community level for materials relating to community history, and there is usually no one to supply those materials. Indeed, this thirst for "local history" is one of the explanations for the general success of the many student "Foxfire" publications (see below). Even in the case of communities which are fortunate enough to possess a body of local historiography, this is often a higly selective and "lily-white" history that neglects the historical contributions of Blacks, Mexican-Americans, and other minorities. The student project may generate materials that help to fill this historical gap. This local history collection could be based in the community library or at a local college or university, and it might serve as a tangible reminder to successive generations of students that their labors, and the products of those labors, were not just "for drill" but "for real."

(3) *A Foxfire-Concept Journal.* Finally, student oral history projects might culminate in the publication of a student journal of oral history, folklore, and folklife patterned upon the journal *Foxfire.* Some seventy of these student publications are now in production within secondary schools in the United States. Despite the obvious difficulties of researching and producing such a journal within the real world of the public school, the Foxfire-pattern has spread far and wide across the United States, and even abroad. Most of these journals are self-supporting (by way of over-the-counter and subscription sales); and some, like *Salt* and *Bittersweet,* are joining *Foxfire* itself in the pleasant position of extreme fiscal solvency. *Foxfire*'s annual book royalties now are a considerable sum.

Launching an Oral History Project

What Equipment Do I Need?

Many oral history programs use reel-to-reel tape recorders to ensure the best possible recording. School programs, on the other hand, often find cassette tape recorders easier to use. A cassette tape recorder can be used with great success if a few simple rules are observed.

1. Use the best equipment available. Poor quality recording equipment produces poor quality recordings.
2. Use a high-quality, thirty-minute cassette tape. The forty-five minute per side cassette tape may be too thin, depending on the brand used.
3. Use an external microphone, preferably dual lavalier microphones, to get the microphone as close to the speaker as possible. (Built-in microphones, in contrast, often pick up recorder noises.)
4. Try to arrange an interview setting which is as quiet as possible.

Do I Need a Legal Release?

A legal release is necessary to clarify the conditions under which a tape-recorded interview is made. Generally, individuals who agree to an interview are willing to give the school the contents of that interview. However, some people are legitimately concerned about being quoted out of context, or about being made to appear foolish or uneducated. A legal release can help avoid such misunderstandings. While a sample release form is included, the final form should be cleared with a school district legal officer. The release form should include a place for restrictions or special conditions attached to a particular interview. Some interviewees may wish to review the tape prior to release. Some interviewees may wish to read the transcript. Others may simply want to see any material which is placed in the public domain. . . .

What About Record-keeping and Storage?

As an oral history project gets underway, tapes begin to accumulate faster than one can keep track of them. Record-keeping, thus, is an im-

Release Form

Date: _____

I hereby give to (name or school) _____,
for whatever scholarly or educational purposes may be determined, the tape recordings, transcriptions, and contents of this oral history interview.

_____   _____
Signature of interviewee   Signature of interviewer

_____   _____
Name   Name

_____
Address

Special restrictions:

_____

_____

_____

_____

_____

Figure 32.1. Sample release form

portant part of any oral history project. The best recording in the world is of little value if it is lost.

The interviewer should do two things. First, clearly label each tape with the name of the interviewee, date, name of the interviewer, and tape number if there is more than one tape. Second, each interviewer should fill out an interview data sheet in order to preserve details about interviewee and the interview itself. A sample data sheet is reproduced on this page.

Donated Tapes Collection
Regional Oral History Office

The Bancroft Library
University of California at Berkeley

General Topic of Interview _____
Date _____ Place _____ Length _____
Narrator *Interviewer*
Name _____ Name _____
Address _____ Address _____

Name & address of relative, friend

Relationship to narrator (friend, neighbor, etc.) _____

Birthplace _____
Birthdate _____
Occupation(s) _____

Length of acquaintance _____
Occasion of interview _____

Interview Data
Subjects covered, in approximate order, spelling out names of persons and places mentioned.

Estimated time on Tape   *Contents*

Use back of sheet if necessary

Figure 32.2. Oral history data sheet

Once tapes are brought back to the classroom from the field, they should be logged in some master file. The tapes may then be stored. Ideal storage conditions of constant temperature and humidity are generally not possible for most school projects. However, tapes should be protected from extreme temperature variation. . . .

How Do Students Learn To Interview?

The interview situation provides one of the greatest single opportunities for student learning. Interviewing must be approached carefully if valuable interviews are to result. The most important key to successful interviewing is training.

Training for interviewing begins by ensuring that students understand the goals of the project. If students are involved in the selection of a project, they will be better acquainted with the kind of material which they need to collect in their interviews. Are life histories the focus, for example? Or are the project participants seeking only specific experiences during World War II?

In addition to understanding the projects, students should also have some historical framework in which to ask questions. An interview with a woman who was a housewife during World War II is greatly enhanced if the interviewer knows something about rationing for civilians during the war.

Once the interviewer understands the goals of the project and the historical framework, the real training begins. The teacher might start by asking the class to generate a list of possible interview questions. These questions should be open-ended, allowing the interviewee to respond fully. This interview guide must not be used mechanically. The guide is not a list of questions to be worked through, after which the interview is over; it is only a listing of the areas to be covered. However, sometimes some preplanned questions used with follow-up questions make students more comfortable in initial interview situations.

Students should have opportunities to practice before the interviews begin. Students could begin by interviewing one another or a family member. Role-playing might be used to help students avoid difficulties, such as initial shyness. Any students who interview should also be asked to listen to early interviews to help improve later interviews. Sample interviews could be brought to class as a review activity.

Often, students feel more comfortable in an interview situation if someone else is along. Some teachers send out interviewing teams, usually composed of two persons. The advantage to having two persons at an interview is that one, as principal interviewer, can focus on the substance of the interview; while the second student keeps track of tapes, takes photographs, or tries to ensure optimum conditions for the interview.

Each tape should begin with an introduction identifying interviewee, interviewer, date, location, and subject of the interview. A checklist for each interviewer helps standardize the introduction. The introduction might appear as follows:

This is an oral history interview with _____
conducted by _____on _____ at _____.
The subject of this interview is _____.

The checklist might also remind the interviewer about the legal agreement, recording level, or other easily forgotten matters.

When the interviewer begins the interview, she or he should test the equipment with a short recording in the presence of the interviewee. Such a procedure eliminates the horror story of a beautiful interview which is somehow inadvertently never recorded because the tape recorder was not working. In addition, testing seems to relax some interviewees.

Interviewing, as your students will find out, is interesting and difficult work. The interviewer must be attentive to what is being said, listening for clues to follow-up questions or hearing omissions which can be filled in later. The interviewer must also indicate—by eye contact, nodding, and making appropriate comments to keep the speaker talking—that she or he is listening. At the same time that the interviewer is listening carefully and showing that she or he is doing so, the interviewer is also formulating new questions and ensuring that the interview is progressing well. Interviewing is like performing in all three rings of a circus—at the same time!

33

Oral/Aural History:
In and out of the Classroom

Don Cavallini

One of oral history's great strengths is its ties to the living history beyond the classroom doors, and this next article offers educators a creative guide to sound-collecting field trips. Don Cavallini, a social studies teacher, reports here on a series of innovative exercises he has developed to stimulate students to explore, listen to, and record their sound environment. In the past, teachers and historians alike have tended to ignore the historical context of sounds, smells, and sights. If sounds are beyond the usual definition of oral history, they nonetheless carry information which may be as central to the historical experience as the words which oral historians customarily preserve. And for teachers, they offer a powerful motivating device for students.

The author offers lesson plans for specific school projects: oral autobiography/biography, oral validity in history, and oral war accounts. He suggests that teachers encourage students to collect and study the raw sounds of history which once surrounded us: the freight train's moan, the streetcar's clang, the whine of fast-disappearing farm machinery: earwitness accounts.

Don Cavallini teaches at Lexington High School in Lexington, Illinois. His dissertation, at Illinois State University, was entitled "Using Oral History in College and High School: A Model for studying the Great Depression" (1980).

"Oral/Aural History: In and out of the Classroom" was originally published in Social Studies *70 (May 1979), pp. 112–17.*

ORAL HISTORY, as defined by Vaughn Davis Bornet, "is a spoken reminiscence which has been recorded with the aid of a trained interviewer-historian in accordance with recognized ethical and procedural standards and typewritten under his supervision."[1] That, of course, is a highly clinical definition of the term but it does go to the heart of oral history. For researchers and purists Bornet's definition is certainly satisfying. But for teachers of oral history, one may find the definition of Willa K. Baum's more useful and practical. She has said, "oral history is a method of collecting historical information . . . the method includes planned-in-advance, tape-recorded interviews with someone who has firsthand knowledge of an event or a way of life that's of some historical interest."[2] Oral history is a methodology, a process, or a procedure which can be used by classroom teachers as a way to reveal some interesting truths about the subject matter or content they teach every day.[3]

Since there is more to reconstructing the past than the recording of the human voice, oral historians (and teachers of oral history) need also consider the word of the aural historians. The latter involves the taping of sounds with historical significance. This may range from the wailing whistle of a steam engine, when railroad locomotives used coal as fuel, to the whirr of an old fashioned telephone being cranked. The aural historian is primarily interested in the preservation of historic sounds along with the meticulous collection and analysis of current sounds.

Used alone oral history offers some highly promising teaching possibilities; the same is true for aural history. But used together even more fascinating and exciting options become apparent. The following narrative will include a description of classroom projects using the oral/aural technique. The projects are divided into three classifications: (1) oral history, (2) aural history, and (3) oral/aural history.

Oral History Projects

Project 1: "Oral -autobiography/biography." Students are asked first to read published accounts of well known people. Next they write a book review and together as a class discuss the biographical approach to history. Following this students tell about themselves on tape. From this point they are to compare what they have to say about themselves by making a tape on their own life through interviewing their parents, relatives, and friends for biographical information. The two tapes are played in class for a comparison of viewpoints. The class then conducts an analysis of the tapes to check for varying viewpoints, conflicting facts, and different opinions. The student who made the tapes then writes a critical reaction to the interviews and draws his own conclusions about the oral history as a tool in writing biographical accounts.

Project 2: "Oral validity in history." Students begin selecting an event from the twentieth century in which they are interested. Research is conducted on this event using traditional methods. To motivate students have them listen to Studs Terkel's oral history record "Hard Times," a two-record *Caedmon* album. After listening to selected interviews students make a list of questions that they would consider asking older people about the depression years. Compile all of these questions and encourage students to analyze them to see if they are closed or open ended—that is if they would encourage people to talk or not.

Next invite someone from the community to come to your class and be interviewed using the best of the student formulated questions. Record the interview. Then analyze the tape later in class to determine the effectiveness of the interview. Now permit students to interview their own prospective narrators concerning the topic they originally selected. Finally, have students analyze their own tapes comparing the verbal information to the written evidence they uncovered while researching the topic.

Project 3: "Oral war accounts." Have students interview veterans of World War I, World War II, Korea, or Vietnam. Keep a chart relative to differences in experience, length of service, rank, branch of service, length of service, attitudes toward the conflict, and reaction to battle experiences. The chart is posted on a bulletin board and filled in by every student after conducting each interview. All of the class may interview veterans who participated in the same war so as to permit comparisons or merely make conclusions about veterans in different wars. . . .[4]

Aural History Projects

Project 1: "The Earwitness Account." As an exercise leading up to more complete aural listening skills and as a general introduction to aural history projects, teachers should introduce students to the earwitness account. An earwitness account is a written description by someone of a sound that can no longer be heard. The World Soundscape Project has compiled a list of earwitness accounts of sounds that were once frequently heard at an earlier time in history. A few of these accounts originally printed in *The Vancouver Soundscape* have been selected to demonstrate precisely what an earwitness account is. A set of exercise-questions have been compiled for teachers to use in their classroom when discussing and analyzing these aural history documents.

The Streetcar

The conductor at the back of the streetcar had a hand bell to signal the motorman at the front. A single bell meant to stop at the next corner, two bells signalled the start, three bells signalled an emergency stop. The interurban cars had a very distinctive whistle sound, produced by an airwhistle. For some reason they had two different codes. When they were in town they used—just like the streetcars—one signal for stopping at the next street. But once they were outside of town they used three whistles as a stop signal,—From Gordon Odlum (1973) reminiscence pre-1955.

The Train

You don't realize what you have until you no longer have it. Noise is so all-pervasive now that the tendency is not to listen. In the past the trains either whistled more or we heard them better. In any case they seemed to be announcing their arrivals, starting from a long distance away, and we heard the steam whistles, then all that snorting and puffing. They had more personality.—From Mrs. Donald B. Grant, reminiscence of the 1920s.

Horses

There were still lots of horses until after the First World War—horse pulling delivery wagons. Every grocer had a delivery cart with one horse. They'd never move faster than a walk and on these cobbled streets that were just stones set in, sort of rough, the horses' iron shoes made quite a row. We've got to bear in mind that at that time there wasn't any noise anywhere, so one horse going along a block or two could be heard easily.—From Joe Simson (1972) reminiscence.[5]

EXERCISE-QUESTIONS SET FOR EARWITNESS ACCOUNT:
1. Underline all words that describe or identify a sound.
2. Guess at what approximate time in history these sounds would have been heard.
3. What sounds exist today that did not exist 100, 50, 25, or even 5 years ago?
4. How important is sound to the quality of life today?
5. What are some "controversial" sounds of the 1970s that some people perhaps wish could be eliminated from the environment? Why are these sounds disturbing?
6. Write an earwitness account of your own describing a sound with which you are very familiar in the 1970s. Be very specific so that a person living 100 years from now, when the sound you are describing no longer exists, can really "hear" this sound.
7. What makes sounds obsolete and disappear from the environment?

Project 2: "The Sounds of Yesterday." Many long familiar sounds are disappearing. Students with their tape recorders can preserve a valuable part of history by recording vanishing sounds. The sounds would become an historical artifact. Small research papers could be written around old sounds. The World Soundscape Project gives some examples of "endangered" sounds: the ringing of old cash registers, butter being churned, hand coffee grinders, school hand bells, and razors being stropped—just to name a few. Your students could think of other sounds and quickly build an entire treasury of sound artifacts.[6]

Project 3: "City/Country Sounds." Students in urban settings could easily record the sounds of a busy city street. Captured sounds might include: traffic, horns of taxis, and cars, elevated trains, buses, and police sirens. With the sounds as an introduction, an oral commentary could be made explaining why and how the sounds depict city life. Perhaps even an exchange program between urban and rural schools could be worked out in order to exchange sounds of different living environments. Rural students could record the sounds on a farm and make an oral commentary. As a side feature of this project, students could be introduced to other students many miles away. Each would have a greater appreciation of the other students' environment and lifestyle.

Project 4: "The Soundwalk." A complaint that teachers often make is that students do not really listen. Perhaps it is because they have never learned how to listen. In which case the soundwalk will be a new and revealing experience. The soundwalk is an explanation of the soundscape. Students are given maps of a locale—perhaps near the school—and are directed to the symbols which call the listener's attention to the sounds to be heard along the way. The soundwalk requires that the students be quiet so that tape recorders can pick up the designated sounds on the map. Upon returning to class, students should listen to the tapes and describe in writing the sounds they heard. As a supplementary assignment, students can draw their own maps and create their own sidewalks to be shared later with other in the class. A class discussion can then result comparing the soundwalks and the significance of the various sounds heard. . . .[7]

Spin-Off Projects: Using oral/aural history as the motivating device here are some other possibilities that could relate to various topics in consumer economics.

1. "The Sounds of the Stock Market." Ticker tape machines, floor conversation, and an oral history interview with a stock broker describing the function of the machines and the services of a stock broker along with the history of the stock market.

2. "The Sounds of Industry." Blast furnaces, printing presses, etc., all would make ideal recording subjects. Interviews could then be conducted with workers and management. Related topics for recording might include job requirements, description of the nature of the work, problems in the industry, labor-management confrontations.

3. "The Sounds of Agriculture." Tractors, combines, the shelling of corn, etc., would all be desirable sounds to capture on tape. Interviews with farmers about their machines, their work, problems, role in the country's economic life would prove to be valuable oral history material.

The possibilities are only limited by one's imagination. No matter what the economic subject chosen the format would remain essentially the same:

1. Teacher recording the sounds of various machines.
2. Oral history interview conducted with a selected individual.
3. Students guessing of the sounds.
4. Students listening to the interview.
5. Completion of a handout by students while listening to the tape.
6. A field excursion to the place of business.
7. Follow up activities which could include a quiz involving the sound/slide/function of the machines.
8. Follow up with a test covering the content of the field excursion experience and the taped oral history interview.

Oral/aural history then can enrich our social studies curriculum in numerous ways. It certainly will not solve all our teaching problems, but it can offer students another method of understanding a little better the world they live in and the world in which their parents and grandparents lived.

Notes

1. Vaughn Davis Bornet, "Oral History Can Be Worthwhile," *American Archivist* 18 (July 1955), p. 241.

2. Willa K. Baum, "Looking at Oral History," *Social Science Education Consortium Newsletter,* September 5, 1975, p. 1.

3. The reader is referred to the following authors who have written articles about the teaching of oral history in the classroom: William Cutler, "Oral History as a Teaching Tool," *Oral History Review* 1 (1973), pp. 29–47; Cullom Davis and James Krohe, Jr., "History with a Tape Recorder in the Community and in the Classroom," *Illinois Journal of Education* 63 (May/June 1972), pp. 7–11; Michael H. Ebner, "Students as Oral Historians," *History Teacher* 9 (February 1976), pp. 196–201; Charles T. Morrissey, "Oral History as a Classroom Tool," *Social Education* 32 (October 1968), pp. 446–49; John A. Neuenschwander, *Oral History as a Teaching Approach* (Washington, D.C.: National Education Association, 1975); John A. Neuenschwander, "The Use of Oral History in Teaching," *Oral History Review* 3 (1975), pp. 59–67; Richard F. Newton, "Oral History: Using the School as an Historical Institution," *Clearing House* 48 (October 1973), pp. 73–78; Beatrice Spade, "Americans in Vietnam: An Oral History Project," *History Teacher* 8 (February 1975); and Margaret Sullivan, "Into Community Classrooms: Another Use for Oral History," *Oral Hsitory Review* (1974), pp. 53–58.

4. Baum, "Looking," p. 4.

5. R. Murray Schafer, "Listening," *Sound Heritage* 3:4 (1974), pp. 10–17.

6. Schafer, "Listening," pp.10–17.

7. Schafer, "Listening," pp.10–17.

34

Introduction to *The Foxfire Book*

Eliot Wigginton

Our final article on schooling tells the history of a sweepingly successful experiment in education through oral history and folklore. The work of Foxfire originator Eliot Wigginton has had controversial and far-reaching effects: hundreds of thousands of copies of the Foxfire series were sold; a play based on these folk narratives opened on Broadway; and between 1971 and 1977, eighty of these student-oriented collecting projects began around the United States.

Academic critics have called the results of these projects "fakelore" and have rejected the impressionistic field-collecting procedures. Advocates have called the approach "one of the nicest things to have happened to schools since they put backs on benches." Together with books by our con-tributors Neuenschwander (Oral History as a Teaching Approach, 1976) and Mehaffy, Sitton, and Davis (Oral History: Projects for the Class-room, 1983), the Foxfire series may represent a new movement in commu-nity education.

The Foxfire program is, in the words of its founder, "a grassroots attempt to evolve innovative patterns of community oral history intended for com-munity consumption"; many of its supporters are educators impressed by the program's success in motivating student interest in community tradi-tions. The Ford Foundation has funded the use of this model in demonstra-tion schools nationwide.

Here is Wigginton's own account of the founding of the first Foxfire proj-ect. Whether this proves to be a teaching approach of limited applicability or the beginning of a widespread revival of rural and oral traditions, only time can tell.

B. Eliot Wigginton, a high school teacher in Georgia, started Foxfire *magazine in 1966 to help his students explore their own Appalachian cul-ture. Since then he has set up a foundation, the Foxfire Fund, and projects in community television, record recording, environmental education, and community development, all based on the ideas first articulated here.*

The Foxfire Book *was published in 1972 (New York, Doubleday).*

THE CONTENTS OF this book need little introduction; they stand on their own as helpful instructions and enjoyable reading. But what is not immediately apparent is that the material here was collected and put toegether almost entirely by high school students. And that makes the book a little special—for me at least, since they were kids I was supposed to be teaching.

It was 1966, and I had just finished five years at Cornell. I had an A.B. in English and an M.A. in Teaching, and I thought I was a big deal—a force to be reckoned with. So I went to Georgia and took a job at the 240-pupil Rabun Gap-Nacoochee School where I taught ninth and tenth grade English, geography, and had about ten other side responsibilities. Rabun Gap is right in the Appalachians. God's country, as they say here, and I'll go along with that.

About six weeks later, I surveyed the wreckage. My lectern (that's a protective device a teacher cowers behind while giving a lecture nobody's listening to) was scorched from the time Tommy Green tried to set it on fire with his lighter—during class. Charles Henslee had already broken off the blade of his Barlow knife in the floorboards. Every desk was decorated with graffiti. My box of yellow chalk was gone, and so were the thumbtacks that had held up the chart of the Globe Theatre. The nine water pistols I had confiscated that very afternoon had been reconfiscated from under my nose.

And it was with a deep sigh that, as I launched one of several paper airplanes within easy reach, I began to ponder greener pastures. Either that or start all over.

The answer was obvious. If I were to finish out the year honorably, it would be necessary to reassert my authority. No teenagers were going to push me around. Besides, my course was too important. First offense would be an "X" in the grade book. Second, a paddling. Third, to the principal. Fourth, out of class for two weeks.

It frightens me to think how close I came to making another stupid mistake. First, I had bored them unmercifully. Now I was about to impose a welcome punishment. Two weeks out of that class would have been more pleasure than pain.

Those who cannot remember the past not only relive it; they tend to impose it, mistakes and all, on others. My own high school— monumentally boring texts and lectures, all forgotten; punishments and regulations and slights that only filled a reservoir of bitterness; and three blessed teachers who let me make things, helped me make them, and praised the results.

Luckily, it took only a few rewards to keep me going. How many students were denied even those few scraps of self-esteem from anyone other than their peers? And how many was I now denying?

I am not sure what the magic formula is or whether I have it pegged yet, but it involves a chemistry that allows us to believe we may have worth after all. Someone says, "You've done well," and we hunger to make that happen again and again. Too often we, as teachers, slip, and that first flush of success our students get comes after they've survived a night of drinking Colt 45, stuck up the local gas station, or taken two tabs of acid and made it out the other side alive.

We could catch some of those if we would.

The next day I walked into class and said, "How would you like to throw away the text and start a magazine?" And that's how *Foxfire* began.

From the beginning, the idea was to involve everyone. (It hasn't always worked, but we try.) We decided to print one issue put together by all of us as a class and during class time. If that issue did what I hoped it would do for my ailing classes, we might try to make it a regular thing. But for the time being, one issue only.

The contents? There were lots of possibilities. Many older people in this area, for example, still plant today by the signs of the zodiac and the stages of the moon. I had heard them mention it, but I didn't know what it meant. Rather than interrupt a conversation to find out, I figured I'd get my students to tell me. They'd probably know since it was mostly their parents and grandparents who were doing it. But my kids didn't really know what it was either, and soon they were as curious as I was. Why not find out and turn the information into an article?

So they went home and talked—really talked—to their own relatives, some of them for the first time. From those conversations came superstitions, old home remedies, weather signs, a story about a hog hunt, a taped interview with the retired sheriff about the time the local bank was robbed—and directions for planting by the signs. It was looking good.

Another possibility was poetry. Many of my students hated the stuff. I suspect one of the reasons was that they were forced to read pages of sentimental greeting card verse before they ever got to high school. In any case, working with poetry from an editor's point of view might be one way to overcome an already deeply rooted bias, and they were willing to try. So we added poetry too. Some was from our school (and some was from notably bad students in an effort to give them a boost they were hungry for). Some of it was from students in other schools in the state. And some was even from practicing poets. As we said in the first issue, "We hoped that they would remember their own beginnings and their own battles to be recognized and not to be too proud to provide us with examples to follow—pieces we could aspire to in our own work."

The name? Each student submitted three choices. Duplications were eliminated, a master list was mimeographed and passed out, the obviously unworkable ones were dropped, and the kids voted from among those left. They chose "foxfire," a tiny organism that glows in the dark and is frequently seen in the shaded coves of these mountains.

And money? The school could provide no support at all. Any financial obligations would be my problem—not theirs. Looking back, I can see what a blessing in disguise that was. It meant the magazine had to sell, and that literally forced us to emphasize folklore rather than poetry, for magazines devoted to verse almost never survive for very long on the market. It also meant the kids had to find the money for that first issue themselves, and that made them more determined to see the magazine go than anything I could have said.

And so they hit the streets after school. Any donor, no matter how small his gift, would be listed in the issue, and he would receive a free copy signed by all the kids.

They collected four hundred fifty dollars. The local printer said that was enough to print six hundred copies photo-offset. So we printed six hundred copies, sold out in a week, and printed six hundred more.

It sounds simple doesn't it? I can promise there were times we almost chucked the whole thing and went back to *Silas Marner.* In our total ignorance we made some colossal blunders. We went broke a couple of times, for one. People like John Dyson and groups like the Coordinating Council of Literary Magazines came along and pulled us out of the mud, brushed us off, and wound us up again.

And each time we flopped, we got up a little stronger. Now, in Rabun Gap, there exists a magazine that has subscribers in all fifty states and a dozen foreign countries. It has been written about in magazines like *Saturday Review, New Republic, National Geographic School Bulletin, Scholastic Scope,* and *Whole Earth Catalogue.* It has received two grants from the National Endowment for the Humanities, one of them for $10,000. But most important, it is run by high school students—students who are going on to college knowing that they can be forces for constructive change; knowing that they can *act* responsibly and effectively rather than being always *acted upon.*

Looking beyond Rabun Gap and *Foxfire,* I can't get over the feeling that similar projects could be duplicated successfully in many other areas of the country, and to the genuine benefit of almost everyone involved.

Daily our grandparents are moving out of our lives, taking with them, irreparably, the kind of information contained in this book. They are taking it, not because they want to, but because they think we don't care. And it isn't happening just in Appalachia. I think, for example, of numerous Indian reservations, Black cultures near the southern coasts, Ozark mountain communities, and a hundred others.

The big problem, of course, is that since these grandparents were primarily an oral civilization, information being passed through the generations by word of mouth and demonstration, little of it is written down. When they're gone, the magnificent hunting tales, the ghost stories that kept a thousand children sleepless, the intricate tricks of self-sufficiency acquired through years of trial and error, the eloquent and haunting stories of suffering and sharing and building and healing and planting and harvesting—all these go with them, and what a loss.

If this information is to be saved at all, for whatever reason, it must be saved now; and the logical researchers are the grandchildren, not university researchers from the outside. In the process, these grandchildren (and we) gain an invaluable, unique knowledge about their own roots, heritage, and culture. Suddenly they discover their families—previously people to be ignored in the face of the seventies—as pre-television, pre-automobile, pre-flight individuals who endured and survived the incredible task of total self-sufficiency, and came out of it all with a perspective on ourselves as a country that we are not likely to see again. They have something to tell us about self-reliance, human interdependence, and the human spirit that we would do well to listen to.

Is the subject, English, ignored in the process? Hardly. In fact, the opposite is true. English, in its simplest definition, is communication—reaching out and touching people with words, sounds, and visual images. We are in the business of improving students' prowess in these areas. In their work with photography (which must tell the story with as much impact and clarity as the words), text (which must be grammatically correct except in the use of pure dialect from tapes that they transcribe), lay-out, make-up, correspondence, art and cover design, and selection of manuscripts from outside poets and writers—to say nothing of related skills such as fund raising, typing, retailing, advertising, and speaking at conferences and public meetings—they learn more about English than from any other curriculum I could devise. Moreover, this curriculum has built-in motivations and immediate and tangible rewards.

The project also has benefits for the community at large. The collection of artifacts, tapes, and photographs is a valuable addition to any community museum Furthermore, many still culturally distinctive areas, cut off from the main thrust of our country, are also economically and educationally deprived. Articles about local craftsmen and craft cooperatives, to give only one small example, can result in a welcome flow of income from a population grown weary of a plastic world. And the education the students can acquire in the process can be a welcome supplement to their ordinary routine.

And the whole thing doesn't cost that much. In pure business terms, you can get a staggering return from a relatively small investment.

The kid who scorched my lecturn had been trying to tell me something. He and his classmates, through their boredom and restlessness, were sending out distress signals—signals that I came perilously close to ignoring.

It's the same old story. The answer to student boredom and restlessness (manifested in everything from paper airplanes to dope) maybe—just maybe—is not stricter penalties, innumerable suspensions, and bathroom monitors. How many schools (mine included) have dealt with those students that still have fire and spirit, *not* by channeling that fire in constructive, creative directions, but by pouring water on the very flames that could make them great? And it's not *necessarily* that the rules are wrong. It's the arrogant way we tend to enforce them. Until we can *inspire* rather than babysit, we're in big trouble. Don't believe me. Just watch and see what happens. We think drugs and turnover rates and dropouts are a problem now. We haven't seen anything yet.

Foxfire obviously isn't the whole answer. But maybe it's a tiny part of it. If this book is worth anything at all, it's because every piece of it was put together and handled and squeezed and shaped and touched by teenagers.

And it's been a long time since I found a paper airplane under my desk.

PART SIX
Oral History and Libraries

35

The Implications of Oral History for Librarians

Martha Jane Zachert

Previous sections have discussed the history of oral history; its interpretation and design, and its relation to other disciplines. All of these are important issues, but most will come to naught if the oral history collected does not find a good repository—a library—where the materials are housed and distributed. Library handling and retrievability, the subject of the next articles, is the key to whether the whole enterprise is useful.

Research librarians have a particular interest in oral history. In 1968, Martha Zachert, a teacher of library science, published this early acknowledgment of the importance of oral history for librarianship.

The author lists five major implications of oral history archives for librarians. (1) Librarians can create, not just acquire primary research materials. (2) Librarians must furnish access bibliographically to these new materials. (3) Librarians should study problems of bibliographical control. (4) Oral history collections offer new possibilities of service and new responsibilities. (5) These collections also pose problems of integration into main library collections.

For many libraries, oral history programs offer an effective avenue into widened public access (and interest in) their collections. By initiating community participation in community history projects—including media programs—by recording and circulating information about the lives of well-respected citizens, and by holding workshops for local teachers on ways of using their collections, librarians have the opportunity for an active, creative role as a storehouse of community tradition.

Martha Jane K. Zachert teaches at the College of Librarianship at the University of South Carolina. In recent years she has worked on community and continuing education projects and has been a research fellow at the British Library in London.

"The Implications of Oral History for Librarians" first appeared in College and Research Libraries 29 *(March 1968), pp. 101–103.*

ORAL HISTORY is no longer an experiment; it is a healthy movement. A group of historians, librarians, doctors, psychologists, and lawyers . . . met [in 1966] at the Second Oral History colloquium[1] to discuss techniques and philosophies and to found the Oral History Association. The papers and discussions at this meeting showed that, as a movement, oral history has significant implications for research librarians, especially those in academic libraries.

Oral history is a record of recall. The record is authored by an individual who participated in, or observed at close range, events whose documentation will aid future researchers in understanding some facet of twentieth-century life. The oral author is aided in his recall by an interviewer versed both in the segment of life to be recorded and in appropriate techniques for creating this unique record. To this extent oral history is a collaboration: the oral author is the contributor of substance, the interviewer is the contributor of recording skill. Practitioners of the art are currently engaged in formulating techniques to safeguard both the accuracy of the record and convenience in its use. For accuracy the record is tape recorded; for convenience it is usually transcribed. Groups of oral history interviewers are usually organized into an oral history "office," "center," "program," or "archives," although loners are not unknown. Groups or single interviewers may be an adjunct of a research library or may more usually be autonomous within an academic context. In either event, tapes, transcriptions, or both almost always come to rest in a library while awaiting their ultimate users.

The alert research librarian will perceive at once that there are many implications in this oral history movement for libraries and for librarians. To an observer at the colloquium's sessions five implications seem of immediate significance.

1. Oral history, for a library, is a way of *creating* primary source materials in contrast to its time-honored responsibility of *acquiring* them. For the librarian, then, building an oral archive becomes a unique opportunity for a creative intellectual contribution. Research librarians are typically specialists, either through academic accomplishment or through informal but penetrating study of the materials in their collections. Typically also, research librarians have a near-intuitive rapport with other individuals that comes from long and intensive public service. To become builders of oral archives librarians must add analytic skill to identify what is significant in our own times in order to define the appropriate scope for each oral history project they undertake. Librarians must also learn interviewing and recording techniques. If research librarians do not rise to this occasion, a rare creative opportunity will escape them.

2. Oral archives offer new service possibilities for research libraries; they also present new responsibilities. The oral author's product is legally

his to deposit or to assign to the institution which houses and services it. In either case—deposit or assignment—the oral author can stipulate conditions under which his material may be used by researchers. Under these circumstances the library must fulfill the author's conditions or be liable for its failure to do so. If the library chooses to copyright the oral history tapes or transcripts, it has the added responsibility to make sure the copyrighted material is used but not infringed. Libraries now receiving oral archives, whether or not they themselves created the materials, have already had these new responsibilities thrust upon them. Libraries contemplating embarkation on a project of their own or cooperation in a project with an academic department should inform themselves in respect to these new responsibilities and vulnerabilities.

3. A further responsibility for the library housing oral archives is that of integrating tapes and transcripts into the collections of primary research materials, while at the same time observing conditions of housing uniquely required by the unusual formats. Most oral history projects generate series of records rather than single items. The name "oral archives" suggests that these materials may be better handled through the archivist's concepts of provenance and record series than as individual items.

4. The responsibility for bibliographic control follows, and again a solution may derive from the archivist's concepts. Oral archives can be, perhaps should be, described as are collections of personal or official papers. But providing intellectual access to primary source materials is only half the battle. Physical access must also be provided for researchers. It is not too soon in the oral history movement to recommend the inclusion of oral archives in the *National Union Catalog of Manuscript Collections*. Lending themselves to the same kind of description as that used for papers, oral archives can be included without requiring any modification in the format of NUCMC. Their use along with the kinds of materials already described in NUCMC stipulates their inclusion for the convenience of the researcher. Why should he have to search different tools for such closely related primary materials? The fact that inclusion of oral archives is already under discussion between oral historians and NUCMC suggests that all research librarians need to keep an eye on the situation. Even those librarians whose own institutions do not include oral archives will want to be able to direct their patrons to collections that can aid research under way.

5. Finally, oral history archives offer librarians opportunity for research into the problems of retrieving information from additional storage media—tapes and transcriptions. All appropriate techniques, including machine techniques, should be investigated while the total body of oral archives is relatively small. The urgency to index in depth may not be

apparent with the present volume of material. But one lesson that seems clear is that the body of material is growing rapidly with no endpoint in sight. Lessons expensively learned from journal and technical report literature seem appropriate for modification in the new context.

Lest research librarians feel helpless in the fact of these implications, the following readings are suggested for an orientation.

Note

1. The Second Oral History Colloquium was held in New York at Arden House, November 18–21, 1967, under the sponsorship of Columbia University.

Bibliography

Bingham, Walter, and Bruce Moore. *How to Interview.* 4th ed. New York: Harper, 1959.
"Goals and Guidelines for Oral History." Mimeographed. Los Angeles: Oral History Association, 1967. (See part 7 of the present volume)
Gottschalk, Louis R., et al. *Use of Personal Documents in History, Sociology, and Anthropology.* New York: Social Science Research Council, 1945. (Paperback)

36

The Expanding Role of the Librarian in Oral History

Willa Baum

In our second article, Willa Baum, author of two classic manuals on oral history, discusses the responsibilities of librarians in creating, curating, consuming, and counseling with respect to oral history. She explores the special problems libraries face in caring for and publicizing oral history holdings, then points out how the library, through setting standards of acceptance, can play a part in encouraging well-researched oral history.

Willa K. Baum, head of the Regional Oral History Office of the Bancroft Library, University of California, Berkeley, served on the first and subsequent councils of the Oral History Association. Active in the field since 1954, she has played a major role in developing the technique of oral history through her two guidebooks, Oral History for the Local Historical Society *(1969) and* Transcribing and Editing Oral History *(1977), and through her many journal articles and lectures.*

"The Expanding Role of the Librarian in Oral History" is adapted from a 1976 lecture at the Louisiana State University Library School, published in Library Lectures 6 *(1978), pp. 33–43.*

IT APPEARS to me that the greatest need in oral history is to engage the knowledgeable participation of librarians in oral history, especially librarians in the smaller local and regional libraries. Two things especially concern me:

1. the preservation and use of oral history tapes after they are produced and
2. the quality of the interviews being produced—I refer to the content of the interviews, not the quality of the sound recording, although that matter also requires attention.

I have recently been working with a library school student who has chosen as her field study assignment the compilation of a directory of all the oral history tapes in the San Francisco Bay area. She has been discovering, and I think the San Francisco area is in this respect fairly representative of other regions, that oral history tapes are being produced by a myriad of individuals and temporary groups, that the tapes are getting into local libraries, and that there they are lost. They are not irretrievably lost, but lost to use—uncatalogued or inadequately cataloged, often unshelved, undescribed as to subjects discussed on the tapes or how they came to be there at all, and with no information regarding access and restrictions on their use.

Another problem is that while the oral history tapes being recorded are often very good in terms of documenting local landmarks, the community's colorful characters, both praiseworthy and notorious, and major events, such as the earthquake and fire, the flood, and the opening of the bridge, the tapes are neglecting less dramatic but possibly more significant material. An interview with the town's chief of police for forty years, for example, includes no discussion of changes in law enforcement problems or police methods during those four decades.

It seems to me imperative that librarians play a greater role in oral history if oral history is to fulfill its promise of providing a medium whereby all of the people and the regions and the occupations of this diverse nation are to be documented and their stories preserved and used in the telling of our nation's history. I mean to limit my remarks here to defining that role.

The Three Steps of Oral History

There are three major steps to oral history, the "three C's," you might call them. In chronological order they are "creating," "curating," and "consuming." To this I will add a fourth, "counseling." By counseling I mean providing the advice, the readings and background material, and the on-going supervision that will aid the creators of oral history in producing acceptable interviews that elicit the most useful information from the narrators.

Creating is not essentially a library function, though in fact many oral history projects emanate from a library, our own office included. But the counseling component of creating, although it could be done by another agency such as the history department of a college, will probably fall to the local library. Therefore I will discuss that function in some detail, and I include a bibliography of manuals on oral history that the librarian can provide for prospective interviewers.

The "consuming" of oral history materials is a laissez-faire situation, with librarians as welcome to participate as anyone else. It is not un-known for librarians to moonlight as writers of historical articles and editors of historical books. Librarians appear in the rolls of writers of historical fiction and even more so among the authors of children's books. The new breed of audio-visually trained librarian is even appearing in the ranks of the producers of radio and television programs and educational AV materials. In all of these areas, oral history materials provide a source of fresh, lively material. The librarian can make a vital difference in the quantity and quality of use of oral history materials by serving as a broker between creator and consumer of oral history.

But it is in the area of "curating" that the librarian is essential; at least, if we accept as part of the definition of oral history that it must, now or later, be available for research use, then it must be accessioned, preserved, made available by information retrieval tools, and serviced.

Definition of Oral History

Before I use the term "oral history" again, I should define it. Or perhaps I would be wiser not to define it, for among oral historians there is no agreement as to precisely what oral history includes and excludes. At the first gathering of persons doing what they called oral history, a meeting called by UCLA in 1966, the definition was hotly debated. Did it include tape-recorded folk tales and songs; surveys on tape of all the inhabitants of South Dakota more than eighty years old on "badmen I have seen"; taped interviews with farm families on why they decided to plant the south forty in wheat instead of rye; intimate probing by a psychoanalyst historian into the dreams of a great leader; or the neatly typed transcripts of much-rewritten interviews, the tapes from which they were prepared having been erased? We could not agree then (we cannot wholly agree now), but we did applaud the late Dr. Philip C. Brooks, then director of the Truman Library, when he said, "I do have a naive feeling that oral history ought to be *oral*, and it ought to be history."

Yet recent events have caused us to discard even Brooks's vague defini-tion. The Watergate tapes are without a doubt *oral* and without a doubt *history*, yet there is no oral historian who would accept them as oral history. They fail in the most basic tenet of oral history—that the parties being recorded know they are being recorded and that they agree to make the information they convey available for research.

Without trying to delineate any exact boundaries, let me define oral history as:

1. a tape-recorded interview, or interviews, in question-and-answer format,

2. conducted by an interviewer who has some, and preferably the more the better, knowledge of the subject to be discussed,
3. with a knowledgeable interviewee, someone who knows whereof he or she speaks from personal participation or observation (sometimes we allow a second-hand account),
4. on subjects of historical interest (one researcher's history could be everyone else's trivia)
5. accessible, eventually, in tapes and/or transcripts to a broad spectrum of researchers.

It is this fifth qualification that differentiates oral history from the time-honored method used by a researcher who asks the people who witnessed an event what happened. It presupposes a certain degree of selflessness, first, in asking questions which may not be of special interest to the interviewer but which are designed to provide information for many users, both present and future, and second, in depositing the product in a library or archive for use by others. And it is in this second step that the librarian becomes key to the value of oral history.

The Popularization of Oral History

The first oral history projects were aimed at the "movers and shakers of society." The presidential libraries sought the chief lieutenants and, sometimes, the chief opponents of their particular president. Special projects such as the John Foster Dulles Project or the General George Marshall Project likewise documented a great man, while multipurpose projects like Columbia's recorded the distinguished citizens of a given region. Our own office, the Regional Oral History Office of the University of California (Berkeley), came into being in 1954, charged by the regents with "tape recording the memoirs of persons who have contributed significantly to the development of the West and of the nation." But in the past ten years the trend has been more to "people's history," to collecting the self-told tales of Indians, migrant workers, coal miners, mountain dwellers, sharecroppers, groups which would otherwise never be documented except by a few brief public records as birth, marriage, death, welfare rolls, or social security rolls.

The scholarly books drawing on oral history have multiplied geometrically with each year following 1960, the first year Columbia University issued a report of its holdings. Books drawing heavily on oral history include T. Harry Williams's biography, *Huey Long,* 1969; Vivian Perlis's *Charles Ives Remembered: An Oral History,* 1974; Fawn Brodie's *Richard Nixon: The Shaping of His Character,* 1981; David Dunaway's *How Can I Keep from Singing: Pete Seeger,* 1981; G. Edward White's *Earl Warren: A*

Public Life, 1982; and, for librarians, Guy R. Lyle's *The Librarian Speaking: Interviews with University Librarians,* 1970.

Oral historians had always aimed for such use, although we initially assumed it would be future use, and we continue to be startled at the rapidity with which our materials are snapped up by current researchers. We did not anticipate the tremendous popularity of lay volumes based on "people's history" such as Studs Terkel's *Hard Times* (1970) and his *Working* (1974); Theodore Rosengarten's *All God's Dangers: The Life of Nate Shaw* (1974); Al Santoli's *Everything We Had: An Oral History of the Vietnam War* (1981); and Eliot Wigginton's *Foxfire,* seven volumes of interviews with Georgia folk done by his high school students.

The popularization and profitability of books derived from oral history may indeed prove damaging to the original concept of oral history's purpose, which was the obtaining of very candid remarks on historical events (to be seen only by a limited group of qualified scholars). Certainly the response has increased the problems of librarians, who must now worry about literary rights, royalties, libel, and invasion of privacy far more than in the early days of oral history.

Curating Oral History

Whether they be accounts of "movers and shakers" or of "the people," oral history tapes and transcripts must find their way into a library or an archive if they are to serve any purpose at all. This need brings us to the essential library function of curating.

Let me illustrate with an example. A professor from a nearby university deposited in the Donated Oral Histories Collection of the Bancroft Library the best tapes produced by students in her course in women's history. One tape recorded a woman who was and is an active trade unionist, first in Idaho and for the past thirty-five years in the San Francisco area. She is one of the prime movers in the founding of Union WAGE (Union Women's Alliance to Gain Equality), an alliance of trade union women to fight discrimination on the job, in unions, and in society. On the tape she tells of her first unionizing experience in 1933 when, as a waitress in a small cafe in Idaho serving CCC boys, she refused to work seven days a week. Later in the tape she tells how she managed to support her children in a man's world and describes the ins and outs of union politics. In a very personal and understandable way, she takes the listener back in time to the beginnings of mass unionization in the depression era, to the CCC days, to the mobilization of all man and woman power during World War II. What a teaching resource this tape would be if the secondary teachers knew of its existence! Surely a librarian would be delighted to participate in bringing this sort of interview into being by working with the teachers, the volunteer oral historians, and the students who would be recording the interviews. Now, consider the problems raised by the donation of this tape:

1. Who owns it?
2. Who can grant permission to reproduce it in tape or transcript for scholarly use, perhaps for commercial publication?
3. How should it be cataloged? Must the librarian listen to a tape for the full hour and a half to determine the major subjects? Suppose that with the tape comes a file of photographs, a scrapbook of newspaper clippings about the narrator, and many official documents relating to the trade union struggles she was involved in. How shall these be cataloged? How shelved?
4. The narrator was at the time of the recording involved in a bitter struggle within her union, and she insisted on stating her case. Could the library be held actionable for slander if one of the opposing union officials learned of the tape?

Headaches? Challenges? Maybe entertainment for the librarian bored with dealing with books that come with LC numbers, catalog cards, and neatly excerpted book reviews on their jackets. There are no accepted solutions to these problems. Nonetheless, I will plunge in and give you my own suggestions.

Accepting the Tapes and Transcripts

Be prepared to cope with some of the problems of ownership, provenance, and cataloging at the time the oral history materials are offered to the library.

Gift Forms. Ownership of the tapes should be signed over to the library, unless the group that produced them is an on-going organization that will be able to administer the interviews in perpetuity. Ownership can be established by having the interviewer and the narrator sign a gift form. The wording of the simple donor form used by the Bancroft Library is as follows:

We, _____ (narrator) and _____ (interviewer) do hereby give to the Bancroft Library for such scholarly and educational uses as the director of the Bancroft Library shall determine the following tape-recorded interview(s) recorded on _____ (date(s)) as an unrestricted gift and transfer to the University of California legal title and all literary property rights including copyright. This gift does not preclude any use which we may want to make of the information in the recordings ourselves. (Signed by narrator and interviewer and accepted by the librarian)

To this gift form can be added any special restrictions the narrator or interviewer may request, such as:

Closed: The entire tape and transcript shall be closed to all users until 1995. (Do not use vague expressions like "until the death of the narrator" unless one librarian will be permanently assigned to obituary watching.)

Some pages closed: The following transcript pages and the tape relating hereto shall be closed to all users until _____ (date) except with the written permission of _____ (narrator). Transcript pages:.

Open for research, requires permission to quote: The tape and transcript are open for research but may not be quoted for publication except with the written permission of _____ (narrator or interviewer) until 1990 (in the event the narrator or interviewer are preparing a publication that will draw on the interview).

Insistent as the library should be on accepting only interviews with gift forms signed by narrator and interviewer, the occasion will arise when a collection is offered for which there are no signed gift forms and the narrators are dead or have dispersed. Should it be accepted? Yes, with prudence. Obtain a signed gift form from the interviewer on the assumption that the narrators gave their accounts to the interviewer and the material is now his or her property to donate. Try to obtain some evidence that the narrators intended to make the recordings available. Perhaps the letter asking them to participate in the recording program said it was for historic preservation. Perhaps the uses of the material are discussed on the tape.

Then, depending on the nature of the material, make the recordings available with care. For example, researchers may be required to identify the source of a quotation as anonymous if the material is personal or to draw general conclusions without providing specific, identified examples. Since the object of library oral history collecting is to make the material as widely useful and easily accessible as possible, the fewer limitations on use, the better.

Provenance and Topic Summary

The library should request a written description of the major topics covered in the interview, who the narrator is, who did the interviews, and why. Obtaining this information will greatly reduce the time required by the cataloger, who otherwise might have to listen to all the tapes to establish subjects. The information about the narrator and interviewer will enhance the value of the tapes to the user as well as aiding the cataloger.

This information also can most easily be obtained by having a blank ready for the donor to fill out (see Figure 32.2 in this volume). Sample forms are available in the manuals listed in the bibliography. Be sure to ask for collateral material such as photographs, scrapbooks, and so forth if they seem appropriate.

Shelving and Cataloging of Tapes and Collateral Material

Tapes, photographs, and papers all survive well under the same housing conditions, that is, in a clean environment (no smoking, no eating) with stable humidity (40–60 percent) and stable temperature (60–70 degrees Fahrenheit). They could all be stored together in closed manuscript boxes. But for purposes of more compact storage, tapes are often separated from papers. This separation is no problem as long as they are so cataloged that all the elements of one collection can be reassembled.

The card catalog determines whether the oral history materials will prove an exciting new resource or will be lost on some dusty shelf. Whatever catalog system you use, the most important thing about an oral history collection is the information it contains, not the fact that it is on tape. Do not bury oral history in an audio-visual materials catalog; file the catalog cards in your main subject/author catalog. The entries should relate to:

1. the narrator (author);
2. major subjects discussed;
3. the producing group (i.e., Baton Rouge Architectural Heritage Committee);
4. the subject "oral history" so that the material will be retrievable as an audio resource as well.

A sample of catalog cards for a transcript with tapes from the manuscript catalog of the Bancroft Library appears in figure 36.1. Note that the transcript's catalog card indicates that there is a tape available; that there is a legal restriction; and that there are supporting materials. The tracings indicate cross-referenced subject catalog entries. In this instance, the interviewee's name is the major entry; it is a 184-page transcript with a well-known person. In other projects, the interviewees may not be well known and the major entry would relate to the topic; for example, "San Francisco Earthquake and Fire, 1906, recollections of."

Servicing

Oral history materials are like other manuscript materials: they are unique and for safety's sake cannot be permitted to leave the library. In addition, the tapes require a tape recorder and headphones that may be used by patrons. And the library that receives tapes all in one format is lucky; more likely they will come on cassettes and on mono and stereo reels at all speeds from one and seven-eighths to seven and one-half inches per second, making necessary several playback machines or a way of duplicating tapes for patron use. Ideally, the archival or master copy of the recording will be held on reel-to-reel tapes, with copies duplicated on

---

Partial phonotape also available
Please inquire at Desk

> 72/105   Rinder, Rose (Perlmutter)
> C   Music, Prayer and Religious Leadership, Temple Emanu-El, 1913-1969. Berkeley, Calif. 1971.
>   [44], 1841. Ms. 28 cm.
>   Photocopy of typed transcript of tape-recorded interviews conducted 1968-1969 by Malca Chall for Bancroft Library Regional Oral History Office. Introduction by Rabbi Louis I. Newman, Photographs inserted.
>   SEALED UNTIL JANUARY 1973 EXCEPT WITH MRS. RINDER'S WRITTEN PERMISSION.
>   CONTINUED ON NEXT CARD

Notation: Phonotape available
Notation: Interview sealed until specified date

> 72/105   Rinder, Rose P. Music Prayer . . . (card 2)
> C   Recollection of the years she and her husband Cantor Rueben Rinder were associated with Temple Emanu-El in San Francisco; their participation in musical life in the Bay area; their friendship with many musicians including Ernest Bloch, Yehudi Menuhin, Isaac Stern and others.
>   Copies of letters, programs, and other documentary material inserted.
>   (OVER)

> 1. Rinder, Reuben, 1887-1966   2. Jews in California   3. San Francisco, Temple Emanu-El x-3. Templ-El. San Francisco   4. Music—San Francisco 5. Musicians—Correspondence, reminiscences, etc.   6. Bloch, Ernest, 1880-1959   7. Menuhin, Yehudi, 1916-   8. Stern, Isaac, 1920-
> I. Bancroft Library.   Regional Oral History Office   II. Newman, Louis Israel, 1893-

Tracings—Rinder, Rose. Cards crossfiled under these entries.

Figure 36.1. Sample oral history manuscript catalog cards

cassettes for patron use. If patrons use the master tape, be sure the playback machine has a lock on the "record" button so that the tapes cannot be accidentally erased.

If there are restrictions on the use of tapes or transcripts, they must be clearly marked on both the catalog cards and the tapes or transcripts so that the librarian cannot bring them to a patron without noting the restrictions.

Legal Considerations

We have now reached the question of restricted use and the possibility of libel or invasion-of-privacy lawsuits. Restrictions requested by the narrator or the donor are necessarily involved in oral history. If we are going to ask narrators to give a candid account, then we must have a way to protect them or the people they discuss. We therefore offer "seal privileges"—the opportunity to close the manuscript for a specified number of years, usually until the date when it may reasonably be expected that all the participants in an event will have died. Then, too, the donor may be a researcher who is willing to donate the tapes now but would like to reserve the exclusive right to publish from them for a specified number of years. Such a stipulation is fair enough. These situations can be covered by the above-mentioned clauses on the gift forms. But what about a case involving a narrator who was very outspoken about other persons in her union and did not accept the offer of seal privileges? The library may occasionally find itself in possession of unrestricted accounts of long-forgotten tales of scandal or incompetence or sharp business practices that could be actionable as slander, libel, or invasion of privacy or could reactivate old community feuds.

Legal considerations that relate to the ownership and use of oral history tapes and transcripts are many and complex. I will skirt the issue by providing a bibliography of articles on legal considerations of oral history, none of which can provide definitive answers.

Legal problems are a danger more in principle than in practice. There seems to be a well-established conspiracy by which both interviewers and narrators seek to clothe the past in rosy hues, to people the "good old days" only with heroes and heroines, and never to say anything bad about the dead. The problem is likely to be how to get a realistic picture of the past.

But though the danger of libel suits is rather remote, there may be some danger of "social injury," especially at the local or family level. Therefore, the wise librarian will always be alert to the content of the tapes and will exercise prudence in making them available. I recommend retaining in principle the right to place library-imposed restrictions on oral history materials. This right should be exercised only in the interest of preventing social injury, never to give some preferred scholar or group priority rights on use (unless, of course, they are the producers of the tapes and the restrictions form part of the gift agreement). In practice, all libraries have a backlog of cataloging, and the prudent librarian may just shift sensitive tapes to the bottom of the cataloging priorities and may simply avoid giving them the extra publicity that brings the users in.

Publicizing

While the card catalog essentially determines the retrievability of oral history materials, cards alone are not enough.

Data Bases. Oral history collections should be reported to suitable data bases. Some states have a central reporting agency for oral history: they include Alaska, Colorado, Idaho, Illinois, Louisiana, New Jersey, and Washington, with more to come. If the collection numbers ten or more transcripts, it should be reported to the Library of Congress for inclusion in the National Union Catalog of Manuscript Collections (NUCMC will not report tapes), so that it enters the mainstream of primary source retrieval.

Public Use. Beyond library channels, full use of oral history materials requires that their existence be made known to the local community of prospective users, and this could involve some hustling for publicity on the part of the librarian who has a talent for it. A printed catalog of the library's oral history holdings could be circulated among libraries and in the community. The accession of a group of oral history materials could be announced in the local newspaper, the library newsletter, local or state historical newsletters, and journals in the field of the materials. If the materials are rich in local history, the librarian might call or send a note to the elementary school curriculum adviser, to high school or junior college teachers who include local history in their courses, and to the local radio station. A list of the most topical, famous, notorious, or otherwise enticing interviews could be sent to all local broadcasting stations, with a call to the public affairs or program directors thereafter to discuss how the interviews could be incorporated into radio programs. It is this final push that can involve the library in an active way with the community (for better or for worse, depending on the limitations imposed by the workload of the library staff.)

Citing Oral Histories. Oral history is very often used as a source of quotations for publication in books, journals, newspapers, museum catalogs, exhibits, and so forth. Once an interview has been cited in a publication, its uses will multiply. Future users become aware of its existence and content if the citations are clear.

Footnote and bibliography manuals do not yet give an accepted form for oral history citations. The librarian can increase access to the oral history collections by, at the time of granting permission to quote for publication, recommending a citation form. The form recommended by the Bancroft Library is as follows:

Paul, Alice, "Conversations with Alice Paul: Woman Suffrage and the Equal Rights Amendment," typescript of an oral history conducted 1972, 1973 by Amelia Fry, Regional Oral History Office, The Bancroft Library, University of California, Berkeley, 1976, 674 pages.

Counseling: The Librarian's Role in Creating Oral Histories

Having considered the essential library functions of curating oral history—accepting, cataloging, servicing, publicizing—let us return to creating, that first step of oral history. I have described creating as "not essentially a library function." Most of us find the idea of creating something more exciting than the idea of tending it properly after it has been created.

Or is there some self-selection factor among librarians that makes "tending" an equally satisfying function? I doubt it, for over the years I have met with many librarians, and usually their chief interest lies in "getting oral history going" in their communities. To the extent that they have channeled this drive into prodding some other group to initiate a project with the advice and guidance of the library, they have been successful; and to the extent that they have tried to sandwich oral history interviewing and processing in with their own too many other duties, adding to the burdens of their own overworked clerical staffs and their own overstretched library budgets, they have been disappointed. But even if the oral history program does not emanate directly from the library (and of course, many programs do), the librarian can and must taken an active part in its creation. The degree of creative participation by the librarian will often spell the difference between excellent oral history and mere tape recordings of conversations.

The creation of well-done oral history memoirs requires a knowledge of oral history methods, of historical background, and of current research trends and findings as well as continual monitoring of feedback from users. Colleges and universities or historical societies can offer some counseling, but they, too, will depend on their institutions' librarians for materials. And in the absence of faculty guidance, the librarian may stand alone as chief consultant. Such vicarious creating I have called counseling, and it is almost as essential as curating in the role librarians must play in oral history. What sorts of counseling aids, then, can the librarian be expected to provide?

Research Materials

Let us assume that an organized group is already eager to do oral history, perhaps a committee of the local historical society, and comes to the library for help. First, the library should be able to provide several different manuals on how to do oral history. The more manuals the group can see, the better. Every oral history project has different goals, different capabilities, and different situations in which to work and access to a number of manuals will enable people to select the procedures best fitted to their needs. A full set of all the oral history manuals listed in the bibliography will cost less than a few popular hardbacks.

Next, the oral history group will need assistance in finding materials on the locality and on the persons and subjects on which the interviews will focus. A librarian could compile a list of items in the library's collection—county histories, old "mug books," a run of the local newspaper, a collection of pamphlets issued by the chamber of commerce, genealogy materials, state histories, and general American histories. Such holdings can be outlined, first, in a general way as the oral history group defines topics and starts to select narrators. Once the project is under way, the librarian can help find background material for specific interviews.

As an example of such cooperation between librarian and oral history committee, I mention the recent visit to our office of a two-woman oral history committee (one of the women was past seventy and a member of a pioneer family) and the librarian of the county public library with whom the women work. The two oral historians had in one year tape-recorded sixty-five old-time residents of the county, an incredible feat, considering the amount of time required to research and then to arrange appointments for one interview. They could not have accomplished the task without having worked very closely with the librarian, who assembled family history and background materials on each narrator before the interview.

In addition to specific topics, a creative librarian can recommend reading in more general fields which will broaden the oral history interview. For example, "The American Family in Past Time" by John Demos, an article published in the summer 1974 issue of the *American Scholar*, raises many questions about the actual rather than apocryphal habits, the real life, of American families. Historians are studying them using demographic methods, census studies, court records on marriage, divorce, desertion, and so forth. Oral history could produce much information about the twentieth-century family if the interviewer is alerted to the pertinent questions.

The Librarian's On-Going Supervision

Let us assume next that the finished oral history tapes and collateral materials have been promised to the library. The librarian should immediately indicate the need for a legal release and should help the oral history committee select a suitable form from the samples in the manuals and should have blank forms prepared. The interviewer should discuss the legal release with the narrator before the interview, and the release could be signed by the narrator at the close of the interview session. At each step the fact that the form has been, first, discussed and, second, signed will keep the narrator and the interviewer aware of the fact that the tape recording is intended for permanent retention and historical use. The reinforcement of that fact alone will help keep the interview from deteriorating into a rambling conversation, and it will also help minimize casual attacks on other members of the community, thereby reducing the possibility of libel or slander.

The librarian will also want to work with the oral history committee to devise a set of procedures for describing the interview—provenance, major subject headings, and a subject-name index to the interviews. A blank interview description form provided by the library will list interviewee and interviewer with some information on each, the project title (if this is one of a series on a particular theme), and major topics, this information to be used for subject and cross-reference cataloging. Establishing the main subject headings will require thought. They should be coordinated with subject headings used by the library for other books and materials.

The form can then provide space for an interview index, a listing of the names and subjects discussed in the order they occur on the tape. This interview index will be useful to the transcriber and the cataloger; it can also serve as a summary of the interview if the transcript is not indexed. It may, in fact, be the only guide to the interview if the oral history project is not able to prepare transcripts and users must find their information on the tape. The librarian will want to work with the committee in establishing subject entries for the index.

Developing description procedures and subject entries is a useful exercise for the oral history committee. Even more instructive to the interviewer is the experience of listening to his or her completed interview for the purpose of completing the interview description form. In preparing the list of topics covered, a task which may initially seem routine, the interviewer will be forced to assess his or her own interviewing techniques and to distill from the chatter the subject headings that are most applicable. (Listening is often a sobering experience—the most common shock is to find that one's own voice is heard a greater proportion of time than the narrator's.)

Thus the library's requirement that the forms be filled out will, in effect, force the oral history committee to listen to its own tapes and thereby to learn from them and to consider the topics on which information is being collected. The librarian should be a party to this process as the work progresses—do not wait until the project is completed. The librarian's involvement could, for example, include examination of the interview description forms to see whether the topic entries conform to the topic entries used in the library's subject catalog.

Sponsorship

So far we have been assuming that an organized group is ready to commit oral history and that the librarian becomes a key adviser to that group and is eventually the recipient and curator of the collection—probably an overoptimistic assumption. More likely someone, and that someone may well be the librarian, sees the need and value of such a program and tries to organize a small number of interested persons to create an oral history program. What can the library do to aid such a group?

It is nearly impossible for a group to find any support or to establish credibility unless it has some institutional affiliation. Funding agencies regard temporary groups with suspicion. What will happen to the equipment they purchase? Will the entire project collapse half-finished if the volunteers shift their enthusiasm elsewhere? Narrators may likewise wonder what will become of their historical accounts. Who will be around to see that no one quotes from their accounts without permission?

For such an unaffiliated group, library sponsorship could mean the difference between success and failure. Sponsorship might involve use of the library's letterhead for official correspondence, a permanent address and telephone number, a cabinet in which the group's tape recorders and supplies can be stored, a definite depository for the tapes with permanent housing and staff to administer any agreements with narrators, and the continuity of one permanent, paid staff librarian. That librarian might have no other responsibility to the oral history program than that of keeping loose track of what the group is doing and of referring calls and mail to the proper group member, but such continuity is essential. With library sponsorship, the group can apply for funds from local and state agencies or from private donors. (Tax deductibility becomes important if the group seeks private funding.)

Public Presentations

From time to time the library can provide exhibit space for the oral history group's products or facilities for a demonstration program. An annual reception held in the library on a Sunday afternoon to honor oral history narrators and their families is a splendid way to bring the younger generations into contact with the older, linking the present with the past and the library with the community—depending on the selection of narrators, perhaps a segment of the community that is unfamiliar with the library. Radio, television, or tape-slide programs produced from the oral history collection offer a means of reaching an even broader segment of the community.

Collecting Oral History from Elsewhere

The library can perform another service as well by making oral histories produced elsewhere available to its patrons, either by collecting bibliographies and catalogs of oral history collections or by acquiring copies of oral history interviews which are especially pertinent to the library's own collections or to the interests of its patrons. Many collections are available for purchase in photocopy from the originating program or on microfiche from the Microfilming Corporation of America. The question of permission to quote from such secondary holdings may arise. As with holdings of microfilm or photocopies of manuscripts, requests for permission should be referred to the original holders of the materials.

Conclusion

As I come to the end of this exhortation, I hope I have not frightened anyone away from oral history. Many tasks are involved in the proper care and feeding of oral history, and I know that most libraries are understaffed and underbudgeted, with overworked staffs. Nonetheless, oral history, even the curating and especially the counseling, can offer to the librarian the sort of community involvement and one-to-one relationships with both the older actors in their communities' on-going history and the younger teachers and learners of that history for which he or she may have hoped when selecting librarianship as a profession. To be sure, oral history is fun, and we all need a little fun in our workday lives. And it can be personally satisfying to serve as a catalyst to the preservation of the oral literature of one's region.

Through oral history, every library in the country can hold special and unique materials especially related to the community it serves and can provide services and satisfactions to a non-book-using clientele. And every library, by careful preservation, by developing an adequate information retrieval system, and by serving as a creative agent between creator and user of oral history can play a part in the writing of this nation's history.

In closing, I would like to relate an anecdote from one of our oral memoirs. It indicates the sort of human insight that oral history can add to the cold facts of history. The speaker is Clara Shirpser, Democratic national committeewoman for California, describing a whistle-stop campaign trip with President Harry Truman in 1952. She had joined the train at Eureka, where she met Truman for the first time, and the party was then staying overnight in San Francisco.

So early this morning there was a knock on my door, and I answered it—I think I was in the middle of eating breakfast in my room, but I was dressed. (I usually had breakfast sent up, because it was quicker, if I ordered it the night before, and I'd be ready in time.) You had to be packed and have your luggage in the lobby at a given early hour, too, so it meant getting up very early. There stood a Secret Service man, and he said, "President Truman wants to see you in his suite." Immediately I thought, "Oh, I've done something that is wrong. What have I done? The President of the United States is calling me at this hour of the morning. Something must be wrong."

With some fear I walked to President Truman's suite. Mr. Truman was walking up and down, in the central room, looking agitated, and he turned to me. I said, "Good morning, Mr. President. Is something wrong?" He said, "Am I President of the United States or am I not, Mrs. Shirpser?" I said, "Well, of course you're President of the United States, Mr. Truman." This was my first president, too, the first President of the United States whom I knew, and I was in awe of him. He said, "Would you go into Margaret's room, and would you tell her that the President of the United States says that she has been late in starting every time, every place we have been so far, and that the President of the United States says he is going to leave this room in ten minutes, whether she's ready or not." So I said, "Are you sure you want me to tell her this? She'd pay much more attention if you told her that." He said, "Like hell she would."[1]

Note

1. Clara Shirpser, "One Woman's Role in Democratic Party Politics: National, State, and Local, 1950–1973," an oral history conducted 1972–1973 by Malca Chall, Regional Oral History Office, Bancroft Library, University of California, Berkeley, 1975, p. 174.

Bibliography

Selected Oral History Manuals

Allen, Barbara, and Lynwood Montell. *From Memory to History: Using Oral Sources in Local Historical Research.* Nashville: American Association for State and Local History, 1981.

Baum, Willa K. *Oral History for the Local Historical Society.* Nashville: American Association for State and Local History, 1974.

———. *Transcribing and Editing Oral History.* Nashville: American Association for State and Local History, 1977.

Cash, Joseph, Ramon Harris, et al. *The Practice of Oral History: A Handbook.* Glen Rock, N.J.: Microfilming Corporation of America, 1975.

Cutting-Baker, Holly, et al. *Family Folklore Interviewing Guide and Questionnaire.* Washington, D.C.: U.S. Government Printing Office, 1978.

Davis, Cullom, Kathryn Buck, and Kay MacLean. *Oral History: From Tape to Type.* Chicago: American Library Association, 1977.

Deering, Mary Jo. *Transcribing without Tears: A Guide to Transcribing and Editing Oral History Interviews.* Washington, D.C.: George Washington University Library, 1976.

Epstein, Ellen Robinson, and Rona Mendelsohn. *Record and Remember: Tracing Your Roots through Oral History.* Washington, D.C.: Center for Oral History, 1978.

Ericson, Stacy, comp. *A Field Notebook for Oral History.* Boise: Idaho State Historical Society, Oral History Center, 1981.

Handfield, F. Gerald. *History on Tape: A Guide for Oral History in Indiana.* Indianapolis: Indiana State Library, 1979.

Hoopes, James. *Oral History: An Introduction for Students.* Chapel Hill: University of North Carolina Press, 1979. (See chapter 31 of the present volume)

Ives, Edward D. *The Tape Recorded Interview: A Manual for Field Workers in Folklore and Oral History.* Knoxville: University of Tennessee Press, 1980.

Jenkins, Sara. *Past, Present: Recording Life Stories of Older People.* Washington, D.C.: St. Albans Parish, n.d. (Order from National Council on Aging, 600 Maryland Avenue, S.W., Washington, D.C. 20036)

Key, Betty McKeever. *Maryland Manual of Oral History.* Baltimore: Maryland Historical Society, 1979.

Kornbluh, Joyce, and M. Brady Mikusko, ed. *Working Womenroots: An Oral History Primer.* Detroit: University of Michigan-Wayne State University, Institute of Labor and Industrial Relations, Program on Women and Work, 1979.

Lance, David. *An Archives Approach to Oral History.* London: Imperial War Museum, and the International Association of Sound Archives, 1978. (See chapter 11 of the present volume)

Moss, William W. *Oral History Program Manual.* New York: Praeger, 1974.

Neuenschwander, John A. *Oral History as a Teaching Approach.* Washington, D.C.: National Education Association, 1975.

Oblinger, Carl. *Interviewing the People of Pennsylvania: A Conceptual Guide to Oral History.* Harrisburg: Pennsylvania Historical and Museum Commission, 1978.

Shopes, Linda. "Using Oral History for a Family History Project." Technical Leaflet 123. Nashville: American Association for State and Local History, 1980. (See chapter 22 of the present volume)

Shumway, Gary L., and William G. Hartley. *An Oral History Primer.* Salt Lake City: Primer Publications, 1973.

Whistler, Nancy. *Oral History Workshop Guide*. Denver: Denver Public Library, Colorado Center for Oral History, 1979.

Selected Works Addressing Legal Considerations

Eustis, Truman W. "Getting It in Writing: Oral History and the Law." *Oral History Review* 4 (1976), pp. 6–18.

Hamilton, Douglas E. "Oral History and the Law of Libel." In *The Second National Colloquium on Oral History*, ed. Louis M. Starr. New York: Oral History Association, 1968. (See pp. 41–56)

Horn, David E. *Copyright, Literary Rights, and Ownership: A Guide for Archivists*. Indianapolis: Society of Indianapolis Archivists, 1978.

Moss, William W. *Oral History Program Manual*. New York: Praeger, 1974. (Discusses legal considerations on pp. 14–18, 55–57, 104–107)

Romney, Joseph. "Legal Considerations in Oral History." *Oral History Review* 3 (1975), pp. 66–76.

———. "Oral History: Law and Libraries." *Drexel Library Quarterly* 15 (October 1979), pp. 34–49.

Society of American Archivists. *Forms Manual*. Chicago, 1973. (Contains sample legal agreements)

Welch, Mason. "A Lawyer Looks at Oral History." In *The Fourth National Colloquium on Oral History*, ed. Gould P. Colman. New York: Oral History Association, 1970. (See pp. 182–95)

Selected Works on Oral History and Libraries

Baum, Willa K. "Building Community Identity through Oral History—A New Role for the Local Library." *California Librarian* 31 (October 1970), pp. 271–84.

Catholic Library World 47 (October 1975).

Cullom Davis. "Tapeworms and Bookworms—Oral History in the Library," pp. 102–103.
Sister John Christine Wolkerstorfer. "Oral History—A New Look at Local History," pp. 104–107.
Betty McKeever Key. "Telling It Like It Was in 1968," pp. 106–109.
John W. Orton. "Oral History and the Genealogical Society," pp. 110–12.
Willa Baum. "The Librarian as Guardian of Oral History Materials: An Example from Berkeley," pp. 112–17.
William W. Moss. "Oral History: A New Role for the Library," pp. 118–19.

Drexel Library Quarterly 15 (October 1979). Edited by M. Patricia Freeman. Issue on "Managing Oral History Collections in the Library."

Carroll Hart. "The New Documentation: Oral History and Photography," pp. 1–11.
Mary Jo Pugh. "Oral History in the Library: Levels of Commitment," pp. 12–28.
F. Gerald Handfield, Jr. "The Importance of Video History in Libraries," pp. 29–34.
Ernest J. Dick. "Selection and Preservation of Oral History Interviews," pp. 35–38.
Joseph B. Romney. "Oral History, Law, and Libraries," pp. 39–49.
Peggy Ann Kusnerz. "Oral History: A Selective Bibliography," pp. 50–75.
Dale E. Treleven. "A Brief Description of the TAPE System" [alternative to transcribing tapes], pp. 76–81.

Filipelli, R. L. "Oral History and the Archives." *American Archivist* 39 (October 1976), pp. 479–83.

Horn, David E. *Copyright, Literary Rights, and Ownership: A Guide for Archivists.* Indianapolis: Society of Indiana Archivists, 1978.

Key, Betty McKeever. "Oral History in the Library." *Catholic Library World* 49 (April 1978), pp. 380–84.

Lance, David. *An Archive Approach to Oral History.* London: Imperial War Museum and the International Association of Sound Archives, 1978. (See chapter 11 of the present volume)

McWilliams, Jerry. *The Preservation and Restoration of Sound Recordings.* Nashville: American Association for State and Local History, 1980.

Morrissey, Charles T. "Oral History: More than Tapes Spinning." *Library Journal* 105 (April 15, 1980), pp. 932–33.

O'Hanlon, Sister Elizabeth. "Oral History and the Library." *Catholic Library World* 51 (July–August 1979), pp. 26–28.

Pfaff, Eugene, Jr. "Oral History: A New Challenge for Public Libraries." *Wilson Library Bulletin* 54 (May 1980), pp. 568–71.

Society of American Archivists. *Forms Manual.* Chicago, 1973.

Stewart, John F., and the Committee on Oral History of the Society of American Archivists. "Oral History and Archivists: Some Questions to Ask." *American Archivist* 36 (1973), pp. 361–65.

Zachert, Martha Jane K. "The Implications of Oral History for Librarians." *College and Research Libraries* 29 (March 1968), pp. 101–103. (See chapter 35 of the present volume)

Directories, Collection Guides, and Bibliographies

Cook, Patsy A., ed. *Directory of Oral History Programs in the United States.* Sanford, N.C.: Microfilming Corporation of America, 1982.

Fox, John. "Bibliographic Update." In *Oral History Review, 1977.* Denton: Oral History Association, 1977.

Mason, Elizabeth, and Louis M. Starr. *The Oral History Collection of Columbia University.* New York: Oral History Research Office, 1979.

Meckler, Alan M., and Ruth Mullin, eds. *Oral History Collections.* New York: Bowker, 1975.

New York Times. Oral History Program. *Columbia University Collection.* New York: New York Times, Library Information Services Division, 1972.

———. *Oral History Guide No. 1.* Glen Rock, N.J.: Microfilming Corporation of America, 1976.

———. *Oral History Guide No. 2.* Sanford, N.C.: Microfilming Corporation of America, 1979.

———. *Oral History Guide No. 3.* Sanford, N.C.: Microfilming Corporation of America, 1983.

(The New York Times Oral History Program guides list oral histories available on microfiche and microfilm from oral history offices nationwide.)

Riess, Suzanne, and Willa K. Baum, eds. *Catalogue of the Regional Oral History Office, 1954–1979.* Berkeley: University of California, Berkeley, Bancroft Library, 1980.

Shumway, Gary L., *Oral History in the United States: A Directory.* New York: Oral History Association, 1971.

Stenberg, Henry G. "Selected Bibliography, 1977–1981." *Oral History Review* 10 (1982), pp. 119–32.

Waserman, Manfred, comp. *Bibliography on Oral History.* Oral History Association, 1975.

37

Soundscapes

W. J. Langlois

Interview with Imbert Orchard

Our final essay is for librarians and sound archivists interested in including both historical reminiscence and sound documents of their time.

Among oral historians in the United States, there has long been a controversy over which was the primary source document: the tape of an interview or its transcript. In the United States the transcript more commonly circulates; in Britain and Canada, for instance, the tape is distributed. In Canada one result has been "aural history," emphasizing the history of sounds rather than the sounds (words) of history. Thus an aural historian might record an important speech for historical preservation and might file it alongside a record of the sound environment of the speaker's subject. Aural history has more in common with sound archiving than with tape recording oral recollections, and some Canadian aural historians belong to the International Association of Sound Archivists (IASA).

To illustrate, we include here an interview with the World Soundscape Project of Vancouver conducted by the man who coined the term "aural history," documentary producer Imbert Orchard. As the introduction to this piece states, this approach to sound preservation may seem tangential to some oral historians; nevertheless, the ideas are novel, and documenting the sounds of a culture—in addition to its historical memory—is a valuable effort, as contributor Don Cavallini noted earlier in this volume.

Imbert Orchard, a Cambridge-trained historian, has produced hundreds of documentaries based on oral history recordings for the Canadian Broadcasting Corporation.

William Langlois served as the former director of the Aural History Programme at the Provincial Archives of British Columbia in Victoria, where this selection was first published. "Aural History and the World Soundscape Project" appeared first in Sound Heritage *3 (October 1974), pp. 1–9.*

T HE WORLD SOUNDSCAPE PROJECT, located at Simon Fraser University, is an organization dedicated to the quality of the sound environment. Their aim, as defined by R. Murray Schafer, is "to bring together research on the scientific, sociological and aesthetic aspects of the environment." Their aim is not merely research but also the creation of analytical tools by which the sonic environment, or soundscape, can be studied and its optimum condition determined and promoted as an ideal toward which individuals and acoustic designers should consciously strive. . . .

To those oral historians, whose goal has been primarily to produce typescripts of interviews, the connection between their work and the World Soundscape Project may seem tenuous. Oral historians often make the point that listening is important, but they have not generally given much consideration to sound quality, the importance of inflection or dialect or idiosyncrasies of speech, or to what the Soundscape Project calls the "perceived image" of a sound as opposed to its physical, technically measurable qualities. . . . [This article] on the Soundscape Project will stimulate oral historians to think more about the quality of the sound they record, and perhaps cause them to extend the definition of the types of sounds that they are interested in.

Those who have declared themselves to be aural historians, that is, who have become involved in the collection of many types of sound documents, and who consider the tape to be the final product of their work, may more easily perceive their relationship to the Soundscape Project, but undoubtedly, their horizons will be further broadened by exposure to this approach to sound recording.

The members of the World Soundscape Project are genuine aural historians in their efforts to record and preserve historic sounds, and in their careful collection and analysis of contemporary sounds, but, unlike many aural historians, they also take a position advocating social change. This will undoubtedly be of interest to all our readers, who have a personal if not professional concern with the quality of the environment.

The following is a transcript of a conversation between Imbert Orchard, aural historian, and two members of the World Soundscape Project research group, Howard Broomfield and Barry Truax. The conversation took place August 7, 1974 at Simon Fraser University, and was centred around the relationship between aural history's attitude toward sound recording, and the environmental sound emphasis of the World Soundscape Project in Vancouver, Canada.

Interview with Imbert Orchard

MR. ORCHARD: The way I look at it, there actually is no boundary between aural history and the study of the soundscape. We are all concerned with sounds in general, but you approach a sound, partly for its own sake and partly for what it suggests, what it manifests of social history, of location, of all of the things that are implied in the sound. The sound itself, therefore, is pre-eminent. Whereas from the aural history point of view, speech—what people are saying—is the pre-eminent thing. A person speaking may describe sounds, whereas you are concerned with the sounds themselves, including the sound of the human voice. Of course, I know that your work extends into a concern with speech as the communication of meaning, just as my work extends sometimes into the use of sound for its own sake. Consequently, I feel that there are whole areas where you, the soundscape people, and myself and other aural historians can collaborate and influence each other. I think particularly of your emphasis on the *quality* of sound: the perfection you are striving for. I feel we could together expand the whole sound-speech documentary process into something very rich and comprehensive.

MR. TRUAX: Well, the technology then can be used to help us. We can go from, say, seventy-five yeras ago, when you would be essentially writing down what you heard, then perhaps you could start recording with the portable phonographs they had, then with the tape recorder single channel, and a limited spectrum. We want to extend this out into as close to a re-creation of an environment, or creation of a new environment, as possible, so we always use two or four channels, and a full frequency spectrum. The whole technological development parallels the kind of interest we have in documenting . . . going from the reduced, one or two-dimensional aspect of speech or environment to as complete an experience as possible.

MR. ORCHARD: This is indeed aural history, a-u-r-a-l history, sounds of all kinds. . . .

MR. BROOMFIELD: I see a dialect going on between the voice and the soundscape. There's a kind of history that transcends language and transcends words and is realized best in hearing the way a voice relates to its ambience. There's a history of man in the field, in the life-world, that comes across just in terms of the way his tone relates to the tones around him. *Now* the human voice is smothered by machinery and that's a kind of history that most people wouldn't think to talk about linguistically.

MR. ORCHARD: You say "now", because we're sitting out here on the lawn beside Simon Fraser University, but the traffic isn't far off. And there's also a noise, a keynote, that comes off the building, a general hum, and so we're by no means in silence here, and we relate to that with our voices. But in general we have psychologically to shut our ears, which is what people, of course, are doing all the time.

MR. BROOMFIELD: What's even worse is that there seems to be a deadening of the voice that goes along with the livening of the machine soundscape. The voice starts to take on the characteristics of the machine, rather than have the fluence it would have in a natural environment where the sounds are more varied. I think that people learn how to speak, not only by listening to other people's voices, but by listening to the natural sounds around them. If you listen to a Squamish Indian speak, you'll hear a lot more wind and water in his voice than you will in our voices. We've been living with typewriters and machines like that, so we talk in long lines.

MR. ORCHARD: That's very interesting, and very true, and very relevant to this aural history approach, looking at it from my side, because obviously we don't usually take great account of the place where we are recording or the speaker's background. I mean, you jsut are there and you're just interested in what they have to say. Yet the whole tone of voice is very important as meaning; and if, for instance, there was a lot of mechanical noise, our voices would take on a different colour, than if we were sitting in the woods somewhere.

MR. BROOMFIELD: We have to raise our voices above the machines, we have to fit ourselves into the parts of the frequency spectrum which the machine leaves out, just so we can be heard!

MR. TRUAX: The basic point we're making is that people are not aware of how sound affects them, all the time, every day, not only the sound they focus on, such as speech sounds that you normally bring out of the ambience into the foreground of perception. The general rise of the ambient noise level of society in the last fifty years or so not only reflects the technological advance, but also is the same kind of evolution that our consciousness is going through . . . the paradox of constant bombardment with more and more stimuli, and the necessity of shutting out most of those stimuli that are not necessary for existence. So, we see this, or rather we hear this as a problem of feedback, you might say: the more one is shutting out, the less aware one can be of the sounds of the environment, because one is less disposed to listen to them. Therefore, the environment can become chaotic without your getting up and saying, "Stop! I can't tolerate this any more!" We feel this kind of deadening, and perhaps you might link this to the loss of oral tradition in our kind of society, if only because it's just harder to hear people speak. And, as Howard suggested, what we call the "flat line" or "long line" of drones and hums from mechanical and electrical apparatus seems to be reflected in North American speech patterns.

MR. BROOMFIELD: I'm not sure when written history began, but it seems that history really is an oral thing, not a written thing, that once history starts being written it starts getting overly concerned with facts and not concerned with human history . . . but people nowadays who are carrying on the oral tradition are the people who are the most disenfranchised from society. If you want to get a fast oral history of Vancouver, the best place to go is down to where the winos and the drunks hang out, because they always have the stories and they may not be true stories, but they're passionate stories, and they're stories that they've been building for years and years and years, because they have no fact to hold on to . . . they have to invent history.

MR. ORCHARD: It's the myth, really, rather than the history; and the myth, of course, is a very important part of the background of any area, any country, any town. We often ignore it, but possibly we will become more aware of it now because we have this sound recording apparatus.

MR. TRUAX (to Mr. Orchard): Talking about the past, and the way that you have used sounds for the past, and the way we are using sounds now, take *The Vancouver Soundscape* for example . . . what is your reaction to our use of sounds in terms of history? In fact, because the tape recorder is recording what is in the present, would you be critical of us as being too present-oriented because of our emphasis on sounds, or do you get a sense of history from what we've done so far?

MR. ORCHARD: I think very much you're documenting history, because from this point of view, as soon as you document anything it becomes history, it's fixed in time as of that particular moment; and even if the moment was a mere five minutes ago, it's still history, but not very long from now it is going to be fifty years from now, and that sound which was Vancouver at that time becomes a historical document. I'm also aware that you're tremendously interested in a sound as it was described by someone, a sound that can no longer be heard. Someone has described it in writing, and often in so doing they reveal their attitude toward the sound.

MR. TRUAX: These are what we call "earwitness accounts"; by analogy to eyewitness, an earwitness is someone who reports about what he or she has heard, what they remember about sound or sound experiences they have had. We've gathered these from literary sources; for instance, in *The Vancouver Soundscape*, the first ones are from the journals of Vancouver and Menzies, the original voyages. Then we come right up to people who are alive today, reminiscing about what it was like in the twenties, the thirties and so on. *The Vancouver Soundscape* is already an historical document, it was recorded roughly a year ago now, and some of the sound, for instance the Point Atkinson lighthouse diaphone, in a few more months will not be heard likely again, it's already a disappearing sound; the 9 o'clock gun too at this moment is not sounding. All the sounds within the next few years will probably change, an evolution will go on. Because you're recording and making this instantaneous image of a sound, you put it on tape and you make it an object; the object survives, therefore the sound survives in some sense. Now, have you noticed though, we also have this ability to take the sound out of time and out of context and isolate it, what we call a "sound object", and then we can transform that object into something unrelated, at least in the aural impression, to what we had before. We call this an "imaginary soundscape", where we're using sounds and making something derived from a reality, but in fact it is creating a new reality.

MR. ORCHARD: Well that's getting into another space altogether; it's becoming very creative and much more than mere documentation. One is reaching out into the manipulation of sound for aesthetic reasons, partly for the sake of the sound itself . . . the quality that it has. In my field, putting together this sort of radio documentary, one that includes voices *and* sounds. Perhaps you've recorded a particularly beautiful voice, just as you might pick up a particularly beautiful sound, and then you edit it in such a way that its natural rhythm is enhanced, or you splice in other voices or cross fade them and all that becomes a creative process in which you're using sound partly for its own sake. For instance, once I recorded the sound of the Skeena River rushing through the Kitselas Canyon, and during production I added the voice of an Indian giving the right pronunciation of Kitselas, which is *"Git-se-laaass"*; and the voice had been put on echo and mixed with a few raven cries, also from the area—and you got a sound that was weird and ghostly. And I used this to introduce a programme that was about the canyon, and set the mood, you see.

MR. BROOMFIELD: Something that you just did, I wonder if many aural historians are getting into and that's working with the voices that you've recorded and heard, to make those voices your own, to become an embodiment of the history as well as a collector of the tapes, to be able to feel and to speak with the voices of the people who've spoken. Somehow that seems as important as writing it down. If just a few people learn to speak with the voice of the past. . . .

MR. ORCHARD: As an aural historian I'm not much concerned with transcribing. The academic approach to this, taking its cue from Columbia University apparently, where it started, is to get the tape transcribed and then it can be picked off the shelf, and read at leisure by people who haven't got any ears. There's nothing wrong in that except it's a very incomplete process. When you're writing something you're careful to arrange it so that its full meaning is apparent when someone else reads it. But if you transcribe something that somebody has spoken, you're only getting a relatively small portion of the meaning, because a great deal of this meaning is in the inflection of the voice, in the rhythm of the voice, in the pauses, the volume, the emphasis.

MR. BROOMFIELD: The way that would get into writing is a poet's job, not something a secretary or someone untrained in language can do. The person who's operating in the field has the opportunity to become a germ-cell of history: they can carry the history in their own voice with them, to make history a part of now.

MR. ORCHARD: Anyone who's describing an event is re-living it, and that re-living is not only being communicated to the person who's listening, but is being fixed on the tape at that moment, so that every time the tape is played there's a kind of bringing of the past into the present in the voice itself.

MR. TRUAX: We want to take the person into the original environment, not bring the original environment into his own. It is much more effective to go into the past as directly and completely as possible, to recreate the soundscape in which those sounds occurred.

MR. ORCHARD: Well this is true. Somebody merely describing something is a limited process. You don't get the sounds that they are describing.

MR. TRUAX: But there you must be careful. You must recreate the sound in the way people remember it, not in the way the tape recorder would have picked it up at the time. People remember things in a way that is, in fact, not the way they actually occurred. They simplify things: first of all the background goes out, all the inessential things are omitted. Long-term memory tends to "idealize" and isolate those sounds, so when we put sounds together, often we are deliberately appealing to the way people will have remembered these sounds, or perhaps just the opposite, for a sort of "shock effect". But our whole basis, at least from my point of view, is that the soundscape is essentially the interface between the real environment and the inner environment of how people remember, imagine, and make fantasy about sound, the perceptual and cognitive process, so even when we go into the past, which past are we going into, the tape recorder past, or the imagined-remembered past? We must understand how people understand sounds in the first place and then how they remember them, how they recreate them. This is really the only true past there is: what resides in the mind. . . .

APPENDIX

Goals, Guidelines, and Evaluation Criteria
of the Oral History Association

Goals and Guidelines of the Oral History Association[1]

The Oral History Association recognizes oral history as a method of gathering and preserving historical information in spoken form and encourages those who produce and use oral history to recognize certain principles, rights and obligations for the creation of source material that is authentic, useful and reliable.

Guidelines for the Interviewee

The interviewee should be informed of the purposes and procedures of oral history in general and of the particular project to which contribution is being made.

In recognition of the importance of oral history to an understanding of the past and in recognition of the costs and effort involved, the interviewee should strive to impart candid information of lasting value.

The interviewee should be aware of the mutual rights involved in oral history, such as editing and seal privileges, literary rights, prior use, fiduciary relationships, royalties, and determination of the disposition of all forms of the record and extent of dissemination and use.

Preferences of the person interviewed and any prior agreements should govern the conduct of the oral history process, and these preferences and agreements should be carefully documented for the record.

Guidelines for the Interviewer

Interviewers should guard against possible social injury to or exploitation of interviewees and should conduct interviews with respect for human dignity.

Each interviewee should be selected on the basis of demonstrable potential for imparting information of lasting value.

The interviewer should strive to prompt informative dialogue through challenging and perceptive inquiry, should be grounded in the background and experiences of the person being interviewed, and, if possible, should review the sources related to the interviewee before conducting the interview.

Interviewers should extend the inquiry beyond their immediate needs to make each interview as complete as possible for the benefit of others, and should, wherever possible, place the material in a depository where it will be available for general research.

The interviewer should inform the interviewee of the planned conduct of the oral history process and develop mutual expectations of rights connected thereto, including editing, mutual seal privileges, literary rights, prior use, fiduciary relationships, royalties, rights to determine disposition of all forms of the record, and the extent of dissemination and use.

Interviews should be conducted in a spirit of objectivity, candor and integrity, and in keeping with common understandings, purposes and stipulations mutually arrived at by all parties.

The interviewer shall not violate and will protect the seal on any information considered confidential by the interviewee, whether imparted on or off the record.

Guidelines for Sponsoring Institutions

Subject to conditions prescribed by interviewees, it is an obligation of sponsoring institutions (or individual collectors) to prepare and preserve easily useable records; to keep careful records of the creation and processing of each interview; to identify, index and catalog interviews; and, when open to research, to make their existence known.

Interviewers should be selected on the basis of professional competence and interviewing skill; interviewers should be carefully matched to interviewees.

Institutions should keep both interviewees and interviewers aware of the importance of the above guidelines for the successful production and use of oral history sources.

Oral History Evaluation Guidelines[2]

The Oral History Association, in furtherance of its goals and guidelines and in support of its evaluation service, has developed guidelines for the use of those called upon to evaluate existing or proposed programs and projects. The outline may also be used by individuals to test their own procedures and by funding agencies to appraise proposals.

Recognizing that the ultimate measure of oral history lies in its reliability as a source for historical understanding, the Association submits that conscientious consideration of every step in its creation is a professional obligation, and that careful attention to the factors raised in the following outline substantially increases the probability of enduring value.

Therefore, the Association has developed the following guidelines to be used in the evaluation of programs and projects producing oral history sources and to provide standards for new and established programs. The text is intended to suggest lines of inquiry by evaluators, who should, however, recognize the need for flexibility in applying them to specific projects. The guidelines will be subject to continuing review by the Oral History Association.

Program/Project Guidelines[3]

Purposes and Objectives
   a. Are the purposes clearly set forth? How realistic are they?
   b. What factors demonstrate a significant need for the project?
   c. What is the research design? How clear and realistic is it?
   d. Are the terms, conditions and objectives of funding clearly made known to allow the user of the interviews to judge the potential effect of such funding on the scholarly integrity of the project? Is the allocation of funds adequate to allow the project goals to be accomplished?
   e. How do institutional relationships affect the purposes and objectives?

Selection of Interviewers and Interviewees

   a. In what way are the interviewers and interviewees appropriate (or inappropriate) to the purposes and objectives?
   b. What are the significant omissions and why were they omitted?

Records and Provenance

   a. What are the policies and provisions for maintaining a record of the provenance of interviews? Are they adequate? What can be done to improve them?
   b. How are records, policies and procedures made known to interviewers, interviewees, staff and users?
   c. How does the system of records enhance the usefulness of the interviews and safeguard the rights of those involved?

Availability of Materials

   a. How accurate and specific is the publicizing of the interviews?
   b. How is information about interviews directed to likely users?
   c. How have the interviews been used?

Finding Aids

    a. What is the overall design for finding aids?
    b. Are the finding aids adequate and appropriate?
    c. How available are the finding aids?

Management, Qualifications and Training

    a. How effective is the management of the program/project?
    b. What provisions are there for supervision and staff review?
    c. What are the qualifications for staff positions?
    d. What are the provisions for systematic and effective training?

What improvements could be made in the management of the program/ project?

Ethical/Legal Guidelines[4]

What policies and procedures assure that each interviewee is made fully aware of . . .
    a. his/her rights and interests?
    b. the purposes of the program/project?
    c. the various stages of the interviewing and transcribing process and his/her responsibilities for participation in that process?
    d. the eventual deposit of the interviews in a suitable depository?
    e. the possible uses to which the material may be put?

What policies and procedures assure that each interviewee is made fully aware of . . .

    a. his/her rights and interests?
    b. his/her ethical and legal responsibilities to the interviewee?
    c. his/her ethical and legal responsibilities to the program/project?

How does the program/project secure a release from the interviewer?

What policies and procedures assure that for each interviewee an adequate deed of gift or formal contract transfers rights, title and interests in both tape(s) and transcript(s) to an administering authority?

    —In lieu of a deed of gift or contract, what other evidence of intent of gift does the program/project rely upon? Is it legally adequate?

How does the program reflect responsible adherence to ethical and legal standards? Specifically . . .

    a. How has the staff been impressed with the need for confidentiality of interview content until the time of release?

b. How has the staff been impressed with the need to conduct interviews in a spirit of mutual respect and with consideration for the interests of the interviewees?
c. How does the program/project demonstrate its ability to carry out the provisions of legal agreements and protect the tapes and transcripts from unethical use?
d. What steps are taken to assure that the staff recognizes its responsibilities to gather accurate material, to process it as quickly as possible, and to make it available for use to the widest possible audience?

Tape/Transcript Processing Guidelines

Information About the Participants

a. Are the names of both interviewer and interviewee clearly indicated on the tape/abstract/transcript and in catalog materials?
b. Is there adequate biographical information about both interviewer and interviewee? Where can it be found?

Interview Information

a. Are the tape, transcripts, time indices, abstracts and other material presented for use identified as to the project/program of which they are a part?
b. Are the date and place of interview indicated on tape, transcript, time index, abstract, and in appropriate catalog material?
c. Are there interviewer's statements about the preparation for or circumstances of the interviews? Where? Are they generally available to researchers? How are the rights of the interviewees protected against the improper use of such commentaries?
d. Are there records of contracts between the program and the interviewee? How detailed are they? Are they available to researchers? If so, with what safeguards for individual rights and privacy?

Interview Tape Information

a. Is the complete master tape preserved? Are there one or more duplicate copies?
b. If the original or any duplicate has been edited, rearranged, cut or spliced in any way, is there a record of that action, including by whom and when and for what purposes the action was taken?
c. Do the tape label and appropriate catalog materials show the recording speed, level and length of the interview?
d. Has the program/project used recording equipment and tapes

which are appropriate to the purposes of the work and use of the material? Are the recordings of good quality? How could they be improved?

e. In the absence of transcripts, are there suitable finding aids to give users access to information on tapes? What form do they take? Is there a record of who prepared these finding aids?

f. Are researchers permitted to listen to the tapes? Are there any restrictions on the use of tapes?

Interview Transcript Information

a. Is the transcript an accurate record of the tape? Is a careful record kept of each step of processing the transcript, including who transcribed, audited, edited, retyped, and proofread the transcript in final copy?

b. Are the nature and extent of changes in the transcript from the original tape made known to the user?

c. What finding aids have been prepared for the transcript? Are they suitable and adequate? How could they be improved?

d. Are there any restrictions on access to or use of the transcripts? Are they cleary noted?

e. Are there any photo materials or other supporting documents for the interview? Do they enhance and supplement the text?

Interview Content Guidelines[5]

Does the content of each interview and the cumulative content of the whole collection contribute to accomplishing the objectives of the project/program?

— In what particulars do the interview and/or collection appear to succeed or fall short?

In what way does the program/project contribute to historical understanding?[6]

— In what particulars does each interview or the whole collection succeed or fall short of such contribution?

— To what extent does the material add fresh information, fill gaps in the existing record, and/or provide fresh insights and perspectives?

— To what extent is the information reliable and valid? Is it eyewitness or hearsay evidence? How well and in what manner does it meet internal and external tests of corroboration, consistency, and explication of contradictions?

— What is the relationship of the interview information to existing documentation and historiography?

— How does the texture of the interview impart detail, richness and flavor to the historical record?
— What is the basic nature of the information contributed? Is it facts, perceptions, interpretations, judgments, or attitudes, and how does each contribute to understanding?
— Are the scope and volume, and where appropriate the representativeness of the population interviewed, appropriate and sufficient to the purpose? Is there enough testimony to validate the evidence without passing the point of diminishing returns? How appropriate is the quantity to the purposes of the study? Is there a good representative sample of the population reflected in the interviews?
— How do the form and structure of the interviews contribute to make the content information understandable?

Interview Conduct Guidelines

Use of Other Sources

a. Is the oral history technique the best means of acquiring the information? If not, what other sources exist? Has the interviewer used them, and has he/she sought to preserve them if necessary?
b. Has the interviewer made an effort to consult other relevant oral histories?
c. Is the interview technique of value in supplementing existing sources?

Historical Contribution

a. Does the interviewer pursue the inquiry with historical integrity?
b. Do other purposes being served by the interview enrich or diminish quality?
c. What does the interview contribute to the larger context of historical knowledge and understanding?

Interviewer Preparation

a. Is the interviewer well-informed about the subjects under discussion?
b. Are the primary and secondary sources used in preparation for the interview adequate?

Interviewee Selection and Orientation

a. Does the interviewee seem appropriate to the subjects discussed?
b. Does the interviewee understand and respond to the interview purposes?

c. Has the interviewee prepared for the interview and assisted in the process?

Interviewer-Interviewee Relations

a. Do interviewer and interviewee motivate each other toward interview objectives?
b. Is there a balance of empathy and analytical judgment in the interview?

Adaptive Skills

a. In what ways does the interview show that the interviewer has used skills appropriate to . . .
— the interviewee's condition (health, memory, mental alertness, ability to communicate, time schedule, etc.)?
— the interview conditions (disruptions and interruptions, equipment problems, extraneous participants, etc.)?

Technique

a. What evidence is there that the interviewer has . . .
— thoroughly explored pertinent lines of thought?
— followed up significant clues?
— made an effort to identify sources of information?
— employed critical challenge where needed?

Perspective

a. Do the biases of the interviewer interfere with or influence the responses of the interviewee?
b. What information is available that may inform the users of any prior or separate relationship of the interviewer to the interviewee?

Notes

1. Original version adopted November 25, 1968, with minor revisions since then.
2. A task force of the Oral History Association met at the Wingspread Conference Center of the Johnson Foundation July 27-28, 1979, to draw up and submit the evaluation guidelines to the membership. The guidelines were approved unanimously at the annual colloquium of the Oral History Association in East Lansing, Michigan, on October 27, 1979.
3. *Project* is here defined as a series of interviews or a single interview focused on a particular subject, theme or era. *Program* is defined as a set of projects under one management.

4. Reference should also be made, in the course of evaluation, to the Goals and Guidelines of the Oral History Assocation.

5. These guidelines were originally cast as statements and were recast as questions by William W. Moss following the instructions of the annual business meeting in East Lansing. They are subject to further review and approval.

6. Some programs have an explicitly instructional, therapeutic or other purpose which may make evaluation of content by historical standards secondary in importance. Oral History Association evaluators should limit themselves to evaluations form the historical perspective and should encourage programs wishing to be valued for other purposes to seek evaluation and counsel elsewhere.

ACKNOWLEDGMENTS

The editors are grateful for permission extended to reprint the copyrighted works that appear in this volume.

"Oral History" by Louis Starr is reprinted from the *Encyclopedia of Library and Information Sciences,* vol. 20 (New York: Marcel Dekker, 1977), pp. 440–63. Reprinted by courtesy of Marcel Dekker, Inc.

"Oral History: How and Why It Was Born" by Allan Nevins is reprinted by permission from the *Wilson Library Bulletin* 40 (March 1966), pp. 600–601. Copyright © by the H. W. Wilson Company.

"History and the Community" by Paul Thompson, copyright © 1978 by Paul Thompson, is reprinted from *The Voice of the Past: Oral History* (Oxford: Oxford University Press, 1978) by permission of the author and Oxford University Press.

"Some Words on Oral Histories" by Samuel Hand originally appeared in *Scholarly Publishing* 9 (January 1978), pp. 171–85. It is reprinted by permission of the author and the University of Toronto Press.

"Reliability and Validity in Oral History" by Alice Hoffman first appeared in *Today's Speech* 22 (Winter 1974), pp. 23–27, and is reprinted by permission of the author and *Communication Quarterly.*

"Distinguishing the Significant from the Insignificant" by Barbara Tuchman appeared in *Radcliffe Quarterly* 56 (October 1972), pp. 9–10. Copyright © 1972 by Barbara W. Tuchman. Reprinted with the permission of the author and the *Radcliffe Quarterly.*

"Accuracy in Oral History Interviewing" by William Cutler III, from *Historical Methods Newsletter* 3 (June 1970), pp. 1–7, is reprinted by permission of the author.

"Oral History: An Appreciation" by William Moss appeared in *American Archivist* 40 (October 1977), pp. 429–39. It is reprinted by permission of the author and the Society of American Archivists.

Jan Vansina's "Oral Tradition and Historical Methodology" appeared in *Oral Tradition: A Study in Historical Methodology,* trans. H. M. Wright

(Chicago: Aldine, 1965). Copyright © Jan Vansina. Reprinted by permission of the author.

"A Note on Oral Tradition and Historical Evidence" by Ruth Finnegan, from *History and Theory* 9 (October 1970), pp. 195–201, copyright © 1970 Wesleyan University, is reprinted by permission of the author and *History and Theory*.

"Oral History Project Design" by David Lance is reprinted from *An Archive Approach to Oral History* (London: the Imperial War Museum and the International Association of Sound Archives, 1978) by permission of the author and the publishers.

Saul Benison's introduction to *Tom Rivers: Reflections on a Life in Medicine and Science* (Cambridge, Mass.: M.I.T. Press, 1967) is reprinted by permission of the author and the M.I.T. Press.

"Theory, Method, and Oral History" by Peter Friedlander is reprinted from *The Emergence of a UAW Local, 1936–1939: A Study in Class and Culture* (Pittsburgh: University of Pittsburgh Press, 1975). Copyright © by the University of Pittsburgh Press. Reprinted by permission of the University of Pittsburgh Press.

"Oral History and the California Wine Industry" by Charles Morrissey appeared in *Agricultural History* 51 (July 1977), pp. 590–96, and is reprinted by permission of the author.

"Reflections on Ethics" by Amelia Fry first appeared in *Oral History Review* 3 (1975), pp. 17–28. It is reprinted by permission of the author and the Oral History Association.

Lynwood Montell's preface to *The Saga of Coe Ridge: A Study in Oral History* (Knoxville: University of Tennessee Press, 1970), copyright © 1970 by The University of Tennessee Press, is reprinted by permission of the author and the University of Tennessee Press.

"The Folklorist, the Oral Historian, and Local History" by Larry Danielson originally appeared in the *Oral History Review* 8 (1980), pp. 62–72, and is reprinted by permission of the author and the Oral History Association.

"Documenting Diversity: The Southern Experience" by Jacquelyn Dowd Hall first appeared in the *Oral History Review* 4 (1976), pp. 19–28, and is reprinted by permission of the author and the Oral History Association.

"Oral History and the Writing of Ethnic History" by Gary Okihiro was first published in the *Oral History Review* 9 (1981), pp. 27–46, and is reprinted by permission of the author and the Oral History Association.

Theodore Rosengarten's preface to *All God's Dangers: The Life of Nate Shaw* (New York: Alfred A. Knopf, 1974), copyright © 1974 by Alfred A. Knopf, Inc., is reprinted by permission of the author and Alfred A. Knopf, Inc.

"What's So Special about Women? Women's Oral History" by Sherna Gluck is reprinted from *FRONTIERS: A Journal of Women Studies* 2 (Summer 1977 Special Issue on Women's Oral History), pp. 3–13, with the permission of the author and *FRONTIERS*.

"Using Oral History for a Family History Project" by Linda Shopes originally appeared as Technical Leaflet 123 (Nashville: American Association for State and Local History, 1980). It is reprinted by permission of the author and the American Association for State and Local History.

"The Search for Generational Memory" by Tamara Hareven, from *Daedalus* 106 (Fall 1978), pp. 137–49, is reprinted by permission of the author.

"Black History, Oral History, and Genealogy" by Alex Haley was first published in *Oral History Review* 1 (1973), pp. 1–25, and is reprinted by permission of the author and the Oral History Association.

"The Oral Historian and the Folklorist" by Richard Dorson appeared in *Selections of the Fifth and Sixth National Colloquia on Oral History* (New York: Oral History Association, 1972). It is reprinted by permission of the Oral History Association.

"Oral History as Communicative Event" by Charles Joyner was first published in *Oral History Review* 7 (1979), pp. 47–52. It is reprinted by permission of the Oral History Association.

"The Anthropological Interview and the Life History" by Sidney Mintz appeared in *Oral History Review*, 7 (1979), pp. 18–26. It is reprinted by permission of the author and the Oral History Association.

"Three Ways of Reminiscence in Theory and Practice" by Marianne Lo Gerfo was published in the *International Journal of Aging and Human Development* 12 (1980–81), pp. 39–48. Copyright © 1980 by Baywood Publishing Company, Inc. Reprinted by permission of Baywood Publishing Company, Inc.

"Oral Historians and Long-Term Memory" by John Neuenschwander originally appeared in *Oral History Review* 6 (1970), pp. 45–53. It is reprinted by permission of the author and the Oral History Association.

"Oral History for the Student" by James Hoopes was first published in his *Oral History: An Introduction for Students* (Chapel Hill: University of

North Carolina Press, 1979). Copyright © 1979 The University of North Carolina Press. It is reprinted by permission of the author and the publisher.

The excerpt from "Oral History in the Classroom" by George Mehaffy, Thad Sitton, and O. L. Davis, Jr., that is reproduced in this volume originally appeared in *How to Do It* 2 (Washington, D.C.: National Council for the Social Studies, 1979). It is reprinted with the permission of the authors and the National Council for the Social Studies.

"Oral/Aural History: In and out of the Classroom" by Don Cavallini first appeared in *Social Studies* 70 (May 1979), pp. 112–17, a publication of the Helen Dwight Reid Educational Foundation. Copyright © 1979 by the Helen Dwight Reid Educational Foundation. Reprinted by permission of the author and the Helen Dwight Reid Educational Foundation.

Eliot Wigginton's introduction to *The Foxfire Book* (Garden City, N.Y.: Doubleday, 1972) copyright © 1972 by Eliot Wigginton, is reprinted by permission of the author and Doubleday & Company, Inc.

"The Implications of Oral History for Librarians" by Martha Jane Zachert first appeared in *College and Research Libraries* 29 (March 1968), pp. 101–103. It is reprinted by permission of the American Library Association and the author.

"Soundscapes" by W. J. Langlois originally appeared in *Sound Heritage*, 3 (October 1974), pp. 1–9. It is reprinted by permission of the author and *Sound Heritage*.

INDEX